Royal Commission on
Electoral Reform and
Party Financing

Commission royale sur
la réforme électorale et
le financement des partis

CANADA

FINAL REPORT

VOLUME 4

Royal Commission on
Electoral Reform and
Party Financing

Commission royale sur
la réforme électorale et
le financement des partis

CANADA

REFORMING

ELECTORAL

DEMOCRACY

VOLUME 4

WHAT
CANADIANS
TOLD US

Available in Canada through
Associated Bookstores
and other booksellers

or by mail from
Canada Communication Group – Publishing
Ottawa, Canada K1A 0S9

Catalogue No. Z1-1989/2-4-1991E
ISBN 0-660-14248-1 (vol. 4)
    0-660-14244-9 (set)

Canadian Cataloguing in Publication Data

Canada. Royal Commission on Electoral Reform and Party Financing

  Reforming electoral democracy : final report

  Chairman: Pierre Lortie
  Partial contents: vol. 3: Proposed legislation; –
  v. 4: What Canadians told us.
  ISBN 0-660-14244-9 (set);
  0-660-14245-7 (vol. 1); 0-660-14246-5 (v. 2);
  0-660-14247-3 (v. 3); 0-660-14248-1 (v. 4)
  DSS cat. nos. Z1-1989/2-1991E (set);
  Z1-1989/2-1-1991E (vol. 1); Z1-1989/2-2-1991E (v. 2);
  Z1-1989/2-3-1991E (v. 3); Z1-1989/2-4-1991E (v. 4)

  1. Elections – Canada. 2. Election law – Canada. 3. Advertising,
  Political – Canada. 4. Campaign funds – Canada. 5. Voter
  registration – Canada. I. Title.

JL193.C35 1991   324.6'0971   C91-098741-6

Royal Commission on
Electoral Reform and
Party Financing

CANADA

Commission royale sur
la réforme électorale et
le financement des partis

TO HIS EXCELLENCY
THE GOVERNOR GENERAL IN COUNCIL

MAY IT PLEASE YOUR EXCELLENCY

We, the Commissioners, appointed by Order in Council dated 15th November 1989, as revised and amended on 3rd October 1990, to inquire into and report on the appropriate principles and process that should govern the election of members of the House of Commons and the financing of political parties and of candidates' campaigns

BEG TO SUBMIT TO YOUR EXCELLENCY THIS REPORT.

Pierre Lortie, Chairman

Pierre Wilfrid Fortier

William Knight

Robert Thomas Gabor

Lucie Pépin

November 1991

171, rue Slater St., Suite 1120
P.O. Box/C.P. 1718, Stn./Succ. "B"
Ottawa, Canada K1P 6R1

(613) 990-4353 FAX: (613) 990-3311

500 Place D'Armes
Suite 1930
Montreal, Canada H2Y 2W2

(514) 496-1212 FAX: (514) 496-1832

CONTENTS

PART 4: APPENDICES

INTRODUCTION

D<small>EMOCRACY DEMANDS MORE</small> than the occasional casting of a ballot. It requires citizen participation in the processes that lead to public policy formulation; it is built upon open communication through which our aspirations and needs are expressed and translated into action. A Royal Commission is one such avenue of communication.

Because needs and aspirations evolve over time, the process of designing and redesigning the structures and rules that govern relations in a democracy is continuous. Our democratic principles and traditions are secure, but there are always new pressures and new requirements emerging in a democratic system. It was in response to these new pressures and requirements that the Royal Commission on Electoral Reform and Party Financing was appointed in November 1989.

The legitimacy of the electoral system depends on Canadians' trust and confidence in its fairness and integrity. Recognizing from the outset that our recommendations for electoral reform would have to meet with the approval of voters, the Commission designed a public consultation process to reach as broad a cross-section of Canadians as possible and to include people with a wide range of experience in the electoral system, as voters, candidates, party workers, or election officials.

Early in our mandate, in January 1990, the Commission placed an advertisement in national newspapers inviting Canadians to submit briefs on any matter pertaining to reform of the federal electoral system and party financing. To complement the advertisement, the Commission Chairman sent more than 7000 letters to potentially interested individuals and groups across Canada, including Members of Parliament, senators, political parties, constituency associations, candidates, official agents and auditors involved in the 1988 election campaign, academics, national, regional and local associations, chambers of commerce, trade unions, and numerous private citizens.

Judging by the response to the Commission's invitation for public participation, Canadians have a keen interest in improving the electoral system. As soon as the advertisement hit the newsstands, the Commission began receiving requests for information from across Canada. Briefs started to arrive almost immediately. Ultimately, Commission staff registered more than 900 briefs, including 233 from groups and associations, 195 from political practitioners and organizations, and 466 from election administrators and private citizens.

The Commission's initial schedule of public hearings called for 28 days of sittings in 25 cities across Canada. Given the overwhelming response and the heavy demand for appointments to speak to the Commission, evening sessions had to be added in most locations, as well as extra days of hearings in some cities. The Commission made a determined effort to hear everyone who wanted to be heard, often sitting late into the evening to accommodate those who showed up to share their views.

By the end of this first round of consultations, the Commission had held 42 days of hearings in 27 cities, most between March and May 1990. A total of 523 groups or individuals appeared before the Commissioners to present their views. The record of this testimony extends to some 14 000 pages.

At the Commission's first meeting it was decided that hearings should be as informal as possible and should avoid a court-like atmosphere. The key was to encourage as many people as possible to come forward and express their views. In this regard, we hope that comments like the following reflect the experience of most participants:

> First of all, I would like to extend my congratulations to this Commission for its hearings, for its very relaxed atmosphere.... We are very grateful to be able to participate. I want to thank you for the atmosphere you have created and for the fact that small [political] parties like ourselves really have an opportunity for input.

And this one from a participant in Moncton:

> I wanted to add that I feel very comfortable here, especially having watched you at work for a few hours this afternoon. I found you very good listeners, very sensitive to what was being said here. And I've learned a lot myself today and I thank you for it.

The Commission heard from Canadians who sent brief letters, perhaps only a paragraph or two, as well as from individuals and groups that presented lengthy briefs. People described personal experiences and frustrations with rules or procedures and sent us detailed proposals for wholesale change in the system. Interest and participation in the consultations surpassed our expectations, not only in quantity but also in the quality of interventions. Everywhere, the Commissioners were impressed by the sincerity of interveners, their concern for the health of our electoral system, and their desire to help improve it.

Interveners ranged from those who longed for simpler times ...

> I came to Canada in 1958 and I worked at the National Research Council on Sussex Drive. Very frequently I left the lab late and I would often meet Mr. Diefenbaker, walking his dog, without a bodyguard. Once in a while we even exchanged a few words, and I had a feeling I knew the man. Now ... I do not think that I know any of them. All I know about them I get through the media.

... to those who look to an electronic future:

~ The new election procedure should include a permanent computerized voters list with special identity cards based on SIN numbers; a permanent election system consisting of selected polling stations, accessible to the disabled; computer election ballots based on SIN numbers; and customized questions allowing quick tabulation and verification of multiple referendums with touch-of-screen technology and a manual check of SIN numbers with a printed voters list.

Some interveners had no difficulty zeroing in on the source of their frustrations with the electoral system. This comment, in both content and tone, was typical of many we heard:

~ The [Canada Elections] Act as a whole is unquestionably one of the most difficult pieces of electoral legislation anywhere. Over two or three elections, I found the best way to settle arguments with angry electors – one of whom wanted to break a chair over my head – was simply to bring out the Act and say, "You try to make sense of this thing."

Commissioners were also enlightened and entertained by those who had worked in past elections. Through anecdotes like the following, the size and diversity of the country quickly came home to us. In the Northwest Territories, for example, election rules that make eminent good sense in most of Canada may present some difficulties:

~ I was asked if I would go to a community some 89 air miles from here and enumerate for the election.... I arrived at Lake Harbour in the morning. I got off the boat plane. It was then mid-September 1966. Walked up to the beach from the canoe and was met by this fellow who wanted to know what I was doing in Lake Harbour. I said I'd come to enumerate for the election. "The election? What election?" I said, "The territorial election." "Oh, well, we had that yesterday." "Yesterday?" I said. "Yes, sure." I said, "How did you manage to do that?" "Well, we heard there was an election and I went up to the school, got an exercise book, wrote the names of the two candidates down on these pieces of paper and got the people in from the camps, the outpost camps, and they came and voted. Didn't you get the results?" he asked, "We sent them over on the radio." I said, "No, we didn't, and there are three candidates." "Oh, well, who is the other one?" So all forces were reassembled, and we brought the people back in from the camps, and we went through the proper procedure with a ballot box and everything. And of course the results were exactly the same, right to the very vote. Six weeks later I was eventually rescued by boat and arrived here on the 10th of November.

Part 1 of this volume tries to convey to readers the flavour of the many thousands of pages of testimony and written submissions the Commission heard and read. An attempt was made to cover all the major topics raised by participants, and a selection of quotations from briefs and testimony has also been included. As the hearings were open to the public and press, and the letters, briefs and transcripts of the hearings are public documents, individual interveners have not been identified in this account; instead this volume focuses on the ideas presented and the suggestions made by the Canadians who spoke to us.

It is the Commission's hope that this sampling of briefs and testimony does justice to Canadians' interests, reflects fairly the range of their concerns, and provides an authentic representation of their views. Undoubtedly there were people who would have liked to voice their opinions but were unable to do so. This is unfortunate, because the Commission found Canadians singularly knowledgeable and helpful. Many thanks are due to those who took the time and made the effort to contribute to the work of the Commission.

Readers should keep in mind that many of the changes recommended by some participants drew no response from others. This is not surprising, in that most interveners focused on the areas they believed needed improvement and tended to ignore areas where they were satisfied with the status quo. Fixed election dates and the right to recall a Member of Parliament are two examples of issues where virtually the only interveners mentioning them were those advocating their adoption.

The account shows where consensus appeared to emerge and where opinion remains divided. But no effort was made to keep score of how many interveners advanced a particular position or favoured a specific course of action. Nor was there an attempt to weight the selection of quotations to reflect the number of people advocating one view or another. Just as the hearings revealed varying views from individuals with different experiences in the electoral process, this account reflects the range and variety of those views, rather than the extent to which they are held by Canadians generally. In making selections, the Commission tried to ensure that participants would see their own views reflected – though perhaps not their actual words – and that all readers would find an informative and representative account of the information, opinions and ideas received from the public.

The first round of public consultations was followed by a process of summarizing and synthesizing the evidence that had been gathered. A major study identified the values underlying the presentations Canadians made to the Commission. With these in mind an extensive research program was designed to explore issues in greater depth and from a comparative perspective. What emerged from the research program – published in the form of the 23 volumes of research studies listed later in this volume – was the framework for the Commission's recommendations.

Thus, participants' contributions were valuable not only because of their ideas and opinions, but also because they helped the Commission develop a research program that encompassed all aspects of the electoral system. The Commission also met with all chief electoral officers from across the country. Their suggestions formed an important backdrop against which to view the public consultation process.

This first phase enabled the Commission to define priorities for electoral reform, delineate the principles that should govern reform, and identify the specific initiatives that could be taken to effect reform. Six major desirable characteristics of electoral democracy emerged from the initial public hearings and some 50 issue papers we requested from academics specialized in certain aspects of constitutional law, party and election finance and the electoral process. The six characteristics suggest important ethical values and objectives for the electoral system. These objectives in turn provided a framework to guide the analysis and assessment of various options for reform:

1. To secure the democratic rights of voters.
2. To enhance access to elected office.
3. To promote the equality and efficacy of the vote.
4. To strengthen political parties as primary political organizations.
5. To promote fairness in the electoral process.
6. To enhance public confidence in the integrity of the electoral process.

As the framework for the recommendations began to take shape, the Commission organized an extensive round of consultations in the form of research symposiums and practical seminars involving academics, political practitioners, including Members of Parliament, election officials, journalists and others with experience in various aspects of the electoral system. Presenting preliminary research results to those with practical experience was intended to ensure that the Commission's recommendations were based on a solid intellectual and empirical foundation and firmly anchored in reality. Speakers from other countries provided opportunities for exposure to comparative experiences and a chance to assess unfamiliar systems and procedures for possible relevance to Canada.

Another series of seminars with practitioners involved returning officers, candidates' official agents, other election officials, Commissioners and staff. These sessions focused on current election administration rules, processes, procedures and on options for reform.

The symposiums were designed to contribute to the Commission's deliberations on its recommendations and final report and also to develop awareness and discussion of the major questions and options under consideration by the Commission. As such, the symposiums were intended to help in building consensus, particularly among political parties and interest groups, on the issues central to the Commission's mandate.

Part 2 of this volume consists of summaries of discussion at the symposiums and seminars organized by the Commission. Each summary explains the purpose of the symposium or seminar, sets out the central issues under discussion, and outlines the principal points raised. The major areas of consensus and disagreement and the conclusions, if any, are noted, and issues remaining to be resolved are identified. A more detailed examination of these issues is available in the Commission's published research studies. Participants in the symposiums are listed in Part 4 of this volume.

Another consultative process also contributed to our deliberations. More effective representation for the Aboriginal people of Canada was identified as an important objective of electoral reform by a number of witnesses early in the Commission's public hearings. Among those testifying to this need was Senator Len Marchand, who in 1968 had been the first Indian person elected to the House of Commons. Senator Marchand pointed out that Aboriginal people have never been represented in the House of Commons in proportion to their numbers and put forward a proposal for improving this situation through reform of the electoral system.

In Sydney, Nova Scotia, this concern was expressed another way:

> Why is it that we as a people do not have representation? Why? Because under the current system of representation in Parliament, the elected Members of Parliament, through no fault of their own, believe they represent the view of a majority of their geographic constituents. And they do not and cannot understand the result of their actions on a piece of legislation when they are so far removed from its effects, being a different people.

The Commission made a special effort to obtain comments from a wide range of Aboriginal people. Toward the end of the hearings, several interveners from Aboriginal organizations urged that there be more substantive consultations on Aboriginal issues than had taken place in the hearings process. At the final hearings in Ottawa, a representative of the Native Council of Canada recommended that the Commission establish a joint working committee with representatives of Aboriginal organizations to develop specific recommendations for Aboriginal representation in the House of Commons. The argument was made that it would be easier to reach consensus on a proposal if it were made jointly with Aboriginal representatives than if it originated unilaterally with the Commission.

Using Senator Marchand's brief to the Commission as a basis for discussion, the Commission asked him to consult more widely with Aboriginal people to determine the extent of consensus on his proposal for improving Aboriginal representation in the House of Commons. In January 1991 Senator Marchand consulted national and regional Aboriginal leaders and found concrete support for his approach. Subsequently, Senator Marchand and four current and former Aboriginal Members of Parliament formed the Committee for Aboriginal Electoral Reform.

Senator Marchand chaired the Committee, whose membership consisted of Jack Anawak, Member of Parliament for Nunatsiaq; Ethel Blondin, Member of Parliament for Western Arctic; Willie Littlechild, Member of Parliament for Wetaskiwin; and Gene Rheaume, former Member of Parliament for the Northwest Territories, which at the time was a single constituency.

The Committee developed a more detailed proposal for Aboriginal constituencies and designed a program of consultation with Aboriginal peoples and national, regional and local Aboriginal leaders. In May 1991 the Committee began consultations, publishing their reform proposal in the Aboriginal press and meeting Aboriginal leaders across the country. By September 18, the Committee had completed its discussions, submitted its report to the Commission and made it public. The report of the Committee for Aboriginal Electoral Reform, with its observations, findings, conclusions and recommendations, makes an original and significant contribution to the challenge of improving our system of electoral democracy as it applies to the Aboriginal people of Canada. As Part 3 of this volume, we present the Committee's report, including the discussion paper used as a basis for their consultations.

The results of these various consultations are presented in this volume, which provides background on one aspect of the process the Commission went through in formulating recommendations and preparing its final report. It is not an exhaustive document, in the sense that not every witness is quoted and not every brief is cited. But it does provide a sample of the ideas and opinions the Commission received and conveys the flavour of the public debate on the issues we were asked to address. The volume is presented in four parts:

- **Part 1** is an overview of Canadians' ideas and opinions on the electoral system, expressed to the Commission in briefs, letters, and testimony at our public hearings.
- **Part 2** presents summaries of the proceedings at our symposiums on various aspects of the electoral system and the financing of parties and candidates.
- **Part 3** contains the discussion paper and report submitted by the Committee for Aboriginal Electoral Reform.
- **Part 4** contains appendices, including a detailed list of the individuals and groups that took part in our public consultation process by submitting briefs or letters, appearing at the hearings, participating in the symposiums or in meetings.

Public consultation is essential to the democratic process. The response to the Commission's extensive consultations demonstrates that Canadians are concerned about the future of our electoral democracy. They recognize that the rules governing this essential feature of our system of government must reflect the social, demographic, constitutional, and technological evolution of our country.

Commissioners were impressed not only with the number of people who came forward to present their views orally or in writing, but also with the thoughtfulness and thoroughness of their interventions. Public consultations gave the Commissioners invaluable insights into how Canadians would like to see the electoral system fashioned to meet their needs and expectations. For this, Commissioners congratulate and thank all those who participated.

The Commission would also like to thank its staff for the special effort they put into making the public hearings, the symposiums and other meetings a success. Commissioners saw first-hand the tremendous amount of time, energy and logistical ingenuity required to keep the show on the road and make it run smoothly. A special thanks to the staff for the many ways in which they made life easier for weary and travel-worn Commissioners.

No matter where presentations were made or in what language they were presented, views expressed across the country were remarkably consistent. This undoubtedly reflects the fact that Canadians share the same traditions and expectations of the electoral system at the federal and provincial level throughout the country, even if the legislation varies with respect to specific provisions. The message the Commissioners received in all parts of the country is that the need for electoral reform is urgent. As one Member of Parliament told the Commission,

> You are here to recommend fundamental reform. Your job is to show Canadians a vision of the future that will enable us, as politicians, to be better MPs and better Ministers, our fellow citizens to be better electors, and Canada to move closer to the democratic ideal we all share.
>
> To get there, we'll need concerted political will. I believe that the Commission's work will encourage this political will to emerge in a way that it has not done until now.

On many issues, Canadians showed a significant degree of consensus on how the electoral system falls short of the ideal and what should be done to improve it. In areas where disagreement remains, there may still be lively public debate. This is as it should be, for the essence of our system of governance is that all those who wish to be heard should have an opportunity for input before decisions are made.

The responses of Canadians to the issues we were asked to address will shape our electoral system into the twenty-first century. With their contributions, the Commission was able to develop a blueprint for an electoral law that will meet the needs of Canadians, reflect their values and democratic principles, and reinforce confidence in our system of governance. The new *Canada Elections Act* must build on the ideals of democracy while reflecting our common values as Canadians looking ahead to the next century. It was these common values that the public consultations were designed to elicit, and it is these values that helped to shape the Commission's recommendations for electoral reform.

PART 1

WHAT CANADIANS TOLD US AT THE PUBLIC HEARINGS AND IN THE WRITTEN SUBMISSIONS

~

1

ON WHO SHOULD VOTE

In some countries, ... people are willing to die for the ability to vote in free elections to determine the government of their choosing.

In Canada, we are led to believe that every Canadian citizen over the age of 18 has the right to vote. On paper, this is true. Our Charter of Rights and Freedoms stipulates that all Canadians are guaranteed this right. However, in practice this is far from true.

As this comment from a Member of Parliament points out, most Canadians assume that we have always had the right to vote. But until relatively recently this right was not protected by law and did not extend to everyone. And while it's true we have no history of a long, divisive struggle to guarantee this basic right, groups such as women and Aboriginal people had to struggle for many years for the right to vote. The Commission saw evidence of a deep belief that the right to vote is fundamental to Canadian citizenship. This was perhaps best summed up by a resident of Winnipeg, who told the Commission, "The act of voting is the most fundamental and direct participation in the process of government."

Canadians who believed that they had been unfairly denied the right to vote, or who had lost the right to vote because of administrative policies and practices, showed up in large numbers at the public hearings to argue their case for changes in law and regulations. Representatives of a Nova Scotia constituency association told us, "We start with the premise that it should be no less worrisome to see a person lose her right to vote as a result of the bureaucracy of Elections Canada, than it would be if the right were taken by a totalitarian regime."

Typical of the strong feelings expressed by many individuals was the presentation by a naturalized Canadian from London, Ontario. Everyone in his apartment block was left off the voters list during the 1988 general election, missed the revision because they didn't realize they weren't on the list and, as urban voters, couldn't be sworn in on election day.

Now, it is very hard for a person who leaves his country and adopts another country, because of a better life, to be forbidden to vote. It is the worst thing that can happen to that citizen.

An election is something you are happy to be able to pursue, participate in and be able to vote for the person you want. That is freedom. The moment you cannot do that, you are not a free person. You can say what you want, but you are not free.

Faced with the question of extending the right to vote to those currently excluded, most participants responded sympathetically, but expressed concerns about cheapening or otherwise abusing the right to vote. For example, the Saskatchewan Association of Rural Municipalities told us, "Canadians living abroad who can prove they have a legitimate reason for doing so should not be disfranchised. Reasons for living outside Canada, such as employment or health, should be acceptable. Canadians living outside Canada for purely social or personal reasons should be required to return home to the constituency to exercise their franchise." And in Moncton one group argued, "We believe that habitual and/or violent criminals, and those without any remorse whatever for their criminal activity, should not be qualified to vote at any time during their incarceration."

> "The act of voting is the most fundamental and direct participation in the process of government."

On the other side of the issue of broadening the franchise, one participant suggested:

I cannot come up with any particularly good reasons why people in prisons and the mentally handicapped should not vote. And I can come up with one good reason [why they should]; namely that it would help their human development in some small way, were they entitled to vote.

Discussion of who should vote focused on five key issues: the voting age, Canadians abroad, persons with intellectual or psychological impairments, prisoners' rights, and the voting rights of judges and returning officers.

> "I cannot come up with any particularly good reasons why people in prisons and the mentally handicapped should not vote."

THE VOTING AGE

The *Canada Elections Act* sets a minimum voting age of 18 for federal elections. The minimum age in provincial elections is either 18 or 19. Members of the Canadian forces, including students at Canada's military colleges, have the right to vote even if they are not yet 18.

The *Canadian Charter of Rights and Freedoms* bars discrimination on the basis of age unless it can be demonstrated that there is a reasonable and justifiable purpose in doing so. No court challenges have been launched by persons under the age of 18 seeking the right to vote.

In practice, an individual may vote for the first time in a federal election when he or she is anywhere from 18 to 22 years of age, depending on the timing of the election and the person's birth date.

The Commission received proposals ranging from setting no minimum age to raising the minimum age to "age 55. That would have many benefits, such as enhancing the value society attaches to experience, to maturity, to our elders."

The Taddle Creek Greens summarized their support for a lower voting age, stating:

> We picked 16 because that is the age at which you no longer have to stay in school; it's the age at which we feel in society you are responsible enough to drive a vehicle on the road; it's an age at which you can do many things in our society. And we feel that the young people are the ones who are going to inherit this horrible mess that we're creating for them. The young people are very concerned about our earth and what we're doing to it and feel they should have a voice.

In response to a question from the Commission on retaining the right of Canadian forces personnel to vote at an earlier age, one Member of Parliament said, "I think it goes without saying that if we expect people to serve the country in an armed conflict, we ought to have confidence that they can cast an intelligent ballot as well."

Student representatives spoke both for and against a lower voting age. In Montreal, a student said, "Electing our own government – it is not a privilege that has been given to us and can be taken away from us by the House of Commons, it's the most basic of our human rights. I always thought that human rights started the minute you were born, not the minute you turn 18."

> "I always thought that human rights started the minute you were born, not the minute you turn 18."

By contrast, a student in Regina, answering a question from the Commission on extending the vote to those under 18, suggested, "I think that's too young. You're not even out of high school.... I feel that at least you have to have some life experience.... A lot of 18-year-olds may still be in high school but ... they're graduating, they're coming out into the world. I think they understand a little bit more about what's going on around them."

In Cape Breton, the Royal Canadian Legion observed, "It has been the experience of our society that when allowances are made for members of our community to be accorded privileges by lowering age barriers, the results have been as predicted. For instance, reducing the age of majority from 21 to

18 years had the immediate effect of reducing the age of legality for alcoholic consumption as well."

The Canadian Bar Association based its comments about the voting age on a consideration of the Charter. Responding to a Commission question about the appropriate age, its spokesperson replied:

~ The Association is of the opinion that a voting age could be arrived at by consensus, following consultation with experts in psychological development and social policy.... While it is probably clear that the seven-year-old bracket should not be enfranchised, it may be that the 14- to 16-year-old bracket is worthy of consideration. Evidence of general levels of development should be looked at in conjunction with other social policy goals which may be advanced by enfranchising younger persons. The Commission may wish to consider what role young people play in society and whether it is appropriate to encourage them to participate in the political process. In this context, it is clear that many young people are politically active, both in mainstream party politics and in dissenting groups.

In Vancouver, a case was put for no minimum age:

~ What if a seven-year-old seriously wants to run for prime minister? Well, the checks and balances in the elections act already take care of that. If you can raise the necessary funds to do it, if you can convince a political party to back you, if you can rally troops on your behalf, and, potentially, get elected, based on a well-run computerized campaign, then I'll vote for you. But chances are, that seven-year-old or that 10-year-old or even that 16-year-old won't have the political moxie, at least for the next 50 years.

The Canadian Bar Association summed up the issue facing the Commission:

~ At the end of the day, the only conclusion we came to as a group was that a fixed age of voting would necessarily be arbitrary in the sense that there would be people younger than that age who were highly educated, politically aware and quite capable of participating in a political process, and there would be people older than that age of whom the reverse could be said.

CANADIANS ABROAD

The *Canada Elections Act* makes no provisions for Canadians voting from abroad, except for members of the Canadian forces and federal public servants posted abroad. These special voting rules also apply to their spouses and dependants qualified as voters and living abroad with them.

The Charter guarantees the right to vote for every Canadian citizen. The elections act provides that every citizen over the age of 18 is qualified as an elector. However, it also requires that a citizen be ordinarily resident in a polling division in order to be enumerated and registered; a person who is not registered cannot vote.

Some provinces have extended voting rights to some persons living or travelling outside the province. Most western democracies, including the United States and the United Kingdom, allow their citizens to vote from abroad. The United Kingdom extends the right for as long as 20 years.

Voting rights for Canadians abroad were discussed by some 50 interveners at the hearings. All favoured some extension, but there was a wide range of views on how far to go and how to implement it. In British Columbia an intervener made this argument:

> Generally speaking, I think a Canadian should have the right to vote in an election deciding his country's government because his country's government will have an impact on his citizenship, his rights to work abroad, his taxation rights. I think it's a fundamental right that no Canadian should lose. I think it should attach to citizenship, not residence.

A Member of Parliament offered this perspective:

> I do share the view that Canadian citizens abroad should have the vote. But let me be honest with you. The political parties are resisting this. It's not so much the CUSO worker or the Oxfam worker – they're not worried about that. They're worried about all the people that live in Florida or California.
>
> I would say stick to the Charter and stick to the principle that if you're Canadian you should have a vote.

"I would say stick to the Charter and stick to the principle that if you're Canadian you should have a vote."

Others weren't so accommodating:

> Those Canadians ... abroad on vacation – I don't think there really should be any special preference for these people. An election is called several weeks ahead of time. If they believe strongly in the democratic process then they should actually have to return to the country to vote.

A question from the Commission as to whether the right to vote should be extended to Canadians who had been out of Canada for 25 years elicited this response in the Northwest Territories: "There are people who live outside of Canada who are not at all in touch with the issues and probably ... wouldn't even really know who they should vote for.... I don't know what purpose their vote would serve if they don't even know who they're voting for or what the issues are."

Canadians working abroad for various aid and development groups were well represented at the hearings. A CUSO worker told the Commission, "My own experience working overseas over the years has been that when you are overseas, you are very conscious of the benefits of being a Canadian. It makes you probably a better and more aware Canadian and more, not less, sensitive to the rights and privileges of citizenship. Since the vote is such a pivotal right, it should be available to all Canadians, especially those who are temporarily absent doing what we hope is good work overseas."

The Commission heard many stories of Canadians living or travelling abroad who had been denied the vote.

> While I was in England, a federal election was called and the issue at that time was the stationing of nuclear weapons on Canadian soil. It's a matter that concerned me very greatly at the time. I phoned the Canadian [High Commission] and said, can I vote? And he said, "No, you'll have to go home to vote."
>
> I was in no financial position to do that, and I was absolutely outraged – in fact I'm still outraged today, at the thought that I was not allowed to vote on an issue which concerned me so deeply, simply because I was out of the country when the election was called and held.
>
> I hope the Commission will make recommendations to deal with people who are in that situation. I hope that never happens again to another Canadian anywhere in the world.

An intervener who works abroad for the federal government explained why he was unable to vote even though many of the people he worked with could:

> In our three major embassies there are a large number of Canadian citizens who are members of the locally engaged staff. These Canadians are in a sort of a limbo land. They are not Department of External Affairs employees, although they are employed by the Department of External Affairs. They are not generally residents of the country in which they are employed. They are Canadian citizens, pay full Canadian taxes. These Canadians have not been permitted to vote.

The Native Council of Canada explained: "There is a particular problem that Aboriginal people have with regard to the out-of-country [vote], because there is such a constancy of movement across the medicine line between Canada and the United States ... and increasingly between Greenland and Denmark, and the eastern Arctic, amongst the Inuit."

Interveners also talked about how to organize voting by Canadians abroad. There were proposals that this be carried out by a mail ballot, similar to that used for the military and for public servants posted abroad. Other solutions included registering on an offshore voters list before leaving Canada, or at a Canadian office abroad, and letting eligible voters outside Canada vote at a Canadian office abroad, using a mail ballot or proxy voting. As one person concluded:

 This [loss of the right to vote while living abroad] was perhaps acceptable in an era when communications technology didn't allow us to obtain information quickly enough to avoid the possibility of fraud when Canadians were voting from abroad. But today technology enables us to get any information we need virtually instantaneously from almost anywhere in the world.

PERSONS WITH MENTAL DISABILITIES

The elections act bars voting by any person who is "restrained of his liberty of movement or deprived of the management of his property by reason of mental disease."

Although the law has not been changed, it was struck down during the 1988 election following a court challenge launched by the Canadian Disability Rights Council. As a consequence, people living in institutions for the mentally disabled were enumerated and allowed to vote, in accordance with guidelines issued by Elections Canada.

More than 40 interveners at the hearings spoke about the franchise in relation to persons with intellectual or psychological disabilities. Most of them represented advocacy groups or groups serving these persons.

Maintaining the present law is not an option, because of the 1988 court decision. The suggestions from witnesses centred mainly on the mechanics of how the right to vote should be applied. Many of the issues raised were practical matters of election administration rather than issues of principle.

The constitutional aspect of the argument was raised by Jean-Pierre Kingsley, Chief Electoral Officer of Canada, who told the Commission: "The provisions in the *Canada Elections Act* excluding judges and persons with mental disabilities from voting should be changed to correspond with the 1988 decisions that found them unconstitutional."

A contributor in Quebec commented that "the right to vote is imperative for people living with an intellectual disability, because this is the initial process that is going to enable them to take their place as full-fledged citizens on equal terms."

Some witnesses contended that there should be an assumption of competence with respect to persons with intellectual or psychological disabilities and that the elections act should abandon the 'asylum complex', which assumes that mental illness makes it impossible for people to function in the community. The Ontario Association for Community Living urged not just an extension of the vote, but that Elections Canada hire people with intellectual or developmental disabilities to work in local returning offices during elections.

Arguing that the definition of what constitutes a mental disability is far too broad, one contributor in Vancouver suggested that "to classify all the mentally disabled in one category is very wrong. I am sure a lot of us get mentally disabled at some time or other with all the stresses and distresses in our lives, but we still function."

"To classify all the mentally disabled in one category is very wrong."

Opinion was divided on whether to deny the vote to persons found incompetent under a judicial process, such as the new Quebec law on legal guardianship. The Public Curator of Quebec estimates that under the new law about 7000 people in Quebec would be deprived of their right to vote for that reason, out of 21 000 now under various forms of guardianship. Other provinces do not have such fully developed systems. An intervener in Victoria contended that even if people have been judged incompetent, they could still have "areas of excellence" and be able to vote.

Another intervener argued that "only those who have been restrained of their liberty of movement or deprived of the management of their property should be deprived of their right to vote." This view was supported by a Winnipeg resident: "As a lawyer, I do this on a regular basis. If a person is mentally incompetent, they cannot handle their own affairs. We get a court declaration and that is the end of it. They cannot handle their financial affairs, they cannot sell their property, they cannot mortgage their property.... Why should they be able to vote?... That is really a good question."

Opinion was also divided about whether there should be some sort of test of mental ability to be allowed to vote. Several interveners suggested that if a test were to be required, it should also be given to other voters. In Moncton we were told, somewhat wryly, "If we do not test the voting competency of the [general] public, then what right do we have to test it on certain groups or individuals such as a person who undergoes treatment in a psychiatric hospital?" This point was reinforced by a Winnipeg participant: "Clearly, requiring the answers to such questions places a higher onus on persons labelled mentally disabled than that placed on the general electorate and represents a prime example of discrimination."

The Canadian Bar Association at the Ottawa hearings suggested:

> The difficulty is that any test you put in place for the mentally disabled will be challenged by somebody else. If you need some kind of a certificate of competency from a physician before you can get on the enumeration list, you are opening up a can of worms which we find to be intolerable.

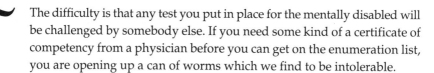

Those who supported a testing procedure generally felt that it should be minimal or that the questions asked of other voters at enumeration – name, address, citizenship and approximate age – were sufficient. As a group in Montreal told us, "This would mean ... that to be excluded from the right to vote, a person would be unable to communicate verbally, in writing or by any other means, his or her identity and address."

More pointedly, we were told, "Regardless of whether it's a demented patient, an elderly senile individual, or an acute psychotic individual in an institution – if they can answer simple questions accurately, they should have the right to vote." Another intervener pointed out that people living in the community can be put on the voters list by a relative without even being seen or questioned by the enumerator.

A Quebec City participant suggested that the ability to go to a poll on election day and cast a ballot constitutes a form of "implicit test". Both the Canadian Bar Association and the Canadian Human Rights Commission pointed out that any test of capacity to vote, beyond the questions needed for enumeration, would be open to challenge under the *Canadian Charter of Rights and Freedoms*.

The argument was summed up in Toronto by an intervener who suggested: "It is really not possible to develop a test to ensure a person's capacity to participate in the electoral process. If there are to be any restrictions placed on this right, those restrictions should apply to all Canadians who are entitled to vote, regardless of disability. The test itself must not focus on the level of intelligence."

The Yukon Association for Community Living and other interveners were critical of the guidelines issued by Elections Canada during the 1988 election with respect to persons with mental disabilities. Enumerators were told that "only those who asked to be enumerated should be listed." Witnesses appearing before the Commission argued that this requirement was unfair because many of the people affected had never voted before; the guidelines had the effect of denying them the assistance they might need to vote.

> "If there are to be any restrictions placed on this right, those restrictions should apply to all Canadians who are entitled to vote, regardless of disability."

Canadians expressed widespread concern about the quality of enumeration as it affected persons with mental disabilities. In one British Columbia institution, only eight of 270 residents were enumerated, according to the British Columbia Association for Community Living. A returning officer in Quebec was turned away by the director of an institution when he tried to conduct an enumeration. Some interveners suggested that all residents of institutions should be enumerated; at the very least, all residents should be seen personally by enumerators, instead of enumerators relying on lists provided by staff.

Institution staff expressed concern about providing lists of residents for reasons of confidentiality. There was an added concern in psychiatric institutions where residents might not wish to reveal the fact that they had been mentally ill.

A number of interveners recommended that the principle of 'reasonable accommodation' should apply to persons with mental disabilities or people who are illiterate. This would entail receiving assistance to vote, including help in marking the ballot if necessary. The Manitoba Association for Community Living recommended that several options be available, enabling a person to seek help from a friend, a relative, or the deputy returning officer, adding that the process of seeking assistance should be simple enough not to present an obstacle to voting.

Another person pointed out: "Everyone has the right to walk, but if you have no legs, it's pretty difficult – you have to use a device. This is what I'm suggesting. If people who are mentally disabled need a device to help them find out about the election law, but they are unable to use this device, then the device is not very useful."

A member of the staff of a Quebec psychiatric hospital suggested that a simple change in the ballot might help achieve this objective: "It would be much easier for people in this group to vote if the ballot had logos of the parties or candidates' photographs on it."

Some concern was expressed about the potential for undue influence on the vote of a mentally disabled person. The British Columbia Association for Community Living suggested that such a risk also exists when persons with physical disabilities are given assistance to vote. A representative of the Canadian Disabilities Rights Council said society has to be prepared to accept certain risks in the interests of guaranteeing the right to vote to persons with disabilities.

A participant in the Ottawa hearings discounted the seriousness of this risk:

> My inclination would be to give someone who was mentally disabled his or her ballot and point them in the direction of the voting booth and hope that they would mark the ballot appropriately. If they were unable to do that, it would be unfortunate, but that would be the end result. If they were able to, they would bring it back and deposit it in the ballot box. So I don't know that we have to have a basic test other than that they should have a right to vote.

In Montreal, an intervener associated with an institution for the mentally ill related the following anecdote:

> The evening before the election, we had invited the nine candidates running in the riding to come to the hospital, and the Rhinoceros candidate showed

up too. Instead of making a speech, he did a magic trick. Well, I can tell you, we were upset afterwards; we told ourselves, "That's it – tomorrow they'll vote for the Rhinoceros Party." But they surprised us by voting ... for the Progressive Conservative candidate, who was voted in.

In Ottawa, a member of a hospital volunteers' committee stated: "We are fiercely opposed to voting by proxy [for persons who are mentally ill]. We believe that the right to vote is essentially personal and can be exercised only by the holder of the right, not by a third party. The psychiatric population is very vulnerable, and the risks of abuse are higher than for so-called normal people."

A number of interveners urged that there be special training of returning officers, enumerators, and other election staff with respect to the needs of persons with intellectual or psychiatric disabilities. More appropriate information about the electoral process needs to be made available to them, and leaflets and other election material, as well as the ballot itself, should be designed to be more accessible to this group.

Others were concerned that there be some assurance that institution staff could not influence the votes of persons in their care: "Since persons with mental disabilities have now received the right to be registered voters, there must be legislation guaranteeing no interference in the right to vote from care-givers and/or administrators of institutions."

Participants in the hearings made other specific suggestions, such as allowing people living in institutions to identify themselves by whatever name they commonly use and to use the name of the institution as their address rather than a street address, which they might not know. They suggested communicating as necessary with disabled persons using Bliss symbols and other forms of non-verbal communication and noted the need for clearer direction to returning officers on how persons with mental disabilities should be enumerated.

The co-ordinator of the Psychiatric Patient Advocate Office in Ontario criticized the practice of designating institutions for the mentally disabled as rural polls in order to permit residents to be sworn in on election day. This is not working because patients may not know one another and nurses cannot vouch for patients because they do not live in the same poll.

A doctor at the Nova Scotia Hospital noted specific problems with respect to short-term patients, who may have no one at home to see that their names are added to the voters list or to cast a proxy vote on their behalf. Patients who were homeless prior to admission are likewise deprived of the right to vote. The Alberta branch of the Canadian Mental Health Association noted a similar problem for patients enumerated while in hospital, then sent home during the course of a campaign.

Some interveners urged that polling places be located in hospitals for convenience and to serve patients who are competent but who are not allowed to leave the hospital grounds; others suggested that polling divisions in hospitals include some residents from the surrounding area so as to keep confidential how hospital residents voted. "We would prefer that there not be a poll reserved exclusively for people living inside the hospital. We would like it to be determined by polling division, once again in order to protect confidentiality," commented one hospital administrator.

PRISONERS

The elections act denies prisoners the right to vote in federal elections, yet section 3 of the Charter gives every Canadian citizen the right to vote and makes no exception for inmates. Federal and provincial inmates have the right to vote in some provincial elections. In some cases this right is set out in provincial law, while in others prisoners have acquired the right by challenging their exclusion through the courts. The provision in the *Canada Elections Act* disqualifying inmates in penal institutions from voting in a federal election was declared invalid by the Federal Court of Canada in 1991. The decision has been appealed.

———

"If our prime object is to rehabilitate prisoners rather than punish them, what better way than to allow them to participate in the democratic process?"

———

Several groups took a strong position in favour of giving prisoners the right to vote. In London, one individual put the case this way: "If our prime object is to rehabilitate prisoners rather than punish them, what better way than to allow them to participate in the democratic process? Why should we take that right away, merely because we have locked them up, because they may pose a danger to society?"

A participant from Quebec advanced the following position:

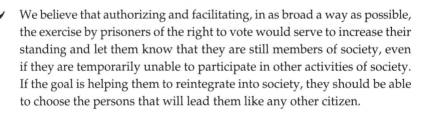

We believe that authorizing and facilitating, in as broad a way as possible, the exercise by prisoners of the right to vote would serve to increase their standing and let them know that they are still members of society, even if they are temporarily unable to participate in other activities of society. If the goal is helping them to reintegrate into society, they should be able to choose the persons that will lead them like any other citizen.

On the other hand, some individuals spoke against permitting prisoners to vote under any circumstances. In Edmonton, we were told, "It's a punishment. The reason why they should not receive a vote is they are not in society in a sense. Until they return to society and act within the confines of our laws, they are barred from certain privileges, one of them being, in my feeling, the right to vote in an election."

In Thompson, Manitoba, the Commission was told:

 We believe that the right to vote is a very special privilege in our country. And we believe that once you break the law of the land, part of the deterrent would be the loss of the right to vote as long as you are in prison. I do not believe the Charter at any point says you have the right to break the law.

Most interveners supported giving prisoners the right to vote, but none advocated allowing prisoners to stand as candidates. The Canadian Bar Association contended that the two issues should be considered separately.

Advocates of voting rights for prisoners acknowledged that there is substantial opposition; a representative of the John Howard Society of Saskatchewan said he would hate to see inmates deprived of the right to vote simply because giving them the right would not be popular. The John Howard Society of Alberta pointed to the need to educate the public concerning penal reform, noting that surveys show that the general level of public knowledge about criminal justice issues is low. Its brief noted that countries such as Italy, Sweden, Norway and Denmark give inmates the right to vote, while other democracies, including the United Kingdom, France, Switzerland and some states in the United States, do not.

Advocacy groups generally opposed the suggestion that prisoners convicted of certain state crimes, such as treason, be denied the vote, as well as the proposal that judges have the option of removing a prisoner's right to vote at the time of sentencing. The John Howard Society of Alberta brief also disputed the argument that prisoners should be denied the vote because they have been denied it in the past, noting that other restrictions from the past, such as denying the vote on the basis of sex or lack of property ownership, no longer apply.

The advocates of prisoner voting rights based their case on the *Canadian Charter of Rights and Freedoms* and on the rehabilitative benefits of allowing prisoners to vote. They argued that the discrepancies between federal and provincial practice violate the equality provisions of the Charter and asked the Commission to reject the concept of 'civil death' by which people lose civil rights because they are convicted of a criminal offence.

The Canadian Bar Association contended that denying prisoners the vote has little social purpose or deterrent value, and that it is an arbitrary rule because prisoners released on discretionary leave can vote even though they have not completed their sentences, while those who are inmates cannot.

 Unless you can come to the conclusion that part of the sanction that is imposed on someone who has offended one of society's laws is to take away that person's right to vote for a temporary brief time, unless that is your logical basis for precluding prisoners from voting, you're not doing something that's very helpful to what is supposed to be one of the prime tenets of sentencing, that is, the rehabilitation of the prisoner.

The Saskatchewan John Howard Society noted that significant change is under way in federal institutions, including better recognition of inmate rights, less intrusion into the lives of inmates, and a greater emphasis on rehabilitation. In its view, voting rights fit into this new trend in corrections. An inmate's vote has no impact on public safety or on the deterrent effect of incarceration, but not being allowed to vote can have negative effects in terms of rehabilitation and subsequent reintegration into society.

It was also argued that denying all prisoners the right to vote is unfair because of disparities in sentencing in different jurisdictions and because people who commit crimes may not be caught, convicted or sentenced. For a given offence, some offenders receive probation while others are jailed. In addition, some types of crime, such as white-collar crime or environmental crime, tend to be treated leniently in terms of prosecution and sentencing.

An inmate appearing before the Commission in Winnipeg put his feelings this way:

> We lose a lot of rights when we come to prison for breaking the law, and I have always known that the main thing is your freedom, your physical freedom. Corrections Canada wants us to re-enter society when we leave prison and hopefully become [responsible] citizens. By taking away our right to vote, that is the last thing we have in prison. We're going to walk back out into a foreign society. In prisons, inmates have access to chapels, libraries, outside newspapers, magazines, self-help groups, programs, meetings, organizations, and are allowed to publish newsletters and articles. Since inmates have access to the media through television, radio, video, film and newspapers, how can one demonstrate or be justified in saying that they are unable to make informed decisions while voting?

The John Howard Society of Manitoba noted that although Aboriginal people account for only 5 per cent of the population in the prairie provinces, they form 32 per cent of the inmate population, and it argued that the denial of voting rights to prisoners mainly affects people of low socio-economic status.

One intervener cited security and administrative difficulties as reasons for not giving prisoners in federal institutions the right to vote. He suggested that the right to vote is a democratic right but not a fundamental one and that losing the vote is less fundamental than losing freedom of movement.

Another argued that prisoners should be denied certain rights because they had denied others a peaceful and secure existence: "It has always been the concept that when a member of the community violates the tranquillity, the security, and the right of others to the ordinary qualities of civilized living, then that citizen should forfeit the same rights, if he is found guilty and committed by his peers."

Other issues raised by witnesses related to the manner of voting, where prisoners' votes should be cast, enumeration in prisons, and the confidentiality of voters lists. Those who supported the vote for prisoners generally thought they should vote in their home constituency, that is, the location of their family or of their last place of residence, rather than in the constituency in which they are incarcerated. Some interveners mentioned potential public concern about a concentration of prison voters in a constituency where a major penitentiary or jail is located.

Many interveners felt that the security problems of conducting the vote in a jail or penitentiary are minimal, although special procedures might be needed, such as closing the polling station once all prisoners who wished to vote had done so.

Corrections Canada maintains a computerized list of prisoners from which voters lists could be drawn up, but there are concerns about making the list public or available to political parties or candidates. Corrections officials were generally open to allowing distribution of party and candidate literature to inmates, but hesitant about allowing access to candidates. However, it was suggested that prisoners can be relatively well informed about politics through their access to the media.

JUDGES AND RETURNING OFFICERS

The elections act denies the vote to certain categories of judges. These provisions were declared invalid by a 1988 Federal Court of Canada judgement. Federal returning officers are not allowed to vote, except when there is a tie vote after a judicial recount.

The question of judges voting was raised by a number of interveners, most of whom were in favour, but the issue was not dealt with at length during the hearings. One participant said, "My suggestion would be that voting would be a matter of personal choice for judges. If judges feel they will somehow be compromised in the way they do their work, because they cast a vote, that can be their decision. However, I do not think it is wise to deny that particular sector of society the right to vote."

> "... disfranchising them is about like disqualifying a judge in a divorce case because he's either divorced or married..."

Another intervener suggested, "I think disfranchising them is about like disqualifying a judge in a divorce case because he's either divorced or married, or in a property case because he owns property or does not own property."

In Halifax the argument was advanced by one intervener that judges should not vote so as to preserve their distance from the political process: "I do not believe that it is important for judges to vote. I like the idea, as manifested in not voting, of [judicial] independence from the rough and tumble of the electoral process."

A few returning officers commented on the question of whether they should have the right to vote. One who argued in favour stated, "I'm asking on behalf of myself and 294 other returning officers to consider us. If judges are to receive the vote; if prisoners are to receive the vote; and all our other citizens are to receive the vote, I think we deserve the right to vote."

2

ON FULLER PARTICIPATION

CANADIANS WHO PARTICIPATED in the Commission's public consultations had no shortage of suggestions about how to increase participation in the electoral process. They were concerned with more than just numbers and voter turnout figures; they wanted to encourage broader forms of participation. There was strong support for greater use of volunteers in the process and for simpler rules to permit more involvement by Canadians.

Proposals to increase the numbers of electors voting at each election ranged from mandatory voting, as in Australia, to a somewhat more novel suggestion made at the Ottawa hearings:

> Voter turnout could be increased significantly by instituting a ballot with an attached receipt to be signed by the returning officer or clerk granting a $100 deduction from tax payable.

Elections Canada's role in encouraging and facilitating participation was examined thoroughly by interveners. Some witnesses argued that Elections Canada should be doing everything in its power to encourage people to campaign and vote for the candidate of their choice. Others argued that this is the exclusive role of the political parties. The majority of opinion fell somewhere between these extremes.

Manitoba's chief electoral officer summed up his case for a more active role on the part of election administrators: "A democratic right is of little value if it is not known to citizens and if that right is not explained in meaningful ways."

Others felt that individuals had to take a greater share of the responsibility. In the words of a Member of Parliament from Nova Scotia, "I say that if we stop spoon-feeding the Canadian people about their right to vote, perhaps Canadians would start to appreciate not only that it is a privilege, but they have some responsibility to exercise it."

On the other hand, Canadians expressed considerable concern about the needs of groups that, for one reason or another, are often excluded from the electoral process. They include the poor, the elderly, members of ethnocultural communities, persons with reading difficulties, people with disabilities, homeless persons, students and Aboriginal people. In Vancouver, a woman who works with low-income people told us:

We need affirmative action policies to make sure that poor people and disadvantaged people are encouraged to vote. Not having these policies will contribute to greater and greater inequality, less participation, and more alienation and violence. And I don't think any of us want that kind of country.

> "A democratic right is of little value if it is not known to citizens and if that right is not explained in meaningful ways."

A New Brunswick returning officer noted that "with the better health care that we have today, we have an ever-increasing senior citizen population. We have to look after that group. We have to make sure that they have the right to vote and that it is easy and it is accessible to them."

Canadians have a good record of participation in national elections by comparison with our neighbours to the south, but our record is not as strong when compared with turnout in other democracies around the world. Canadians representing a wide variety of interests made many suggestions to the Commission about how to increase participation in the electoral process.

VOTER INFORMATION PROGRAMS

Elections Canada conducts a substantial information program during each election campaign. Print, radio and television, as well as the Parliamentary Channel, are used to inform Canadians. The election agency distributes election simulation kits to schools and community groups and maintains a modest information program between elections.

Increasingly, returning officers are called upon to inform the public about the electoral process. The local media and community and special-interest groups are largely responsible for this development; their requests for information between elections are becoming more frequent.

The *Canada Elections Act* requires the chief electoral officer to exercise general direction and supervision over the administration of elections and to ensure effective execution of the provisions of the Act. It does not give any specific mandate to inform the public, nor does it provide in any way for general programs to inform the public about the electoral process.

A substantial number of interveners raised concerns about public information and education in their submissions to the Commission. Most often, the goal was more information for the groups on whose behalf interveners spoke – persons with physical, intellectual or psychological disabilities, homeless people, new immigrants, and so on. In several cases, interveners asked not just for more information but for a full communications strategy and for Elections Canada to be given a broad public information mandate.

In Whitehorse, for example, a political activist suggested, "It's clear that in order to address the increasing disillusionment of many citizens in Canada with the political process, an educational role for Elections Canada should certainly be contemplated."

The National Organization of Immigrant and Visible Minority Women of Canada put this case to the Commissioners: "The onus lies on Elections Canada to ensure that voters are well informed about the general political process, on how to seek nomination, on what a riding association is, etc."

A number of interveners recommended a grassroots approach, with Elections Canada working with community and advocacy groups and using their networks to pursue outreach activities. One Toronto community worker suggested how this might reach some of those normally missed in the electoral process:

> The campaign that I'm recommending needs to be built upon the existing networks of community organizations and services across the country. Networks of places like community centres, hostels, women's shelters and food banks. It's the members and staff of these organizations who have the ongoing connections with the poor and homeless people in our communities, and who are best able to begin this process of voter outreach and voter education.

Several interveners recommended greater use of radio and television. One participant in Winnipeg suggested that "Elections Canada should develop video and written information packages that explain the voting process."

The World Sikh Organization of Canada proposed that Elections Canada start educating potential voters as early as elementary school:

> Since there is always room for improvement, we think recommendations can be made to improve the system simply by raising the interest in it, and this can be best done by education. It should be talked about at the elementary and secondary levels of education. Perhaps Elections Canada could become more involved with our young people at an early stage of their school life.

"... if we are really and truly convinced and dedicated to electoral reform, it is absolutely essential that we consider electoral education."

This view was supported by others who raised concerns about the general lack of knowledge among young people about government and the political system.

> What concerns me a great deal when talking with young people in their third, fourth and fifth years of high school is their total lack of understanding

of our political system, how we are governed and how we should govern.

I think that if we are really and truly convinced and dedicated to electoral reform, it is absolutely essential that we consider electoral education.

An intervener in Vancouver saw an even broader role for Elections Canada. She suggested that "what we really need is media literacy taught in schools. If the media are going to be such a major part of the electoral process, then we need to have an electorate that is versed in the way the media work."

These suggestions were echoed by a number of returning officers who noted an increasing demand for them to carry out public education between elections. At the Halifax hearings one stated, "It is our opinion that the role of the returning officer is acquiring a higher focus, with occasional demands for public input in such forums as schools or university classes, board of trade meetings, and occasional information sessions with political parties."

The point was made on numerous occasions that the effective functioning of our political system relies on tens of thousands of dedicated volunteers, both at election time and between elections. A Winnipeg participant said volunteers are "the backbone, guts, heart and soul of any campaign." Many argued that maintaining this involvement and encouraging even greater participation require that the election law be kept as simple as possible:

We would recommend that the *Canada Elections Act* be redrafted to make it a more understandable document. The Act, as it now reads, is complex and vague, and some sections are subject to various interpretations. Thousands of volunteers need to access, comprehend and understand the legislation which regulates the democratic process in this country. The current legislation makes this comprehension difficult.

In Toronto, one participant suggested, "Do what you can to encourage involvement at the riding level, not to overcomplicate volunteer involvement, and to make it a healthy and acceptable thing to contribute time and money and effort to the election of candidates, regardless of one's political philosophy." Another participant in Vancouver noted, "The Canadian election system is made up of an awful lot of crazy people who for 56 days of every four years give up everything to work in these campaigns, whether it is for the Conservatives, the Liberals, the NDP, the Reform Party – we all rely on [volunteers]. And sometimes, these volunteers are taken for granted."

Witnesses noted that election information must reflect Canada's ethnic and cultural mosaic. Elections Canada first began to direct information about the electoral process to members of ethno-cultural communities in the 1980 election. It spent about $90 000 to reach them during the 1988 election – just under 6 per cent of its advertising budget – and distributed a large number of multilingual booklets on voting in Canada. A participant at the Ottawa hearings urged Elections Canada "to continue to translate voting information into various languages and to use ethnic media increasingly."

The main concern of interveners who spoke on these issues was to increase the flow of information in different languages to people in these communities and to try to promote greater participation. One intervener summed up the requirements in the following manner:

 The model that Elections Canada has at the moment assumes that you've been educated in Canada, you're familiar with what voting is all about, why you should vote, how you do it. That is simply not the case [for many voters]. And the more things you can make more familiar and more consistent, the better.

> "People's first experience with the Canadian political system, the Canadian system of government, should be open, encouraging – they should be welcomed into the process."

People's first experience with the Canadian political system, the Canadian system of government, should be open, encouraging – they should be welcomed into the process. Instead, what they find are barricades, difficulties, and a lot of discouragement.

The National Organization of Immigrant and Visible Minority Women recommended that, to reach as many voters as possible, electoral information be in audio and video as well as in written form, and that organizations representing ethno-cultural communities be asked to help prepare and distribute it.

A Winnipeg constituency association, which carries out its campaign in seven languages because of the ethno-cultural make-up of the riding, was critical of Elections Canada for not being sufficiently willing to help people from other cultures understand the electoral process. On the same point, the Canadian Ethnocultural Council argued:

Elections Canada advertising should reflect the cultural and racial diversity of Canadians in all visual materials. This would fall in line with the federal government's depiction guidelines which call on all federal departments and agencies to accurately reflect the multicultural nature of Canadian society.

Several interveners voiced concern about how people from countries with different traditions and political practices might see the Canadian political system. A participant in the Calgary hearings put it this way:

Language barriers and cultural differences may tend to alienate ethnic minorities from feeling that they're part of Canadian society, and maybe the democratic process as well. As a result, they may not fully understand the significance of the electoral process. Many new citizens come to Canada from societies that are anything but democratic. Therefore, they may view our political system, our electoral process, our voting process – anything that is Canadian – as different, even corrupt. They may not want to voice any of their personal opinions against politics or political leaders, for fear of retaliation.

An intervener in London reflected the thoughts of many others when she said:

The electoral process needs to be inclusive. That is, it must recognize the responsibility to educate more broadly. The parents or older relatives of Canadian citizens must be able to understand the system even if they are not eligible to vote. Their opinions are of vital importance in their households, and the voters are impelled to honour the elders' opinions. Although some sensitization to the needs of a diverse voting population has been demonstrated, the capacity to learn and adapt to linguistic and cultural diversity must increase.

PHYSICAL ACCESS AT THE POLLS

The elections act makes limited reference to the needs of persons with disabilities. It directs that there be level access to at least one advance poll in each urban centre within a constituency. Other advance polling stations shall, "wherever possible", provide "ease of access" to people who are old, incapacitated or in wheelchairs.

The Act also says that regular polling stations shall have "convenient access" or "ease of access" without being more specific. A deputy returning officer or a friend or relative may assist an elector in voting if he or she is blind, unable to read, or "so physically incapacitated as to be unable to vote."

A regular poll in a hospital can be closed so that the ballot box can be taken to patients confined to bed, but there are no other provisions in the Act for mobile polls or for taking the ballot box to the street ('curbside voting') if a voter cannot enter because there is no level access.

In 1988, Elections Canada took a number of steps to improve access to voting for people with physical disabilities. This included providing level access at all advance polls and central polling places and making level access a priority at regular polling stations. This was achieved by moving polling stations or by constructing temporary ramps.

The interveners who spoke on issues affecting voters with disabilities were generally advocacy groups or others directly concerned. As there was little disagreement on the need to improve access to voting, most interventions focused on practical suggestions about how this could be done.

The issues on which there was some divergence of opinion were how far to go in providing level access at polling stations and to what degree Elections Canada, rather than local returning officers, should be responsible for this. As one participant noted, "It would be a real shame if a person capable of voting lost this fundamental right to exercise the franchise just because an architectural barrier got in the way."

In Charlottetown, it was noted that "in past elections, accessibility has only been an afterthought in a lot of areas, and although polling station workers have been very helpful in physically assisting individuals into the voting areas, this is not a very dignified entrance for a Canadian to exercise their right to vote."

Another intervener commented:

> We hope virtually all public buildings will be accessible. This will certainly make voting much easier for many disabled persons. Until that happy day, it will sometimes be necessary to adopt interim measures. Such measures could include mobile polls, the mail-in vote for the severely mobility-impaired, and provision of funding for transportation to accessible polling stations.

The Coalition of Provincial Organizations of the Handicapped, the Canadian Human Rights Commission and several other groups supported requiring level access at all polling stations. An intervener in Fredericton stated:

> Providing advance polls that are accessible is not the final solution. What you are doing is forcing persons with disabilities to make their choice about who they will vote for sooner than the general population, because if they want to access the advance poll, they have to do that at an earlier date.

A participant in Sydney, Nova Scotia, who is directly affected by the need for level access, expressed his feelings this way:

> If I'm going out of town and not going to be at my home riding on the day of election I will vote [at] the advance poll. [But] we have seen many cases where that was used as an excuse not to look further [in providing level access]. We were simply told well, you can vote at the advance poll.
>
> Well, stick it in your ear.... I would like to vote on election day and get caught up with our country's electoral process and be part of it on that day, just like everyone else.

One intervener said it seemed little effort was made in some cases to find a level access polling station. Describing his own experience, he also called for greater flexibility in the law to allow people with disabilities to vote in the absence of level access:

The polling station wasn't accessible. What happened, unfortunately, was to a certain extent a violation of the Act. The polling station was moved into the street so I could vote. I was very relieved, but it's sad that a situation like this means that the person who made the decision actually made it illegally. That time, however, the objective of voting was reached. People in wheelchairs would like to have the choice that other voters have, that is, of voting by proxy or on election day.

_____

"People in wheelchairs would like to have the choice that other voters have..."

_____

The Canadian Paraplegic Association took the position that the Act should make Elections Canada responsible for implementing, monitoring and enforcing the level access provision because of the enforcement difficulties inherent in leaving the responsibility with 295 returning officers.

A number of interveners acknowledged that access to voting for persons with disabilities had improved in the 1988 election. They noted, however, that disabled persons could still lose the right to vote if they moved from an area with an accessible polling station to one where the polling place did not have level access; that the ballot booth was sometimes not accessible even if the polling station was; and that information provided to the public about whether polling stations offered level access was sometimes incorrect. We learned of one example in Yellowknife:

 You can imagine the frustration and anger of one voter who was not familiar with the polling station and arrived and saw a flight of stairs before him. Due to arthritis he was unable to climb the stairs and returned home.

Returning officers had some problems with the proposal that all polling stations have level access. One pointed out that, because of the size of the riding, he could not personally inspect every polling place to ensure it was accessible. Community buildings in northern areas are often built well above the ground because of winter and spring conditions, he pointed out, and it would be easier in these cases to bring the ballot box out to a disabled voter than to construct a costly temporary ramp. Another contended that there was no reason to build ramps to provide level access in communities where there are no persons requiring this service. One explained her experience this way:

I go in good faith to the school board and I rent a school, and I tell them it's necessary, to receive the money, to have access for disabled persons, and they assure me it will be. Then somewhere along the line they give me a room, but there's a detour up three steps and a ramp. Then we get complaints that we didn't abide by the rules, but I can't control it.

PERSONS WITH READING DIFFICULTIES

The *Canada Elections Act* makes one specific reference to literacy. It allows a person to swear an oath that he or she is "unable to read" and to bring a friend to assist at the poll or to have the assistance of the deputy returning officer in voting. The ballot is designed to reduce the possibility of error for persons with reading difficulties; white circles against a black background show clearly where the ballot is to be marked.

Most who spoke to the Commission on literacy issues represented literacy groups, although other interveners raised the topic as well. Their main concerns were to make the ballot and the voting process more accessible to persons with reading difficulties and to improve the way information about the electoral process is provided. According to an intervener in Winnipeg, "Elections Canada has to realize that many Canadians do not have adequate levels of language skills to comprehend and respond to information that Elections Canada does put out."

> "... many Canadians do not have adequate levels of language skills to comprehend and respond to information that Elections Canada does put out."

Interveners estimated that 24 per cent of Canada's population is functionally illiterate. The Yellowknife Chamber of Commerce estimated that 54 per cent of the population of the Northwest Territories, and 72 per cent of its Aboriginal population, cannot read or write English or French, although they may be literate in an Aboriginal language. The clerk of the Legislative Assembly of the Northwest Territories pointed out, however, that turnout in territorial elections is relatively high, at 71 per cent of eligible voters.

If they do not read, interveners pointed out, people may not realize that they have received an enumeration notice and may miss getting on the voters list; they may not be able to find the location of their advance poll or polling station; and they may find changes in constituency boundaries or polling divisions confusing. A spokesperson for the Newfoundland and Labrador Association of the Deaf estimated that 60 per cent of deaf Canadians are illiterate; for many, their first language is American Sign Language rather than English. It would help, he said,

If there were some sort of form that could be sent to the deaf person's home, prior to election day, a form that they could fill out with their names, stating that they are deaf, so that on the day they actually go into this

voting station, the people working there will see their name, know that they are deaf, and then know how to approach them.

The chairperson of a school board in Gatineau, Quebec, concluded that many illiterate Canadians abstain from voting because of the problems involved. The problems can start right from the beginning of the process, with enumeration. "The present enumeration process, done door-to-door in urban centres or by telephone in rural areas, is fine if the person is there. However, if no one is home, the written message left by the enumerators has no meaning for an illiterate person," said one intervener.

On the basis of literacy statistics alone, the possible exclusion of this large a group of voters is a threat to the democratic process. One intervener related what she had been told by a person with reading difficulties:

> The names of candidates are hard to read. For me, it's difficult to read, so when it's time to mark the little box, I'm nervous, and if I make a mistake, I've got no eraser to correct it. Why isn't there any eraser on that pencil, so I could correct a mistake and mark the ballot clearly?

The most frequent suggestion was to put candidates' photographs on the ballot, although the Ontario Literacy Coalition noted that discrimination on the basis of race had the potential to influence voters' choices. Several interveners supported the idea of putting the party symbol or party colour on the ballot along with each candidate's name. A Montreal intervener noted, not without irony, that "world-wide, Canada claims to be one of the great leaders in literacy and, in some developing countries, finances programs so that candidates' photos appear on the ballot; but they don't do that here."

"... Canada, ... in some developing countries, finances programs so that candidates' photos appear on the ballot; but they don't do that here."

A poster with each candidate's photograph in every polling station was suggested as an alternative to photographs on the ballot. The Prince Edward Island Literacy Council suggested having a video in each polling station showing the face of each candidate and a voice message telling people how to vote for that candidate.

The present provisions of the Act were criticized because they make it so obvious to other people that the voter cannot read:

> I am aware that the *Canada Elections Act* does make provision for electors who are unable to mark a ballot paper. But this involves taking an oath in front of witnesses, having their ballot marked in the presence of the poll

clerk and sworn agents of the candidates, or the sworn electors representing the candidates in the polling station. They might as well shout from the rooftop: "Look at me, I'm stupid."

The Greater Moncton Literacy Council urged that election officials be trained to help and not be condescending to people with reading difficulties. It was noted that many people who cannot read can use the telephone and it was suggested that election information, especially in the electronic media, should promote the telephone number. The Commission was told that television was the principal source of information for persons with reading difficulties.

Elections Canada was urged to use television and radio advertising to alert people to its broadcasts on the Parliamentary Channel explaining election procedures; many people are apparently unaware of their existence. Others criticized the dense prose of official election literature and the televised information prepared by Elections Canada, saying that it consists of a written script backed by music and does not take advantage of the dynamic communications potential of television. A Member of Parliament suggested that "the chief electoral officer should launch – and I put great emphasis on this one – a voter education program that is not literacy-based. Videos for community groups should be considered."

The suggestion that community groups be used to circulate electoral information to people with reading difficulties came from many groups. The Sudbury Literacy Coalition recommended the use of a literacy hot-line for election information, but the Ontario Literacy Coalition was sceptical of the idea and said it was more important to provide education about the electoral process through community groups.

POOR AND HOMELESS PERSONS

During the hearings, the National Anti-Poverty Organization estimated that there are between 130 000 and 250 000 homeless people in Canada. Further, an estimated five million Canadians live below the poverty line.

Citizens must be registered to vote, and to be registered they must usually occupy an apartment, house or other dwelling. People living in hostels and lodgings cannot be enumerated if they have not been resident for at least 10 days at the time of enumeration; yet many hostels put a 10-day limit on the period a homeless person can stay.

Voters cannot be enumerated without a street address, although this rule is sometimes circumvented by returning officers and enumerators. Some homeless people may be enumerated using the address of a friend or relative. Toronto and Montreal have attempted to enumerate homeless persons for municipal elections, but no information is available as to their success in registering people and getting them to turn out at the polls.

An Edmonton community worker outlined broad objectives for ensuring that poor and homeless persons have access to the vote: "The opportunity to vote should not be limited by one's reading ability, lack of permanent residence, fear of disclosure of residence, or other identifiable circumstances that exist for any significant group of individuals."

Interveners on these issues included advocacy groups, community agencies, rights advocates, groups representing people with disabilities, political party representatives, election officials and interested individuals. Many of their recommendations dealt with enumeration, revision of the voters list, and voter registration on or just before election day. Some pointed out that poverty in and of itself does not necessarily diminish interest in the electoral process. On the contrary, for many it is part of their struggle for change. An intervener in Ottawa explained:

 Some people of low income care a lot about the issues; they're very politically sophisticated. Some don't care at all because they see it as totally irrelevant to their lives. But I don't think you can generalize. Certainly a lot of them want to vote. And that is why this issue was put on the priority list by our board, who are primarily low-income activists.

Poor and homeless people also face special problems in identifying themselves to enumerators and other election officials; they may not have a driver's licence or credit cards, or their identification may have been lost or stolen. For this reason it was recommended that individuals be allowed to swear an oath to establish their identity, or that less formal kinds of identification be accepted. Alternatively, someone who knew the person could swear to his or her identity.

> "Poor and homeless people also face special problems in identifying themselves to enumerators and other election officials..."

Interveners generally favoured changes in the elections act to extend voting rights to homeless people. But one person at the Toronto hearings raised a note of caution: "It is not [abuse by] the homeless I am worried about. It is the people that might use [to their advantage] the provision that you do not have to have an address. Names of non-existent people might appear [on the voters list]. That is my concern."

The Downtown East Side Residents' Association in Vancouver urged, however, that reforms should open up the electoral process as much as possible to include homeless people, rather than tightening it to prevent one or two abuses:

 One of the things that we really need to look at is that people be allowed to vote on election day, regardless of whether they have been enumerated or not; that they could swear an oath that I am who I am and reside in this community; and that they be able to swear that oath even if they are not able to produce ID or proof of residency.

We should certainly go in the direction of trying to extend the democratic process as far as we possibly can, rather than tightening it up too much in order to keep a few people from abusing it.

A number of practical suggestions were offered for enumerating people without a fixed address. These included listing them but giving no address; listing them at the street address nearest to the place where they normally slept; using a hostel, community centre or agency as their address for enumeration purposes; or listing them with the returning office as their address.

In Winnipeg, the Coalition of Provincial Organizations of the Handicapped said, "We support the position taken by the National Anti-Poverty Organization that encourages looking at alternative solutions to enumeration that would provide an opportunity for those persons who are homeless to be enumerated."

Women living in shelters for battered women have good reasons not to want their address published on a voters list. As one group in Vancouver elaborated, "Women who have left abusive relationships frequently fear the publication of their name and address might be used to trace them to their residence. Women's shelters and transition houses have policies to keep their location secure. Such policies prevent the enumeration of residents due to the required inclusion of an address."

These women face another problem, explained an intervener: "Where a woman is in a battered women's shelter [for less than] the 10-day requirement, she can't vote [because she cannot be enumerated]. She is no less a citizen for the fact that she's had to leave her husband – her family, perhaps – and move into a shelter. But she no longer has the right to vote because she hasn't been there 10 days. So that 10-day requirement has to go."

Interveners pointed out that because enumeration is based on where people live, homeless persons tend to be excluded until it comes time for revision. People who are homeless may be illiterate or have little access to television or newspaper information about how to be registered. Some interveners recommended special outreach programs through community agencies or through Elections Canada. For example, a group in Edmonton recommended that Elections Canada study voter turnout after each election and develop a plan to increase participation by members of groups whose overall turnout is low.

Interveners in Montreal and elsewhere pointed out that enumerators often miss homeless voters staying in hostels because they make their rounds during the day, when the hostels are empty. The problem of access to voters living in low-cost hotels and lodgings was also raised in Vancouver. The Commission learned of problems experienced in enumerating poor and homeless persons, such as risks to personal security in rough areas, the risk of incomplete enumeration in unfamiliar neighbourhoods, language and cultural barriers, and so on. Special training was recommended for enumerators working in these areas:

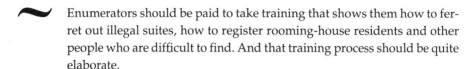 Enumerators should be paid to take training that shows them how to ferret out illegal suites, how to register rooming-house residents and other people who are difficult to find. And that training process should be quite elaborate.

Two anti-poverty groups suggested that free public transport be provided on election day so that people of low income could get to the polls without relying on the parties for transportation.

STUDENTS

The proxy voting rules allow students living away from their home constituency to vote, provided they are studying full-time within Canada and the election takes place during the academic term. To use a proxy to vote in their home constituency, students must have proxy forms certified by their educational institution, a process that takes time and can cause difficulties.

The Canadian Federation of Students estimated the number of postsecondary students in Canada at 892 000; some 60 per cent of these students are studying away from home. Most of the issues related to students and voting focused on this latter group and were brought to the Commission's attention by groups representing post-secondary students. For students studying abroad, the Federation recommended:

There are an estimated 20 000 Canadians studying abroad each year. Unless enumeration and voting take place in the summer months, these students are denied their right to vote. The provision for an absentee vote, similar to that extended to Canadian military personnel abroad, should be made available to these students.

The *Canada Elections Act* provides for voters to be enumerated at their place of ordinary residence on the enumeration date, which is 38 days before election day. This provision is open to interpretation by returning officers and by enumerators; as a result, students living away from home may be excluded from enumeration where they are studying. If they are not put on the list in their home riding by their family, it may be difficult for them to arrange to be added at revision, or a student may miss the deadline for revision. Students at the University of Western Ontario explained:

Our particular student body is probably the most mobile in Canadian society, and as a consequence, frequently gets missed in the enumeration process, or they end up enumerated in a different riding than the one in which they are resident on election day.

Enumeration and proxy voting were the major topics raised by student organizations and other interveners on student issues. It was pointed out that students can have as many as three residences in a typical year, if they take a summer job away from campus and their family home. A students' group at Laurentian University suggested that federal elections not take place in the first or second week of September to avoid problems for students just settling into new living accommodation. Students explained that the problems of enumeration were compounded by the absence of any provision allowing urban voters to be registered after the close of revision, 17 days before election day. Consequently, a group of students in Sydney, Nova Scotia, recommended:

> "Our particular student body ... frequently gets missed ... or they end up enumerated in a different riding than the one in which they are resident on election day."

 In order to prevent so many potential voters from being disfranchised, our Committee recommends that section 47 of the *Canada Elections Act* be extended to include urban as well as rural electoral districts. The provisions of this section permit individuals not on the official list of electors, but otherwise qualified to vote, to register their ballot after providing some proof of identity and meeting residence requirements. We consider this to be an appropriate measure to protect the citizens' right to vote.

Student representatives reported instances where enumeration in student residences had been done carelessly. They also pointed out that depending on the timing of an election, a student might have moved to another riding after being enumerated because of the delay between enumeration and election day.

Although there was no clear consensus, the favoured alternatives were to give students the option of deciding where to be enumerated, or to enumerate them at their place of study unless they chose specifically to be enumerated in their home riding. It was suggested that this choice be explicitly provided for in a revamped elections act.

A number of interveners criticized the proxy system for students because of its time-consuming procedures and the fact that it does not apply to part-time students and to students studying abroad. It was also noted that for students living away from their families – experiencing independence for the first time – it seemed unfair to have to ask a parent to cast their first vote. The preferred solution was to allow students to cast a mail ballot; the Canadian Federation of Students proposed that special polling booths be established on campuses where these ballots could be cast.

Some student groups criticized returning officers for locating polling stations for student residences off campus rather than in convenient locations on campus. Because very few students were living in residence at the time of enumeration for the 1984 election, returning officers may not have realized that the number of voters on campus would increase sharply for the 1988 election, which was held during the school term.

Elections Canada was commended for its literature about the electoral process directed to students, but student groups requested even more material and recommended that Elections Canada support and work with student associations to help educate students about the electoral process.

LANGUAGE ISSUES

Elections Canada seeks to provide services to voters in both official languages where it judges that there is a significant demand (where 3 per cent of a riding's population is from the minority language group). When this standard was set for the 1988 election, it raised the number of bilingual ridings to 98 from 92. Under the previous criteria for a bilingual riding, 5 per cent of the riding population had to be from the minority language group.

In bilingual ridings, Elections Canada policy seeks to ensure that election information and services are available in both official languages. Elections Canada maintains a bilingual telephone information service. There is no bilingual requirement for the returning officer in a designated riding. There is likewise no requirement that parties or candidates carry out a bilingual campaign.

The elections act does prescribe bilingual forms for the ballot and for other material used in elections, but it makes no other direct reference to official languages issues. The form of the ballot is set out in the Act, although it can be changed by regulation. There is no provision in the Act for the ballot to be in languages other than English and French.

The law is not clear about whether voters may bring an interpreter or translator to assist them at the poll. If a deputy returning officer does not understand the language spoken by a voter, the official is required, where possible, to appoint an interpreter. An interpreter may be appointed in other circumstances, but this is not required, even in polls with a high concentration of voters who speak neither English nor French. Some returning officers try to appoint deputy returning officers and enumerators who speak a particular language in certain polls, but this is not obligatory.

The Commissioner of Official Languages reported that the number of complaints about language issues in the electoral system increased from 20 in 1980 to 100 in 1988; he suggested that for every formal complaint, many other voters may have been denied their linguistic rights. The complaints focused on Elections Canada's failure to provide voter information in the minority language in newspapers and on cable television, on the use of unilingual enumerators, and on the lack of minority language services on election day.

The Commissioner reported that unilingual returning officers had been appointed to bilingual ridings in the National Capital Region and in New Brunswick and that the parties did not meet Elections Canada's request that 50 per cent of enumerators and election day officials be bilingual. The Commissioner of Official Languages stated unequivocally that "the electoral process must fully recognize the equal status of French and English by respecting voters' choice of language."

> "The electoral process must fully recognize the equal status of French and English by respecting voters' choice of language."

The Société des Acadiens recommended that returning officers appointed in bilingual ridings be required to be bilingual. The Association de la presse francophone recommended that federal parties be made subject to the *Official Languages Act* and that, in particular, they be required to place advertising in the minority language where there is a minority language newspaper available:

> We believe it is essential that all parties use the main majority and minority language publications if they decide that the written press is going to be one of their vehicles for campaign advertising.

One returning officer raised the problem of finding bilingual enumerators and election day staff in a constituency that is designated bilingual but where the minority language population is concentrated in a few rural areas outside a city where most of the people in the constituency reside. Several interveners suggested that more bilingual election day staff would be available if elections were held on a Sunday, enabling bilingual people with Monday-to-Friday jobs to help out.

The Canadian Cable Television Association said that the policy of cable stations was to broadcast election information videos from Elections Canada in both languages only if the cable service itself was bilingual.

Some interveners suggested that Elections Canada use languages other than English and French. The Canadian Ethnocultural Council asked that Elections Canada continue to translate voting information into various languages. They recommended that the enumeration process be sensitive to language barriers, particularly in the case of immigrant women and seniors. Enumeration in ridings with a high concentration of ethno-cultural communities would improve if workers could speak the language of the community they are enumerating.

Speaking on behalf of Inuit and Innu voters in northern Labrador, an intervener asked that Elections Canada mail information to voters in the language that they can read and understand.

~ Even though 70 per cent of the voters in my district are Inuit and Innu, the information they receive during an election is only in English and French.

Interveners in Iqaluit and Kuujjuaq made a strong case for using Inuktituk on the ballot and in election material used in their area.

~ Things have changed; people are showing more and more of an interest in federal politics. During the last territorial election, ballots were written in Inuktituk, and again, that is an absolute necessity. But a lot of the preliminary information that emanates from Ottawa to all the districts throughout Canada is supplied only in French and English. It would be helpful to the returning officer to have information in Inuktituk that she could send out to [voters].

"It would be helpful to the returning officer to have information in Inuktituk that she could send out to [voters]."

The Northwest Territories recognizes seven Aboriginal languages as official languages. Since 1979, a placard with a photograph of every candidate has been posted in polling stations in territorial elections. One intervener explained:

~ We are faced with a method of recording names that appear in more than one style. We use syllabics for written communication in many communities in the North. We also use Roman orthography; our normal means of writing that we use in English is also adapted to Inuktituk in some areas.

So at the very least, we would require two forms of each name on the ballot and, ideally, a picture ballot, because many of our people in outlying areas are unilingual.

Another suggestion was that returning officers be able to print ballots and election materials in Aboriginal languages and in Braille as necessary to meet the needs of voters. It was also suggested that an oral ballot could be used to make voting more accessible to electors with impaired sight or reading difficulties and to voters who can read neither English nor French. The voter would listen to the names of the candidates, then indicate a choice.

Elections Canada advertised in the Aboriginal press during the 1988 election. Under the Act, polling stations are required to post information concerning an election only in English and French, even in polls where a substantial number of voters are of Aboriginal origin.

POLITICAL RIGHTS

The federal government and several of the provinces have policies that restrict the involvement of their employees in politics. Federal employees may seek leave to be candidates, but they are otherwise prohibited from campaigning for a candidate or a political party. On the other hand, some provinces have policies allowing public servants to participate in a broad range of political activities. A few employers grant political leave as a matter of internal policy, and some union contracts set out specific policies on political involvement. The Supreme Court of Canada has recently given several decisions that appear to limit the ability of governments to restrict political activity by their employees.

The most extensive intervention on political rights came from the Public Service Alliance of Canada. The Alliance asked that federal employees have the same political rights as other Canadians. They argued that any public servant should have the right to be active politically, but recognized that the most senior employees would have to assess for themselves whether political involvement was appropriate.

One intervener raised the problem of employees who are candidates being forced to take a leave of absence when there is a long period between the nomination and the election. Another intervener suggested that public servants wanting to stand as candidates should have the right to a leave of absence, rather than simply the right to request it. It was noted that this is a particular problem in the Northwest Territories because of the higher proportion of public servants.

> "... the government should legislate that a person involved in politics be allowed time away from work without jeopardizing his or her job."

The Sudbury Business and Professional Women's Club stated, "We presently have legislation that states that an employer must give each employee time to vote on election day. We also have legislation that allows an employee to do jury duty without penalty from his or her employer. In this spirit, the government should legislate that a person involved in politics be allowed time away from work without jeopardizing his or her job."

One national organization proposed that employees should have the right to take leave to run for political office and that this should extend to the right to up to six years of unpaid leave if elected.

The Victoria Civil Liberties Union wanted the right of tenants to put up election signs assured. They contended this was a right of political expression, noting that "tenants frequently are not allowed to display political signs in their apartment windows and so forth. We know of instances where landlords have refused them the right to do that…. We would like to see guarantees that allow those people to express their political opinions in the form of signs and so on in [their] residence." Another group asked that the *Canada Elections Act* guarantee the right to put up posters on light standards during election campaigns.

3

On Effective Representation

THE TRADITIONAL CONCEPT of representation for many Canadians has been geographic, that is, being represented as a resident of a community or a constituency. The focus of past representational reform has therefore been on the number of seats for each province and territory and how the boundary lines are drawn between constituencies.

Many of the groups and individuals who appeared before the Commission or submitted briefs based their comments and recommendations on a broader concept of representation. They wanted to reflect on how they were represented in Parliament as members of an identifiable group or community of interest – as members of ethno-cultural communities, as Aboriginal people, as women. The concerns of members of these groups are not always readily understood in traditional discussions of electoral reform:

> Because we've been fixated on geographic representation in Canada, we have developed a very limited range of representational concepts. We have therefore had difficulty understanding the concepts of representation that are held by people who are marginalized from the political system and feel alienated from it.

In putting forward proposals to enhance their representation within parties and in Parliament, many interveners focused on the candidate nomination process. The Canadian Advisory Council on the Status of Women summed up this way: "There is ample evidence to document that winning the nomination is the key to our electoral process. If the nomination process is not fair, the election campaign that follows will be a charade." Proposals ranged from imposing rules on parties to increase the presence of underrepresented groups to adopting an American-style primary system run by Elections Canada. Some suggested regulated representation in parties coupled with proportional representation in elections to the House of Commons, to guarantee the appropriate level of representation for their group.

NOMINATION OF CANDIDATES

The elections act sets out the legal requirements for nominating constituency candidates but makes no reference to the parties' processes for choosing their nominees. Candidates must be endorsed by the party leader, however, if the party's name is to appear on the ballot along with the candidate's name.

A candidate must be a qualified elector and must submit a nomination form signed by 25 qualified electors in the relevant constituency, have these signatures sworn to under oath, pay a deposit of $200, and complete these requirements by the 28th day before the election.

Parties usually hold nomination meetings in each constituency, at which members of the party association choose the candidate. These members are usually residents in the riding, but they may not all be qualified electors and, especially in vigorously contested nominations, may be newly recruited by the candidates competing for the nomination. New members may have to wait a specified period (such as 30 days) before they can vote at a nominating meeting.

> "The Canadian public deserves some assurance that all candidates have gone through a fair, open, and honest nomination process..."

Several interveners perceived problems with the nomination process and proposed specific changes to the elections act to overcome them. The main focus was on ways to improve the process and make it fairer. One put the case for regulation this way:

> The question of nominations is one that we have generally neglected in Canada, perhaps because we haven't recognized how big the country has become and have assumed that the old inbred rules of the game could be accepted – not recognizing that it is the only point of access to the political system and that, if it isn't brought under some form of regulation, the anarchy that often prevails at the present time will continue.

An Alberta intervener recommended that "Elections Canada become involved in party nomination races. The Canadian public deserves some assurance that all candidates have gone through a fair, open, and honest nomination process prior to having their name appear on an election ballot." Not all interveners were so sure, however, that regulation is called for:

> You should definitely raise the issue in your report. By doing that you will warn political parties, as perhaps professions have been warned, that part of the privilege of being self-policing is the responsibility to do just that.

Another was more direct in his opposition to regulation, stating, "How the people who come to stand for public office are placed in that position or place themselves in that position, I don't think is any concern of the law."

A Member of Parliament suggested that many nominations in the 1988 election transgressed any definition of fairness. She gave a number of examples of what she called common abuses in party nominations, including fraudulent memberships, membership applications, memberships that are 'lost' after being handed in, and arbitrary criteria for identifying party members. She called for Elections Canada to regulate the nomination process to maintain its integrity.

With respect to regulation, an Ontario political scientist recommended that nominations be supervised by Elections Canada and administered by the local returning officer rather than by untrained organizers. He also proposed that the rules for nomination be laid down clearly in advance. In Edmonton it was recommended that Elections Canada set standard procedures and monitor both the nomination race and the nomination meeting. In British Columbia a Member of Parliament stated:

> There's nothing that shakes the confidence of the public in our process as much as seeing the unseemly actions that take place, either when a nomination meeting is stacked or when an attempt to do so is made in a federal leadership race. We've had some very immediate examples of problems that arise when thousands of people become new members for a few weeks and then are not heard of again by the party until four years later.

Another Member of Parliament emphasized the need to maintain public confidence in the electoral system, stating that it is essential to take into account the function of political parties in brokering the interests of different regions and groups of Canadians, in developing and explaining policy, and in presenting the public with intelligent and experienced candidates. He expressed concern that the system of nominating candidates fails to achieve this goal:

> I find myself wondering how many Lester Pearsons or Louis St. Laurents, or other people who came into public life, would have done so had they faced the initial hurdle of a modern, costly, time-consuming nomination battle in an urban riding. Parties are no longer very capable of delivering nominations, if they ever were. I am not saying that the nomination process should be totally non-democratic, but I see it as increasingly a problem in the system.

In some constituencies, witnesses pointed out, there is almost no question as to which party will win the election. The real issue is not the election, but the contest for that party's nomination. The Canadian Association of the Deaf estimated that a nomination campaign in a hotly contested riding could cost as much as $40 000 and asked that a spending ceiling of $1000 be set to make nominations more accessible to persons with disabilities. Others suggested limits ranging between $10 000 and $25 000. Another intervener asked that donations to registered parties that qualify for the tax credit be prohibited by the Act from being used in nomination or leadership campaigns.

Some interveners suggested that one way to open up the nomination process would be to make it more like the American system of primaries. A Member of Parliament appearing before the Commission noted that "the Americans enfranchise all supporters of a party by operating a primary system that gives voters the same [voice in the] selection of the candidate. The concept may be well worth exploring for Canada."

Others recommended against a primary system because it would be too long and costly. Another intervener presented this case for maintaining the current process: "The riding association is the democratic and logical place to select and endorse a candidate; only they have the best contact with the citizens in the area, know what they want, raise the money, run the campaign, sell the memberships, vote for their own choice, and pay for their upkeep."

Witnesses also raised the issue of the candidate's deposit which has been set at $200 for more than a century and has become a minor campaign expense for candidates from major parties. The deposit is refunded if a candidate qualifies for federal funds to cover election expenses by obtaining 15 per cent of the vote.

One individual suggested that "the present deposit of $200 seems rather inadequate; it's been in effect for over a hundred years, and there are candidates coming in that tend to degrade the election process. I think it [the deposit amount] should be reviewed."

Another participant suggested that having too many candidates floods voters with choices and leads them to focus on national campaigns rather than on the local candidate. He recommended raising the deposit to $2000 to discourage fringe candidates but returning the deposit if the candidate obtained more than 5 per cent of the vote, rather than the current requirement of 15 per cent. The Institute for Political Involvement recommended raising the deposit to $1000.

Representatives of the Green Party disagreed strongly with the idea of a $2000 deposit. Representatives of the Libertarian Party objected to the current $200 deposit, because it is a major expense when a small party presents candidates in a number of ridings. An anti-poverty group asked that the deposit requirement be removed, since it is an obstacle for an individual or group with limited resources.

WOMEN'S REPRESENTATION

Women are underrepresented in the legislatures of almost every industrial democracy, and Canada is no exception. In the 1988 election, 39 women were elected to the House of Commons; thus they now account for 13.2 per cent of Members of Parliament, the highest proportion achieved to date in Canada. (Women made up 3.6 per cent of the membership of the House of Commons in 1979 and 0.4 per cent in 1968.)

The key issues raised by interveners with respect to women in politics were the structural or systemic barriers facing women seeking to participate in political life and the obstacles to women being nominated in winnable ridings. This theme was sounded by one intervener:

> As it stands, this process will continue to shut out competent women (as well as competent men) and will never guarantee that the best candidates are nominated. If the process is fair and equal and determined ahead of time, then at least women will have the opportunity to start from the same point as everyone else and know what is expected.

At the hearings in Ottawa one participant suggested that "we should take the steps necessary to ensure that money or socio-economic status is no longer an obstacle for women who are interested in getting into active politics." Her comments were strongly supported by another group:

> We strongly urge you to make recommendations that will turn Canada away from money-dominated politics. From our perspective, as women who want to encourage more participation by our sex in public affairs, the present political system is already too much under the domination of a moneyed male elite. As long as ability to raise money is a major criterion for political participation, the corporate male network will decide who represents Canadians in Parliament.

"We should take the steps necessary to ensure that money or socio-economic status is no longer an obstacle for women who are interested in getting into active politics."

The Fédération des femmes du Québec noted that since Agnes Macphail's election in 1921, only 100 women have been elected to the House of Commons. They estimated that "if women continue to gain by 4 per cent each election, and if there is an election every five years, it will be 45 years before 50 per cent of elected members are women, although we believe this is a fairly optimistic scenario, because women are going to continue to encounter obstacles."

A national vice-president of one of the parties outlined some of the difficulties in expanding the role of women:

> I was the only woman on the provincial board of directors. I was the first female provincial vice-president of a political party. I am the first female national vice-president of a political party, and I have worked very hard for the past two years, travelling around the province and trying to persuade women to try for the position of president of a constituency association. Six years ago there were six [female constituency presidents]. Six years later there are still six, though not the same six.

Some interveners contended that many of the barriers to women in politics are comparable to the barriers facing them in other careers: sex-role stereotyping; the difficulty of juggling career, family and political responsibilities; problems of child care; jobs that are less flexible for entering politics than those held by men; negative attitudes within parties; the fact that men tend to have better networks to help them in politics; and the question of how female politicians are portrayed in the media.

As one commented:

> These pitfalls are closely connected to culture, to the way politics is practised, and also to partisan traditions. Parties are organizations led by men, where the mode of involvement is masculine. And the women who have to get involved in this method must get very deeply involved and even, to a certain extent, accept that they must take over and dominate male territory.

Some of these factors translate into a lack of financial resources for women to seek nominations in winnable ridings. One group said that women are rarely offered safe seats and must either run as sacrificial lambs in ridings where there is no hope, or spend large sums to contest a nomination in a winnable riding. A former candidate stated that there is bias against women within the political parties and that women are nominated less often in constituencies where they have a chance of election. Several interveners argued that a higher proportion of women than men are disaffected or alienated from electoral politics. The political system is not an equal opportunity system, they said, and dirty tricks are played against women candidates even in 'lost-cause' ridings.

> "There is a continuing problem that will not go away and that is the small proportion of women in Parliament."

In Iqaluit, the Baffin Women's Association outlined some of the problems facing women in securing nominations and winning elections:

> Women often have no money backing them, from their parties, over and above the monies that are generally available to candidates. Women need to be able to see that there is more financial backing for them to cover costs such as daycare, since women are the primary caregivers to children, and that is very definitely the case in the North.

A few interveners recommended that Canada adopt a system of proportional representation in which half of each province's seats would be designated for women and half for men. In Kamloops, a former Member of Parliament suggested:

> There is a continuing problem that will not go away and that is the small proportion of women in Parliament. I would like to suggest a very sweeping change to set things right there. The number of constituencies should be cut in half. Each constituency should elect two people, one male and the other female.

The Canadian Advisory Council on the Status of Women recommended a similar system. The Council also recommended that the nomination process be regulated to provide for spending limits, disclosure, and qualifications for voting by constituency association members. The Sudbury Business and Professional Women's Club advanced this case:

> On the average, women earn less money than men and therefore have less personal funds to spend on a nomination race. [This] can be a disadvantage for women who are running against someone who has the means to spend a lot of money promoting his candidacy. Only after a nomination has been won are restrictions placed on the amount of money candidates can spend. Because there are no set limits to the amount of money a potential candidate can spend to get a nomination, the person with greater financial resources is at a definite advantage.

The group therefore recommended that pre-nomination spending by candidates be restricted. Some interveners offered solutions. A political scientist in Ottawa, for example, said that bringing the nomination process under the control of electoral law would be the single greatest contribution the Commission could make to giving women greater access to the political process.

Several interveners recommended that donations to individual election campaigns be eligible for tax deductions or tax credits. A former Member of Parliament, drawing on her experience in the 1988 election campaign, recommended that campaign spending by a candidate be limited for the nomination as well as during the election campaign.

> It's important to act at the nomination stage, to facilitate access to constituency nominations. This is why I recommend, first, funding of expenses involved in this first step in the electoral process and, second, strict regulation of the expenditures allowed at this stage.

With respect to the cost of campaigns, the Canadian Advisory Council on the Status of Women recommended that reimbursement of campaign expenses be raised to 75 per cent for men and 100 per cent for women candidates and that parties whose candidates are at least 50 per cent women should have their campaign expenses reimbursed at a rate of 50 per cent rather than the current level of 22.5 per cent for all parties eligible for reimbursement. Others recommended different types of financial incentives to political parties to take concrete steps themselves to encourage greater access by women.

The Committee for '94 recommended more public funding as a means of encouraging women candidates, while a Nova Scotia intervener called for strict limits on campaign spending to make politics more accessible to women. Another intervener noted that the special fund set up by the three national political parties to help women pay their election expenses gave each candidate between $500 and $600. None of these funds is intended to assist women with the costs of seeking a nomination.

One participant summed up her objectives:

> Not only do we want more women to participate in the electoral process, we want equal representation of women in the House of Commons. We want a "triple E" House of Commons in which women are elected, equal and effective.

Many of the proposals to assist women in politics involved various forms of affirmative action, either by encouragement or financial incentive. Another participant disagreed, arguing that people should not vote on the basis of gender and that the evidence was that women could get elected if they were competent and able.

A recommendation to eliminate linguistic sexism from the *Canada Elections Act* was made by the Nova Scotia Advisory Council on the Status of Women, which also recommended that unpaid volunteer work by women in election campaigns be assigned a monetary value and be treated as a political donation.

REPRESENTATION OF ABORIGINAL PEOPLE

Since Confederation only 12 self-identified Aboriginal Members of Parliament have been elected to the House of Commons, nine of whom have been elected since 1962. Three Métis Members of Parliament from Manitoba were elected in the 1870s, including Louis Riel.

The first Indian person elected to Parliament was Len Marchand from British Columbia. Until 1960, status Indian persons living on reserves were not entitled to vote in federal elections unless they gave up their status and the rights and privileges that status implied. Now a member of the Senate of Canada, Senator Marchand told the hearings:

> For the vast majority of Aboriginal Canadians, Parliament is seen in the distance, but there is no trail to get there. In an equal democracy, the majority of the people, through their representatives, will outvote and prevail over the minority and their representatives. But does it follow that the minority should have no representation at all? Because the majority have all the votes, must the minority have none? Put another way, must the majority have all the representation, Aboriginal people none?

Of the nine Aboriginal Members of Parliament elected since 1962, six have been elected in the Northwest Territories, where Aboriginal people form the majority. There are currently three Aboriginal Members of Parliament in the House of Commons – two from the Northwest Territories and one from Alberta.

Many interveners, including a number of Aboriginal organizations, spoke about Aboriginal issues at the hearings. Their major concern was to ensure better representation for Aboriginal people in Parliament, although a number of interveners emphasized that their first priority remains the achievement of Aboriginal self-government. Several of these interveners favoured the creation of Aboriginal seats, similar to the system for the Maori in New Zealand.

The New Brunswick Aboriginal Peoples' Council suggested that the New Zealand system helps to account for the success of the Maori in New Zealand society. In their brief to the Commission, they stated:

> Traditionally, native turnout has been relatively low, simply because people do not feel that that process is their process. There are a lot of reasons why they haven't voted. Some of it is people not talking to them in their Aboriginal language; people not talking about issues of concern to them.
>
> The Aboriginal people of this country not only have the collective right, but also a need, socially, economically and politically, to participate in the Canadian political process, the very process that elects governments, that governs this land, that makes laws that impact on all citizens, and that has for far too long trod upon the rights of Aboriginal people.

Another intervener outlined how the Maori have frequently been able to influence legislation and government policies through their members. It was noted that Nicaragua, Fiji, New Zealand and the state of Maine make provision for some form of representation for Aboriginal groups.

On the question of Aboriginal representation there was no shortage of comments:

> I am here today to testify before this Commission because I am an Indian and, as an Indian, my vote does not count. I cannot vote for a candidate of my choice, I have never seen the name of the person who represents my people or myself on a ballot, and I am effectively disfranchised.

"I cannot vote for a candidate of my choice, I have never seen the name of the person who represents my people or myself on a ballot, and I am effectively disfranchised."

> Although we now have the right to vote, the social attitudes and political policies which stood in the way of our right to participate in the political process for more than one hundred years still dominate the electoral process in this country and still prevent our free participation in government.

Some pointed to specific remedies:

~ Representation structures must reflect and accommodate equally the demographic realities of the Aboriginal population through the use of a national
Aboriginal voluntary voters list, a model similar in principle to the New
Zealand model, but with some variations. Aboriginal people do wish to
survive in the next half-millennium and fundamental reform is urgently
required. We think that the public spirit, public reception for fundamental change, is there, and 1992 is an ideal time to do it.

Others presented several alternatives:

~ In my view there are three ways of focusing to achieve enhanced political
representation of Aboriginal groups.
　　　Firstly, you could look at means of redressing current underrepresentation through such measures as adjustment of constituency boundaries, increasing party nominations to accommodate Aboriginal interests,
or looking at alternative electoral systems. You could look, secondly, at a
guaranteed representation in legislatures and [at] according to Aboriginal
representatives non-voting participation. That's a system that has been
debated and looked at in various jurisdictions at various points in time.
　　　And thirdly – and in my view, this is the only one that has any real
prospect of achieving an objective of enhanced political representation –
is the creation of a separate and parallel electoral system which ties into
the mainstream system in a very clearly defined way.

Some interveners expressed reservations about the New Zealand model.
One was a Yellowknife resident who argued, "You're going to have a few
ghettoized members who aren't part of caucuses, who aren't part of the
power mechanism at all in the operation of the federal Parliament and are
going to be very much off on their own."
Another was a political scientist from British Columbia:

~ I'm uncomfortable with New Zealand's special constituencies for the
Aboriginal people, the Maori, as it mixes two principles of representation:
representation by community and representation by group.

The alternative of creating northern ridings with Aboriginal majorities
was supported by the Grand Council of the Crees and by other interveners
at the Commission's hearing at Kuujjuaq, south of Ungava Bay. They criticized the fact that electoral boundaries in northern Quebec had been drawn
so as to link northern areas with southern cities, thereby making Aboriginal
people a minority in two constituencies.

~ It's been well said that we are far too few people occupying vast stretches
of geography. This has its inherent problems in providing for adequate

representation in the House of Commons. It's complicated, irritated and compounded by the fact that we are divided north/south into two federal ridings. We have pleaded and ranted and raved at the previous three hearings to have the boundary changed to an east/west orientation on the 55th parallel and, if need be, to have a special exemption from the regular electoral laws that apply in the country to make this possible.

The Métis Society of Saskatchewan recommended that the boundaries of the northernmost riding in Saskatchewan be redrawn to give it an Aboriginal majority, but the Society's preference was to provide Aboriginal representation on the New Zealand model. The Native Council of Canada supported amending the *Electoral Boundaries Readjustment Act* to ensure that redistribution accommodates historic and existing Aboriginal communities of interest.

Two other approaches to providing more effective Aboriginal representation were put forward. The Siksika Nation Tribal Council recommended creating electoral districts based on treaty areas throughout Canada in which only Indian candidates and Indian voters would be allowed to participate; the Council also expressed interest in representation on the New Zealand model. The Baffin Regional Inuit Association recommended the creation of a new riding of Nunavut in the eastern Arctic to provide parliamentary representation for the area's Inuit.

The issues of how a special electoral roll for Aboriginal voters should be drawn up and who should be eligible to be listed on it were dealt with only briefly. The Siksika Nation Tribal Council suggested that only status Indians should be eligible. The Native Council recommended that Aboriginal voters lists be drawn up on the basis of self-identification rather than on criteria from the *Indian Act*. It recommended the creation of an Aboriginal electorate program to encourage community-based voter registration and electoral participation by Aboriginal people.

"We need Members of Parliament who do not have to be taught who we are, what we want, and why we are important to this country."

The question of Indian self-government was raised frequently by interveners on Aboriginal issues, but improving Aboriginal representation was seen generally as complementary, not contradictory, to the goal of self-government. At the final Ottawa hearing, the Commission was told that Aboriginal leaders may not be ready to make Aboriginal representation in Parliament a priority because their focus has been to achieve self-government. On the other hand, a member of the Manitoba Keewatinowi Okimakanak, Inc., representing 23 Cree bands in northern Manitoba, said:

Throughout our mutual history, our side of the benefits ledger has never been properly recorded, much to our disadvantage and our detriment. Today we are faced with the consequences of years and years of neglect and oppression. We need Members of Parliament who do not have to be taught who we are, what we want, and why we are important to this country. We need our people in Parliament in greater numbers than is possible under the power or influence that our votes are reduced to, even in ridings like Churchill [in northern Manitoba].

The New Brunswick Aboriginal Peoples' Council asserted that a guaranteed right of representation in political institutions flows from the Aboriginal right of self-government – although it is no substitute for the constitutional recognition of Aboriginal self-governing institutions. A representative of the Native Council of Nova Scotia said she did not believe that Aboriginal peoples could achieve self-government without co-operation from legislatures, and that required having Aboriginal representatives present in those legislatures.

Throughout the hearings, interveners from Aboriginal organizations emphasized the alienation of Aboriginal Canadians from the electoral system and the inadequate representation of Aboriginal people in Parliament in relation to their numbers. The Liberal Aboriginal Peoples Commission argued that electoral boundaries commissions had created ridings to recognize the interests of ethno-cultural communities in major cities, but not to deal with the group rights of Aboriginal people. Another intervener judged that the participation of Indian persons in the electoral process since 1960 had not resulted in political power or in any substantial influence on Indian policies.

Chief Ovide Mercredi spoke of a growing feeling among Aboriginal leaders that they were wasting their energy and resources trying to find acceptance in a political system that does not want Indian people. For Indian persons, the one person-one vote rule of elections translates into non-Aboriginal majority rule:

The boundaries have to be re-examined; they have to be changed so that our vote does make a difference, so that our people will have a sense of confidence that by going to the polls they are not wasting their time, but they will in fact be sending their representative to Parliament.

A member of the Siksika Nation Tribal Council told the Commission that the federal government had routinely violated both the letter and the spirit of its treaty with the Blackfoot Confederacy. Indian people, he said, had been denied the rights expressed in their treaty because life on reserves had come to be controlled by the *Indian Act*, and because Indian people had been denied the right to effective representation in Parliament.

A representative of the Assembly of Manitoba Chiefs, expressed concern that the Commission had invited Aboriginal representatives to testify so as to legitimize a process that would once again deny Aboriginal people their proper place in the country.

In Kamloops, a member of the Shuswap Nation Tribal Council argued the need for an "honourable accommodation" with his people that would encompass every element of the relationship, including land, resources, services, political powers, and representation, and that would be enshrined by treaty with the federal government.

REPRESENTATION OF ETHNO-CULTURAL COMMUNITIES

It has long been common for political parties to make special efforts to attract the support of Canadians who are immigrants or members of ethnic or cultural minorities. In recent years, candidates and leadership campaign organizers from various parties have been criticized for recruiting so-called 'instant' members, often from a single ethnic group, to vote in nomination meetings or in the selection of leadership delegates. The Commission was told that this technique has been used not just to nominate candidates from traditional backgrounds, but as a means to enable minority candidates to win nominations, sometimes over the opposition of the local party establishment.

One participant put the question of ethno-cultural participation in a wider context. Democracy is an ideal toward which we must strive continuously, she argued. Demographic change and the new make-up of our society must be taken into account. If substantial portions of the population continue to be excluded from the political system, can there still be a democratic and representative electoral system?

> No integration of ethno-cultural groups or of women in the political system is possible, no representation is possible, unless all groups in society, men and women, white men and black men, Asians [and other groups] too have the opportunity to have a voice in Parliament and to be represented in Parliament.

She noted that research on the question of political participation by minorities has been limited, and that researchers seem to have assumed incorrectly that the social and economic integration of minorities would lead to political integration. She recommended that affirmative action measures and financial incentives be considered to increase the participation of minorities in political parties, but she had not reached a conclusion about whether this should be pursued voluntarily by the parties or whether it is a matter for regulation through the *Canada Elections Act*.

Several interveners representing ethno-cultural communities urged that the parties make room for people from their communities to participate in a genuine way rather than just using them as instant members. These interveners suggested that the period of membership before members could vote at a nomination meeting be extended to as long as one year.

The Canadian Ethnocultural Council also recommended that the parties adopt affirmative action policies to increase the number of candidates from ethno-cultural communities in winnable ridings, as well as to increase the participation of minorities within party organizations.

 The first step is to educate and push and lobby political parties to not just bus in truckloads of members of visible minorities and ethnic communities, but to actually involve them at higher levels of the political process and as candidates in winnable ridings. We have three visible minority Members of Parliament, which in a Parliament of nearly 300 is simply shocking.

The World Sikh Organization also called for reforms in party nomination processes, arguing that democracy is not served by using minorities as "pawns to be exploited and then forgotten in the game of leadership." Its representatives urged that voting in nomination meetings be restricted to persons who are citizens and at least 18 years of age. To promote consistency and fairness among parties, they recommended that the minimum age for party members be established through the elections act.

> "We have three visible minority Members of Parliament, which in a Parliament of nearly 300 is simply shocking."

One person defended allowing non-citizens to become members of constituency associations and to vote in party nominations, on the grounds that this is a good way for them to learn about the electoral process while they are waiting to become citizens.

Another person said that some backlash would be normal once minority groups started to work together to compete for power within the parties. Interveners from some minority groups objected to 'power brokers' from ethnic communities mobilizing support for a candidate or for leadership delegates, then failing to encourage continued activity in the party after the event:

When that preliminary selection process is over, there is very little role allowed for all these individuals. As an expression of that frustration, you see various ethnic groups hijacking ridings, threatening to take them away from sitting members – it is really an expression of frustration that we are not being allowed to play a more meaningful role within the process.

ELECTORAL BOUNDARIES READJUSTMENT

Canada's electoral map is revised after every decennial census by a boundaries commission established in each province and the Northwest Territories under the *Electoral Boundaries Readjustment Act.*

The number of seats in Parliament for each province and territory is determined by the *Constitution Act, 1985*. The average population per seat in each province is calculated using the most recent census. No riding may vary more than 25 per cent from the average for its province as a result of redistribution, except where a boundaries commission finds that there are extraordinary circumstances. Members of Parliament can appear before a boundaries commission along with the public at large.

On the issue of redistribution there was a sharp divergence of opinion between interveners advocating representation by population and those more concerned with ensuring that communities of interest and identity are represented and with the problem of representing large rural and sparsely settled ridings when strict representation by population is adhered to.

A Member of Parliament who represents a northern riding argued, "It is critical that geographic size continue to be a key element in this calculation. Without such guarantees, I predict that over a period of time, pressure will mount to reduce the number of seats allocated to areas like northern Ontario."

Another intervener said, "I believe that with the changing population and growing size of our cities, it is getting very difficult for rural representation to be able to deliver the message of the regions from the country." From the opposite perspective, a participant in the Calgary hearings

"We want to ask that the fundamental principle of democracy, which is one person–one vote, be revisited."

said simply, "We want to ask that the fundamental principle of democracy, which is one person–one vote, be revisited." Another argued, "Regardless of how you set riding boundaries, they have always distorted election results. They will never be able to really represent the communities, which are all of different sizes. If votes are to have equal value, you cannot have ridings of different sizes."

Their arguments were reinforced by the mayor of Vancouver, who said:

> We have to recognize that representatives of urban cores face a whole raft of individual problems. And, in fact, if you have a larger number of electors in the urban core, because somehow it seems easier to walk 10 blocks than to fly a thousand miles, I think we're missing the fundamental link between the constituent and the Member of Parliament. A Member of Parliament is expected to service those people. When we went through the electoral reform commission earlier, we found our constituencies were 20 to 25 per cent larger than other constituencies in the province of British Columbia. And I don't believe that that's good enough.

A number of interveners who attached greater importance to the principle of representation by population asked that more resources be provided to help Members of Parliament serve their constituents in sparsely settled and northern ridings.

Some questioned the rules guaranteeing that provinces will not lose House of Commons seats if their relative share of the population declines and suggested that reductions should be possible, though by no more than one seat per province every 10 years.

A few interveners favoured allowing the population of redistributed ridings to vary by no more than 10 per cent from the provincial quotient. Others spoke against the 'extraordinary circumstances' clause, which permits the creation of ridings larger or smaller than the current 25 per cent limit would allow. A former boundaries commissioner said, "I would suggest to you that the extraordinary circumstances clause that was added in 1986 to the *Electoral Boundaries Readjustment Act* is really superfluous. I do not see any need for it." In Moncton, it was suggested that Parliament should define these areas in legislation rather than leaving the decision up to boundaries commissions. Speaking in favour of the present variation of plus or minus 25 per cent, one intervener commented:

Let's analyse the level of representation and look at cases where there are 27 000 electors for one MP and 45 000 for another. If you look at the geographic size of these ridings and the way the population is scattered, a population of 27 000 electors in ridings like the Gaspé, Abitibi, and Northern Quebec seems appropriate, especially when you consider how difficult it is for their representatives to reach them. Compare that to someone living in Montreal, where a constituency has 40 000 to 43 000 electors, and the MP can tour the entire riding on foot. You can't do that in the Gaspé or on the North Shore. So achieving fair representation really justifies the allowable variation of plus or minus 25 per cent.

Figures were cited to show that after the 1987 redistribution, two-thirds of all federal ridings were within 10 per cent of the electoral quotient for their province and that only two dozen of the 295 ridings were more than 20 per cent above or below the provincial quotient. In Saskatchewan, the boundaries commission created ridings with only a 5 per cent variance.

In British Columbia, a Member of Parliament pointed out that under the present system a vote in Kootenay East is worth about 40 per cent more than a vote in Vancouver Centre. Another intervener pointed to a 44 per cent difference after redistribution between the population of the Restigouche and Moncton ridings in New Brunswick, based on the 1981 census population of the two ridings.

Two interveners asked that northern Ontario retain its 11 seats in Parliament, despite the faster growth of urban areas in southern Ontario, pointing out that their area constitutes 88 per cent of the land area of the province. The Commission was also asked for legislated guarantees that the three seats in the two territories would be preserved, despite their relatively small population.

Several interveners in Iqaluit made the case for creating a third riding in the Northwest Territories to be known as Nunavut, which would take in the Inuit population of the eastern Arctic and would follow the traditional lines of communication in the North. The Iqaluit Chamber of Commerce said the current division into two ridings seems to be a logical arrangement.

In Kuujjuaq in northern Quebec, interveners also made a case for improving Inuit representation by creating a new Quebec riding out of the northern portions of the Abitibi and Manicouagan ridings.

~ The land, people and resources of the North are intricately related and cannot be ignored as part of the political equation of Canada. If this requires changes to legislation to allow for a unique situation for direct representation in the House of Commons – so be it.

In the Churchill riding in Manitoba, an intervener asserted that the requirement that boundaries commissions consider maintaining a "manageable geographic size" for sparsely populated ridings had been ignored in 1987. Churchill covers more than 500 000 square kilometres, and over the objections of many people in the riding, 15 isolated communities on the east side of Lake Winnipeg had been added to the riding during redistribution.

The redistribution process was criticized for taking too long and for being based on outdated census figures. Some interveners suggested that the size of ridings be based on the number of registered voters at the previous election rather than on total population. Another suggested more frequent census-taking or using population estimates based on aerial photography or real estate data.

A former member of a boundaries commission spoke about the lack of resources given to the commissions to do their job. Another group urged that redistribution take place within one year of census results being published. Both urged that the role of Members of Parliament in the process be reduced.

In Victoria, it was suggested that the practice of using geographical names for Canadian constituencies be reconsidered and that the Australian and Quebec practice of naming electoral districts after eminent artists, writers, politicians or historical figures be used instead. If community names were not used, it was argued, changes in constituency boundaries would not necessitate name changes.

OTHER PROPOSED REFORMS

Witnesses raised several other issues related to representation, including the desirability of an electoral system based on proportional representation and of mechanisms of direct democracy such as recall of Members of

Parliament, referendums and voter initiatives, and protest votes. Canada's system of electing one member per constituency is based on the British model and dates back to the beginning of parliamentary institutions in Canada. Many industrial democracies, however, elect their legislatures through some form of proportional representation.

A number of states in the United States provide for some form of recall of representatives. A petition by a certain number of voters can be used to force a sitting legislator to resign and seek re-election.

Several Canadian provinces have legislative provisions to allow the holding of referendums. There is no specific provision in the *Canada Elections Act*. The 'initiative' is used to give voters an opportunity to raise issues for consideration and determine policy issues directly through a vote rather than through elected representatives.

There is no provision in the current law for a voter to cast a protest vote. An individual can refrain from voting or can spoil the ballot, but these actions are not recorded as protest votes.

Several interveners supported some form of proportional representation, arguing that legislative representation would reflect the make-up of the electorate more accurately as a result:

> The need for proportional representation is not a quest for power by fringe parties. It is a recognition that a diversity of ideas presented at the highest levels of government is more likely to enhance the capabilities of Canada to meet the challenges the world is presenting to us. The present electoral system only reinforces an inadvisable protection of the status quo.

Some pointed to specific situations that could be corrected by proportional representation:

> It shouldn't be the case, as it was here in New Brunswick, that only one Liberal Member of Parliament was elected at the 1984 general election when a third or more of the province's population voted for the party. It makes no sense that we have one member out of 10 when our share of the vote was better than 30 per cent. A proportional representation system would ensure that there would not be only two strong parties and only one smaller party with a chance of representation. Parties would be more representative and people would be able to vote for a winner to a greater extent.

"It makes no sense that we have one member out of 10 when our share of the vote was better than 30 per cent."

On the other side of this issue, a Halifax intervener cautioned:

> It appears to me that the Canadian voter expects and demands as funda-
> mental the accountability that each Member of Parliament owes to his or
> her constituency. That direct access to the legislative process for any voter
> in that riding is crucial. I think that the advent of a proportional system
> perverts that relationship. And I think anyone who advocates that sys-
> tem must tread very carefully.

A Montreal participant emphasized the importance of the individual relationship between Members of Parliament and their constituents, pointing out that "electing an MP in a riding is like having a good parish priest; you can confide in him and he keeps his trap shut and doesn't tell everybody everything."

A number of interveners recommended that Canada adopt the German system, where half the members are elected from constituencies and half by proportional representation: the latter seats are allocated to balance the results of constituency elections according to the proportion of the total vote cast for each party. Several interveners recommended the use of a single transferable vote system, which counts voters' second and even third preferences if no candidate has a majority after first-choice votes are counted.

In Regina, a group of political scientists recommended that

> The House of Commons consist of 310 members to be allocated in the
> following manner: 10 MPs representing Indian, Inuit and Métis peoples;
> a further 300 members, 150 of whom are elected as representatives from
> local constituencies, and 150 from lists presented by the parties.
>
> Each voter then would have two ballots, one to choose the constituency
> representative and the other to choose the party.

The Council of Canadians was one of several interveners recommending the use of run-off elections on the French model, where a second election is held a week after election day in constituencies where no candidate won a majority of the vote. One group suggested that, although it was better to expand facilities for Members of Parliament than to expand the House of Commons, 30 seats should be added to increase the representation of parties winning more than 10 per cent of the vote but whose proportion of seats in the House is less than their share of the popular vote. Each party's unelected candidates with the highest share of the vote in their riding would take these seats.

The Reform Party recommended the introduction of a number of instruments of direct democracy, including the use of referendums and plebiscites, and the initiative and the right of constituents to recall their Member of Parliament. They argued these were needed to counter the trend to executive federalism and unrepresentative decisions by Parliament.

Others also argued for recall provisions and greater use of referendums to make Members of Parliament more accountable, to encourage participation, and to make the electoral system more democratic.

One argued, "We need a recall system for politicians who lie. As one of our Board members said, 'If you buy a frying pan, and it doesn't work, you can get your money back, and it should be the same with politicians.' "

A Member of Parliament who had presented a draft bill to permit national referendums on important issues noted that the power to hold referendums now exists in seven provinces. A Toronto political scientist recommended that Canada allow for referendums on issues such as the free trade agreement to accompany a general election, although he thought that the results should be advisory, not binding on government:

> "A more modest step in that direction would be to allow Parliament, through a process defined in advance, to put important questions on the regular election ballot."

 A more modest step in that direction would be to allow Parliament, through a process defined in advance, to put important questions on the regular election ballot. This would achieve many of the gains to be made from a referendum device, without incurring the additional expense of more frequent elections.

Some interveners aired more general concerns about the electoral system. These included the low value people attach to parties and candidates and their lack of understanding of what politicians do. Concern was also expressed about the degree to which political parties seem to prefer the glamour of politics over the substance. In Winnipeg an intervener suggested:

 The adversarial scenario in Parliament is contradictory to the democratic process; it should be dropped. Political party alignments are all right to help you get elected, but after an election that alignment should switch to informal, so co-operation becomes the order of the day, to run the country based on the consensus of all the ridings in Canada.

Other interveners recommended that voting be mandatory, called for an elected Senate, and suggested that the prime minister be elected separately and not be a member of the House of Commons. Others recommended that party leaders sit in Parliament but not be required to represent a constituency because of their other responsibilities.

A former Member of Parliament from British Columbia warned that if the Senate were elected, it would no longer be a chamber of sober second thought but would gain greater power than the House of Commons, as is the case in the United States. He suggested the Senate would be improved if each province were allowed to name half its senators.

The most substantial submission advocating a protest vote came from a Montreal political scientist who contended that dissatisfied voters have very few options; it takes too long to create a new political party or gain control of an existing one, and most people do not have the time or resources to run as independent candidates. To spoil a ballot is a negative act not easy to interpret, and no message is left by a voter who simply stays away from the polls.

> It is a serious weakness in our electoral system that it does not adequately allow for dissent from the established political parties. This weakness limits democratic expression and disseminates an inaccurate perception of public attitudes. Fortunately, there is at least one obvious solution: provide a place on the ballot for those who wish to reject all candidates.

The witness went on to say that should protest votes be in the majority, a second election would have to be held.

Support for a protest vote or for leaving a space on the ballot for 'None of the above' came from several other interveners. One participant argued, "Providing a 'none of the above' option on the ballots used to select members of the House of Commons provides an opportunity for dissenting voters to be recorded and not to be mistaken or dismissed as illiterate or apathetic."

4

ON POLITICAL PARTIES

CANADIANS WHO SPOKE to us about the role and regulation of political parties can be loosely categorized into two groups, not so much because they represented opposing points of view but because they offered different perspectives on political parties.

One group consisted of people who work in and with political parties, many of whom are volunteers. They argued for stronger political parties, more resources and simpler rules. A prominent Canadian put her case this way: "What I believe should be a focal point of your report is the need to encourage and strengthen major political parties, and not merely to throw open the political forum to any and all groups concerned solely or mainly with one issue and one point of view."

A Member of Parliament offered the following perspective:

> Ideally, both the electoral system and political parties should become perfect conductors, transmitting the public will to the state with a minimum of resistance.
>
> The clash of ideas and personalities, the freedom to help determine the future of one's country, the precious liberty to vote for or against a platform or person, all of these are unthinkable without the assistance of political parties.
>
> Given the crucial mediating role between rulers and ruled, political parties must conform to the highest democratic ideals. If the people's tools are blunted, then the house of democracy will be ill-fashioned.

The second group consisted of people interested in the political process but not necessarily involved directly in partisan politics. They were concerned with regulating the struggle between the parties and with ensuring access for all Canadians to the political process and consequently to political parties.

Party financing was a pivotal issue. Proposals ranged from withdrawing all public funding to providing total funding. The issue of who should be able to contribute to political parties and whether there should be limits on contributions sparked vigorous discussion.

Several interveners recommended regulating leadership campaigns. They argued that because someone can be chosen to head a federal party and in this way become prime minister without a national election, some form of regulation is needed. Others contended this is an internal matter for each party.

There was also considerable discussion of the requirements for official recognition of political parties. The benefits and responsibilities that follow recognition, including free-time election telecasts and public funding, were also raised by many interveners.

Finally, several interveners discussed party issues at the local or constituency level, raising questions about the level of public financing that should be provided and the disposition of surplus campaign funds.

PARTY FUNDING

Registered political parties are reimbursed for 22.5 per cent of their expenses during an election campaign, provided they spend at least 10 per cent of the campaign limit (about $8 000 000 in 1988 for a national party contesting every seat). The limit depends on the number of seats contested, but there is no requirement for a party to receive a minimum percentage of the vote.

Contributors to political parties are eligible for tax credits, both during campaigns and between elections, but there is no policy of direct annual funding for national political parties.

Candidates, on the other hand, are reimbursed for 50 per cent of their election expenses, provided they receive at least 15 per cent of the vote. Contributions to candidates at election time are eligible for tax credits.

No public funding is provided for nomination campaign expenses, which are not limited by law, except when political parties allow donations which qualify for tax credits to be used for nomination campaign expenses.

The question of public funding was raised frequently at Commission hearings across Canada. Two of the key issues were annual funding for political parties and expanding or enriching reimbursements for election expenses.

A former provincial party leader contributed a personal insight to the discussion:

> I once looked upon the financing situation from the standpoint of an incumbent minister and a fairly strong government with a lot of financial resources available. As time unfolded, I ended up being leader of an opposition party with a huge debt and an inability to raise money. Funny how that changes one's perspective on these issues.

Another politician was equally candid in recounting his party's changed fortunes:

> Unfortunately, we in the Liberal Party have had the experience, which has lasted much longer than we would have hoped, of being an opposition party for five or six years already. The Commission should examine the fate of opposition parties in our system. Parties like the NDP have much more experience than we do, they have perhaps succeeded in resolving this problem. For financial and other reasons, we have found it very difficult to be in opposition.

In contrast, one provincial party leader expressed opposition to any funding scheme: "I would not prohibit people saying what I find to be hateful, but I do not want to finance it. And you are making me finance it. That is the difference." This sentiment was echoed by the leader of a national party, who said, "We do believe that, increasingly, they should get their funds from the people they purport to represent rather than from the taxpayers."

Several interveners spoke in support of annual direct public funding for political parties. They argued that it is necessary if parties are to fulfil their role in the political process between elections. The need for annual funding would be even greater, it was argued, if limits were imposed on contributions, resulting in reduced party income.

> "We do believe that, increasingly, they should get their funds from the people they purport to represent rather than from the taxpayers."

Interveners pointed to the examples of Quebec and New Brunswick, both of which provide annual funding to parties according to the number of votes received in the last election. Some expressed the opinion that New Brunswick's $2 per vote was too high.

One intervener suggested:

~ The notion of a checkoff system [on the personal income tax form] should be looked at very carefully, because I think all parties need more financial support if they are going to be active on a year-to-year basis, and that may be one way in which individuals can express support for the party of their choice.

Both the Canadian Labour Congress and the federal New Democratic Party commented on the disparity in the subsidy for local and national campaigns. They said that it results in constituency associations being relatively well off while national parties are left impoverished. The Congress recommended that spending ceilings be raised at both levels and that expenses be reimbursed at a rate of 50 per cent up to the present ceiling, then at 25 per cent for expenses up to the new ceiling. In Yellowknife, a participant suggested that local and national campaign expenses be reimbursed at the same rate, 33.3 per cent.

Two participants recommended full public funding. They cited figures to show that the reimbursement of election expenses plus the tax credits on political donations amounted to 66 per cent of the parties' spending in the 1988 federal election. One argued:

~ As taxpayers, women help pay for a system that underrepresents them. As citizens, they deplore a system that forces candidates to raise money

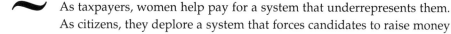

up front, and in the process become indebted to special interests. We now get the worst of both worlds. We, as members of the public, pay for a back-door form of government funding of the electoral process, and much of that public funding goes out in the form of tax credits to wealthy party insiders to help them buy private influence with our politicians.

Another participant recommended:

~ The 50 per cent reimbursement of national expenditures should be allo-cated according to the percentage of votes that a political party gets in a province. Then it would be based on provincial results instead of being calculated globally, from the national point of view. Everyone knows per-fectly well that in certain provinces there are parties that can hardly elect a soul or that get very few votes.

On the question of reimbursement of campaign expenditures at the national level, it was suggested:

~ The emergence and nurturing of new political parties takes time. New parties may not, in fact, be able to raise 10 per cent of their allow-able spending limit. By denying them rebates for allowable expenses below this level, Canada is making it unnecessarily hard for them to establish themselves.

Several suggestions were made to improve the formula for reimbursing election expenses. These included reducing the threshold to 10 per cent of the vote and introducing a sliding scale for candidates who receive less than the required threshold. Others suggested moving to full public funding of candidates' campaign expenses.

One constituency association recommended annual funding for local riding associations and suggested raising the reimbursement rate for local campaigns to 60 per cent, but only for expenses not financed by corporate donations. The association suggested that this restriction would lead to lower, rather than higher, overall subsidy costs.

Several other interveners asked that specific expenses be met using public funds. The Prince Edward Island Federation of Labour suggested that people who take time off from their job to stand as candidates be reimbursed for living expenses. Another intervener suggested that party scrutineers who work on election day be paid out of public funds, as is the practice in Quebec. A Green Party supporter recommended pub-lishing a federal newspaper in each constituency with information on each candidate, and a group of Saskatchewan riding associations recom-mended that local constituency associations be entitled to several free mail-ings each year to balance the mailing privileges of incumbent Members of Parliament.

THE TAX CREDIT

The federal tax credit on political donations was introduced in 1974 as part of election expenses legislation. The system gives individual and corporate donors a tax credit of 75 per cent on the first $100 donated, 50 per cent on the next $450, and 33.3 per cent on the next $600, for a maximum of $500 in tax credits annually for donations of $1150 or more to federal political parties and candidates. Corporate political donations are eligible for this tax credit but are not a deductible business expense. The tax credit is available only if federal tax is payable. Federal law does not prohibit donations made to a federal party that qualify for a federal tax credit from being used for provincial party purposes. However, some provinces have rules respecting the transfer of federal party funds to a provincial party.

The tax credit for political donations provoked much discussion. One participant stated, "Canada's progressive policy of making it easy for ordinary Canadians to participate fully in the political process through a system of tax deductions for financial contributions to political parties and candidates should be expanded." Critics either opposed any public funding of political parties and candidates or asked that donations to political parties be treated for tax purposes in the same way as donations to charity.

> "Canada's progressive policy of making it easy for ordinary Canadians to participate fully in the political process through a system of tax deductions ... should be expanded."

On several occasions, Commissioners asked why political donations up to $1150 should be treated more generously than donations to charity. Interveners defended the disparity on the grounds that the tax credit is intended to encourage participation in political parties – a fundamental requirement for a strong democratic system. Others pointed out that substantial contributors receive more favourable tax treatment for charitable donations. However, one charitable organization opposed giving any tax concessions to political parties, arguing that all non-profit organizations benefiting from tax concessions should be barred from demonstrating any support for a political party.

A representative of the National Citizens' Coalition argued against the political tax credit system:

> I find it outrageous that political parties would put themselves in a preferential position, as far as tax treatment goes, over the Salvation Army. Why should they get such exceptional treatment? Why should it make more sense to me to give a dollar to political parties than it makes to give

a dollar to the Salvation Army? I would just suggest you treat the two the same.

Another participant stated, "I would expect political contributions to go way down if we were treated exactly the same as charities are right now."

Several interveners advocated enriching the tax credit system; several said the credits should be indexed. One group calculated that a $100 donation in 1974 would be the equivalent of $309 in 1991 because of inflation, and recommended a new tax credit schedule at about three times the present level. Others recommended that tax credits be given for donations up to $2500. A few interveners also recommended that the credit be refundable so that the system would not discriminate against people whose income is too low to pay federal tax:

~ Tax credits presently in place are very good, except when I helped my wife fill out the income tax I realized that, although she gave to a party, she could not claim because she has no income. So I think that could be something that you could look at. It could be like the child tax credit, where if she gave $100 to a party she could get $75 back.

Several interveners suggested that priority be given to increasing the amount eligible for the 75 per cent tax credit. Others recommended that new parties be allowed to issue receipts for donations for tax credit purposes without having to wait until an election is called.

A Newfoundland and Labrador political association recommended establishing a mechanism to allow federal campaign funds to be contributed directly to provincial riding associations, since there is no provincial tax credit in Newfoundland. In Winnipeg, a former Member of Parliament disagreed, saying the provinces had adequate resources to establish their own tax credits; the use of federal tax credits should be confined to federal electoral politics.

DISCLOSURE

A number of interveners made comments on the disclosure provisions of the *Canada Elections Act*. When individuals or organizations contribute more than $100 to a registered political party in a given year or to a candidate during an election, their names must be reported. These reports are available for public scrutiny. An intervener in Toronto highlighted the importance of disclosure in our system of election financing:

~ We believe that the publication of donors' names allows public scrutiny of the process, and thereby controls abuses of the process, particularly as the vigilance of our Canadian media and political parties in this respect is second to none.

The $100 disclosure threshold for political contributions was set in 1974. Since then, inflation has tripled nominal money values. Several interveners suggested a new threshold of $250, while one suggested doing away with disclosure and instead limiting contributions to a maximum of $1000.

One riding association suggested raising the threshold for disclosing donor names to $250, the same amount it suggested be eligible for a 75 per cent tax credit. Another suggestion was that donations to leadership campaigns be eligible for credits at half the usual rate, but that disclosure not be required for donations below $500, so that party members would not have to identify the candidate they supported.

> "The intention is laudable, but for all practical purposes, the *Canada Elections Act* does not allow the identity of party backers to be revealed."

The Fédération professionnelle des journalistes du Québec criticized the disclosure law because it does not require the address of contributors. One member explained:

> The intention is laudable, but for all practical purposes, the *Canada Elections Act* does not allow the identity of party backers to be revealed. In fact, the Act does not require backers' addresses to be disclosed. The name of a person or a company can just as easily be from Yellowknife as Sept-Îles; it's meagre information and difficult to use.

Another expressed concern that people must reveal the political party they support when filing their income tax return because tax receipts identify the party to which a taxpayer has contributed, and he offered this solution:

> It would be easy enough to design a system of identical government-issued tax receipts; the people who would need to know would be able to tell from a serial number what party issued it, Liberal or Conservative party or any other. This would avoid revealing contributors' political allegiance. I think this should be done in a democracy.

THE SOURCE AND SIZE OF CAMPAIGN CONTRIBUTIONS

The *Canada Elections Act* limits the amount a national party or local candidate may spend during an election campaign and requires disclosure of all contributions to a party or candidate that exceed $100, but the Act does not distinguish between corporate, trade union or individual donations, nor does it set a ceiling on the size of contributions.

Several provinces restrict the size of contributions. Under Quebec's system of election financing, provincial parties and candidates are allowed to receive contributions only from electors, and each elector can give a maximum of $3000 in political contributions each year. Quebec also provides annual public funding to the parties.

Many interveners commented on limiting contribution size, barring corporate and union contributions to political parties, and the Quebec model of political financing. One Member of Parliament expressed support for a funding policy similar to Quebec's:

 [Voters] do not believe that an engineering firm that gives $100 000 to a political party or that makes a bunch of people available to a political party in an election campaign does not expect to get engineering contracts afterward. And it's the same for paper companies and for lawyers. No, Canadians won't believe that.

Companies that want to participate in the political process have many other ways of doing so. If they want to do it by lobbying, let them follow the law on lobbyists that Parliament has just passed.

Other interveners based arguments for banning corporate and union contributions on general concerns about undue influence. Some were concerned about drifting toward the American political model; others expressed a general desire to clean up Canadian politics. One expressed concern about the overall process: "Politics in Canada is becoming a rich man's game. When candidates for nomination or leadership are dependent on the financial assistance of corporations and corporate interest, they become beholden to the public policy prospectus of these corporations."

> "... not permitting organizations to make political contributions would be healthy for the system because parties would then have to ... [draw] on individual support."

One participant expressed concern for personal freedom of choice: "What we're trying to get at is the right of individuals who belong – and often have no choice in the matter – to organizations, such as trade unions, where membership is compulsory, not to make political contributions."

Another intervener suggested, "I believe that not permitting organizations to make political contributions would be healthy for the system because parties would then have to become much more active in drawing on individual support."

A Member of Parliament argued that the perception of the donation is itself a problem:

 Even in good faith, a contribution by a land developer to a municipal politician, by a beer company to a provincial candidate, and by a bank to a federal candidate, is not healthy no matter how one wants to proclaim that every citizen is entitled to make a contribution.

Several interveners said it would be easier to justify restricting corporate and union support for advocacy groups at election time if their contributions to political parties were also restricted. Some interveners believed that the Quebec model of political financing would make politics more accessible to women. An intervener from Quebec suggested that limits on donation size could not be enforced if corporate donations were permitted.

A number of presenters spoke out against restrictions such as those imposed by the Quebec model:

Right now we see the spectre of Members of Parliament going out and raising money for their parties; that's not their job, they're supposed to be legislating.

If we lessen or narrow the base of our contributions, then we will have elected politicians who will be spending more of their time fund raising for their party to help others who are not so well off or to help the party that may be in debt. That's not the job of a politician.

Another intervener said, "One thing is clear: the solution to this dilemma is not a return to fund raising exclusively from individuals. This option is impractical. It is clearly true that one cannot run a national campaign on the proceeds from selling fudge." These comments were echoed by another participant who suggested, "While a perfect world would make only individual donations acceptable, we do not believe that this is a practical or realistic goal at this time."

> "It is clearly true that one cannot run a national campaign on the proceeds from selling fudge."

Several interveners favoured barring corporate donations at the local level, but not nationally. There was considerable support, however, for setting limits on political contributions rather than banning certain contributions altogether. One participant suggested that "large political donations by special-interest groups, labour unions, or corporations should not only be reported but also limited in dollars."

Another suggested that the current level of corporate donations does not threaten the system, but advocated setting a $10 000 limit on contributions to counter the perception that there may be problems. Another suggested that a limit – but not a ban – on corporate donations would probably be acceptable under the Charter.

Several participants suggested a ceiling of $5000. One intervener suggested that no corporate donations to local campaigns be allowed and that the national limit be $50 000. Another suggested that small business be able to make contributions locally and suggested a ceiling on donations of $1000 locally and $20 000 nationally.

Several interveners were concerned about foreign influence on Canadian politics and recommended that no foreign contributions to a party or candidate be allowed. Others suggested that a vote by union members or shareholders be required to authorize a political donation by a union or company.

One intervener stated, "If the source of funding is wholly outside Canada, of course it should be banned. However, a subsidiary corporation that resides in Canada should have the same right as a Canadian corporation. After all, we allow them to set up and carry on their business under Canadian law." Another argued that "it is really expensive to run the parties in this complicated, regionally diverse country. And if I can find some company in Cleveland, Ohio, that doesn't mind having its name in lights for giving $10 000 to our party, why not?"

> "... if I can find some company in Cleveland, Ohio, that doesn't mind having its name in lights for giving $10 000 to our party, why not?"

Many believed, however, that the current system is satisfactory. The Canadian Labour Congress stated, "We recommend the Commission repeat the Barbeau Committee recommendation that no restriction as to size or source of political contribution be initiated, and all individuals, corporations, trade unions and organizations be encouraged to support the political party of their choice."

Others felt that the alternatives suggested weren't practical:

It's easy to be naive about the political process, and one thing that it is easy to be naive about is that if unions and corporations are restricted from providing money, those with money and interest in getting money to political parties will find other means to do so.

Representatives of the business community questioned the apparent contradiction between being good corporate citizens and not being allowed to participate in electoral politics through financial support for parties. Some interveners suggested that because corporations pay tax, they should be allowed to play a role in the political system. One said, "I think that any limitation on [corporations'] spending would negatively affect the involvement of people in the political process and if there is concern, it should be addressed by further disclosure."

The Montreal Chamber of Commerce warned that limitations could lead to underground donations. Another participant told the Commission:

It doesn't take a genius to figure out how to put money into a campaign without exceeding an arbitrary limit imposed by statute. Caps would clearly drive contributors underground, and the devious aspects of political fund raising would come into play. Much simpler, much easier and much more open, is a system of full disclosure of campaign contributions.

An intervener argued that Quebec no longer has genuine *financement populaire* because social fund-raising events are used to bring together Cabinet ministers and business people: "The weight of the evidence is that it is not popular fund raising in the Quebec sense. The feature of these activities is that they are graced by the presence of Cabinet ministers. As a result, businessmen pay inflated prices for access to the ministers."

Others suggested that limiting the size of contributions could have adverse effects on the operation of modern political parties. One intervener commented, "The strength of the current system, when it comes to contributions, is the requirement for public disclosure. I caution against introducing new limits that may prove to be impractical in the real world of election campaigns and party financing. Contribution limits may seem desirable, but they must not be looked at in isolation."

Another intervener echoed these concerns:

 What is essential, what constitutes the brakes and is our best guarantee of political morality, is transparency. When things are transparent, people draw the conclusions they want to draw when the facts are placed in front of them. Imposing a ceiling on contributions made each year is a measure that your Commission will have to study carefully, taking into consideration the fact that the lower the maximum, the more we will have to search for other ways to finance political parties during and between election periods; this means public funding, in my opinion, because the democratic system has to function through the parties.

> "What is essential, what constitutes the brakes and is our best guarantee of political morality, is transparency."

Others agreed that more public funding for parties would be needed if a form of political financing like the Quebec model were introduced. A national party official said that a survey of the federal ridings in Quebec showed that 80 per cent no longer supported the concept of *financement populaire* because it had not been successful. These same ridings had endorsed the concept in the summer of 1988, and many had tried to raise their campaign funds that year through this method. The official concluded that there should be limits on contributions but that donations from business should not be banned.

A constituency association offered its own version of *financement populaire*: corporate donations would still be permitted, but with a lower public subsidy than that given for individual donations.

LEADERSHIP CAMPAIGNS

Federal law does not regulate leadership campaigns. They are governed entirely by the political parties, albeit under the scrutiny of the media. Tax credits are not allowed on donations made directly to leadership campaigns. However, credits are available on donations made through a registered party and passed on to a candidate.

Many interveners supported some regulation of the leadership process, although this view was by no means unanimous: "It is every Canadian's business because the person who spends his or her way to the top could be the next prime minister. It is our business to find out how that was done," stated one supporter of intervention. Another intervener argued that internal party processes should conform to the public desire for openness because of the crucial role parties play in a democracy. One participant commented:

> Party leaders have considerable power in our system. We hear more and more about how our system is becoming presidential, with the party leader playing a major role in the election campaign. If these leaders owe favours once they reach office, whether it's to powerful interests or to the mysterious fundraisers who made it possible for them to win the leadership, it's no more healthy than if the parties themselves were being financed in this way.
>
> A new electoral law should deal with the financing of leadership contests in the same way and with the same requirements as the financing of political parties.

Another participant disagreed:

> Parties should continue to operate under the current system, free of government regulation in relation to the selection of party leaders. Political parties are increasingly aware of the public's interest in this area, and I anticipate that responsible parties will themselves increasingly set guidelines or regulations relating to the process of leadership selection.

Those against regulation suggested it was either unnecessary or might drive contributions underground. One participant warned of excessive regulation, and urged the Commission not to venture into this area, noting that few other democracies regulate leadership campaigns.

Outlining his views on what form regulation should take, one participant stated, "Although I would certainly not wish to impose uniformity on the different political parties, it is essential that there be some standard regulations on the financing and regulation of leadership conventions.... I am suggesting that [Elections Canada] should have a role in the administration of the leadership conventions – that it's a natural extension of skills that they already have."

One intervener recommended that rules for leadership races be harmonized with the rules governing contributions to parties and candidates. He proposed a ceiling of $5000 on contributions to leadership campaigns and suggested that donations of more than 20 volunteer hours be disclosed. He also urged detailed disclosure in sensitive areas such as 'instant' party memberships, delegates' convention expenses, and contributions by ethnocultural organizations.

"... it is essential that there be some standard regulations on the financing and regulation of leadership conventions."

A participant suggested a ceiling of $500 000 on spending in a leadership campaign and said that anything beyond that is excessive. The Nova Scotia Advisory Council on the Status of Women suggested a $250 000 ceiling; another group suggested $100 000.

One participant suggested that the disclosure rules should differ from those for other political contributions:

> At the very minimum, there must be requirements for disclosure of the names and contributions; perhaps contributions over $500. I don't think you can buy a Canadian political leader. So I think there is still a private aspect to political parties and would argue for a $500 limit. I have been anxious to encourage general participation in the political process. My judgement is that this is a reasonable balance.

Another intervener suggested that ceilings on contributions would be acceptable if tax credits were available for donations to leadership campaigns.

In recent leadership conventions, the three largest parties allowed party members to take part in delegate selection or to be delegates even if they were not eligible voters because they were under 18 or not Canadian citizens. On the question of letting people who are not eligible to vote participate in leadership campaigns, one person said:

> I'm not sure that we can dispossess them or tell them, because you're 14 years of age or because you haven't yet got your citizenship, you shouldn't be involved in any part of our election process. They can't vote, but they can certainly come in and support a candidate and work their buns off for him or her. I don't want to minimize the importance of Canadian citizenship,

but I want part of becoming a Canadian to be involvement in the process. So as you're working toward becoming a Canadian, or until you're old enough to vote, take part in a nomination meeting.

One intervener suggested that, for constitutional reasons, Canada will eventually adopt a uniform process for selecting candidates and leaders. Another intervener recommended that Canada give the public a role in choosing leadership delegates through a process similar to U.S. primaries.

OFFICIAL PARTY STATUS

Under the *Canada Elections Act*, registering a new party is a two-stage process. A party has to apply for registration, giving its name and the name of its leader, its officers, its official agent and auditors, as well as the signatures of 100 members. But it can be registered only when it has officially nominated candidates in 50 federal constituencies after a general election is called. This rule means that a party formed between elections cannot be registered and therefore cannot issue tax receipts for donations until it embarks on its first election campaign with at least 50 candidates. A registered party that fails to confirm its registration at election time, or to present a minimum of 50 candidates in that election, may be de-registered unless it has at least 12 members in the outgoing House of Commons. Not surprisingly, this issue was of interest mainly to interveners representing smaller parties, who were generally critical of these rules. Not being able to be registered before an election is called makes it more difficult to raise funds, because parties cannot issue official receipts entitling donors to a tax credit for contributions.

The Communist Party said that the requirement for 50 candidates is undemocratic and forces smaller parties into activities beyond their means or their provincial or regional base. As an alternative, they proposed a party be required to have 10 000 signatures to be registered.

The Reform Party took a similar view, suggesting that 1000 signatures be required, but the party did not oppose a higher number. They suggested that if registration is made easier, it should also be easier to de-register a party once it is established.

Manitoba's chief electoral officer suggested that the *Canada Elections Act* follow Manitoba's model for registering new parties – new party status is granted when a party has 2500 signatures on its application.

The Parti nationaliste recommended that a regional party be recognized if it presents candidates in 15 per cent of the ridings in a particular region. It also suggested that minor parties be represented on the House of Commons Standing Committee on Privileges and Elections and that decisions to de-register a party should be made only by this committee.

Another intervener expressed this view: "If a party can elect 12 members from 12 different ridings and be established as a recognized political party in Parliament, it doesn't make any sense not to accord them the right to be recognized as such on a ballot."

Some interveners suggested increasing the requirement for registering a party to 75 or 100 candidates, but also suggested expanding new parties' rights. One recommended that a party also be required to have an annual convention to maintain its registration.

CONSTITUENCY ASSOCIATIONS

Unlike political parties, constituency associations are not required to register or report under the *Canada Elections Act*; nor are their operations and financial affairs generally open to scrutiny. Constituency associations cannot issue tax receipts for political contributions, but local candidates have this right during election periods.

Some local associations have substantial financial resources, raised using their federal party's tax receipt and from surpluses generated during election campaigns. The Canadian Institute of Chartered Accountants reported that in the 1988 election, 723 candidates, or 98 per cent of those entitled to federal funds for election expenses, had a surplus in their campaign budget after receiving the subsidy. The total surplus was $9.6 million. The use of these funds is virtually unregulated, although they are usually passed on to the constituency association or used to defray pre-election expenses.

Some Members of Parliament and members of the Canadian Institute of Chartered Accountants strongly supported requiring local associations to register and file annual returns. One intervener suggested that registration be required if a constituency association wishes to issue tax receipts, but otherwise should be voluntary. The main argument put forward was that candidates receive public funds through the tax credit system and through the reimbursement of election expenses. These are passed on to the local association. Thus, because they receive public funds, albeit indirectly, they should be accountable. One intervener said that constituency associations should be registered because parties are in business 12 months a year, not just during elections.

An auditor for candidates in Ontario suggested that the financial activities of constituency associations during election campaigns be reported when candidates report their election expenses. Ontario has required that local associations be registered since 1975, he said, and there have been no problems.

One constituency association recommended that all surplus campaign funds be transferred from the candidate to the local constituency association. In Alberta, it was suggested that these funds be held in trust for the next election campaign, or that rules be introduced to exact accountability for these funds.

A smaller group of interveners recommended that local associations be permitted to issue tax receipts for political contributions made between elections. One commented that this was needed to reverse the increasing centralization of party finances. Another said that it would avoid the 'taxing' of local associations, in which the national party takes a portion of any political donation to the constituency. Still another supported the change because every time he gave a contributor's name to the national party so that he or she could receive a tax receipt, he lost a donor because the person was then bombarded with appeals for funds from the national level.

OFFICIAL AGENTS

Under the Act, a candidate's agent is responsible for all financial aspects of a candidate's campaign and is subject to heavy penalties for failing to comply with the Act. In certain cases, a candidate who is elected can be removed from office if an official agent has failed to comply with the Act. The agent's responsibilities include receiving all contributions to the candidate's campaign; maintaining the bank account for the campaign; controlling all payments made by the campaign; keeping expenditures under the ceiling set by law; submitting the candidate's return; and receiving allowable reimbursements. Unlike those of most election workers, the agent's responsibilities extend beyond election day and must be fulfilled whether the candidate is elected or not.

Issues surrounding the role and responsibilities of official agents were raised by several interveners but not discussed at length. The most common concern was the need for Elections Canada to give official agents much better training and to pay them because of the unusual nature of their responsibilities. One returning officer stated, "Sometimes people acting as official agents are asked to take time off from work to fulfil their electoral responsibilities. And after the election is over, the official agent still has work to do, often for quite a long time. Official agents have a lot to do; their responsibilities are serious, and there are forms and questionnaires and a great deal of paperwork to be completed."

> "As the official agent ... you are trying to make sure that people do not spend money that you are not aware of."

It was recommended that agents be paid an amount equal to 2 per cent of the candidate's election expenses, up to a maximum of $1500.

Two accountants said they had declined to be official agents in the 1988 campaign because of the nature of the agent's responsibilities and the difficulties of interpreting the Act and because the agent has little or no control over the actions of campaign workers for whom he or she may be responsible. Another described his experience:

 As the official agent you are always in a bad position. Your candidate is yelling at you to spend more money and you are trying to control the costs so that you do not go over. You are trying to make sure that people do not spend money that you are not aware of.

You have not lived until you have waited until after an election for the bills to roll in, to see if there are some bills that you had not known anything about. You just wait and pray that nobody has done it, even though you tell everybody, "Do not buy anything without me knowing it." And then on top of that you have to decide whether some costs are an election expense and some are not an election expense.

A former official agent contended that agents are under great pressure to see that a candidate does not exceed the spending limits by so much as one dollar. He said this was far more burdensome than normal accounting procedures, where auditing is done to specified levels of materiality. He suggested that a definition of materiality that allowed for a 10 per cent margin of error would be reasonable. This margin should apply only to questionable judgements made by official agents in calculating election expenses.

One intervener recommended that the official agent for each candidate be a neutral and non-partisan appointee named by Elections Canada rather than being appointed by the candidate. A group asked that the Act be amended so that official agents not be found guilty of an offence as long as they act in good faith and take reasonable steps to avoid overspending.

The submission of the Canadian Institute of Chartered Accountants dealt mainly with the issues of defining and reporting election expenses, but it also touched on the role of official agents. The Institute urged that reforms be introduced to improve accountability for the use of campaign funds, because they often include public money given to parties or candidates as reimbursement for election expenses. The Institute also suggested that official agents and candidates be required to confirm that their returns cover all campaign donations and expenditures. In addition, such items as computer equipment and software that are subsequently used during a campaign should be counted as a campaign expense to the extent that they are used during the campaign.

A returning officer in Halifax recommended that agents and auditors reside in the province in which their candidate is running and that a person be allowed to work as an official agent for only one candidate. An official agent noted the difficulties posed by having to obtain a judge's order to make payments more than four months after the election. He recommended that payment be allowed with the returning officer's consent or be permitted up to one month after reimbursement has been received from Elections Canada.

5

ON FAIR CAMPAIGNS

M ANY INTERVENERS RAISED the issue of fairness in the electoral process. With the 1988 election still fresh in everyone's mind, it's not surprising their arguments for change were based on an assessment of the strengths and weaknesses of that campaign.

The 1988 campaign featured a major issue – free trade. But one of the most controversial questions of the campaign was whether advocacy groups should be allowed to promote their points of view in the media unrestricted by spending limitations such as those imposed on political parties. One side argued that the other had much more money and had influenced the outcome. In Montreal one intervener argued, "It's distorting the debate and distorting the democratic process not to impose a spending ceiling on an organization created specifically to promote and advance a pivotal issue in an election."

Those on the other side argued there was no evidence to support this and that, in any event, it was the right of individuals and groups to make their positions known. An intervener in Calgary told the Commission, "Voters are imbued with ultimate common sense and, given the opportunity to have access to a free and open debate with as much information as possible, will make decisions in a fair and reasonable manner."

Many interveners spoke about the complexity of the regulations limiting party and candidate expenses and argued for simpler rules. The adequacy of current limits was also raised. Many pointed to the cost of campaigns in the United States as an example they did not want copied in Canada. In addition, the current arrangements for investigation and enforcement troubled several interveners.

The question of formalizing leaders debates during election campaigns drew many comments. Predictably, much of the discussion focused on who should be allowed to participate. Opinion was also divided on the question of whether to permit the release of public opinion survey results during election campaigns.

ADVOCACY GROUPS

Amendments to the *Canada Elections Act* in 1974 prohibited independent spending during an election campaign by any advocacy group or individual to directly support, promote or oppose a candidate or political party, unless they could show that their expenditures were incurred for the purpose of gaining support for their views on policy issues or for advancing the aims of a non-partisan organization. In 1983, this qualification was removed and no independent expenditures were permitted if they directly promoted or opposed a candidate or party. Independent spending was still allowed, however, if it simply promoted issues.

> "I don't think you can allow, in the interest of freedom of expression, non-party groups to have a totally free ride."

This section of the Act was struck down by an Alberta court in 1984 in the National Citizens' Coalition case. The decision has not been appealed. In the 1984 and 1988 campaigns, no attempt was made to prohibit what has come to be called third-party involvement, and advocacy groups had a high profile in the 1988 election campaign during the vigorous debate for and against free trade.

These issues attracted more interest from interveners than any other issue before the Commission except campaign and party financing. Many witnesses were concerned about the influence of advocacy groups on the outcome of the 1988 election. Here is a brief sampling of their arguments:

We cannot stress too strongly our conviction that the unlimited third-party expenditures that are not a hallmark of Canadian election campaigns pose a significant threat to Canada's political democracy. Freedom of expression is central to our political democracy. That is why we must not allow freedom of expression to be limited to those who can afford to purchase access to the means of expression.

I believe that the harm to society that occurs when the purveyors of the corporate agenda are given a free hand to influence the results of an election has been demonstrated. Like the purveyors of hate literature, the purveyors of the corporate agenda seek to wrap themselves in the *Canadian Charter of Rights and Freedoms* for protection. And like the purveyors of hate literature, they must not be afforded such protection.

I think that you should be quite strict and not allow third parties to make uncontrolled expenditures for which they are not accountable to the chief electoral officer, when at the same time, political parties are accountable. I don't see why you would allow these groups to do things that political parties cannot do.

You cannot have people in a race and then people standing on the sidelines tripping them as they run by, which is effectively what happens in third-party advertising.

I don't think you can allow, in the interest of freedom of expression, non-party groups to have a totally free ride. It's as though the political candidates were in the boxing ring with their gloves on, and then one of the fans comes into the ring and hits one of the candidates over the head with a frying pan.

Others attached greater importance, however, to maintaining individual rights of freedom of expression. These are some of the arguments we heard from different interveners across Canada:

~ I do not believe a credible case can be made to ban all efforts by interest and advocacy groups to put their views across to Canadians in a non-partisan way at election time. Such a step would amount to a Draconian and unprecedented attempt to muzzle the vast majority of Canadians who are neither members of political parties nor particularly active in a partisan way during an election.

Third-party expenditure is a way that voters have of expressing the intensity of their preferences, and it is a necessary outlet when voters believe candidates are not responsive enough to what they are saying. It is a necessary outlet and a platform or vehicle for voters' views.

> "The complexity of Canadian society and its issues has proved the political parties incapable of being the sole vehicles for debate."

The complexity of Canadian society and its issues has proved the political parties incapable of being the sole vehicles for debate. Although the parties will always be the most important players in an election, there is an expanding list of concerned activists, and any system must recognize that.

I want to see wide public debate on all the issues. And if some of that comes by privately funded money, whether it be a teachers' association, a union or a business association, as long as they are identified as to who they are and what the membership is, then I'm happy with that. Otherwise you are stifling the debate.

It is absolutely ludicrous to assert – and the Charter does not assert – that we have the fundamental freedoms of speech and expression *except* during an election.

Former Chief Electoral Officer Jean-Marc Hamel told the Commission that the issues of limiting election expenses and regulating advocacy groups are linked. He recommended that the Commission examine whether the principles of fairness, openness and equal access advanced in the Barbeau Committee report and embodied in the present legislation were still valid. If so, he said, the Commission should seek to regulate political activity by advocacy groups. Several other interveners took the same position. Some contended that the issue amounts to choosing between individual rights and the communal or collective right to a fair electoral process not unduly influenced by financial constraints.

Several interveners suggested ways to regulate the activity of advocacy groups. Some participants recommended that all intervention by advocacy groups be barred during a campaign, while others suggested that spending by advocacy groups be permitted only if included by a party or a candidate as part of their election expenses. A few interveners recommended that the National Citizens' Coalition judgement be referred to the Supreme Court of Canada. Some argued there were already ample opportunities to express one's views under the current system. One intervener told us:

> We believe political parties are the key to effective participation. There are currently 15 parties registered under the Act. We believe that if a "third party" cannot find one that represents their view, they can do one of three things. They can change an existing party; they can found their own party; or they can run as an independent.

Whether they supported or opposed restrictions on advocacy group election activity, several witnesses thought these groups should be required to report spending and disclose the source of contributions. Some interveners suggested disclosure of the financing of advocacy groups as an alternative to more restrictive regulation of advocacy group spending. One participant stated, "I would suggest that we do not ban third-party advertising, but during the electoral period we require people who had advertised with intent to influence the electoral process to register and report their expenses to Elections Canada." Another participant suggested that, "with respect to media and advertising that are provided by third parties, reference to the parties involved should be included in the media or television releases." Others, such as this intervener, felt disclosure alone would not solve the problem:

> Some people believe that the disclosure of how much a party spends in the campaign is enough. But this does not address the problem one single bit. Simple disclosure would not erase the unfair advantage given to one party, simply because it is the richest party and is the best organization that money can buy.

One intervener proposed use of the Charter's notwithstanding clause to limit the rights of advocacy groups to advertise during an election campaign, but other interveners differed sharply on this point. The Council of Canadians contended that the notwithstanding clause was a non-issue because regulation of advocacy groups was a reasonable restriction under the Charter. This position was also taken by several other interveners who favoured regulation, one of whom suggested that "if we are going to limit the activities of candidates and political parties, a way must be found within the limits of the *Canadian Charter of Rights and Freedoms* to regulate the activities of third parties as well."

Other interveners had a different reaction when asked about recourse to the notwithstanding clause: "I wince when you say that. I wince out of a natural repugnance that I have to that notwithstanding provision. I just find it repugnant, and ... I don't think that is a way out."

> *"... a way must be found within the limits of the Canadian Charter of Rights and Freedoms to regulate the activities of third parties as well."*

Those favouring regulation of advocacy groups argued that the electoral system is not fair if private interests can spend freely. They argued that the system will not be democratic if groups cannot participate effectively because of lack of resources. The situation has changed since 1984, they said, when the courts ruled against regulating advocacy groups; the change was particularly evident in the 1988 campaign. One intervener made this observation and recommendation:

> Unregulated third-party advertising could become a way in which recognized political parties circumvent the *Canada Elections Act* and the expense restrictions. This would not be acceptable. We are, therefore, recommending that some form of regulation be placed on third-party advertising, which could comply with the *Canadian Charter of Rights and Freedoms* and respect an individual's right to freedom of expression. As well, we are recommending that penalties be imposed against recognized political parties who have co-operated with special-interest groups, or vice versa, in the publication and dissemination of promotional material.

Another argued, "If interest groups are perfectly free to advocate their policies or programs or points of view for 46 out of 48 months, what is the problem with living with some restrictions during two out of 48 months?" Still others combined both arguments, as in this assessment:

The absence of limitations on third-party spending results in a functional right to free speech for rich and powerful organizations and no meaningful degree of freedom of speech for those less financially secure. It also creates a substantial loophole that can undermine the intent of limiting election spending by candidates and parties through proxy spending by third parties.

_____

"If interest groups [can] advocate their policies ... for 46 out of 48 months, what is the problem with living with some restrictions during two out of 48 months?"

_____

Interveners opposed to restrictions argued that advocacy groups force candidates and parties to face issues they might prefer to ignore, such as abortion. Several interveners contended that corporations should have a right to participate directly in elections because they pay taxes or because they are, in effect, associations of individuals. Some interveners suggested that the rise of special-interest groups reflects a failure of the parties to represent all the concerns of Canadians, or the fact that the issues have become too complex to be handled solely by the parties. One intervener summed up the argument this way:

 Why should an interest group that has dedicated itself [to an issue] and developed some degree of credibility not be permitted to speak out on an issue? After all, the people who made the argument for free trade were those who were most profoundly affected by it in many respects: those who had to decide whether to invest; those who had to decide whether they would be able to trade; those who had to decide whether their products would, in fact, have access to the market. These are people who had some natural affinity for the issue. Why should they fall back and leave to elected representatives ... the final and only word on an issue as complex as free trade? Not only would it be a derogation of democratic principles, but also it would be a derogation of common sense.

The Saskatchewan Pro-Life Association pointed out that it was precisely at election time that it needed to be active if it was to promote the election of Members of Parliament who share its position. Noting that political parties receive significant public funding, it argued:

 It seems very unfair that the interest groups funded by the government [political parties] can have a captive audience, or at least because of this power [can] get their point of view across, and those groups that do not get government funding and just want to spend the money that they can scrape up from honest citizens are unable to advertise.

Others argued that the issue is not one of freedom of expression:

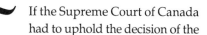 For us, there is a definite distinction to be made between freedom of expression and freedom to invest millions, supposedly to buy freedom of expression for oneself. The latter is a freedom available only to a minority, and we do not think the *Canadian Charter of Rights and Freedoms* sanctions the freedom to invest millions, even if it does guarantee freedom of expression.

Commissioners suggested to some witnesses that the reverse might also apply. If advocacy groups were allowed to spend freely, the case could be put that spending limits on candidates or parties should be removed. One intervener responded:

> "For us, there is a definite distinction to be made between freedom of expression and freedom to invest millions, supposedly to buy freedom of expression for oneself."

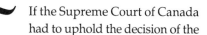 If the Supreme Court of Canada had to uphold the decision of the Alberta court, I think we would definitely have to abandon the idea of limiting election expenses, because it would become a monumental farce. Not only could groups other than political parties make these expenditures, but political parties with more election funds would quickly establish their own groups – they're not stupid. The groups would spend the rest of the funds that the parties could not otherwise spend. In this case, you can't have your cake and eat it – either you respect each clause of the *Canadian Charter of Rights and Freedoms* or you don't.

The Canadian Bar Association spoke in favour of a "principled balance" between the right of free expression and the need for fairness:

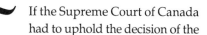 The balance between regulation and freedom of speech and association must be made in a principled manner. This balance can be achieved by weighting the legitimate state interest in regulation against a concept of freedom of speech which includes recognition of the value of the equality of participants in the political process.

The Council of Canadians also suggested a compromise that would allow local activity by advocacy groups: "We propose to permit other groups and individuals, so-called third parties, to undertake person-to-person communications. These might include articles, reports, lawn signs, bumper stickers, hand bills, etc."

Some interveners suggested treating advocacy groups like political parties:

~ . The rules should be the same for everybody. During election campaigns, the rules should be the same for third-party advertisers [as for political parties]. And between elections, the same organizations that are very active in Ottawa lobbying should be subject to the same legal constraints that registered political parties are.

Another intervener suggested it was acceptable to permit popular groups and community-based organizations to take part in the electoral process, but not well-financed business lobbies.

Another argued, "Why should I, as the candidate, be limited in the amount I can spend to tell voters how good I am, when someone else can spend without limit to tell the voters how bad I am?"

> "Why should I, as the candidate, be limited in the amount I can spend to tell voters how good I am, when someone else can spend without limit to [say] how bad I am?"

Collaboration between parties and advocacy groups and the creation of advocacy groups specifically to get around spending restrictions on parties were also cited as potential problems. The issue of interest groups ganging up on a particular candidate or targeting constituencies was also raised, but no specific restrictions were suggested.

Those who argued for regulating advocacy group activities during election periods focused most often on the large, national groups that participated in the 1988 campaign. A Member of Parliament from Nova Scotia pointed out that great care should be taken to define what we want to regulate:

~ You have got to be pretty clear when you're talking about third-party advocacy groups; there is quite a distinction to be made between the group assembled for the purpose of [promoting] free trade and those assembled because they belong to the Canadian Legion. There is a big distinction between those two groups.

One intervener raised the issue of foreign companies, individuals and special-interest groups taking part in Canadian election campaigns, stating, "What is probably more frightening than anything is ... the involvement of [foreign] interests in advertising without any accountability."

Some witnesses proposed a partial blackout, allowing advocacy groups to advertise during the first part of a campaign, but not after the parties begin advertising, or for the last two weeks before the election. If it is reasonable to ban party advertising during a certain period, they contended, then a blackout on advocacy group advertising should also be considered reasonable under the Charter.

Although generally opposed to restrictions, a representative of the Canadian Alliance for Trade and Job Opportunities said, "I think it makes sense to impose restrictions on all partisan and issue-oriented advertising in both print and broadcast media during the last few days leading up to an election. Perhaps 72 hours would be an appropriate cut-off point."

A pollster who took no position on regulating advocacy group activities told the Commission that advocacy advertising played a significant role in the 1988 election and may have made the difference between a minority and a majority government.

LIMITING CAMPAIGN EXPENDITURES

The *Canada Elections Act* sets a limit on election spending by local candidates based on the number of electors on the preliminary list in that riding. The limit on a registered political party's election expenses is also determined by the number of voters on the preliminary lists in all constituencies where the party has officially nominated candidates. Limits on spending by candidates and parties are adjusted on April 1 each year. The adjustment is based on the average increase in the Consumer Price Index for the previous 12 months. In a typical riding, the ceiling for candidates was about $45 000 for the 1988 campaign. Parties were permitted to spend 47 cents per elector for a total of $8 005 799 for a party with a candidate in every constituency.

The Act defines an election expense as any amount paid "for the purpose of promoting or opposing, directly and during an election, a particular registered party, or the election of a particular candidate." Certain expenses related to a campaign are not subject to the ceiling. These include some expenses of the candidate and the cost of local and national polls. Expenses incurred by parties and candidates before the writs are issued are not regulated.

A person who works full-time on a campaign while on holiday is considered a volunteer. If people are paid by their employers to participate in a campaign, however, the value of their time is considered an expense and is subject to the expenditure ceiling. The volunteer contribution of a self-employed person must be counted as election spending if that person normally charges for the service being provided. There are also complex rules for accounting for election expenses in such grey areas as the use of borrowed office furniture and office equipment, the re-use of equipment or signs from previous campaigns, and the provision of services to a campaign at below commercial value.

Although many interveners agreed on some form of control of campaign expenses, their views were far from unanimous. As one intervener put it:

 In a democracy such as Canada, both rich and poor should have the opportunity to serve our country as elected representatives to Parliament, so there must be strict election expense controls established. These controls must take into account population, size of the area, and local costs that might vary across our country. These allowable election expenses must be sufficient to inform the electorate but not to the extent that one party or one candidate can exercise unfair advantage.

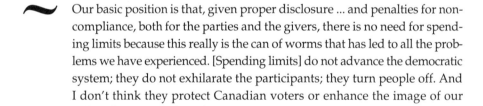

"High spending limits and expensive campaigns really deter the development of new political forces in the country and new political parties."

Another suggested, "High spending limits and expensive campaigns really deter the development of new political forces in the country and new political parties. I'd hate to think that the existing big three political parties have the exclusive right to represent the political spectrum of Canada forever. Things evolve."

In contrast, an intervener advanced this case against spending limits:

 Our basic position is that, given proper disclosure ... and penalties for noncompliance, both for the parties and the givers, there is no need for spending limits because this really is the can of worms that has led to all the problems we have experienced. [Spending limits] do not advance the democratic system; they do not exhilarate the participants; they turn people off. And I don't think they protect Canadian voters or enhance the image of our political system in Canada.

In the 1988 election, only the three largest parties spent sufficient funds on their national campaigns to approach the spending limits. In their appearances before the Commission, all were careful to point out the direct link between what was considered an election expense and what would be a reasonable limitation on expenditures. If the definition of an election expense were broadened to include significant new items, or if the period during which expenditures are deemed reportable were extended, they argued, this would have to be reflected in higher limits.

One intervener commented:

 Any system of limits must also provide a mechanism for such limits to be adjusted regularly so that they can keep pace with the cost of conducting campaigns. Just to give you an example, in 1984, using that as a base, compared to 1988, the cost of buying the same advertising would be somewhere between a 36 and a 48 per cent increase. In the cost of renting the same aircraft, it was 100 per cent more. What I'm saying is that even a normal inflation consideration sometimes doesn't address the additional costs of running a national campaign.

A number of interveners, including the Canadian Institute of Chartered Accountants, asked that ambiguities in the Act concerning the definition of election expenses be resolved. Particular concerns included the re-use of election signs and other material, loans of office equipment to a campaign and gifts in kind. Also mentioned were issues such as honorariums paid to scrutineers on election day, to secretarial help and to candidates. A Halifax constituency association counted seven categories of expenses for official agents to deal with, each subject to different rules. An intervener at the Fredericton hearings explained the current complexities:

> "Election expenses should include all expenses incurred between issuance of the election writ and closure of the polling stations, except for items specifically excluded..."

~ A lawyer can come in and sign all your Commissioner of Oath statements, give you all the advice in the world, and that is not considered an expense on the basis that he is doing it as a party supporter rather than a lawyer. However, if a taxi driver takes a day off and drives a car for us, that is an election expense because he is a taxi driver. There seems to be a little oddness to the Act that way. We just want it to be clarified a bit.

The Ontario Commission on Election Finances recommended that federal law follow the Ontario model in defining election expenses, that is, that all expenditures by or on behalf of a candidate be counted as an election expense unless specifically excluded. A former Member of Parliament supported this view, saying, "Election expenses should include all expenses incurred between issuance of the election writ and closure of the polling stations, except for items specifically excluded in the Act." Representatives of the federal parties emphasized the importance of this issue, one stating:

~ We believe that it's one of the most fundamental issues that's facing the Commission and the country. No single issue has confounded the fair and consistent application of the *Canada Elections Act* more than the interpretation of the definition of election expenses.

This view was supported by another party spokesperson:

> The definition of "election expense" in the *Canada Elections Act* has simply defied comprehension. Anybody can give it a meaningful explanation to advocate their own point of view, because it is so broad. I hope that you are addressing this issue.

A number of interveners suggested that certain campaign expenses be excluded from the spending limit. Examples were office expenses, rent, phone banks, taxi fare home for staff and volunteers working at night, and coffee and snacks for campaign volunteers. In British Columbia, federal New Democratic Party riding associations asked that full-time campaign workers not count as an expense.

A fundraiser from Manitoba asked that volunteer labour not be counted as an election expense; the system should not penalize the enthusiasm and initiative of election workers, it was argued. The Alberta Progressive Conservatives urged that no volunteer work be counted as an election expense. The Alberta Federation of Labour recommended that the services of anyone loaned to a campaign be counted as an expense, no matter who the employer may be. Another participant asked that self-employed people be able to work as volunteers in their area of expertise without being counted as an election expense. By contrast, the Canadian Human Rights Foundation supported the present rule related to the self-employed.

Some interveners asked that pre-writ campaign expenditures be limited. But the Canadian Labour Congress disagreed, saying it was impossible to police spending before the writs are issued. A former Member of Parliament wanted a limit so that a candidate could not 'buy' a riding before the election was called.

On the other hand, one intervener argued that sitting Members of Parliament have a built-in advantage that should be addressed, commenting, "If it is inevitable that there be campaign ceilings, these campaign ceilings should at least take into account inter-election spending by incumbents who can take advantage of parliamentary facilities."

The Nova Scotia Advisory Council on the Status of Women recommended that unpaid work by women volunteers be treated as a campaign donation so that women would receive more recognition for their work in politics:

> Much of the work that women do, both in the political process and outside of it, is of a support nature. What this means is that very few women have the opportunity to gain the kind of experience that will qualify them in the eyes of the party as desirable candidates. Recording the volunteer work of women in election campaigns as a political donation is a first step in recognizing and valuing women's unpaid labour for what it is, political involvement.

The cost of running elections in remote and northern ridings with scattered populations is higher than average because of problems in communications and long-distance travel. The problems associated with the unique circumstances of sparsely settled ridings, often with highly mobile populations, were conveyed in almost every submission to the Commission related to northern and remote ridings. Candidates and local riding associations noted the costs of campaigning in areas where a return trip between two parts of a constituency could cost as much as $800 (Iqaluit and Pond Inlet) and where one riding (Nunatsiaq) covers four time zones.

The major concern about election financing in these ridings was making spending limits high enough to be realistic yet finding the means to pay the bills. In Yellowknife, interveners for the three major parties recommended increasing spending limits for these constituencies. Interveners at the Thompson, Manitoba and Yellowknife hearings spoke of the difficulties of fund raising in a northern riding. In addition, there is less time to raise funds because of the difficulties of running a campaign in a large, thinly populated riding. In Iqaluit, the Baffin Regional Inuit Association recommended that the parties increase their funding for candidates because of the high costs of campaigning in the North.

Several Members of Parliament and former candidates questioned the current spending limits on constituency campaigns. In Nova Scotia, a Member of Parliament said the five provincial constituencies within his federal riding had a combined campaign spending limit of more than $170 000, compared to the federal limit of $48 000 for the same area. The provincial limits are too high, he said, but the federal ceiling is too low. Another indicated that the federal spending limit was about $50 000 in his riding, while the limit on the six provincial ridings was about $175 000. He recommended a 25 per cent increase in the federal ceiling.

> "I am not talking about a lot of bells and whistles; at $45 000, you are talking a pretty bare bones campaign."

Arguing that the spending limits for candidates are too low for a modern election campaign, an intervener in Sudbury came right to the point: "I am not talking about a lot of bells and whistles; at $45 000, you are talking a pretty bare bones campaign." The Canadian Labour Congress recommended that spending limits on local campaigns be increased by 50 per cent. Other proposals were more modest; one suggested that a $5000 increase would be enough to allow campaigns to include expenses now considered to fall in the grey areas. A representative of the Green Party suggested, however, that limits should be reduced.

INVESTIGATIONS AND ENFORCEMENT

Investigations into possible breaches of the *Canada Elections Act* are carried out by the RCMP, because Elections Canada does not have the necessary powers. Cases under the Act and other election-related legislation are normally heard by a county or district court judge.

Interveners' major concerns about election law investigations and enforcement were decriminalization and simplification of the *Canada Elections Act*, but other concerns were raised as well. Former Chief Electoral Officer Jean-Marc Hamel stated:

~ It is hard to believe that a simple and minor violation of the blackout provisions of the Act has to be tried in a criminal court. The investigative and enforcement provisions found in the *Canadian Human Rights Act*, for instance, could easily be adapted to meet the requirements of the *Canada Elections Act* and serve as a model.

Another participant supported these comments, stating, "It has always bothered me that a minor election expense violation would result or could result in the declaration that the seat was vacant. The penalty seemed way out of proportion to the offence."

Commissioner Norman Inkster of the RCMP supported transferring investigations under the Act from the RCMP to Elections Canada:

~ I am not at all satisfied with the present system in which the RCMP investigates administrative and statutory violations of the *Canada Elections Act*. Investigations under the *Canada Elections Act* should be the responsibility of the staff of the Commissioner of Canada Elections.

This recommendation was supported by another intervener, who said, "The Commission must also have its own officers trained to investigate election fraud and the power to investigate all allegations. Such a mechanism will help to ensure that election offences do not occur, and that when they do, the allegations are investigated fairly and promptly, and that when false allegations are made, those accused are quickly cleared."

The Chief Electoral Officer of Canada, Jean-Pierre Kingsley, proposed:

~ As for certain offences, such as failure to submit an election expenses report on time, I would consider appropriate the imposition of civil sanctions in the form of reasonable fines. In all other senses of non-compliance with the Act, I would favour the use of administrative tribunals, as is the case in the area of human rights.

Support for this view came from a Member of Parliament, who suggested, "If there have been administrative offences or infractions on the part of a candidate or those working for him, they could have a hearing before a tribunal instead of being dragged into court."

Several interveners complained about the complexity and difficulty of interpreting the Act, as well as about last-minute changes in interpretation by Elections Canada. We heard this comment at our hearings in Ottawa:

We must have a system that encourages participation of all Canadians without fear of being the subject of criminal investigations for inadvertent breaches of overly complex and, in some cases, bizarre rules. Volunteers are the very essence of our democratic political system. Their day-to-day lives, however, are far removed from an in-depth comprehension of Canadian electoral law in its detail. The complex rules and the enforcement provisions of the current Act combine to discourage many potential excellent and qualified volunteers from participating in the process.

> "It has always bothered me that a minor election expense violation ... could result in the declaration that the seat was vacant. The penalty seemed way out of proportion to the offence."

The federal Liberal Party supported the idea of Elections Canada directing investigations and prosecution under the Act, but the party wanted the means of enforcement defined in the Act, not left to the government. This idea was opposed by the federal New Democratic Party, which favoured expanding the powers of the present Commissioner of Elections Canada and moving judicial review to the Federal Court of Canada.

An individual who had come under RCMP investigation after the 1984 campaign described the experience and asked that a Member of Parliament be informed if an inquiry is taking place and when it has been concluded. Another suggested that a seat vacated because of illegal practices should be awarded to the candidate who came second.

REGULATING ELECTORAL BROADCASTING

The current *Canada Elections Act* provisions regulating broadcast media were drafted initially for radio and were not altered significantly in subsequent revisions. The regulations focus on advertising, free-time election broadcasts and premature broadcasting of election results (for example, before the polls close in western Canada). Partisan advertising is prohibited for the first half of the election period and for the last 24 hours of the campaign, leaving an advertising "window" of 28 days for parties and candidates.

The Act requires broadcasters to make available for purchase up to six and one half hours of prime time for paid political advertising during an election campaign. This time is apportioned amongst the parties by unanimous agreement of the registered parties or, failing agreement, by the Broadcasting Arbitrator. The Act provides for the appointment of a Broadcasting Arbitrator by agreement of representatives of the registered parties holding seats in the House of Commons or by the chief electoral officer if the parties cannot agree on a candidate. If the registered political parties cannot agree on a division of paid advertising time, the Arbitrator makes a binding allocation based on a formula set out in the Act. The formula apportions the time on the basis of the number of seats and the proportion of the popular vote won by each party at the last general election. The number of seats contested in the previous election is also considered, but at one-half the weighting given to the other two factors. No party may be allocated more than half of the time available. Smaller parties have access to a minimum of advertising time, usually two minutes.

The major networks, but not individual stations, are also required to make free time available to the parties. The amount of free time varies among networks and is divided in proportion to each party's allocation of paid time.

On the allocation of free time, one contributor suggested:

> Free-time broadcasts are allocated among the registered political parties according to a formula based on the number of seats held in the last Parliament, share of the popular vote in the previous election, and the number of seats contested in the current election. Such a policy has an inherent bias against minority parties.

Another suggested an alternative:

> Right now the Parliamentary Channel is being under-used and it is being wasted. To turn it on and see nothing but "Parliament will resume at 2 o'clock" is a total waste of time, when video clips submitted by Canada's registered political parties, including minor ones, could be running on a rotational basis.

The CBC supported the present system of allocation, but it recommended that free-time party broadcasts deal with issues and be run in three- or four-minute blocks to avoid confusion with regular commercials. CTV endorsed the concept of giving political parties equitable treatment, but it resisted any suggestion of equal time.

A former Libertarian candidate acknowledged that some regulation would ensure that broadcasters provide time to political parties in preference to advertising already booked when an election is called. The Parti nationaliste called for an increase in the broadcast time made available to the parties. It pointed out that the networks make free time available to the parties only on a national basis. It recommended that airtime be allocated on a regional basis.

Broadcasters in Chicoutimi made the strongest case for eliminating the regulations on electoral broadcasting. Because the number of stations and advertising time available are no longer limited, they argued, there is vigorous competition among broadcasters. Less money is spent in the regions on political advertising because the parties spend most of their money on network television.

Minor parties were concerned about the limited amount of free and paid broadcast time allocated to them. One intervener described the situation this way: "In the current system, small parties with no money don't have access to seats, and then they don't have money because they don't have access to a seat; it's a vicious circle that keeps new ideas from getting into Parliament."

> "In the current system, small parties with no money don't have access to seats, and then they don't have money because they don't have access to a seat; it's a vicious circle..."

The minimum of two minutes provided to each smaller party in 1988 resulted in their free-time broadcasts being so short that many observers felt they were hard to distinguish from commercials. A number of interveners from smaller parties complained about the limited broadcast time allotted to them under the present system. Representatives of the Reform Party and the Green Party recommended that time be divided equally among all registered parties; Station VOCM in St. John's also recommended equal division, but confined to parties with seats in Parliament.

The Communist Party said its efforts to make known its alternatives to the free trade agreement were frustrated by its limited access to the media under the *Canada Elections Act*, as well as by its limited resources. A former party candidate described his experience:

I have also run as a candidate and I can tell you, when you are given 120 seconds, one crack, you can't stutter – one shot, 120 seconds, to outline your program for the country and you wonder why nobody takes you seriously.

The Vancouver Libertarians contended that there should be no limits on advertising by any party. The British Columbia Green Party recommended all parties should get equal free time on the broadcast media – a position supported by the Reform and Christian Heritage parties.

A representative of the Green Party commented, "Because 60 per cent of all voters get their political information from television, access to television is fundamental in this democracy. To give the Conservative Party 195 minutes and the Green Party two minutes, regardless of whether they can afford to pay for it, is just fundamentally wrong."

The Communist Party proposed a revised system of allocation: one-third of the time provided by broadcasters would be divided equally among registered parties; one-third would be allocated according to the number of votes in the previous election; and one-third would be divided according to the number of seats held. This kind of formula was endorsed by one representative of the Green Party as an alternative to the equal sharing of time, provided the threshold for a candidate to receive a public subsidy was lowered to 3 per cent of the vote, so that they might even be able to afford some television advertising.

"To give the Conservative Party 195 minutes and the Green Party two minutes, regardless of whether they can afford to pay for it, is just fundamentally wrong."

Commissioners asked on several occasions and in different provinces how television advertising time had been allocated among the parties in provincial elections where there are no regulations, but there were no reports of difficulties.

The CBC was strongly criticized by interveners in Yellowknife and Iqaluit for not allowing local campaign advertising on its northern network. Interveners noted that native broadcasting stations did not carry advertising either, because of their CRTC licence or transmission agreements with the CBC. A number of interveners recommended that the CBC allocate more free time to candidates in the North, rather than confining its local election coverage to news broadcasts controlled by CBC staff.

Representatives of the CBC said that discussions on this issue had been under way since 1979. However, it was CBC national policy not to sell time to the parties beyond what is required by law. The CBC had made provisions for remote regions to have more free time for political broadcasts, but in the 1988 election it was decided to step up local news coverage of the campaigns rather than make more free time available.

Some interveners said funding is a major problem for northern broadcasting services. One recommended the establishment of an all-candidate forum during elections. A journalist said the northern media lacked the money to organize such a debate. One intervener made the following suggestion:

I think CBC has a mandate to offer equal time to candidates. Certainly in the south, they do it on a regular basis on the TV network on Sunday evening. And politicians have access to the CBC. But that is very carefully controlled and it's not considered – not in the normal fashion – campaign advertising.

Maybe we should waive some of the stringency and say, look, there is a certain amount of time that is going to be given to each candidate to use in a freer manner to get across the key components of his or her campaign, prior to an election – so that it is used in some ways similar to the way a candidate would use a commercial radio facility.

Several broadcasters raised technical issues relating to their contract responsibilities and their obligations under the *Broadcasting Act*. The CBC requested that broadcasters not be held liable for the content of political advertisements they have accepted in good faith. The Mid-Canada Network asked that the *Canada Elections Act* be amended to relieve broadcasters of liability to clients whose advertisements are pre-empted with little warning when advertising time must be made available for election purposes.

CTV asked that the networks not be required to give free time to political parties that fail to become registered. The CBC suggested that smaller parties need to show more initiative in arranging their free-time broadcasts and should not leave that task to the network.

One intervener suggested that a provision be added to the *Canada Elections Act* requiring that networks provide facilities for political parties to make their advertisements. He also maintained that the amendments would remove broadcasters' obligations to provide equal time to the parties during election campaigns.

Interveners suggested that broadcasters have an obligation to provide news coverage of smaller parties during campaigns as part of their commitment to fairness in broadcasting. Several representatives of minor parties said there is systematic discrimination against smaller parties in the media. One commented, "At present, winning seats is the sole pursuit of political parties. Without seats in the legislature, a party has no voice and is virtually invisible. Witness the almost complete exclusion of all but three main parties from significant media coverage."

A member of the Green Party argued that the lack of news and public affairs coverage for minor parties violated the obligation of broadcasters under the *Broadcasting Act* to provide equitable treatment. He noted that the only national coverage of the Green Party on the CBC during the last election came when it threatened to sue the CBC for lack of coverage.

One broadcaster responded:

I think that during an election period, we should devote our energies to informing the public about the election campaign as such and, to a certain extent, to encouraging all political parties fairly.... If on top of this we have to include everyone who wants to have his say during an election campaign, and if we have to give about the same amount of airtime to everyone, it becomes impossible.

Many witnesses opposed the rules restricting release of election results in areas where voting is still taking place. Only one intervener urged that the present regulations be retained. The Canadian Cable Television Association and several broadcasters asked that they be scrapped. To overcome the problem, CTV suggested that voting hours be standardized across the country or that ballots be sealed in eastern Canada until polls close in the West. As a Regina television executive told the Commission, "It's galling to realize that a U.S. competitor, coming out of Detroit no less, can tell our citizens, my potential viewing audience, what is happening in the election in Atlantic and central Canada while I'm sitting here with my mouth zipped."

> "It's galling ... that a U.S. competitor ... can tell my potential viewing audience what is happening ... in Atlantic and central Canada while I'm sitting here with my mouth zipped."

There was mild opposition from broadcasters to the blackout on party advertising on the broadcast media and in newspapers in the first three weeks and final day of the campaign. Two participants recommended that the blackout be eliminated altogether, but they suggested that the campaign period be shortened. The blackout also drew this favourable comment, however:

The blackout is a good idea because it creates a cooling-off period – it allows people to have the freedom, without being bombarded with information, to make choices based on their own feelings and not on all the confusing elements coming at them from every direction.

The Association canadienne de la radio et de la télévision de langue française recommended that the *Canada Elections Act* provide a national system for collecting election results to replace the independent arrangements now made by the news media. This proposal was also supported by CTV. The costs would be paid by the networks, but the system would work better with pooled resources.

We hope that one day there is only one system for collecting election results on a national scale. It wouldn't be anything new; the Americans have operated like that for years. The big American networks and the big wire services formed a company whose sole purpose is to compile election results and input them in a central computer to which ABC, NBC, CBS, CNN, AP and UPI have access and for which they split the bill.

In recent years there has been a substantial increase in government-sponsored advocacy and information advertising on such issues as national unity, tax reform, free trade and the goods and services tax. Saskatchewan law restricts all government advertising during an election campaign, but there are no such provisions in the *Canada Elections Act*. Several interveners in Saskatchewan and Alberta, along with the Council of Canadians, criticized the Alberta government for advertising its support for free trade during the 1988 election campaign. They estimated that the advertisements cost between $500 000 and $600 000 and called this intervention inappropriate. An Edmonton Member of Parliament recommended that provincial and municipal governments be prohibited from intervening in federal elections.

LEADERSHIP DEBATES

The *Canada Elections Act* makes no reference to televised leaders debates. Televised debates among the leaders of the three largest parties have been held in four of the last seven federal general elections. Similar debates have been held in a number of the most recent provincial elections. They have been organized by the television networks, with the format negotiated between the parties and the networks. Participation by the party leaders is by invitation and is voluntary. A fourth leader, Réal Caouette, took part in the leaders debate on one occasion, in 1968.

There was lively discussion in our public hearings about whether and how to regulate the leaders debate. Both private and public broadcasters were opposed to the idea. Those in favour of a regulated debate contended that, under the present system, the governing party has the advantage in negotiations about the format for the leaders debate because opposition parties cannot afford not to participate. Because election campaigns are highly regulated, they argued, it follows that the leaders debate should fall under the law too. One intervener commented:

> Probably the pivotal event in every election campaign, the leaders debate, is not predetermined [though most other aspects of the campaign are]. That doesn't make sense to me. It should be on a fixed date, at a fixed time, at a fixed location and during a period when no party, whether the incumbent or the challenger, will be seen to be at an advantage.

Another intervener was not sure that the legislation should specify a format but agreed with the suggestion that the broadcasting arbitrator might make the final decision if the networks and the parties could not agree. The Canadian Labour Congress suggested the parties should be consulted before any rules on timing, the number of debates and participants are enshrined in law. Another intervener argued, "The CRTC should require the television networks to include all party leaders, should a debate be held. If numbers make this difficult to organize, then more than one debate should be held."

A former journalist made this case:

> It is my contention that the debates become far too important a question to be left in the hands of the government, that leaving it there makes the

electoral process less democratic, and that it is time to include nationally televised leaders debates in the structure of our national campaigns.

Broadcasters contended that the leaders debate is information programming and should not be subject to regulation, as political advertising and free-time broadcasts are. The Fédération professionnelle des journalistes du Québec suggested the law should promote the free circulation of information rather than imposing restrictions, as did the following intervener:

> The broadcasters feel they are, and always have been, the people who are most suited to determine what public affairs programming should be carried. They will carry debates that the electorate has an interest in. And they are the appropriate people to determine the nature and scope of the leaders debates.

The CBC stated its position as follows:

> The CBC is firmly opposed to any legislation that would require television coverage of leaders debates or impose conditions regarding the format of, or access to, such broadcast debates.
>
> We believe that televised leaders debates are a purely journalistic undertaking, an integral part of the media's proper role in the dissemination of information and opinion to the public.

Another intervener spoke from personal experience: "I participated in four negotiations concerning leaders debates, two federal and two provincial. Two took place and two didn't, which means I'm batting .500. My suggestion about the *Canada Elections Act* is along the lines of what the journalists were saying this morning: above all, don't get it mixed up in this."

"... it is time to include nationally televised leaders debates in the structure of our national campaigns."

On the question of who should take part in a leaders debate, one intervener suggested a common-sense, case-by-case approach. The Canadian Labour Congress suggested including parties that were represented in the House of Commons or had more than 10 per cent of the vote in the previous election. Another intervener suggested that smaller parties be allowed to participate equally in the debates if they met certain requirements, such as holding annual membership meetings and fielding a certain number of candidates.

The Reform Party suggested it was impractical to have 10 or 12 leaders in a televised debate and recommended that some other way be found:

~ I do think it is important for new parties to get some national exposure, if only for people in the rest of the country to find out what these things are about. And there should be some midway point between the current debate, which focuses exclusively on the three national parties, and going as far as having a debate involving all the leaders.

The Confederation of Regions Party suggested the smaller parties be given more free time as an alternative to participating in the debate. One Member of Parliament suggested a special debate for leaders of the smaller parties only; another suggested that leaders of "serious" small parties, like the Reform Party and the Green Party, be included; a third suggested pro-rating the time given to leaders of smaller parties. The Green Party recommended that all leaders participate equally in the televised debate.

The Canadian Association of Broadcasters and CTV urged that broadcasters retain copyright control of the contents of the leaders debate, so that excerpts could not be used in election advertising, as the Liberal Party attempted to do in the 1988 campaign. But another witness countered that the debate is a public document, like an article in a newspaper, and that political parties should have the right to clip and use parts of the debate.

PUBLIC OPINION POLLS

There were 11 national opinion polls published during the 1988 campaign and 22 in the 1984 campaign. There is no regulation of opinion polls in the *Canada Elections Act* or any other federal legislation. The issue of regulating opinion polls during election periods drew substantial comment at the hearings.

One pollster said that there are tremendous pressures on polling firms to be accurate and objective, so it is unnecessary to regulate polling. Other interveners favoured some form of ban or restriction on publishing poll results during campaigns. One group commented, "Public opinion polls serve no useful purpose other than to provide jobs to the pollsters and media hype for the press, radio and television."

> "Public opinion polls serve no useful purpose other than to provide jobs to the pollsters and media hype for the press, radio and television."

Another intervener explained her reasons for supporting a ban: "The banning of polls during elections would give the citizens time and space to reflect on the issues as they are presented in the political arena instead of being stampeded by the pollsters and their sponsors in whatever direction they want people to go."

A former party leader suggested that, in his experience, "the polling results shaped – and dramatically hurt – our ability to get the message out.... I regret to have to say that I don't think polls are a constructive part of having a level playing field. A level playing field does not exist when the public believes the game is over."

> "Any attempt to limit or restrict opinion polls will only serve to interfere with the public's right to know."

Polling firms, broadcasters and journalists voiced most of the objections to restrictions on publishing polls, but they were not entirely alone in this view. In Yellowknife, one person explained, "An attempt to prevent the publication of polls during an election would lead to an information differential. There would be people in Canada with access to information relevant to the electoral process that other people did not share. I think that would be extremely dangerous."

The Canadian Association of Broadcasters commented:

~ With respect to opinion polls, the CAB has expressed its serious concern with any proposal that would have the effect of controlling, restricting and then potentially eliminating conventional news and public affairs coverage of opinion polls by broadcasters. I think the right to publish polls should continue in the public interest. Any attempt to limit or restrict opinion polls will only serve to interfere with the public's right to know. There is no evidence to support the notion that polls influence the vote.

And a pollster argued:

~ I believe strongly that any action to censor or ban the publication of public opinion polls would definitely be a case of the cure being worse than the disease. How could a democratic society like ours justify such an outright assault on freedom of information and speech? How would journalists and voters weigh the leaked claims of party-sponsored polls, if there were no properly run media polls to refute or confirm their results? If we ban the Canadian media from broadcasting or publishing poll results during campaigns, would we impound at the border copies of the *New York Times* reporting on the results of Canadian voters, or would we jam the satellite signal broadcasting a CNN poll on Canadian politics? I think it would be like trying to keep rock and roll out of Kiev.

On the question of requiring polling firms to explain their methodology when the news media report on an election survey, the Gallup representative said his firm already publicizes its methodology with each political poll it releases and deposits the results with the National Archives. Omnifacts Research made the following proposal at the St. John's hearings:

~ Those responsible for conducting the poll should be prepared to have their name or names associated with the poll. Sufficient information should be provided with the poll results to allow a knowledgeable person to determine the credibility of the poll. This would include the dates when the data were collected; the methodology employed; the sample size; the representativeness of the sample compared with the population in terms of age, gender, geographical distribution, etc., as appropriate; the exact wording of the questions; and, ideally, a copy of the complete questionnaire so that a person could judge whether any bias may have been injected by the order [in which] questions were asked.

In Victoria another intervener suggested:

~ Polls are predicated on what is asked in the question, and what we get is the summation of the pollster's idea of what went on – the pollster's interpretation of the answer to that question. But we never get the question. And so, if they're going to publish a poll, it might be worthwhile to publish the questions asked along with the answers.

The polling firms argued that publication of polls encourages strategic voting, gives voters more information, and allows them to understand the dynamics of the campaign. Moreover, most people believe other people are influenced by polls but say they are not influenced themselves. One pollster suggested, "There is a great deal of hypocrisy about polling. Some of Canada's leading figures criticize it publicly, and then they sneak into the pollster's haunts at night to get some advice and sometimes even utilize the services."

Others questioned the motives of news media that rush to publish polling results:

~ I know that when I express this opinion, I'm swimming against the professional tide. But I think that the profession, or at least those who work in the large news organizations, are much more concerned with or interested in the surge of popularity with either their readership or their listening audience that they get by publishing polls on the eve of an election.

Some interveners supported a short blackout on the publication of public opinion polls just before election day. There was general support, however, for a ban on publishing exit polls before the polls close on election day. Said one intervener, "I have a problem with exit polls ... I know it's done in the United States constantly ... but it's a private matter. I don't feel that you want to catch some individual coming out of a polling booth and ask them how they voted."

A participant in the Montreal hearings proposed that an independent commission on polling be established, similar to one operating in France, to monitor the quality of published polls. Its aim would not be to censor polls but to ensure that their methodology and results were reliable.

Polls are not considered election expenses for political parties or candidates. Citizens Concerned about Free Trade suggested that fewer polls would be taken if their publication were banned during an election campaign and if parties had to count the cost of polling as an election expense.

6

ON RUNNING THE ELECTION

~

M ANY PEOPLE TURNED out to suggest how the election process could be
improved. Their presentations usually centred on a perceived problem,
with most interveners offering practical solutions. There was general agreement, however, that elections in Canada are well run.

A number of interveners, including election officials from across the
country, discussed the process of appointment of election officials and
the role of political parties in that process. While most take on these jobs for
the satisfaction it gives them, they did express concern about remuneration.

The issue of the timing and length of election campaigns was raised frequently. The enumeration process and the compiling of the voters list was
another major topic discussed by interveners. The possibility of a permanent
voters list was raised for a variety of reasons, most frequently because of
its potential to shorten election campaigns. The overriding concern was that
the enumeration process be as complete and accurate as possible.

Because many urban Canadians failed to get on the voters list and were
unable to vote in 1988, there were many requests to allow urban voters to
register on election day in the same manner as rural voters. Much discussion centred on advance polls and other special arrangements for voting,
such as proxy voting, mail-in ballots, mobile polls, hospital polls, and the
military vote.

Staggered voting hours were suggested as a solution to the problem
of results being available in eastern Canada before the polls close in the
West. Some interveners suggested that elections always be held on Sundays
to encourage the largest possible turnout and to ensure a larger pool of
potential election day workers. Others rejected this proposal on religious
or other grounds.

Other issues raised included the sale of beer and alcohol on election
day and the organization of Elections Canada and how it relates to the constituencies and regions.

APPOINTMENT OF ELECTION OFFICIALS

The chief electoral officer is appointed by resolution of the House of Commons
and can be removed only for cause by joint resolution of the House and
the Senate. Returning officers, on the other hand, are named by the government and normally hold office until age 65, unless they move from the
riding or are removed for incompetence or incapacity. The government
must also appoint a returning officer for any electoral district that is changed

through redistribution. This latter rule accounts for the largest number of changes.

Enumerators are nominated in each riding by the two candidates who received the greatest number of votes at the previous election. If they do not recommend enough enumerators by the prescribed deadline, the returning officer may recruit and appoint them independently.

The Act provides that the returning officer appoint deputy returning officers and that they in turn appoint their poll clerks or assistants. Election staff working in the returning office are appointed by the returning officer. The election clerk or assistant returning officer is appointed by the returning officer.

One intervener questioned having the government of the day nominate the chief electoral officer, even if the actual appointment is made by resolution of the House of Commons. He recommended that the nomination be made by the Speaker of the House of Commons after consultation with the parties in Parliament.

There was significant support for making non-partisan appointments of returning officers and enumerators or for adopting Quebec's system of public competition for returning officer positions. This support was summarized by an intervener in Ottawa:

> Probably one of the biggest concerns we have with the whole question of returning officers is the process by which they are nominated. We don't feel that the political parties, regardless of which political party it is, should control who the returning officers are, who the deputy returning officers are, or who the poll clerks are. There should be a fair and open competition amongst qualified Canadians.

"Returning officers who are performing their duties satisfactorily should be protected, and they should be replaced only for due cause."

Another intervener suggested that the parties draw up a list of three nominees for returning officer in a constituency where the position is vacant and that the appointment be made from that list by the chief electoral officer.

Winnipeg returning officers spoke of the added pressures on Elections Canada created by the delayed appointment of returning officers. They recommended that vacancies be filled by the chief electoral officer if the government has not nominated anyone within 60 days. They also said that Elections Canada should be allowed to recommend the replacement of incompetent returning officers.

Jean-Marc Hamel, the former Chief Electoral Officer, contended that the government's power to appoint returning officers is abused when ridings are changed at redistribution. He recommended that the chief electoral officer have the power to reassign returning officers when new ridings are created and that the government appoint only when there is a genuine need for replacement.

A Member of Parliament supported this position, stating, "Returning officers who are performing their duties satisfactorily should be protected, and they should be replaced only for due cause. In other words, if they are good, keep them, regardless of which party they might come from."

Only a few interveners suggested that the candidates should not nominate enumerators. However, some suggested that returning officers be given more power to appoint; that the parties be required to name their enumerators earlier in the campaign; or that all candidates be entitled to nominate enumerators rather than just the two who led the polls at the previous election. One of the problems returning officers raised on numerous occasions was having to wait for the parties to forward names before they can appoint enumerators. In New Brunswick, returning officers explained:

> "One of the worst jobs ... of running a campaign at the local level is being charged with [finding] 120 or so names of individuals to participate in the enumeration process."

~ If they are going to have to go door-to-door, they should at least be able to walk. And believe me, I have had some who were going with two canes. Now these people can't possibly go out and enumerate 350 people, but they are good party workers. By the time you get those names you're so darned glad to have them that you're not going to dispute them.

A party official told the Commission that constituency campaign managers consider the task of supplying enumerators a real burden: "One of the worst jobs, they say, of running a campaign at the local level is being charged with the task of providing the returning officer with the 120 or so names of individuals to participate in the enumeration process."

Not all Members of Parliament like being involved in the process. In the words of one:

~ One thing that frustrates me is the role that Elections Canada expects the incumbent to play in terms of submitting lists of names for enumerators and poll clerks. That really cheeses me off, quite frankly. I am in the

business of running a campaign and not finding workers for Elections
Canada to be their enumeration and poll clerks.

Several returning officers recommended that enumerators be appointed
and trained before the election is called, and some suggested that preparing
for an election would be easier if there were a fixed term for election staff.

Increasing difficulties in recruiting enumerators and extracting nominations from the parties were noted. One returning officer recommended
moving to one enumerator per poll, with 60 per cent named by the governing
party and 40 per cent by the opposition. He also pointed out that many
16- and 17-year-olds are hard workers and easy to train and he recommended that they be permitted to work as enumerators, poll clerks and
deputy returning officers. This is already allowed in Manitoba, where the
test is competence rather than age.

With the exception of one returning officer appearing before the
Commission, there was strong support for better financial compensation.
Some returning officers noted that they do a great deal in organizing the
revision process, finding staff and office space and performing other tasks,
yet they are paid only on the basis of the number of names on the preliminary voters list; they are not rewarded for doing an effective job in adding
voters through revision:

> A federal returning officer's pay is based on the preliminary list. If enu-
> meration is done in the summer and half the world is away from home,
> you don't get much. If at least we got paid for the names we collect during
> revision or, at worst, we got something for the demanding work that we
> do in revision, that would be a first step in the right direction. I don't mean
> to say that this would straighten out the problem completely, but at least
> it would be a good start.

In Halifax, returning officers suggested that they be paid for responsibilities that continue between elections. No specific pay scale was proposed
for returning officers, although some comparisons were made with Quebec's
pay scale. In Edmonton, one returning officer estimated that he was paid
only about $2.44 per hour. Several, like this intervener, commented on other
aspects of the job:

> A returning officer does not just work at an election. I myself have
> been called on by community groups, citizenship groups and schools
> to discuss the electoral process. These people respect our appointed
> position, and some even feel we're powerful because we administer
> a democratic process. The public relations of Elections Canada goes
> on all year. Therefore, a returning officer should receive adequate
> remuneration.

One returning officer said that if the present budget arrangements continue in effect, he will not be able to keep his returning office open for the hours recommended by Elections Canada during the next election. In Toronto, a returning officer said she would need to pay a minimum of $12 an hour for election staff in the next election, twice what was paid in the 1988 election.

The issue of enumerators' compensation was also raised. Some interveners suggested that income earned by enumerators be tax-exempt or eligible for a tax credit so as not to affect other income, such as welfare or pension supplements. One intervener recommended that party scrutineers on election day be paid by Elections Canada, as is the practice in Quebec elections.

TIMING AND LENGTH OF ELECTION CAMPAIGNS

The *Canada Elections Act* sets the length of federal campaigns at 50 days, although it may be longer because of the timing of the announcement. Provincial election campaigns are generally much shorter.

The timing of elections in Canada derives from the British parliamentary system. Elections occur when the governing party calls one or, on occasion, when the governing party loses the support of the majority of members of the House of Commons. In any case, general elections must be held every five years in Canada and the date for by-elections must be announced within six months of the seat being declared vacant by the Speaker. The actual date chosen for a by-election may be several months later, however, sometimes resulting in long periods where a constituency is without representation.

A number of interveners strongly supported reducing the length of election campaigns:

 Why should we indulge in such long campaigns in Canada that cost Canadians so much and that often, by the end of the campaign, result in rather disgraceful spectacles? When parties' resources run out, they are always tempted to sink to personal attacks and similar tactics. There is no reason to have such long election campaigns. What purpose do they serve? As far as voters' intentions are concerned, by the end of a campaign, people often return to the voting intentions they already had at the outset.

> "It appears to us that shorter election campaigns would be more effective and less expensive..."

A member of the news media was concerned about the cost: "It appears to us that shorter election campaigns would be more effective and less expensive for us and the political parties. It costs an arm and a leg to cover an election campaign and [shortening the campaign] would probably help maintain a constant level of public interest right up to election day."

Arguments for a shorter campaign boiled down to the fairly universal conviction that 50 days was just too long to maintain the enthusiasm of the candidates, the media and the public. In Montreal, senior citizens pointed to the cost of a long election period and asked why so much time is needed when people already receive an abundance of information through radio and television.

> By the last week of an election campaign, most people are sick and tired of hearing the same old song day after day and meeting after meeting. Television should say things once or twice. You have to assume that tax-payers and voters have a minimum level of intelligence.

Other interveners said long campaigns become exhausting tests of endurance and make it difficult to keep volunteers involved. Broad-casters wanted a shorter campaign to reduce costs and keep the public's interest.

Opposition to shorter campaigns came almost exclusively from the North. Interveners argued that communication and transportation problems would make a shorter campaign even more difficult for northerners. The Iqaluit Chamber of Commerce expressed reservations about shortening the campaign period because of the time needed to visit every community in the Nunatsiaq riding. A former elections worker in the Iqaluit returning office said the campaign would still need to be at least 35 to 40 days long, even after enumeration is finished. Another said it would take a minimum of 45 days to run a campaign in the Nunatsiaq riding using commercial airlines for transportation.

Three arguments were advanced for holding federal elections on a fixed date: it would make it easier to administer and organize elections; it would allow for better enumeration; and it would be more democratic because it would remove the ability of the party in power to call an election at the most favourable time. A Green Party representative said that his party supported the idea:

> It is a system that most democracies in the world use. I believe only the systems based on the British parliamentary system have the situation now where the government can be opportunistic in that they can call an election when things look good. And they can manipulate the system, so they can basically do all sorts of unpopular things, have a cooling-off period, and then call an election.

Another intervener stated, "The election process would be better served if elections were held every four years, at a given time, as is the case in the United States, rather than being called at the whim of the party in power.

If this were the case, perhaps they could be called at the time of year when weather would be better for enumeration." A third intervener suggested:

> With a fixed date for an election we can remove some of the power of political parties, who may now compel their caucus members to vote according to the wishes of a strong cabinet for fear of defeat of the government and an election. With fixed dates, the defeat of a bill would be just that; it would not necessarily be the defeat of the government or an election call. This would allow MPs to vote according to the wishes of their ridings.

Although most of the calls for a fixed date came from representatives of smaller parties, the suggestion was not restricted to them. The three largest parties did not deal with this question, but it was raised by a few other groups.

"... long periods of time ... between a vacancy being created and the calling of a by-election effectively denies the citizens ... their voice in the government of the nation."

One student group discussed the timing of by-elections. Their representative argued, "The present system of filling empty parliamentary seats between general elections is too vague and open to abuse. The current practice of allowing long periods of time to elapse between a vacancy being created and the calling of a by-election effectively denies the citizens of the affected riding their voice in the government of the nation."

ENUMERATION PROCESS

Canada's system of enumerating voters after an election call has been described as unique among industrial democracies. Under the *Canada Elections Act*, enumeration must be done between the 38th and the 32nd day before election day. In urban areas, two enumerators canvass every residence. In rural areas, enumerators are not obliged to visit every residence and may use other means to draw up the preliminary list of voters.

In Sydney, one intervener summed up the reaction of many to the current system: "The electoral process at the federal level is lengthy and cumbersome. It is exacerbated by the necessity of enumerating each qualified elector in the 295 electoral districts in the preparation of the preliminary list of electors. This is followed by a period of revision and finally the addition and deletions to the final list of electors." The solution proposed by most was to improve the present system, not to exchange it for another.

Interveners from several constituencies said that large numbers of voters had been left off lists because of faulty enumeration. The estimated number of electors affected ranged from 4000 in Caribou–Chilcotin and 5000 in Winnipeg North Centre to 14 000 in the riding of York North. A participant in the Halifax hearings claimed that 340 000 eligible Canadians had not been enumerated in the 1988 election. Several interveners had unsuccessfully challenged their disfranchisement in court after being left off the voters list. They complained of poor enumeration among seniors, in areas of low-income housing, in rooming houses and residential hotels, in large apartment buildings, and among Aboriginal people and members of ethnocultural communities.

A Member of Parliament with extensive experience at the community level argued, "The mechanism for a voter to be added to the list, once they have been missed, discriminates against the elderly, persons with disabilities and the poor, for whom it is difficult or impossible to get to the returning officer."

Concern was also expressed that large numbers of Aboriginal people are not enumerated, whether because the population is mobile and difficult to enumerate, because band councils do not permit enumerators to operate on band land, or because Aboriginal people resist participating in an alien electoral system.

To overcome these kinds of problems, one intervener recommended that a preliminary enumeration be carried out in the year prior to an election to make sure everyone is on the list and aware of the need to be on the voters list if they want to participate in the coming election.

> "... we tend sometimes to forget that we ... have a responsibility to be registered on the voters list and that the government shouldn't be expected to do everything for us."

The chief election officer of Ontario suggested that criticism of the federal system may be an over-reaction to the extensive media attention to cases of voters missed by the enumerators. Such criticism overlooks the fact that millions of electors are enumerated in a very short period, most without problems, and that the Canadian system is considered a model in the United States.

Some, like this Vancouver intervener, thought that people expect too much: "I think that we tend sometimes to forget that we, as Canadian citizens, have a responsibility to be registered on the voters list and that the government shouldn't be expected to do everything for us." Others thought we should continue the present system but just do it better:

In this country, we have spoiled our electors. They expect a whole lot from the electoral system, and they expect to be chased down and practically cajoled to have their name on the voters list. And I don't think we should change this. I think we should continue to pamper our electors in this country but should bring the pampering up to date so that we can do it efficiently and inexpensively.

A Member of Parliament suggested that our system offers certain advantages: "The state approaches citizens to ask them to register for the voters list. This system offers greater opportunities for citizens to participate in the electoral process than does the U.S. system, for example, where the proportion of eligible electors is much lower than in Canada."

Others wanted to involve more people and agencies in the process:

 I have absolutely no idea how many people are missed by enumeration, but I do think that making greater use of community groups, of the services that these people use, would reach many of them. I like the idea of sending out reminders with family allowance cheques. They could be included with things like social assistance cheques.

Several theories were offered to explain enumeration problems. It was suggested that the parties are less interested in finding enumerators than election workers at the start of the campaign; that enumerators are harder to find because more women are working outside the home; that people are afraid to enumerate in certain areas for reasons of personal safety; that people cannot be reached because they are away from home more often; that individual polls have grown too large; and that the pay is too low. It is also difficult to get two enumerators to find time to work together and to match enumerators with the right language skills in bilingual or multilingual areas.

There was significant support for enumerating before the writs are issued rather than after the campaign has begun. Some interveners suggested enumerating at regular intervals, perhaps every 12 or 18 months. One person suggested that voters be registered annually by party to allow the assembly of membership lists for nominations and leadership campaigns, but that this registration be voluntary.

The proposal to reduce the number of enumerators in urban areas to one per poll, as is the current practice in rural polls, drew strong support from election officials. Newfoundland was reported to have used one enumerator per poll for 40 years without any problems. But one returning officer contended that it is critical for the integrity of the enumeration process that there continue to be two enumerators per poll. She also spoke of the increasing difficulty of recruiting competent enumerators. An intervener from Regina stated, "I would support two enumerators. I think that you get a fairer system. It may be more cumbersome and more time-consuming to do the enumeration, but it's a check."

Interveners called consistently for better training and supervision for enumerators. This was one reason for suggesting that enumeration take place before the writs are issued. Mention was made of the role of enumeration in alerting voters to a coming election and in providing them with information about the electoral process. In addition, it was proposed that language skills be improved where they are needed, that members of ethno-cultural communities be used to enumerate in areas where there are high concentrations of these groups, and that hospital patients be employed to enumerate in psychiatric wards. A representative from the Psychiatric Hospitals Branch of the Ontario Ministry of Health suggested:

~ We would recommend that all enumerators, deputy returning officers and poll clerks undergo a special orientation covering basic modes of mental disorder, communication concerns, institutional structure, etc. – basic issues that would assist the enumerators in fulfilling their function within the hospital.

Several interveners in the Toronto area questioned whether enumerators should be able to ask voters to produce evidence of citizenship. Some were concerned that non-citizens may be gaining the right to vote. Others felt that requiring proof of citizenship might discriminate against immigrants or members of visible minorities. For example, in Ottawa we heard this opinion:

~ Any exhortation in the Act requiring proof of citizenship is meaningless. It just isn't there. I don't have any proof of my citizenship. I don't carry it with me. And in a riding such as mine, if you are thinking of imposing a burden such as that, you have to be careful that you don't alienate new Canadians.

The Canadian Association of the Deaf expressed concerns about the enumeration process as it affects hearing-impaired people, noting that they cannot hear the doorbell. The literature left by enumerators may pose additional problems, because many hearing-impaired people have reading difficulties as well.

PERMANENT VOTERS LIST

The *Canada Elections Act* makes no provision for a permanent voters list or for any form of enumeration before the writs are issued. The idea of a permanent list drew strong support from many individuals and groups that submitted briefs to the Commission. This concept appealed to some interveners because it would allow for considerably shorter election campaigns. Other advantages were also suggested:

~ The permanent voters list wouldn't be a panacea; it wouldn't take care of all the difficulties, but gradually it would allow greater levels of participation. Lack of enumerators and people able to do part-time work is another reason why we believe that a permanent voters list would go a long way toward meeting some of the difficulties we've encountered. The establishment of a permanent voters list itself would be of assistance to Elections Canada in establishing polling division boundaries. It wouldn't simply be there for voting day, but would serve other purposes as well.

Those who opposed a permanent voters list did so almost exclusively because they believed that this would result in a lower participation rate. One person suggested, "In a society with such a high rate of mobility as ours, a permanent voters list is a contradiction in terms." This view was echoed by another participant: "The enumeration process is the most effective and accessible registration system. A move to replace it with a permanent voters list would be detrimental to the basic principle of ensuring an accessible electoral process."

> "In a society with such a high rate of mobility as ours, a permanent voters list is a contradiction in terms."

There was significant support for using a permanent list for municipal and provincial elections as well. In Montreal, one intervener strongly supported a permanent list for all levels of government on the basis of economy and practicality:

> If Canada wants to have a permanent voters list, the federal, provincial and municipal governments should share the expense. The list could also be used for school board elections, municipal plebiscites, jury lists, and so on. For once, you've got someone suggesting saving, not spending.

Some interveners said they would support a permanent list if it were as accurate as enumeration or if it did not cost more. Others insisted that voters be able to register on election day as a condition of moving to a permanent list.

There were several recommendations for computerizing a permanent voters list. One person commented, "To establish voters lists in their ridings, returning officers should have the appropriate human, material and financial resources. This is the computer age, and each riding should be able to use micro-computers with standardized software prepared by Elections Canada for processing their data."

There was also significant support for giving every elector a voter's identity card or for using the social insurance card for voting purposes. Support for this came from an intervener who suggested, "I don't think that Canada would become a police state if people had a voter's card. The first advantage of having a voter's card is being able to vote." The chief electoral officer of Quebec suggested:

> Perhaps the solution is a voter's card – not a card issued for another purpose and used for voting as well, but a separate voter's card. This might be one way of promoting confidence in the electoral system. If people don't have confidence in the system, they won't allow their names to be put on the voters list. It's the democratic process that will suffer as a result.

One Member of Parliament put forward a detailed proposal for creating a permanent voters list based on data from government departments. He proposed that people's names and addresses be obtained from income tax records through Revenue Canada, supplemented by data from other government departments about people who become citizens or who die and by information from Canada Post about people who move. He noted that, in 1988, there were 17 million tax returns filed, compared with 17.6 million Canadians who were enumerated, and that a number of tax returns also contain information about taxpayers' spouses not in the paid labour force or dependants. There would be no breach of confidentiality because only people's names and addresses would be taken from the tax returns. This proposal received direct support from an intervener who stated, "The suggestion does warrant a little further study, but I like the idea of using information that the government has already paid for."

"I don't think that Canada would become a police state if people had a voter's card."

Some interveners in British Columbia expressed concern about the number of people left off that province's permanent voters list and, in particular, about the decision to discontinue election day registration. They noted that about 150 000 voters used this provision in the 1986 provincial election. The acting chief electoral officer of British Columbia said the permanent list seemed to be registering as many voters as were recorded by the federal enumeration. About 50 municipalities, including Vancouver, are planning to use the permanent list for forthcoming local elections. The public apparently reacted very positively to the introduction of voter identification cards last fall. A representative of the Union of British Columbia Municipalities commented, "Surrey, the fastest-growing municipality in British Columbia, had its list of electors updated. The list had 101 000 electors [and was completed] for a cost of under $700. Think of what an enumeration would have cost!" In Kamloops, one intervener recommended basing a permanent list on government data banks, augmented by door-to-door enumeration after an election is called and registration booths in public places.

The Nova Scotia Progressive Conservatives were among several groups expressing concern about the confidentiality of a permanent list: "We suggest to you that if a list is adopted, the Commission may wish to consider allowing voters to veto the right [of election officials] to give information pertaining to them to any third party, including a political party."

The chief electoral officer of Newfoundland described what he termed a semi-permanent voters list now being used in that province. This list is updated from motor vehicle registrations, vital statistics and medicare records, as well as registration at the polls on election day. Newfoundland is considering enumerating people at work because of difficulties in trying to enumerate them at home during the day.

In the late 1970s, Quebec spent about $4 million developing a permanent list system that was never implemented. Quebec's chief electoral officer offered to share that province's experience if a permanent federal list is to be created. On the other hand, the chief electoral officer of Saskatchewan contended that enumeration is cheap and fairly efficient compared to the development of a permanent list. He offered suggestions for computerizing and streamlining the current system.

Reservations about computerized lists included cost and accuracy. In British Columbia, it was argued that low-income people and tenants who move frequently would be more likely to be left off a permanent list than homeowners who stay at one address for many years.

A representative of a literacy group saw little effective difference between the current enumeration system and a permanent list. But the group strongly opposed a voluntary registration system such that of the United States.

Some interveners also expressed concern at losing the personal contact between enumerators and electors at the start of an election campaign.

REVISION AND ELECTION DAY REGISTRATION

Under the *Canada Elections Act*, voter registration for those left off the preliminary list of voters is different in urban areas (population over 5000) and in rural areas. Revision in rural areas is handled by the enumerator for each poll. Voters in rural polling divisions left off the list may still register to vote on election day if they take an oath and are vouched for personally by a registered voter from that poll. Revision in urban areas is handled by a group of revising officers appointed by a senior judge rather than by people named by the returning officer. Once revision ends, 17 days before the election, there is no other way for an urban elector to obtain the right to vote. To further confuse the issue, urban voters can register to vote on election day in some provincial elections.

Many interveners found this system unfair and argued for allowing all urban voters to register to vote on election day. In Quebec City an intervener said, "It is time to end this form of discrimination, especially since this provision in the *Canada Elections Act* could probably be challenged under section 15 of the *Canadian Charter of Rights and Freedoms*." A Charlottetown participant agreed: "To allow people in rural polls to swear onto a list and prohibit people in urban polls from swearing onto a list does not seem to be founded on any logical basis."

In Montreal, one person described his experience with the system:

> I was out of the country. When I came back I thought I would be allowed to vote, but I discovered that if you had not been on the voters list, that you couldn't vote at all. And this I found to be very discriminatory, but what upset me a lot more was that if I had been living in a rural constituency, I would have been able to go to the poll and swear an oath that I was a Canadian citizen and that I was entitled to vote, and I would have been allowed to vote.

It was suggested that the process of registration be simplified and that swearing an oath be allowed even if the voter (such as a homeless person) has no proof of identity. A Vancouver resident put it this way: "Politicians are allowed to go and swear promises all the time that we have to accept as truth, and I think that the average Canadian deserves this same right, to be able to say 'I am who I am and I live here.'"

> "To allow people in rural polls to swear onto a list and prohibit people in urban polls from swearing onto a list does not seem to be founded on any logical basis."

The major reasons offered for allowing election day registration were to ensure a more complete voters list and to avoid depriving people of their right to vote. Several interveners noted how angry and frustrated voters become when they discover at the last minute that they have been left off the voters list and cannot exercise their franchise.

It was suggested that allowing voting day registration would help homeless people gain the right to vote and allow women living alone or in shelters to vote if they do not wish to have their address published on a voters list. Some saw it as an essential step toward adopting a permanent voters list.

The chief electoral officer of Manitoba noted that about 4 per cent of those who voted in the 1988 Manitoba election were sworn in at the polls on election day, mainly in Winnipeg and other urban areas. He had no reason to believe that this ratio would rise greatly in the future. The system of voting day registration in Newfoundland was reported to have worked well in that province for many years. It was pointed out that the electoral system is based essentially on trust, whether people are enumerated at the start of an election or are allowed to register to vote on election day.

A few interveners recommended that registration on election day take place at special locations or at the office of the returning officer rather than at polling stations. One group suggested this was needed to avoid delays for people already registered to vote.

The reasons put forward for opposing election day registration were varied. One returning officer expressed concern that the present system in rural areas leads to cheating, while another preferred to extend the revision period to four days before the election. A Member of Parliament was also concerned about potential abuses and suggested as an alternative that people be required to appear before a judge on election day and pay a fee if they were left off the list and wanted to be registered. A former Member of Parliament commented on the present system:

"... the electoral system is based essentially on trust, whether people are enumerated at the start of an election or are allowed to register to vote on election day."

 We don't have the right to ask voters for identification ... but we do have the right to make them swear an oath. What a mess! Frankly, someone who is determined to use another person's vote will take any oath – he'll take 50 in the same day! That wouldn't bother him because we never ask for identification.

Several interveners recommended extending the revision period to just before the election. It was suggested that voters lists still be revised even if urban voters are also allowed to register on election day, so as to ensure that errors and omissions in the preliminary lists are corrected and that the final lists are indeed complete.

One person suggested that voters see the revision process as something to be avoided and proposed that the procedure be reviewed and perhaps discarded. Two returning officers recommended that revision be carried out by the returning officer rather than by revising officers. A suggestion was made that political parties and community groups be allowed to add people to the voters list at revision. Several interveners questioned the restriction on someone registering a common-law spouse at revision.

ADVANCE POLLS AND SPECIAL VOTING ARRANGEMENTS

The *Canada Elections Act* provides for advance polls to be set up in urban areas and in every community of 1000 or more in rural areas. Voting in advance polls takes place nine, seven and six days before election day. Except for these days, people may also vote in advance at the office of the returning officer, beginning 21 days before election day and ending on the Friday before election day. People may not be able to take advantage of this service, however, in large, sparsely settled ridings.

Commenting on the need for advance polls and their role in improving voter turnout, a Montreal resident said:

> Advance polls should be open to anybody who wants to vote early, it should not be necessary to show that you will be away the day of the poll. It is surely in everybody's interest to have as many eligible voters registered and to encourage people to vote by making it as easy to do so as possible.

Several interveners supported extending the availability of advance polls, with the specific proposal that the Sunday that falls eight days before election day be added. Some suggested extended hours for advance polls to serve shift workers. Extension of voting at the returning office was also supported. Some returning officers pointed out that people are not allowed to vote in a returning officer's sub-office in a large riding and recommended this rule be changed.

Interveners noted that many northern communities do not have advance polling locations because their population is too small. One intervener from Manitoba explained the hardships of not having an advance poll in her community:

> There is one matter with regard to the election process that we would like to bring to your attention. That is the absence of an advance poll in Cranberry Portage. We have approximately 600 voters in our community. At present anyone needing to vote in the advance poll has to travel 120 miles return trip to The Pas. We request that this matter be addressed when reviewing the election process and hope that at the next election there will be an advance poll set up in Cranberry Portage.

In the Churchill riding in northern Manitoba, one of the locations chosen for an advance poll was accessible to people in surrounding communities only by charter flight. In Yellowknife, an intervener described how he had met voters at the airport and escorted them to the returning office between flights so that they would not lose their vote when they were going to be away from the riding on election day on holidays or on business. At the Vancouver hearings, an elector described her route if she wanted to vote at an advance poll in the office of the returning officer:

> Can you imagine the frustration of trying to vote in Powell River when you live in Sointula? For those of you who do not know the geography, Powell River is on the coast and Sointula is an island off northern Vancouver Island. So you have to take a ferry to the north of Vancouver Island, then you have to drive down Vancouver Island, and then you have to ferry across the strait to Powell River.

At the opposite end of the country, the difficulties were similar:

> Advance polls are a little difficult on the Labrador coast. Most communities along the northern Labrador coast are not accessible by road. You have to fly in, or go in over the ice in the winter, or go by boat. The dilemma becomes, do I set up an advance poll in every community? Without them, there is no way for people in these smaller communities to get to an advance poll. So unless advance polls are set up in every community, it is most unfair. It only helps the people in the community where the poll is located.

The solution offered by most interveners was more advance polls. One group recommended that people in remote areas be able to cast an advance vote through the local deputy returning officer. The returning officer for the western Arctic recommended that people be allowed to vote in advance, using an envelope system, at RCMP detachments or at government offices. It was suggested that special voting before election day be allowed in sub-offices established by the returning officer. In St. John's, interveners asked that special voting arrangements be made for deep sea fishermen, who are often away from their homes during an entire election campaign:

> The deep sea fishermen, of whom there are perhaps 1000, are away from port for seven days or 10 days or more at a time. And there was only one election campaign that I am aware of where there was any effort made for those people to vote. And that is when a trawlerman actually ran in an election.

People working in the theatre are in a similar position, explained representatives of the Grand Theatre in London, because many work away from home for lengthy periods every year.

Under the *Canada Elections Act*, people who are sick, students and certain workers may appoint proxies to vote for them if they are unable to vote on election day. Arranging for a proxy vote involves securing a proxy form, obtaining a doctor's or registrar's certificate, and finding someone from the elector's polling division to exercise the proxy. Though there were some concerns about the potential for abuse of proxy votes, most witnesses were in favour of simplify-

> "... categories of persons allowed to vote by proxy are too narrow ... to accommodate the needs of individuals in our increasingly mobile society."

ing the proxy voting system. For example, several interveners suggested changing the rules limiting proxies to two proxy votes and requiring that they come from the same polling division.

Interveners wanted either to extend proxy voting to a broader group of electors or to make it accessible to anyone. One intervener suggested, "Stipulations of the *Canada Elections Act* in sections 139 and 140 regarding the categories of persons allowed to vote by proxy are too narrow ... to accommodate the needs of individuals in our increasingly mobile society." A participant in Kamloops argued, "The reference in the Act to the seven occupations which qualify for absentee voting seems rather outdated and is definitely perceived as discriminatory by the electorate."

Several people expressed frustration at the complications of the present proxy system, which often appears to work against students and other people trying to arrange a proxy vote. The Commission received this proposal in Charlottetown:

> We recommend that you consider some method other than expanding the class of people entitled to cast proxy votes. For example, it may be more appropriate to consider a longer voting period at the returning officer's office, more advance polling days in a greater number of locations, and moving the ballot boxes from place to place to accommodate the infirm.

A Newfoundland resident said that people should vote in person where possible, rather than by proxy:

> Proxy voting is imperfect. It lets someone else in on your secret. The proxy knows how you vote, so their reliability, their integrity and their character really determine if your vote will remain secret. When proxies are sought by political parties in the heat of campaigning, it becomes very dangerous.

Another intervener warned that there is a danger of undue pressure by family or friends on someone who is frail or elderly. He urged that people's right *not* to vote, as well as their right to vote, be sustained and he recommended that it be a criminal offence to solicit a proxy vote.

Several participants preferred the proxy system over a mail-in vote because of concerns about the security of the mail-in vote. We learned that in the Yukon it is acceptable to fax proxy forms to voters, provided they are returned by mail with an original signature. But other interveners preferred a mail ballot or a mobile voting system over the proxy system. In Quebec City, one person told us, "It's better for people to vote for themselves. So it's better to be able to vote at home by mail than to vote by proxy." In Winnipeg, additional problems were pointed out:

> In proxy voting you give someone else your vote to cast and hopefully they do it the way you direct them. But the mail-in vote would be preferable. During the last election we had individuals who were unable to get out to vote and wished to vote by proxy. To do so they were required to get a medical certificate. There are costs to getting out to vote, but for

persons with a disability who wish to use a proxy, there is the additional cost of paying for a medical certificate.

This comment was reinforced by a Vancouver intervener, who told the Commission:

> As things stand now, a person must go to their physician, have a physician fill in a form that says that they are indeed disabled, and they must provide a medical certificate to that effect. There isn't one medical insurance plan in this country, to my knowledge, that will fund such a certificate. The whole cost must be borne by the person requiring the certificate. And it's our contention that this shouldn't be. If a person is held back by the lack of a certificate from taking advantage of their proxy voting right, then there's something very wrong.

There was wide support for the concept of mobile polls being taken to institutions too small to have a polling station and where residents find it difficult to get out to vote. The idea of taking a mobile poll to the homes of people who cannot get out to vote drew more limited support but no opposition. One intervener suggested that this service should be requested during enumeration.

In Yellowknife, an intervener described northern experience with mobile polls:

> The mobile poll is used in the Australian outback and for the nomadic Aborigines who camp in isolated areas. This is also the case in the Northwest Territories. I'm not saying we have a lot of sheep farms in the Northwest Territories – we don't have any as a matter of fact – but there are a large number of fishing or hunting camps and isolated communities in the territories with a small number of eligible voters who have the right to cast their ballot and have expressed a desire to do so. A chartered plane took the election officers and ballot boxes to Bay Chimo and Bathurst Inlet. The people responded with a 100 per cent turnout in Bathurst Inlet and a 72 per cent turnout in Bay Chimo.

The concept was also welcomed in Thompson:

> A mobile advance poll would certainly make the vote accessible to some people – people that knew they were going to be away on election day well ahead of time. It wouldn't help the trapper who decided at the last minute to go out on his line, or the fisherman who was away, but it would enfranchise a lot more people.

Special provisions now being used in northern Canada were recommended for general use in federal elections. In the Yukon, it was reported that a mail ballot is being used for polling districts with up to 25 voters as an alternative to setting up a polling station. The Yukon also proposes allowing people who would be out of touch during an election campaign, such as trappers working in the bush, to assign proxies in advance rather than lose their vote.

The *Canada Elections Act* recognizes special circumstances for hospital voting but does not require that a polling station be located in every hospital. It does permit regular voting in a hospital poll to be suspended temporarily so that election staff can take the ballot box through the wards and let people vote who are confined to bed.

Patients in chronic-care and long-stay hospitals are entitled to be enumerated, provided they have been in the hospital for 10 days or more. This right does not extend to patients in acute-care beds, even if they have been under treatment for a long time or are chronic patients for whom a chronic-care bed cannot be found. Doctors from both Alberta and Nova Scotia questioned the practice of not enumerating patients in acute-care beds. One raised the problem of hospital patients who have no one to cast proxy votes on their behalf; people admitted to hospital who cannot be enumerated because they have no fixed address; and short-term patients with no one at home to submit their names for enumeration.

Unlike some provincial legislation, the federal Act does not provide for mobile polls that go, on or before election day, to nursing homes and other institutions too small to justify polling stations for their residents. One intervener recommended, "The law should provide for mobile polls for health-care institutions and nursing homes where the number of residents does not justify a polling station." In Saskatoon, a returning officer suggested that "consideration should be given to a mail-in type of ballot for the infirm or elderly living at home." Few interveners spoke directly on the question of hospital voting, but there was substantial interest in electoral issues related to persons with intellectual or psychological disabilities living in hospitals and institutions.

"Consideration should be given to a mail-in type of ballot for the infirm or elderly living at home."

Military personnel stationed in Canada use the same voting system as is used by military personnel stationed abroad, but their spouses and dependants must vote in the riding where they are posted. Veterans in veterans' hospitals vote under the military system in their riding of ordinary residence, but they may choose to vote locally if they have been in the hospital for a year or more.

One intervener suggested the special voting rules for veterans in institutions be scrapped; they should vote instead in the riding where they are located. What is important, he said, is to ensure they have access to the vote. If the system continues, then there is room to simplify its procedures, particularly as they apply to veterans in hospitals. He asked, for example:

> Why do we supply blank ballots and require them to fill in the name them-selves? As a previous witness was saying, it was only one per cent of veterans who didn't vote either in their own riding or in hospital and therefore needed a special blank ballot.... I don't see any reason why veterans shouldn't follow the same voting procedures as anyone else in hospital during an election. In my view, we should try to simplify voting as much as possible for veterans. Let's drop the affidavit, the envelopes, the signatures, and all those procedures.

These issues were touched on very briefly at the hearings, with only one presentation from a Canadian forces officer, another from a local Legion representative, and one from an official of the Department of Veterans Affairs. One intervener expressed concern that "if a Canadian forces elector votes in the advance poll at his unit and goes to the polling station in his riding of ordinary residence on election day, he could easily vote twice because his name would have been placed on the civilian voters list."

A former Member of Parliament suggested that military personnel sta-tioned in Canada should vote locally rather than through the special voting rules. In Chicoutimi, a member of the Canadian forces argued the opposite, on the grounds that forces personnel do not have a choice about where they are posted and are stationed there only temporarily.

ELECTION DAY

The *Canada Elections Act* fixes Monday as the day for holding federal elec-tions, except when it is a national or provincial holiday. Voting hours are 9 a.m. to 8 p.m. local time. Votes are to be counted immediately after the polls close. When the count is complete, the results are announced when the deputy returning officer gives a statement of the poll to the candidates' agents. There is no provision in the Act to delay the count of ballots or to delay the announcement of results.

The Act guarantees employees four consecutive hours of time off for voting on election day.

The *Canada Elections Act* makes it an offence to sell or give out alco-holic beverages in any hotel, tavern or public place during polling hours on election day. The same rule applies on voting day to licensed premises in a constituency where a federal by-election is being held.

Opinion among interveners was divided on the question of changing the day of the vote to Sunday. There were various proposals to make voting hours uniform, to reduce the gap between poll closing hours in various parts of the country, and to make the release of results simultaneous in eastern and western Canada. One intervener suggested, "The two main advantages of

Sunday voting are that people then would have the time to vote, and voting hours perhaps could be easily standardized from coast to coast. And this would then result in a decrease of grievances from the western provinces."

The Chamber of Commerce of Metropolitan Montreal argued that Sunday elections would make it easier for citizens to arrange to vote, particularly where both parents work outside the home; would make it easier to use public buildings, such as schools, for polling stations; would free most businesses from the need to release employees to vote; and would help the political parties obtain volunteers to work on election day. Sunday voting would also make it easier to move to uniform voting hours across Canada.

A number of interveners disagreed, however, arguing that Sunday is not acceptable for religious reasons. It was also argued that Sunday is a day of rest and a family day. Interveners in Sudbury and Saskatoon cited the controversy over Sunday shopping in their opposition to Sunday voting.

> "That is not a matter of just convenience, it's a matter of principle. And prudence in this area would indicate that we continue to hold elections on weekdays."

An Ottawa resident agreed: "Putting voting on Sunday, or even Saturday, presents issues to a significant group of the population which just cannot be set aside. That is not a matter of just convenience, it's a matter of principle. And prudence in this area would indicate that we continue to hold elections on weekdays."

Some interveners commented that they did not see a problem with people voting after church or on their way to a family activity. One commented that Sunday voting would do away with long line-ups at the beginning and end of the voting day. Only two interveners justified Sunday voting on the grounds that it would help increase voter turnout, while another suggested that the turnout could be lower.

A representative of the Christian Heritage Party said that holding elections on Sundays would deprive a party like theirs of essential workers who would not participate because of religious convictions. Elections Canada might have similar problems recruiting workers for election day. The party also opposed holding elections on Saturday because it is the Jewish Sabbath. The Reformed Christian Business and Professional Organization in Toronto recommended against holding the election on any day that would affect the religious practices of any group.

One participant conceded that he could see arguments for both points of view:

 From a political strategist's point of view, the option of holding elections on a Sunday is indeed attractive because more people would be available to participate in the process. It offers great flexibility to Elections Canada in securing polling places and relieves the business community of lost productivity. On the other hand, it would serve to cause a heart-wrenching debate in many communities. I do not believe, on balance, the option of conducting elections on Sundays should be pursued.

Many interveners called for uniform voting hours or, at a minimum, a reduced gap between polls' closing times. The feelings of many westerners were summarized by this comment: "There is nothing more frustrating or aggravating for a construction worker in Coquitlam than to leave work at 5:30 p.m., with the intention to vote on his way home, only to hear on his car radio that the outcome of the election has already been decided." In Toronto we heard this observation:

> "There is nothing more frustrating ... for a construction worker in Coquitlam than to leave work at 5:30 p.m., [intending] to vote on his way home, only to hear on his car radio that the ... election has already been decided."

~ I have always felt that election night represents a rare opportunity for Canadian broadcasters to draw this country together. Instead, the process has become a source of irritation for western Canada. It is a divisive element that encourages not only indifference, but even a feeling of alienation. Equity can be achieved by providing for uniform poll closings across the country, or by keeping ballot boxes sealed, perhaps, until all Canadians have cast their vote.

An intervener in Sydney offered the following perspective:

~ Given the increasingly sophisticated nature of the communications and broadcast networks, it is unlikely that the voting results of any region, once known, can be withheld for any length of time. Yet it would do much to alleviate the sense of powerlessness felt by western Canadians if they were not presented with a new government before their votes had even been counted.

Some interveners recommended delaying the count of ballots or the announcement of results in eastern Canada until all the polls are closed. In the words of one intervener in Whitehorse, "We could look at alleviating this and making the West feel that they're more involved ... [by closing] the polls at the regular times, 8 o'clock throughout the country, but [delaying the] counting of the ballots until the polls close in BC and the Yukon and possibly, Alberta."

Another proposal offered to the Commission was this one:

~ The only solution I can see is splitting the voting into two days, so that in the eastern part of the country, voting would start in the late afternoon and continue through the evening and then be available until the early afternoon the next day. That's the only way that you can ensure that all polls close at the same time and that everybody still has any time period of the day, morning, afternoon or evening to vote, depending on their personal responsibilities and commitments.

A few interveners had a different view on this question. One noted, "We are not aware if any definitive research may exist on what actual effect premature publication of election results might have. Our instinctive view, and it is no more than that, is it would probably be minimal or non-existent." Another commented:

~ I do think that beneath and behind the complaint that the election's already been decided by the time we vote out here is really a complaint about the power and the population of this country being centred mainly in Quebec and Ontario, and therefore when those results are in, it's all over.... And that's something that can't be fixed through the electoral law or playing with the hours of opening the boxes.

Some solutions might contain the seeds of future problems. A Newfoundland group noted, for example, that uniform polling hours would mean that Atlantic Canada's results would be overshadowed by Quebec and Ontario results.

The issue of time off for voting was raised by some labour groups. They expressed concern that the four-hour provision for time off should not be changed if election day is changed to Sunday. Some business groups echoed the suggestion of the Montreal Chamber of Commerce that holding elections on Sunday would reduce the disruption of giving employees time off to vote during the week. Others raised concerns about employees and domestic workers having time off to vote and asked that the present law be strengthened.

In Thompson, one person contended that the hours of voting on election day are inappropriate in some smaller communities because the polls are required to stay open all day even after all residents have voted. This was also mentioned as an issue with respect to prison voting where, for security reasons, it was recommended that polls not be kept open after all inmates have voted. It was noted that a mobile poll operating on the train line between Thompson and Churchill had to shut down because it did not fulfil Elections Canada's requirement that each poll be open throughout election day.

According to the Canadian Restaurant and Foodservices Association, five of the provinces now permit sales of liquor during polling hours on provincial election days. The request from industry spokespersons to rescind the ban on alcohol sales on election day was unanimous. The Canadian Restaurant and Foodservices Association estimated that the industry loses $5 million in sales because of the ban and that small businesses would benefit if it were lifted.

> While I admit the issue of election day [bar] closing does not rank up there with some of the other important issues facing our members, it does, however, have some negative impact on our members who in some cases find it rather difficult to deal with any loss of sales.

Other interveners suggested that the law is antiquated and unfair and that Canadian lifestyles and election practices have changed since the law was written.

> The present law forbidding the sale of beverage alcohol during polling hours is both antiquated and unjust. This legislation was introduced in a far different era, both politically and socially, from that which exists today. We believe that the current law should reflect the changes that have occurred in society in general and specifically the changes by several provinces to their own beverage alcohol regulations.

In Montreal, an intervener explained one of the anomalies arising from the rules: "The ridiculous thing about all this is that when you've got a by-election, sometimes it's only the middle of a street that separates two ridings, so that on one side of the street [the bars] are open and on the other side they're closed; it's ridiculous."

The Downtown East Side Residents' Association in Vancouver opposed lifting the ban, however. They urged that the restriction be maintained to prevent people who want to vote from being sidetracked in areas like theirs, where voters have to pass a number of pubs on the way to polling stations.

ELECTIONS CANADA ORGANIZATION

Elections Canada is the non-partisan agency of Parliament responsible for administering the conduct of federal elections in Canada. The agency's headquarters are in Ottawa. It does not maintain permanent regional offices but at each election opens a returning office in every constituency. Many of the procedures Elections Canada applies are set out in the *Canada Elections Act*.

Elections Canada's operations and structure were discussed in a number of contexts. Generally, participants in the public consultation process spoke highly of Elections Canada. Typical of the comments was this statement from a returning officer:

I found it much easier to put in the many hours of work which I do as a returning officer during a federal election because the people at Elections Canada in Ottawa also put in the same hours. They are very dedicated and a very competent group. They make the many decisions they need to make very quickly during elections, and they recognize very clearly the different situations people face.

Several interveners commented on the training of election officials. A Member of Parliament suggested, "The Commission should recommend that all election officials be properly trained, that a course on the election process and their responsibilities be made mandatory, and that no one be allowed to be an election official until that course is successfully completed."

In Vancouver, a participant had a suggestion for increasing the pool of people qualified to work as election officials:

Somewhere within the education system, we could have a two- or three-week course where students can learn how to become a deputy returning officer, a poll clerk or an enumerator.

And then when there is an election, they say, "I took this course and I would now like to be a deputy returning officer or a poll clerk or an enumerator." And it is not to cut out the people who traditionally have done some of these tasks, the retired people and the women working in the household, but it would increase the number of people who are available with some previous experience. And I think it would also raise the level of interest amongst young people in the electoral process.

Interveners from British Columbia and Manitoba were concerned about the difficulty of long-distance communications with Elections Canada during the election period. One group complained of difficulty in receiving rulings from Elections Canada in Ottawa, which in their experience could sometimes take several days. The problem was not only delay, but also the time election organizers took trying to find answers or to locate the right person in a distant office. The Parti nationaliste suggested decentralization.

Another intervener recommended the appointment of regional returning officers responsible for several ridings, who could help new returning officers and those with staffing problems.

The interveners who dealt with computerization of election operations all favoured progress in this area, with the exception of one who had had a bad experience with a computerized system in the 1988 campaign. The Halifax returning officers spoke of the advantages they had enjoyed after computerizing the voters lists in four ridings. Data on electors were entered daily rather than at the end of the enumeration period, and enumerators had two extra days for callbacks because they did not have to prepare their lists on their own. They recommended that the addition of names to the list through revision be computerized as well.

In Kamloops, we heard from one person who had worked on a computerized voters list in the 1988 campaign. He recommended using continuous pre-numbered enumeration forms designed for computerization and producing notices of enumeration on forms that do not have to be addressed separately. He also recommended computerization of revision of the preliminary list.

It was recommended that software be developed to streamline the work of candidates' official agents and to reduce the data entry required after official agents file their returns. It was also suggested that computer technology be used to allow Canadians to vote anywhere in the country regardless of their home riding, similar to the banking machine technology that now serves customers at any location.

Several returning officers suggested they be permitted to rent telephone answering machines and computers to support their work and that election law allow faxed documents to be accepted as originals. Some raised concerns about whether the salaries they are allowed to pay their staff are sufficient to hire people qualified to use computerized systems.

PART 2

WHAT CANADIANS TOLD US AT THE SYMPOSIUMS

~

1

SYMPOSIUM ON THE ADMINISTRATION OF ELECTIONS AT THE CONSTITUENCY LEVEL

**Edmonton, Alberta,
October 21–23, 1990**

THE SYMPOSIUM WAS divided into six sessions covering the entire local election process, from enumeration to voting day:

- Running a Local Election
- Enumeration and Revision: Doing it Right
- Advance Ballots and Proxies: Improving the Process
- Serving Voters with Disabilities and Special Needs
- Election Day Headaches and How to Solve Them
- Improving the Local Election Process: Where Do We Go From Here?

The Commission assembled 30 returning officers from every province and the Northwest Territories, 15 local and national party officials, two Elections Canada officials and three provincial chief electoral officers to discuss how elections work at the constituency level. Participants believed this was the first such symposium ever held in Canada.

RUNNING A LOCAL ELECTION

The opening session focused on running a local election. In her opening remarks, returning officer Ruth Haehnel said that although it is not always easy to be sensitive to political parties, the success of the constituency election process depends on it. Another returning officer said she found that political party representatives know little about election law and often nominate unqualified enumerators.

Party representatives pointed out that providing enumerators is not their top priority and that they do not always assign their best people. Furthermore, providing enumerators does not benefit parties as much as in the past because they can now compile reliable voters lists for campaign operations from other sources, such as telephone companies. Rosemary Dolman of the Progressive Conservative Party said her party wanted to improve voter access, develop some kind of computerized voters list, make enumeration more thorough and efficient, and train election workers better. She also advocated the appointment of 'provincial' or supervising returning officers to improve national co-ordination and hasten responses to constituency queries.

Many participants addressed the issue of communication with voters. Ruth Haehnel said the primary problem in elections today is that too many Canadians either cannot or do not read. Some participants said that because parties emphasize television and radio advertising, Elections Canada's booklets, brochures and posters are outdated as means of communication. Others remarked on the wide variety of languages spoken in Canada and argued for multilingual information programs.

> "... the primary problem in elections today is that too many Canadians either cannot or do not read."

Richard Rochefort, formerly of Elections Canada, described the size of the task Elections Canada faces in an election. He remarked that establishing returning offices across the country after an election is called is like starting up 295 small businesses in a week with little or no notice.

ENUMERATION AND REVISION

At the second session, returning officer Joy Miller suggested that enumeration might be improved by allowing returning officers to nominate enumerators in addition to those nominated by the party and by allowing recruitment of enumerators before a writ is issued.

Miller described enumerators' problems in the field, pointing out that several categories of people are often not listed: those who are afraid to answer the door, people on vacation, people who live in illegal apartments, and people who move frequently. She advocated making revision – the process of adding or deleting names from the preliminary voters list compiled by enumeration – easier for voters, allowing revision until the polls close on election day, and making the returning officer the revising agent for each riding.

Cheryl Hewitt of the New Democratic Party said her party has three major goals at the local level: a broader franchise, an impartial electoral system and improved training of enumerators. She said it should be much simpler to register to vote and advocated voting-day registration in all constituencies, noting that there must be an element of trust in the enumeration system. When parties collect information about names left off the list, there should be a mechanism for sharing it with the local returning office.

Andrée Lortie of Elections Canada described a new computer system that Elections Canada intends to use in future elections. All returning offices would have computer terminals, fax machines and common software to help with enumeration. Parties could buy the software, which would be compatible with the Geographical Information System, to produce precise electoral maps. At each address, enumerators would fill in a slip with the names of all eligible voters. This information would be entered in the computer each day, keeping the computerized voters list up to date.

Keith Lampard, Chief Electoral Officer of Saskatchewan, described the address-based computerized enumeration system he is developing. In this system, enumerators receive lists of addresses with the names of the electors from the last election. The enumerator gives each person enumerated a copy of the enumeration slip to be presented at the poll. Anyone missed can register easily during revision or on voting day. In this system, forms and procedures are simpler, training of enumerators is easier and errors are reduced.

Participants generally agreed that they can live with the current system, although it has problems. Voters know the system, and door-to-door enumeration is effective in ensuring the list is as up to date as possible given that Canadians tend to move often. Participants also agreed that

_____

"... the revision period should be longer and voters should be allowed to register on election day."

_____

the revision period should be longer and voters should be allowed to register on election day. Judges should not take part in revision, and returning officers should have more discretion in voter registration.

Most participants had encountered difficulty recruiting enumerators. As the work force absorbs the people who used to do this work, returning officers have to seek new sources of enumerators. Some participants suggested using service club members (possibly paying them as a group if the club offered its services to raise funds), 16- and 17-year-olds, enumerators recruited independently by returning officers, and enumerators nominated by all parties in a riding, not just the two leading parties. It was also suggested that returning officers should have the discretion to use one enumerator, rather than two, depending on the poll. Participants thought that parties should continue their involvement in enumeration, but they pointed out that most returning officers prepare lists of potential enumerators themselves and do not wait for parties to present theirs.

All participants agreed that preparation is the key to finding enough enumerators. They welcomed any measure that would make preparation easier. Some participants said that when they know an election is coming, they write to people who have done the job well in the past and invite them back. Most enumerators accept when asked in advance.

Participants generally approved of greater use of fax machines and computers. One remarked that in the last election, the first to feature extensive computerization, there were some bugs to be worked out but that, overall, the results were excellent. Now that Canada Post is developing a postal code with an identifying number for every residential building, a permanent computerized voters list looks like a real possibility. Computerization was seen as the way to simple, efficient election administration.

In another workshop, participants lauded Quebec's competitive system for appointing returning officers and thought it should be emulated under the federal law. Qualifications should be clarified, they said, and new returning officers should be tested on their ability to adapt to situations likely to arise during an election.

ADVANCE AND PROXY VOTING

The third session dealt with how to improve arrangements for advance and proxy voting. Although workshop participants agreed that absentee voting and advance voting should be more accessible, they emphasized that advance voting cannot replace election day because candidates and parties must have time to present their platforms.

Some participants pointed out that more and more electors vote at returning offices. One forecast that the advance poll will become increasingly popular because baby boomers are now busy adults who need a more flexible system. A participant suggested adding one day to the advance voting period, making it the Saturday, Sunday, Monday or Tuesday beginning nine days before election day.

> "... the advance poll will become increasingly popular because baby boomers are now busy adults who need a more flexible system."

Returning officer Linda Landry of St. Catharines suggested making advance voting more flexible, but emphasized that the system must guarantee the secrecy and integrity of the vote. She advocated more advance polls and voting at the returning office for 26 rather than 21 days before election day, including a Sunday.

Jack Siegel of the Liberal Party criticized the proxy vote, saying it is sometimes not secret and is open to abuse when used by elderly people or persons with mental disabilities. He suggested limiting the proxy vote to people unable to vote in the advance poll, at the returning officer's office or by mail. He also suggested that students vote by mail instead of by proxy, pointing out that students studying abroad would not be disfranchised if they had this option.

Participants generally approved of the use of mobile polls on election day for small nursing homes and institutions where residents might otherwise not have an opportunity to vote.

In one workshop, participants said that the mail ballot should be considered an extension of normal voting rather than an exception. Using this system would solve many problems because it is easier to administer than proxy voting.

Chief Electoral Officer Richard Balasko of Manitoba contended that the mail ballot is the best way to extend the franchise to voters who cannot get to the polls. He warned against using the mail ballot as a substitute for mobile polls and advance polls, saying that each has its place in the system. Mail ballots are secret because voters can mark their own ballots and seal them in special envelopes. He recommended keeping the proxy system for cases in which a mail ballot is not practical.

Participants generally approved of mail ballots for travellers, students, transient workers and people in remote areas and communities too small to have advance polls, although some had reservations about the mechanics of the process. Some were not sure that the mail ballot envelope could be delivered on time, and some thought mail ballots should be received and counted by Elections Canada instead of by the returning officer. Some said that voters should be allowed to hand-deliver mail ballots to election officials.

Participants also suggested a write-in ballot for people who need to vote before nominations are complete, but one party representative argued that this would discriminate against independent candidates and focus too much on the parties.

The returning officers thought that current procedures to maintain the integrity of the vote avoid fraud and adequately protect the secrecy of the ballot.

VOTERS WITH SPECIAL NEEDS

The session on voters with disabilities and special needs opened with a presentation by returning officer Lesley Singer. She addressed the need for guidelines and extensive training in serving voters with intellectual or psychological disabilities, living in institutions. As one participant pointed out, many people suffer emotional difficulties at least once in their lives, so this group cannot be ignored. Returning officers must choose election staff for institutions very carefully, she said, and parties should be equally selective with scrutineers. She discussed the 1988 election, in which the courts, after regular enumeration was finished, granted the franchise to persons with mental disabilities. This left officials little time to prepare for enumeration. Directions from Elections Canada were not clear enough. In later discussion, a representative of Elections Canada said that elections staff had been frustrated by the difficulties they faced and disappointed in the low participation rate.

Singer congratulated Elections Canada on its multilingual booklet *Voting in Canada*, but said also that it was not comprehensive enough for a riding like hers, which contains dozens of ethnic groups. She called for more information to be provided multilingually, especially about enumeration and the questions enumerators ask, to help ensure that every qualified elector is placed on the voters list.

Noting that 15 per cent of Canadians have permanent or temporary disabilities, she pointed out that mobile polls are excellent for voters living in chronic-care hospitals, nursing homes and seniors' residences. On the other hand, she said, many able-bodied people in urban areas will complain if they have to travel an extra half-mile to vote in a wheelchair-accessible building, as a result of the fact that many urban buildings are not barrier-free.

> "... mobile polls are excellent for voters living in chronic-care hospitals, nursing homes and seniors' residences."

Patrick Ledgerwood, Alberta's Chief Electoral Officer, noted that Alberta rewrote its electoral law in 1980 to modernize the language and again in 1985 to adapt it to the *Canadian Charter of Rights and Freedoms*. In Alberta, rural and urban voters alike can register on election day if left off the voters list. The province dropped proxy voting because it was too vulnerable to corruption and instead uses a mail ballot (similar to Manitoba's) available to anyone who will be absent for the advance poll and on voting day. He described the system as very simple and problem-free.

Homeless people still have serious problems with proof of residence and identification. He agreed on the need to encourage more low-income voters to participate in the election process, but said it is not the chief electoral officer's responsibility to encourage them to take part; that is the job of political parties.

> "... homeless people ... should be allowed to register on voting day, in rural and urban ridings alike."

Larry Brockman, a community worker in Edmonton, focused on the issues of homeless persons and literacy. He acknowledged that no one has had much success bringing homeless and transient people into the electoral system. He agreed that the electoral system is not designed to bring people in to vote, but went on to suggest several ways to improve current practices.

His key recommendation was that homeless people (and others) should be allowed to register on voting day, in rural and urban ridings alike. Although there is some risk of abuse, the guiding principle should be to include as many voters as possible. Safeguards, such as requiring voters without fixed addresses or identification to be identified by registered voters, could be adopted. In discussion, a participant suggested putting polling stations in soup kitchens, because it has already been established that homeless people can be identified and enumerated there.

As elections rely heavily on the printed word, another of Mr. Brockman's key recommendations was that elections material should be written in plain language. Adults with reading difficulties also need information about the issues, the electoral process, the party system and how to get involved in politics. Community groups and government could help; one way would be to provide explanatory videotapes.

During the discussion it was pointed out that about 25 per cent of Canadians are functionally illiterate, and that they must no longer be ignored. A participant asked whether Elections Canada could get more involved in education. Elections Canada representatives reported that they are now preparing a special program for people with low reading skills.

One participant suggested using party symbols on the ballot, to make the process easier for voters with reading problems. He noted that even very young children can learn to recognize symbols, such as the McDonald's sign. When party representatives were asked to comment, one agreed, but others said independent candidates and candidates from small parties would suffer because they have little-known symbols or no symbols at all.

A participant remarked that the government should tell people about the electoral system but leave it to them to choose what to do. Another agreed, saying that both the parties and the returning officers have special responsibilities in communicating how the system works. Electoral officers should have a special mandate – and a budget – to inform the public.

ELECTION DAY

In the fifth plenary session and the workshops that followed, participants proposed improvements in the election-day voting process. These included opening the polls early so people can vote on their way to work, paying poll staff better, permitting only one agent per candidate at each polling station (as more parties contest each election), and permanently locating polling stations in barrier-free buildings familiar to people with physical disabilities. Participants generally approved of allowing voters to register on election day, provided they do not delay pre-registered voters, and as long as the integrity of the electoral process is protected.

"... the idea of holding federal elections on Sundays is too controversial."

Participants felt the idea of holding federal elections on Sundays is too controversial. They said it would result in lower turnout of voters, and that fewer election workers would be available. They did support advance polling on Sundays to help solve the problem of access to the polls. One party representative warned, however, that many voters would not vote on Sunday in summer, spring or fall because they go away on weekends. One participant pointed out that people who have religious reasons for not voting on Sunday would abstain; they belong to a minority that deserves to be treated as sensitively as any other. Another party representative had no objection to Sunday voting, but suggested declaring a national holiday for federal elections to get maximum voter turnout.

Participants tended to favour keeping the current voting hours, rather than trying to reduce the differences in poll closing times that lead to disclosure of eastern Canada's results before the polls close in the West. Some thought that concern about variations in closing times is disproportionate to the problem and expressed the opinion that election staff would have to work too late if the polls closed later in the East. Other participants said western Canadian voters would be even more disadvantaged because they would have to get to the polls by 5:30 p.m. rather than the current 8 p.m. Participants suggested delaying the count in eastern Canada until the polls closed in the West as an alternative to staggered hours.

Terry Stratton of the Progressive Conservative Party pointed out that political parties now concentrate less on enumeration and scrutineering and more on bringing voters out to the polling station. In a shorter electoral period they would have difficulty recruiting volunteers because their recruitment period would also be shortened. He also remarked that parties should retain the responsibility for recruiting election volunteers because parties have the most direct interest in the political process.

Returning officers agreed that they should get more involved in their communities and circulate more information about the voting process between elections. They also agreed that returning officers, deputy returning officers and political parties should communicate better so each group understands the rules, practices and procedures of the others.

The symposium ended with a plenary session to summarize the issues discussed in the workshops. The final discussion produced general agreement that returning officers and party organizers should meet regularly between elections to exchange views on improving the electoral process.

2

SYMPOSIUM ON THE ACTIVE PARTICIPATION OF WOMEN IN POLITICS

**Montreal, Quebec,
October 31–November 2, 1990**

THE SYMPOSIUM ON the active participation of women in federal politics was held in Montreal at the École Polytechnique from October 31 to November 2, 1990. The main objectives of the symposium were to identify the principal barriers confronting women who want to enter federal politics, to find ways to eliminate discriminatory factors, and to study new ways of giving women more equitable access to the political process. The symposium was designed to improve understanding of the situation of women who want to enter politics and to give Commissioners an opportunity to discuss the issue with political and academic experts.

> "Are women just not interested in politics? ... Or is it so difficult for women to have access to the electoral process that they simply give up?"

About 60 participants with varied training and experience related to politics shared their thoughts on the four major topics of the symposium.

- Women and Electoral Politics in Canada
- Women's Participation in Political Parties
- Women and their Candidacy to the House of Commons
- Women Politicians and the Media

Commissioner Lucie Pépin opened the meeting by raising questions about the low participation of women in the political process. Are women just not interested in politics? Do women fear political life? Are women satisfied with the current situation? Or is it so difficult for women to have access to the electoral process that they simply give up? Are the leaders to blame?

Are the local riding associations involved? Do women wish to take up this challenge? What is holding them back?

Sheila Copps, candidate for the leadership of the Liberal Party of Canada, was the guest speaker at the opening session. She told participants that women continue to be relegated to the traditional roles that have been reserved for them for as long as women have been involved in politics. Of the 13.5 per cent of Members of Parliament who are women, 21 per cent are given responsibilities in the social policy fields, such as human rights or multiculturalism, while only 7 per cent are responsible for economic or monetary policy portfolios. In relegating women ministers or critics to topics such as abortion or education and keeping them out of areas such as defence and finance, women are given only partial power, since they do not control the levers that influence the rest of the political agenda.

Speaking more directly to the Commission's mandate, she underlined the importance of quickly removing discriminatory barriers in the Canadian democratic system. She said the nomination process and the financing of candidates are the two areas the Commission should look into first. The regulation of these two elements, which are now controlled by the political parties, should be subject to Elections Canada regulation to clean up these two processes and to legitimize the use of public funds in the form of tax credits for contributors to a candidate's campaign. It is important to understand that the election is not the barrier that limits women's access to political life. The problem lies at the nomination level, and it is at that level that the Commission should take action. Leadership campaigns in all of the parties should also be regulated by the *Canada Elections Act*.

WOMEN AND ELECTORAL POLITICS IN CANADA

Discussion at the first session of the symposium emphasized the need to increase the number of women in Canadian politics, focusing on three major themes: the appropriate role of the state in regulating political parties and elections; the specific barriers to women's entry to political life; and the need for measures to ensure change.

The discussion began with a presentation by Janine Brodie of York University who emphasized that although Canada has made significant progress toward gender parity in its representative institutions, it should not be assumed that these gains are continual, permanent or sufficient. According to her, the barriers to women's entry into the political system include the cost of contesting party nominations and pre-writ spending, as well as the tendency among political parties to ask women to run in marginal ridings.

She argued that the persistent underrepresentation of women in Canadian politics calls into question the legitimacy of our democratic institutions. It is not necessary to demonstrate that women have universal interests that can be represented to justify their entry into politics, since men are not required to demonstrate such unanimity or homogeneity. This thought was echoed by several participants in the discussion that followed.

Brodie also argued that women are underrepresented not only when programs are established and decisions made, but also in terms of the values they want to promote. Again, this observation was echoed by many participants.

Ami Lönnroth, a Swedish journalist, gave an overview of the status of women in politics in Sweden. She attributed the strong representation of women in Swedish politics not to measures that ensure formal equality, but rather to growing corporatism in Swedish life. As economic issues are removed from the political arena and increasingly debated by unions and corporations, moral and cultural issues often associated with women become more prominent in the political arena. Lönnroth maintained that women's entry into politics has thus coincided with a shift in power away from the political arena.

Lönnroth also noted that in Sweden, although political parties do not officially adhere to quotas, many parties voluntarily accept a 40/60 principle, whereby neither sex should account for more than 60 per cent or less than 40 per cent of the names on their electoral lists. The entry of women into politics has also necessitated changes in public life so that it harmonizes with private life. For example, there is now a ban on evening sessions of the Swedish Parliament.

Eleanor Smeal, president of the American organization The Fund for the Feminist Majority, focused on the need for measures to increase the number of women in political parties. She noted that in the experience of both major American parties, voluntary measures to increase the participation of women have never succeeded. Only mandatory affirmative action programs achieved the desired result. She also noted that mandatory measures are often met with attempts to circumvent them, for example, by increasing the number of (primarily male) ex officio delegates to a party convention when a mandatory gender parity rule is imposed on convention delegates. She also observed that in many European countries, it is the smaller parties that adopt reforms increasing the number of women candidates, thereby pushing larger parties in the same direction.

> "... the gender gap has begun to exert an impact on ... American elections, and significant gender gaps have begun to emerge among legislators on issues such as abortion rights."

Smeal emphasized the positive impact that organized feminist activity can have on the integration of women into the political system. She noted that one important activity for feminist organizations is to challenge discriminatory government regulations. Smeal also reminded participants that gender does make a difference: the gender gap has begun to exert an impact on the results of American elections, and significant gender gaps have begun to emerge among legislators on issues such as abortion rights.

The general discussion began with some debate about the degree to which it is necessary to see women as a special-interest group who face barriers to entry into political life. Dorothy Dobbie, Member of Parliament for Winnipeg South, made the case that women face few systemic or systematic barriers. There was general disagreement with her comments.

Jane Jenson of Carleton University suggested that the women who were gathered for the symposium were not representative of all women, in that they had generally been successful within the political system. According to Jenson, statistics show that there is systemic discrimination against women who want to participate in politics. She also noted that the adoption of a system of proportional representation would not be a panacea, since it is not the electoral system but rather the strategic decisions of political parties that affect the number of women elected. Jenson also suggested that the objective is not just to integrate women into the political system, but also to integrate all underrepresented groups.

During the discussion that followed, many participants felt that it was of primary importance that, in its final report, the Commission meaningfully address the underrepresentation of women. A lively debate centred on the appropriate role of the state in regulating parties and elections. A number of participants argued that it is inappropriate for the government to legislate the internal affairs of political parties. They felt that regulated nominations or mandatory quotas would be unacceptable intrusions into the internal operations of political parties. However, the majority of participants argued that such intervention is appropriate given the important role that political parties and their candidates play in the Canadian electoral system and given the fact that these parties and their candidates receive public funding.

Many participants addressed other barriers facing women who seek to enter politics. Among the most important barriers were family responsibilities, which are still shouldered largely by women; financial constraints; lack of employment security; and, in many instances, insufficient support for women candidates at the level of the constituency association.

"... women generally do not have access to the networks of affluent people that provide generous funding for many male candidates."

Concerning financial barriers, participants noted that the cost of nomination campaigns has increased greatly, particularly in urban areas, and stated that women are less likely to be able to raise the necessary funds.

Several participants noted that women generally do not have access to the networks of affluent people that provide generous funding for many male candidates. Some participants suggested that regulating nominations or providing public funds for nomination races would be one way to lessen the impact of financial barriers.

Some participants also blamed the demands of public life, while others suggested that there are elements of the Canadian political system that make it inaccessible to women. It was also suggested that women's entry into the small business and professional sectors made them unavailable for politics at the age when many men enter politics.

Speaking from their experience as party activists, a number of participants indicated that mandatory affirmative action programs were the only effective means of increasing the number of women active in political parties. In the experience of these participants, voluntary measures were seldom effective. Mandatory measures adopted by parties, however, were felt to have had a significant impact on women's participation in political parties. Such measures include requiring that 50 per cent of all convention delegates, committee members or public office holders be women.

According to Lucie Pépin, people are ready to accept women as rightful participants in active politics, but various political party leaders too often wish to retain absolute decision-making power over the choice of candidates and the ridings they are offered. Women are willing and able to perform political duties, but they must be given the opportunity to run for office. It would be unfortunate if the arrival of many women on the political scene coincided with a displacement of power from the political sector to business and unions, as has been observed in some Scandinavian countries. Pépin maintained that if women are given access to active politics by changes in attitudes or by making nominating and financing more equitable, the problem of their underrepresentation would largely be solved.

WOMEN'S PARTICIPATION IN POLITICAL PARTIES

Sylvia Bashevkin of the University of Toronto opened the session with an analysis of the place and role of women at the various levels of political organization. Her research suggests that at the local level, women are still much less likely to hold the position of president or treasurer in constituency associations than they are to fill clerical positions. Although women are increasingly active at the intermediate level (which encompasses such roles as convention delegate, federal or provincial party executive member, and campaign manager), they still occupy the minority of these positions. At the candidate level, women remain poorly represented. Not only do women make up less than 30 per cent of party candidates, they are often nominated in marginal or unwinnable ridings. Certain political parties have undertaken formal and informal reforms. According to Bashevkin, political parties should increase the quantity and quality of female representation in the Canadian political process because voters seem ready to accept women as equal participants in the political process.

Bashevkin's findings were confirmed by the National Vice-President of the Progressive Conservative Party of Canada, Denise Falardeau, and by the former federal Liberal cabinet minister, Judy Erola. Women frequently occupy the lowest rungs in political parties; and the higher you look, the fewer the women you find. Even today, although some progress has been made, women continue to occupy primarily clerical positions in political parties, positions that are essential to the smooth running of the party but do not entail decision-making authority.

"Women frequently occupy the lowest rungs in political parties; and the higher you look, the fewer the women you find."

Denise Falardeau and Judy Erola nonetheless underscored the crucial importance of demystifying the image of political parties as enormous, complex and impenetrable machines to which only a few can have access. They emphasized the need to obtain a good understanding, at all levels, of the operations of political organizations and riding associations. Finally, they mentioned that women of all political parties must work together to improve the status of women in political parties and increase women's access to power.

Abby Pollonetsky, Director of Women's Programs in the New Democratic Party, Sheila Gervais, Secretary General of the Liberal Party of Canada, and Jennifer Lynch, President of the Women's Federation of the Progressive Conservative Party, echoed the previous comments and emphasized the importance of women's commissions within political parties to promote women's interests and ensure equal treatment.

A discussion ensued on the importance of women's commissions within political parties remaining vigilant, focusing on the example of the most recent results in the elections for the executive of the Liberal Party of Canada. Since 1986, the Liberal Party's constitution has stipulated that positions at the vice-presidential level should be divided equally between men and women. But, this requirement for equal sharing of positions was eliminated from the party's constitution in June 1990 and today, the Liberal Party's two vice-presidential positions are occupied by men, while the six regional presidential positions are held by four men and two women. Women are thus far less well represented in the party's decision-making process than they were between 1986 and 1990.

At the nominations level, financial problems are among those most frequently encountered by prospective women candidates. The majority of women have different working backgrounds in administration than men and generally less experience in executive positions. As a consequence, they do not have access to the financial networks that make fund raising easier. It was also pointed out that nomination races are very expensive, sometimes more expensive than the election campaign itself.

Another important factor is the issue of candidates for nomination who bus in newly recruited constituency association members – the so-called instant party members. This can cause a substantial shift in support from one candidate to another. This practice is connected to the financing of nomination campaigns since, in many instances, instant members have their membership paid for by nomination candidates. Another element that can distort the democratic process when it is permitted is the practice of bringing in up to a certain percentage of voting delegates from outside the contested riding.

Proposals to ensure greater equity in financing, and thus to ensure greater access for women to the nomination process, included spending limits for nomination candidates, tax receipts for contributions to nomination campaigns and compulsory disclosure of all donors. Judy Erola also stressed the importance of such measures but warned participants against special treatment for women that could interfere with fair competition for nominations and with the democratic process in general.

Concerning the practice of busing in and the participation of delegates from outside a constituency, it was felt that political party rules must be changed. A number of participants felt that the entire nomination process should be brought under the *Canada Elections Act*.

The proposal for government regulation of parties sparked differing views. One participant felt that political parties are the public domain because they receive special treatment from the government along with subsidies and the right to issue tax receipts. Thus, Canadian citizens have the right to exercise some degree of control over the operations of recognized parties in Canada. Rosemary McCarney, former Vice-President of the Liberal Party of Canada, argued that Canadians have the right to expect some control over political parties, particularly in leadership races, given the importance of this position and the difficulty for parties to exercise sufficient and impartial control over the process.

Carolle Simard of the Université du Québec à Montréal cautioned participants against the dangers of over-emphasizing women's lack of power. While she agreed that they are underrepresented in politics, they do hold power in many other areas.

Pierre Lortie, Chairman of the Commission, concluded the discussions by referring back to several points that had been raised by participants. He pointed out that if the electoral process is open and equitable, on average and over a reasonable period of time, the results should be representative of the diverse components of Canadian society. Canadians should be optimistic, given the high turnover rate of Members of Parliament in the House of Commons following each election, that women should be able to run for a greater number of seats uncontested by incumbents. This situation presents an opportunity to redress more rapidly the inequality that characterizes the representation of women in the federal Parliament, compared with the situation in other countries.

Lortie suggested that although we must recognize the importance of parties in a democratic system, they ought not to be controlled by government. He suggested that the challenge was to balance the need for a regulatory framework for the structure and practices of political parties with the need to ensure that their autonomy is not unduly curtailed and that regulations, if indeed they are introduced, are not cumbersome or otherwise undesirable.

Finally, Lortie raised a point that the session had not considered: the importance of encouraging young women to participate in political life. He cited the results of research prepared for the Commission demonstrating that high school girls show much less interest in politics relative to their male counterparts. One explanation is that the ethical values and behaviour of political parties and the values they promote do not reflect those of today's youth. This lack of interest on the part of young women and other Canadians, the Chairman concluded, cannot be addressed through legislation. Responsibility lies and should continue to lie with the political parties themselves and with Members of Parliament.

WOMEN AND THEIR CANDIDACY TO THE HOUSE OF COMMONS

The focus of the third session was the nomination phase of the electoral process. Winning a party nomination has often been identified as the most difficult challenge of the electoral process for women seeking elected office. Participants in this session based their remarks on their experience as candidates, campaigners and party officials.

The session began with a presentation by Lynda Erickson of Simon Fraser University focusing on the effect that Canada's decentralized nomination system has had on the election of women candidates. Although political parties at the national level have introduced several measures since 1984 to increase the number of women candidates, the fact that the nomination process is controlled by constituency associations has meant that these measures have not resulted in significant increases in the number of candidacies by women. Erickson also noted that the small number of women in politics is more a question of supply than of demand. She suggested that parties could increase the number of women running as candidates by adopting more formalized recruiting procedures designed to identify and recruit women.

> "Winning a party nomination has often been identified as the most difficult challenge of the electoral process for women seeking elected office."

Erickson suggested a number of reforms, including limiting expenditures at the nomination stage, providing centralized funding for nomination contests, and changing the nature of political life in Canada to make it more hospitable to women.

Libby Burnham of the Committee for '94 made the case for increased public funding of the electoral process to improve women's access to the system. She suggested that public financing of elections would open the system to participation by women and other underrepresented groups. She also urged that public funding and expenditure limits be imposed on the nomination process to make this part of the electoral system more open to women. She pointed out that taxpayers are already funding at least 66 per cent of the cost of elections; thus as taxpayers, women are paying for a system that underrepresents them. Burnham also urged that political parties undertake more comprehensive programs to recruit and train potential women candidates.

The need for financial reform at the nomination level was also emphasized by Aldéa Landry, Deputy Premier of New Brunswick. She recommended that political parties work to develop a culture that makes the political process more attractive to women and that women already in the political sphere offer greater support to other women thinking of entering the process.

Albina Guarnieri, Member of Parliament for Mississauga, clearly identified the nomination process as the most formidable barrier to women's entry into politics. Guarnieri advocated a variation of the American primary system: a regulated nomination system administered by Elections Canada that would allow all electors to vote in one party's nomination, with all nomination meetings being held on the same day.

Many of the comments that had been made about the nomination process as women experience it were reinforced by Mary Clancy, Member of Parliament for Halifax. She noted that her own nomination had not been contested, possibly because her party was low in the polls at the time.

Marlene Catterall, Member of Parliament for Ottawa West, spoke about the need to open up the system not only to women, but also to members of other underrepresented groups such as visible minorities. She also spoke about the importance of increasing the number of women in political life to put issues of greater concern to women onto the political agenda.

The New Democratic Party's efforts to increase the number of women candidates were described by Richard Proctor, the party's federal secretary. He also noted that the New Democratic Party national executive, federal council and riding associations all strive for 50 per cent representation of women.

Several participants picked up on the suggestion in Erickson's presentation that political life must be made more hospitable to women. A number of elements of political life were identified as inhospitable to women, including the adversary nature of the political system (as typified by Question Period and strict party discipline), as well as the demands made on the time of Members of Parliament. Participants suggested a number of concrete changes in this regard, including set dates for elections, establishing dates and times for sessions of Parliament, and the use of new communications technologies to allow MPs to spend more time in their constituencies and with their families.

WOMEN POLITICIANS AND THE MEDIA

Gertrude J. Robinson of McGill University presented her research results showing systematic differences between media coverage of male and female politicians. Women politicians are called upon to answer human interest

questions (children, husband, how to balance a political career with raising a family), questions that are asked of men in politics only rarely. Even
today, the media play up a woman's personal appearance, and too often the
contribution of women politicians is relegated to the back pages of newspapers or the tail-end of news reports. Robinson concluded on an optimistic note, however, pointing to the public's positive perception of women
politicians, despite the stereotypes too often employed by the media, and
the opportunity women have to offer Canadians an alternative based on consultation and sharing rather than confrontation.

The evolution of stereotypes applied to women was traced by Armande
Saint-Jean of the Université du Québec à Montréal. Having shed their collective image as housewives and dimwits, women are now classified into
new categories such as 'superwoman' and 'champion', to name but two.
These new stereotypes can be just
as confining as the old ones, but they
also give women greater latitude than
in the past; women appear to have won
the right to have faults individually,
without having those faults attributed
to the entire sex. But if they are talented,
then nothing short of excellence is
expected of them. To be equal, women
must be more equal – that is, better –
than men. She concluded by underscoring the important contribution of
women journalists, who are changing the mentality of the media and producing a more fair and balanced representation of women in politics.

> "To be equal, women must
> be more equal – that is,
> better – than men."

The media strategist for Sheila Copps during her leadership campaign,
Joseph Thornley, stated that women politicians have developed different
approaches and values that appeal to Canadian voters. As Copps was the
only woman candidate for the leadership of the Liberal Party of Canada in
1990, the strategy chosen was to dissociate her from the other candidates
based on her sex and thereby offer an alternative to both the Liberal delegates and Canadians in general.

Another element of the strategy was to accept all airtime made available to the candidate. In addition to increasing her chances of reaching the
greatest number of delegates at the leadership convention, Copps gave
herself national visibility that would follow her throughout her political
career, regardless of the outcome of the leadership race.

Male journalists refuse to criticize women politicians too severely for
fear of being accused of sexism, but each success by a woman in politics will
help to change this mentality in media circles and thus make journalists'
treatment of women politicians fairer.

Rosemary Brown, a candidate for the New Democratic Party leadership in 1975, began her remarks by urging researchers to make a greater effort

to gather the diverse views and experiences of women living outside Quebec and Ontario to gain a broader Canadian perspective. She emphasized the importance of ethnic and geographic diversity in our democratic system. "I found the [symposium] papers were based on the premise that all women politicians are white and live either in Quebec or Ontario. It is not taken into account that there are women politicians outside of the golden triangle."

Women must go out and get what they want, she continued, and not wait for it to be given to them. This applies to the media as well. Women must learn to understand how the media work and overcome their fear of the power of the media while remaining on their guard. During interviews, they should reply in a straightforward and succinct manner and only to those questions they can and wish to answer, and use the remaining time to convey their own views.

Brown said that discrimination in the media does exist; one has only to compare the media treatment of Audrey McLaughlin, leader of the NDP, with that of her predecessor, Ed Broadbent. Every point gained in the polls under Broadbent was attributed directly to his leadership qualities, but rarely is McLaughlin as party leader credited for rising NDP popularity. Participants agreed with panelists that women are discriminated against in the way they are treated in the media.

Mary Clancy noted that the *Canada Elections Act*, like all Canadian laws, must be written in non-sexist terminology. Pierre Lortie, who chaired the session, indicated that the Commission had already agreed to adopt this principle in drafting its report.

Aldéa Landry also pointed out that media image is very important in politics, particularly for women, who are perceived differently by the media than are their male colleagues. Women must learn the underlying rules in the world of communications. A woman politician's appearance can influence voters, much more so than a man's, either for or against her depending on the image she projects. Body language is also perceived differently. Women are more expressive and seldom hide their emotions. They must learn to build a consistent front for the media that will make them less vulnerable to their political opponents and the electorate. They must follow that strategy for as long as the media do not apply the same rules of the game to men and women in politics.

Further to Thornley's comments regarding the media strategy chosen for Sheila Copps' leadership campaign, Rosemary McCarney sounded a note of caution against using female stereotypes to one's advantage as a woman politician. While those stereotypes may have worked in her favour, there is no guarantee that the same strategy will work next time, especially if there are other women running. She also drew attention to Question Period in the House of Commons, saying that it is not a good forum for women politicians. Changes should perhaps be made to that period of confrontation, which does not correspond to the way women are brought up.

The session concluded with one participant stating that women must not let themselves be stereotyped in one image. They must project the image that suits them and reject confining labels. The media reflect society, and until there are more women behind the cameras, women will not be portrayed fairly.

CONCLUSION

Mary Collins, Minister Responsible for the Status of Women, personally contributed to the symposium by stressing many of the barriers women face if they wish to participate in politics. She stated that the Commission will have to make complex and innovative decisions to set up a more equitable system for political participation by women and men. The problem of the underrepresentation of women in politics is not unique to women but is a societal problem; we must try to find a solution that will reflect the values of all Canadians.

Most participants expressed the hope that the Commission's report would bring about many changes that will encourage women to enter active politics in Canada. Women have a strong willingness to participate in the democratic process as candidates or by working within a political party. All too often, however, they face insurmountable barriers of systemic discrimination and financial and organizational constraints. Political parties and governments in Canada must demonstrate a willingness to change and establish mandatory measures that will correct these inequalities.

3

CANADA-UNITED STATES CAMPAIGN REFORM SYMPOSIUM

**Joan Shorenstein Barone Center on the Press, Politics and Public Policy
John F. Kennedy School of Government, Harvard University
Cambridge, Massachusetts, November 19–20, 1990**

THE SYMPOSIUM CONSISTED of four sessions:

- The Financing of Election Campaigns in the United States and Canada
- The Role of the Media in Election Campaigns: A Discussion of Potential Reforms in the United States and Canada
- The Role of Political Parties: A Comparative Perspective
- Symposium Review by Canadian Participants

This symposium brought together prominent academics, journalists and practitioners in electoral politics in the United States with Canadian political practitioners and political scientists. The objective was to develop an understanding of American electoral politics and its relevance to Canada.

The first session focused on the current state of campaign finance in the United States and proposals for reform. Although regulations governing political financing in Canada and the United States are based on different philosophies, both countries face many of the same challenges.

Karl Sandstrom, Staff Director of the House Subcommittee on Elections, indicated that because the mass media provide the only means of reaching voters in a highly mobile society, spending on media accounts for at least 60 per cent of all spending in competitive races. He argued that the costs of campaigns have been increasing, partly as a result of declining reliance on volunteers.

Incumbents are driving up costs in the system, Marc Nuttle, Executive Director of the National Republican Congressional Committee, noted in his opening remarks. He suggested that the benefits enjoyed by incumbents are one reason for rising costs. The name identification associated with being an elected member of Congress is high, which means that challengers must spend $600 000 or more just to achieve the same name recognition. The total value of the franking privilege for all members of Congress is estimated at $130 million.

Frank Sorauf of the University of Minnesota pointed out that campaign spending has been increasing at a rate not much greater than the rate of inflation. The change has been in the pattern of contributions, with the trend toward an increased share of all contributions being enjoyed by incumbents; expenditures by incumbents are increasing at a greater rate than expenditures by non-incumbents. Fred Wertheimer, President of Common Cause, noted that, over time, the gap between funds available to incumbents and to challengers has been increasing, with the trend toward 'de-funding' challengers. The consequence is a lack of competition in the electoral process. Of 406 incumbents in the 1990 election for the House of Representatives, 79 were unopposed, 168 faced challengers who spent less than $25 000, and 124 faced challengers who had less than half the financial resources of the incumbent, leaving only 10 per cent of incumbents in competitive contests.

> "... the gap between funds available to incumbents and to challengers has been increasing, with the trend toward 'de-funding' challengers."

He argued that Political Action Committees (PACs) exist to give money to incumbents, pointing out that although overall contributions to incumbents outweigh contributions to challengers by a ratio of 8 to 1, PAC contributions to incumbents outweigh contributions to challengers by a ratio of 16 to 1. He noted that 96 per cent of House incumbents and 34 of 35 Senate incumbents were re-elected in 1990.

In response, John Motley, Vice-President of the National Federation of Business Free Enterprise PAC, argued that most of the money in American politics comes from individuals and parties, with 60 per cent of House funding and 75 per cent of Senate financing coming from these sources. If the system is skewed toward incumbents, it is not only because of the actions of PACs. He also argued that increasing costs are not the result of PAC activities. Rather, media costs are driving increases in campaign expenditures.

Phil Friedman, an attorney in Washington, D.C., argued that it is rational for PACs to give money to incumbents. Ideological PACs provide an opportunity for individuals to become involved in the political system. Friedman emphasized the importance of disclosure, arguing that informed voters are capable of making their own decisions about the sources of a candidate's funds.

The savings and loan scandal highlighted the inadequacies of the American disclosure system, argued Jill Abramson, a staff reporter for the *Wall Street Journal*. Most of the money in question was 'soft' money and consequently has become public knowledge only because of investigations by journalists and police.

The panelists suggested a wide variety of possible reforms to the American campaign finance system, reflecting their diverse viewpoints and backgrounds. Much of the discussion centred on the question of whether public funding should be provided.

Fred Wertheimer advocated extending the system of public funding in presidential campaigns to congressional elections. This would entail either cash grants or matching funds to participating candidates. Frank Sorauf suggested that implementing a system of public funding and expenditure limits in the United States is a more daunting regulatory task than it has been in Canada because of the size and decentralization of the American system as well as the constitutional constraints. He indicated that his preferred form of public funding would be a tax credit similar to the Canadian system.

Those opposed to public funding contended that the American public is not willing to pay for it. It was suggested that reforms should focus on incumbent advantage, shortening the campaign and requiring candidates to 'zero out' campaign funds after the election and thus prevent them from rolling over huge surpluses that intimidate potential challengers. Phil Friedman advocated eliminating the existing system and relying entirely on a full disclosure system.

Although none of the panelists suggested making PACs illegal, both John Motley and Phil Friedman expressed strong opposition to such a measure, and indicated that if PACs were made illegal, they and their members would find other means of becoming involved in the political system.

Discussion with the Canadian participants began with a question regarding the role of voluntarism in American politics. A panelist suggested that chequebook voluntarism had replaced traditional forms of voluntarism in American politics, noting that some 10 million Americans make political contributions. Another added that the professionalization of campaigning has progressed to the point that campaigns sometimes reject offers of volunteers, preferring cash contributions instead.

"... the professionalization of campaigning has progressed to the point that campaigns sometimes reject offers of volunteers, preferring cash contributions instead."

A question about the popular support for public funding drew a response from Fred Wertheimer. He argued that some poll results suggest there is support for public funding and noted that nine of the 11 public funding proposals that have appeared on the ballot in California have been adopted. He concluded that it was a question of political will and choice. Phil Friedman called public funding fundamentally anti-democratic.

Karl Sandstrom suggested there is a class bias in the contribution system, with the bulk of contributions coming from wealthy white males, with only 1 to 3 per cent of the electorate participating. Marc Nuttle took issue with this, indicating that the average contributor made small contributions, and was older, often retired, and had an income of less than $30 000 annually.

Fred Wertheimer argued it is necessary to ensure organizations making independent expenditures are actually independent and advocated requiring groups making such expenditures to display their name on their advertisements. He also noted that most independent expenditures are made on behalf of incumbents. Another participant said the effects of these expenditures are overestimated. He noted, however, that if other channels were closed through further regulation of contributions or expenditures, independent expenditures would increase.

The trend in Canada toward independent expenditures focusing on individual candidates, with groups starting to target particular cabinet ministers or Members of Parliament, was noted by one participant. Another suggested there is about a five-year gap between the emergence of a phenomenon in the United States and its appearance in Canada. He also asked panelists to discuss the process of electoral reform and the reasons for the failure of American reform proposals.

The argument was advanced that it is necessary to overcome partisanship to achieve electoral reform. At present, neither the Democratic nor Republican party recognizes its self-interest. In fact, it was suggested, neither of the parties' initial assessments of their interests in campaign reform has been accurate. In a similar vein, the Democratic National Committee kept the 'soft' money loophole open and will suffer the consequences for having done so, as this is not in their self-interest. Another suggested that there are very real differences between the two parties and between the two chambers of Congress insofar as campaign finance reform is concerned.

It was suggested that the interests of incumbents are at play and that the current system constitutes an incumbent protection plan. Reform will not occur until incumbents feel threatened.

> "... the 'media maestros' are becoming the new political bosses in the United States."

In response to a question, Karl Sandstrom noted that there are very few advocates of strong parties in the United States. In his view, increasing the strength of the parties would simply mean that money would be washed through the parties and passed on to candidates. John Motley argued that stronger parties would mean a much greater degree of polarization of the American political system, as unions lined up behind the Democrats and business interests lined up behind the Republicans. He noted that this would not be an improvement, particularly because the public no longer trusts political parties to act as aggregators of interests.

Ellen Hume, Executive Director, Joan Shorenstein Barone Center on the Press, Politics and Public Policy, began the second session by underscoring the increasing role of the media in shaping political debate and discourse in the United States. She said the "media maestros" are becoming the new political bosses in the United States. As moderator, she asked the panelists to address four general issues concerning the role of the media in American politics. What are the trends in the free media? What are the trends in the paid media? Should some free airtime be provided during elections? Should leadership debates be reformed?

A staff writer with *The Washington Post*, Paul Taylor, noted that an increasing amount of political information is being transmitted through shorter sound bites. The average television sound bite shrank from 48 seconds in 1968 to 9.8 seconds in 1988. He reviewed how the media have become highly critical and sceptical about politics and politicians, and the carriers and chroniclers of dissatisfaction with political life. The media have fully embraced the 'strategic game' perspective, portraying politics as a horse race, emphasizing drama and theatrics over substance and issues, and searching endlessly for visual sensations. The cumulative impact of this approach has been to make politics more and more irrelevant to the everyday lives of American citizens.

He argued that the attack mentality of the contemporary media can be traced back to the submissive stance of the media during American involvement in Vietnam. Now the media are determined that coverage of the political process will not be manipulated or coerced by political elites.

Most politicians have embraced Roger Ailes's motto that the media are most receptive to "pictures, mistakes, attacks," said Ed Fouhy, Executive Producer of the Concord Communications Group. The 1988 presidential and congressional elections confirm the validity of this motto. He emphasized the role corporate economics play in shaping the election coverage of the three major television networks, which are concerned primarily with profits and are less imbued with a sense of public responsibility and political altruism than previously.

Jim May, executive vice-president (Government Relations) of the National Association of Broadcasters, applauded the expanding role of local networks in election coverage. He noted local networks have been organizing state-wide debates and have made some efforts to improve their reporting of substantive political issues.

Political consultants try to manage what issues and events are considered newsworthy and have had some impact on television news election coverage, explained Ron Rosenblith, a campaign consultant from Washington, D.C. He argued that there is a critical linkage between the news and the credibility of negative ads. To be effective, negative ads need some facts and must refer to actual events. If citizens can identify these facts and events in news stories, then the "spin" put on them by political consultants through negative ads becomes believable.

There are no simple answers to the question of the impact of contemporary media coverage on the way information and ideas are transmitted to voters, cautioned David Yepsen, chief political writer for the *Des Moines Register*. He felt the expanding electoral coverage of the local media means more information is available to voters. Generally, though, he faulted the media for not adequately sorting out the large amount of information available to voters.

Tom Patterson of Syracuse University charged that journalistic values had replaced primary political values as the guiding factors in determining the nature of election coverage in the United States. In his view, the media expend too much energy and resources on irrelevant stories. The media are too dedicated to highlighting the horse-race qualities of elections and too concerned with reporting on the personal foibles of candidates. He noted that 70 per cent of election coverage in the 1988 elections was negative, a change from 1960, when 60 per cent was positive.

Commenting on ways the media could critically assess whether the content and messages of negative ads were truthful and relevant, one panelist said it was improbable the media could be purveyors of truth. He placed less value on the impact of negative ads and more on increasing both the number and substance of leadership debates. He saw these debates as the most important events in election campaigns. Another advised the media to be more sceptical of the role played by "spin doctors" and journalists. Consultants want to sell a story; they want a say in the election coverage of their candidate. The media have to appreciate how consultants manipulate election coverage. Tom Patterson noted negative ads have come to dominate election campaigns in the United States as a result of the transition from issue-centred campaigns to candidate-centred campaigns.

> "The media have to appreciate how consultants manipulate election coverage."

Paul Taylor noted that commercial advertisers are subject to a more restrictive regulatory environment than political advertisers. He believes some free airtime (perhaps five minutes per party per night for the last month of the campaign) would encourage a more substantive treatment of political issues. Ed Fouhy said enhanced use of public television would be a solid first step in achieving substantive political discourse. Several panelists emphasized how the media environment in the United States has become highly fractured. The presence of cable television and speciality channels and the growing influence of local networks have made it exceedingly difficult to transmit political information and values to a large number of diverse audiences. The use of free airtime would be hampered by these structural and technical realities.

Panelists were asked to comment on the impact of public opinion polls on voting choices and whether there is wisdom in banning polls for a certain period during elections. Ed Fouhy said he was not bothered by the possible impact of polls. David Yepsen questioned whether media organizations should be conducting and publishing polls that could have an impact on voting choices and called for the media to be responsible in the use and reporting of polls. Tom Patterson noted that empirical studies have been inconclusive about the impact of published polling results on voting choices. He argued they have an indirect impact by accentuating the reporting of elections as horse races; polls indicate who is leading and who is trailing.

Asked how leadership debates could be made more meaningful, the panelists felt the debates would have more value and legitimacy if they were less scripted and more spontaneous. Conversely, panelists emphasized that the debates will never become more spontaneous because the players would not want to give up the control they now have.

In commenting on whether the media have become too accepting and too dependent on the sound bite, one panelist suggested that the existence of the 9.8 second sound bite simply reflects declining public interest in the political process.

A number of differences were cited between the electoral systems of the United States and Canada in relation to the way the media report on politics. Unlike the United States, where there is considerable symmetry between electoral districts and media markets, Canadian media markets normally extend beyond a single constituency. In Canada, candidates cannot make efficient use of media markets to reach voters as they would often be spending money to reach those who cannot vote for them. A similar dilemma exists in many congressional races, but less so in senatorial and gubernatorial campaigns. Media campaigns in Canada, therefore, tend to be national in scope (except in Quebec, where distinct media campaigns are presented), rather than candidate-centred. And because media campaigns are national, they are more likely to advocate issues, not promote individuals, thus reducing the incentive for negative advertising.

In the third session panelists were asked whether the role of political parties as public institutions has increased or decreased in recent years.

Gary Orren of Harvard University said a number of long-term social, economic and demographic factors have caused parties to decline. Parties are now performing fewer and fewer functions. The state has assumed responsibility for the administration of elections. Civil service reform has deprived parties of an important source of patronage. A better educated electorate has meant weaker party identification. The advent of the mass media has accelerated and reinforced the decline of parties. He labelled parties 'super PACs' which are making increasing use of modern technologies to raise large amounts of money.

Drawing a comparison with the Canadian system he noted, "A lot of functions that parties have performed ... have slipped away to other actors in the [American] political system. You have a much stronger party system and you need to guard against that erosion. I think our elections are the worse for it here and by extension, our governing process is the worse for it."

The school of 're-invigorization of parties' was rejected by Bob Shogan, political correspondent with *The Los Angeles Times*. This view says parties are reasserting themselves as forums for recruiting and training candidates, providing policy research, and giving candidates election campaign resources. He said parties are simply imitating PACs, rather than re-building themselves as credible public institutions, and argued that parties have always been weak in American politics, a fact he attributed to the constitutional and institutional arrangements established by the founding fathers.

Leaders and other candidates do not want strong parties, said Paul Tully, Political Director for the Democratic National Committee. They want to communicate directly with their voters and are leery of using parties for these purposes. He rejected the view that parties are systemically weak in American politics. A number of strong party machines exist in many American suburbs, where parties are important factors in voting decisions and in shaping public perceptions of policy issues. He argued that after race, party identification is the most reliable indicator of voting choice. He said parties do function as loose coalitions out of which legislative majorities are built.

"... after race, party identification is the most reliable indicator of voting choice."

He cautioned it was a mistake to describe parties as monolithic. American parties are organizationally complex; they are made up of a large number of committees and sub-parties. Certain segments of the parties are more influential than others.

Parties do have some carrots and sticks and use their financial and organizational resources to control unco-operative or undesirable candidates. Bernadette Budde, Vice-President of the Business Industry Political Action Committee, listed a number of activities performed by parties – policy research, fund raising, candidate training, contracting of assistance from political consultants, and polling for local candidates. Several other panelists agreed parties have resources that enable them to impose a degree of policy standardization on candidates.

Noting that parties have declined considerably, Jan Baran, General Counsel for the Republican National Committee, stated that parties no longer serve as policy and electoral mediators. The primary function of modern parties is to raise money, and the Republican Party has been far more successful than the Democratic Party. Republican fundraisers have been adroit at building a broad-based donor constituency through aggressive direct mail campaigns. Parties have almost no input on who becomes a candidate.

Asked whether parties and PACs compete, Gary Orren said that parties do less than PACs. Although parties provide some policy cues and ideological cohesion for local candidates, they do not perform four essential functions. They do not communicate with and educate voters; the media and candidates do this. Parties do not evaluate, test or appraise candidates; the news media do. Parties do not select leadership candidates; they simply ratify choices made by voters. And parties do not identify and recruit candidates; candidates make their own choices about whether to run.

Commenting on how parties could be strengthened, Bob Shogan said reform proposals should be modest in scope, perhaps directed at better campaign finance disclosure rules. Jan Baran felt any reforms would have to create financial equity between the Republicans and the Democrats. Currently, the Republicans have money, and the Democrats have seats. The Democrats would not want a more competitive electoral environment if they had far less money than their opponents. Another panelist said PACs would resist any reforms designed to change elections from candidate-centred campaigns to party-centred campaigns.

The panelists were asked for clarification of the role of American parties in policy formation. If parties play only a small role in policy making, where is policy made? The response was that parties no longer have a policy mediation role. Policy is made throughout the executive and legislative branches. Candidates, not parties, make policy selections. It was argued that a substantive policy-making role is alien to American parties; as a result, parties have been less relevant than in other countries.

> "If your parties have a policy function, cherish it and protect it against all enemies."

In response it was noted, "because they [parties in the United States] don't do this, because they don't have any input on policy, they really are not terribly relevant to people. Therefore, they get weaker. If your parties have a policy function, cherish it and protect it against all enemies."

PAC activities are directed almost exclusively at local candidates, Bernadette Budde said in response to a question on whether PACs try to shape policy debates in American politics and whether they influence public opinion. Senators and members of the House of Representatives can make laws and control legislation. PACs want precise, measurable outcomes, not trends in public opinion. PACs give money to those individuals who can make things happen.

Several questions about the role and possibility of new parties in the United States were raised, with panelists replying that the electoral process regulatory regime in the United States makes it difficult for new parties to develop and survive.

Discussion at the final session applied the U.S. experience to the Canadian situation. Participants discussed a number of proposals for reform of the Canadian system, many of which focus on strengthening the Canadian party system. There was consensus among the participants that, in general terms, the Canadian electoral process and party system are much healthier than their U.S. counterparts.

One panelist warned that the American experience shows that weak parties result in "... wealthy and celebrity candidates. You get incumbents. You get political consultants. You get the news media, especially television. You get special-interest groups. Something is going to fill that void."

A brief description of the challenges facing the Canadian political system was given by Suzanne Warren, Ontario Director of Operations for the Progressive Conservative Party of Canada. Widespread voter malaise, a decrease in the number of volunteers, and the rise of regional parties (such as the Reform Party and the Bloc québécois) all challenge the relevance of the major parties as the primary vehicles of access to the political system.

She cautioned that the U.S. experience with contribution limits suggests they are difficult to enforce, and also noted that the American experience with referendums suggests that Canada should proceed with great caution on that front.

The Federal Secretary of the New Democratic Party, Richard Proctor, noted that although Canadian parties are stronger and more policy-oriented than U.S. parties, there has been some deterioration of the Canadian party system; he emphasized the need to strengthen political parties in Canada. To this end, he suggested consideration be given to public funding of political parties between elections. He suggested that the key issue upon which the Commission must focus is interest group advertising during elections.

The value of examining the American experience lies in seeing the future, and in this case the future doesn't work, remarked Tom Axworthy, Executive Director of the CRB Foundation. He noted that the earlier discussion about viable political parties pointed up that while the Canadian system is far from perfect, and there are some discouraging trends, there is still time to prevent Canada from going down some of the roads the Americans have. He also noted that technology affects the nature of elections; within three to five years of a technology's introduction in the United States, it appears in Canada. This suggests that unless certain safeguards are strengthened, Canada may face many of the difficulties experienced by the American system, most notably the decline of the party system.

Underscoring the importance of maintaining a strong party system, Axworthy pointed out that in a society with few truly national institutions, parties are all the more important because they perform the essential function of aggregation from which emerges a concept of national interest. Axworthy recommended that Canada maintain spending limits, retain and enhance public financing, expand the definition of election expenses to include polling, place limits on the use of public funds by political parties, reform the system for allocating media time to minor parties, and limit interest group interventions during elections to maintain the integrity of the system. He advocated full disclosure for interest groups intervening in elections.

Asked how he would deal with regional groups like the Bloc québécois, Axworthy responded that the principle should be that any group with a reasonable following should not face significant barriers to gaining party status. On the question of having to name candidates in all regions of the country in order to gain registered party status, he indicated that, although his bias was toward national parties, it is impossible to deny regional parties the right to organize.

> "... any group with a reasonable following should not face significant barriers to gaining party status."

A participant expressed his view that given current spending limits, polling should not be included as an election expense, because this activity is too crucial to deny to parties. If polling were included as an expense, parties would be prevented from commissioning good quality polling, thereby relegating polling entirely to the media. He also argued that if polling were included as an election expense, parties would avoid the law by having other organizations perform their polling for them.

Axworthy responded that any activity a party pays for is a professional service and should be included as an election expense. Noting that all the parties engage in extensive polling during elections, and referring to polling as "Canada's soft money", he suggested that the integrity of the system would be enhanced by "coming clean" about polling. He also advocated increasing the spending limit to reflect the broader scope of the definition.

As the session concluded, it was noted that in contrast to the previous observations, many of the solutions being discussed by Americans are already in place in Canada, and that these measures have served Canadians well. The strength of the forces of fragmentation within the Canadian political system were noted, and it was suggested there is a need for a better appreciation of the forces affecting parties.

4

SYMPOSIUM ON ELECTION AND PARTY FINANCING AT THE CONSTITUENCY LEVEL

Winnipeg, Manitoba
November 26–27, 1990

THE SYMPOSIUM CONSISTED of three sessions:

- Managing Candidates' Spending and Financing in Federal and Provincial Elections
- Presentation of Draft Proposal from Accounting Profession Working Group on Election/Party Finance Reporting at the Local Level
- Workshops for Official Agents and Auditors to Discuss the Proposal of the Accounting Profession Working Group

The purpose of the first session was to compare federal and provincial practices at the constituency level on issues such as registration and disclosure for local constituency associations, reporting procedures and the definition of election expenses.

Panelist Anthony Toth, a former federal candidate, suggested federal funding for candidates had significantly reduced the barriers for parties that could reach the vote threshold to qualify for partial reimbursement of campaign expenses. He pointed out that candidates may be subject to significant unregulated intervention from single-interest pressure groups and suggested limiting their right to spend independently during campaigns. He also said the definition of election expenses and the method of assessing the value of contributions and assets need to be more precise.

Training for candidates' official agents would be more effective if sessions for experienced participants were separate from those for new agents. He proposed that agents be required to be accredited accountants. Reporting should be computerized, and an effort should be made to create user-friendly forms. The remuneration received by auditors should be increased to compensate them adequately for doing a more complete audit.

Noting that public funds are involved, Toth advocated that federal constituency associations be required to make annual reports on their expenditures. He concluded that despite the current problems, the integrity of our electoral process is intact.

Michael Krashinsky of the University of Toronto said that the current system of reporting is designed for accountants and lawyers, not average citizens. Noting that personal guarantees are usually required for loans to finance election campaigns, he suggested that a sliding scale replace the current 15 per cent of votes cast required to qualify for reimbursements; this would assist candidates in arranging financing.

"... the current system of reporting is designed for accountants and lawyers, not average citizens."

He also advocated increased allowances for auditors, simplified forms, clarification on valuing contributions, and steps to address the question of regulating special-interest groups. A petty cash allowance of $500 to $1000 for smaller items that would not require receipts was a further suggestion.

Pierre Dalphond, a lawyer who has acted as an official agent, proposed that equality, transparency and accountability should be the objectives of election law. He urged that the rules be made as simple as possible. He suggested that competition between candidates and unregulated interest groups results in a basic inequality that does not serve the election process well.

Dalphond supported the concept of reporting at the constituency level. Commenting on Quebec election law, which restricts to voters the making of contributions and limits their contributions, he noted that in some cases contributions are simply spread out over several individuals to get around these restrictions. He recommended that the vote threshold required for reimbursement be reduced to 5 per cent of the votes cast.

John Buckworth, a chartered accountant, suggested that there is an urgent need for clarification of the rules. He noted that many of the forms could be better designed so that they could be computerized more easily. He agreed that training sessions could be improved significantly and suggested they be held earlier in the campaign.

In the discussion that followed it was noted that many official agents are inexperienced volunteers; 30 per cent were newcomers in the last election. One participant suggested that more sample questions and answers, along with charts showing how to value contributions, would be a help to official agents.

Participants did not feel that provincial legislation is any easier to work with than the current federal system. One participant suggested Ontario's system of full reporting allows for much better accounting of contributions and expenditures. It was generally agreed that responsibility for training personnel should rest with the political parties, not Elections Canada.

THE WORKING GROUP PROPOSAL

The second session began with the introduction of the proposal by the Accounting Profession Working Group on election and party finance reporting at the local level. Chairperson Denis Desautels indicated that their final report would include consideration of computerization of the reporting process.

He then outlined the objectives of the Working Group's proposal: clear language, simplicity, accountability for use of public funds, no excessive control or restrictions, full disclosure and transparency, and protection of the public interest. The central features of the proposal were: extension of registration and disclosure rules to constituency associations of registered parties; introduction of more timely detailed reporting for electoral district associations and candidates; use of an all-inclusive definition of election expenses; treatment of certain post-writ nomination expenses as election expenses; and reporting requirements consistent with generally accepted accounting practices. The reporting requirements would entail annual reports from registered constituency associations as well as post-election reports from both candidates and constituency associations.

A few participants said they saw no reason to require constituency associations to file post-election reports, suggesting instead that the official agent report all election expenses. The chairperson responded that this could be done, but that the separate reports called for in the proposal would produce a full picture. When asked why constituency associations' post-election reports need to be audited, a member of the Working Group responded that several items in associations' reports are crucial to complete disclosure.

"... the public has the right to know, particularly because public funds are involved."

Noting that the proposal calls for disclosure of contributors' addresses, a participant remarked that this seemed intrusive. A Working Group member responded that the public has the right to know, particularly because public funds are involved.

Several participants asked about proposed treatment of fund-raising expenses. The Working Group acknowledged that exempting expenditures for fund raising from limitations would include direct-mail solicitation. When asked whether direct mail would remain an unlimited expense if it promotes the candidate as well as soliciting donations, the Working Group noted that Elections Canada now judges whether direct-mail solicitations qualify for the exemption. The Working Group also noted that exempting fund-raising expenses from limits is not based on the purpose of the event, but on whether the event actually raises money. Consequently, a constituency association that loses money on an election period fundraiser could find the expenses of that fundraiser included in its election expenses.

Several participants expressed concern about how the proposed legislation would replace the current system of assessing the value of contributions in the price of tickets to fund-raising events. They noted that many associations work hard to give donors as much of a tax credit as possible on fundraiser tickets. Changes in this system would reduce contributions from the public to candidates and parties.

A number of participants asked about including some post-writ nomination expenses in the total election expenses subject to limitation. One noted that hotly contested nomination races give candidates free media coverage and asked why only 10 per cent of nomination expenses were included as election expenses. A member of the Working Group responded that this provision was designed to set a price on this free media attention and to help level the playing field.

Several participants argued that post-writ nomination expenditures should not be included in election expenses. One pointed out that this provision could drive nominations into the pre-writ period, which would give the advantage to those who can afford to commit to candidacy earlier – especially incumbents and candidates from the party in government. It was also argued that a constituency association's decision to hold its nomination meeting after the writ would affect its candidate's allowable expenses, which would be unfair.

There was considerable discussion about the definition of volunteer labour; several participants suggested that professional services (such as legal advice from a self-employed lawyer to a candidate) should not be considered contributions.

Several aspects of registration and deregistration in the proposal provoked discussion. Participants expressed concern about the requirement that registered parties assume the liabilities of constituency associations after redistribution if a new riding association does not take on these liabilities. A Working Group member commented that this system works in Ontario, and some entity should assume these liabilities; also, parties may now choose not to transfer the assets and liabilities of constituency associations, thus avoiding responsibility.

One participant protested that automatic transfer of liabilities and surpluses from campaigns to constituency associations is unfair because it can force an association that has had no part in running a campaign to assume its liabilities. This participant also proposed giving candidates the option of transferring surpluses to another level of the party.

The requirement that constituency associations report the contributions and expenditures of their auxiliary and affiliated organizations was discussed. Several participants noted that in their party, women's and youth organizations are separate entities; they argued that constituency associations should not have to file reports on these organizations as long as they do not issue tax receipts. Participants noted also that some party organizations, such as campus organizations, cross constituency boundaries.

OFFICIAL AGENTS' WORKSHOP

The Official Agents' Workshop provided an opportunity for official agents to discuss in greater detail issues related to the proposal of the Accounting Profession Working Group. There was considerable discussion, for example, on the question of how to value a computer owned by a constituency association. Issues raised included whether the original value or depreciated value should be used, along with the broader question of whether a portion of its value or the fair market rental value was an appropriate means of including it as an election expenditure.

There was consensus that forms should be as simple as possible and that every effort be made to combine proposed forms to reduce the number to be submitted. The Working Group indicated it was considering a short form or a statutory declaration for candidates and associations that do not spend a lot of money.

> "There was consensus that forms should be as simple as possible and that every effort be made to combine proposed forms to reduce the number to be submitted."

It was recommended that the limit on anonymous contributions be raised from $25 to $100. After discussion, there was consensus at setting the anonymous contribution limit at $50. There was also general agreement that cash could be accepted up to $200, after which contributions would have to be made by either cheque, money order or credit card. One participant thought that limits on monetary donations were inappropriate given that volunteer labour or food can be donated and considered an expense and not a contribution. Another participant reiterated the point and suggested a blanket exemption of $2000. Alternatively, he suggested that services donated by individuals be exempt, but that goods remain included.

AUDITORS' WORKSHOP

The final session dealt with the effects of the Working Group's proposal on the work of auditors. Don Sheehy, a member of the Working Group, indicated some of the principal considerations for the workshop. He outlined the proposed requirements for who may act as an auditor, summarized the general requirements for the returns, and listed the additional returns that would have to be audited and filed under the proposal. He indicated that the criteria to be used in preparing and auditing the accounts would be those generally accepted by the accounting profession, but suggested the completeness of recording may never be fully satisfactory, so that returns may have to include the standard qualification to that effect. Finally, he questioned whether, given the low level of audit fees paid, auditors can be expected to attain a zero level of materiality on returns of candidates and constituency associations.

There was considerable discussion of whether materiality limits should apply to candidate and constituency association returns. One person suggested that auditors would have to work with zero materiality as a result of the strict liability and penalties for exceeding the expenditure limit in the present law. Since no limit is suggested for the expenditures of the constituency association in a non-election year, its audit might allow a materiality limit. Several interveners suggested that guidelines should be issued on these questions rather than leaving it to the auditor's discretion.

In summing up, Don Sheehy noted that many interveners had suggested the need for precise accounting guidance on such issues as pro-rating. Some clarification was reached on who, under the proposal, is responsible for ensuring that a person meets the requirements to be an auditor. Sheehy suggested that the issue of materiality may be beyond the mandate of the Working Group because it relates to decriminalizing offences and Elections Canada's discretionary authority over prosecutions.

There was discussion of the role of Elections Canada in ensuring that spending limits are respected. One participant asked about the discretion the Commissioner of Canada Elections has in deciding whether to prosecute those who exceed the limits. He suggested a distinction should be made between a small amount overlooked and a large intentional infraction, since exceeding spending limits by even a small amount currently constitutes an offence. Such discretion would make auditors more comfortable. It was suggested that the Commissioner has assumed such discretion based on the *Canada Elections Act* which states that prosecutions require his consent.

Some of the pressure could be alleviated if many such offences were decriminalized and heard before an administrative tribunal rather than a criminal court. It was proposed that only in cases of deliberate disregard should the case go to the Federal Court of Canada.

5

Symposium on the Administration of Elections at the Constituency Level

Sherbrooke, Quebec
December 9–11, 1990

T HE SYMPOSIUM WAS organized around six sessions:

- The Organization of Elections at the Constituency Level
- Enumeration and Revision: How Do We Proceed?
- Advance Polls and Proxy Voting: How Can the System Be Improved?
- Service to Voters with Disabilities and Citizens with Special Needs
- Problems Arising on Election Day: How Do We Deal with Them?
- Facilitating Election Operations at the Constituency Level: Where Are We Heading?

This symposium brought together 43 federal returning officers and party and election officials, mostly from Quebec. The subjects covered were similar to those dealt with at the Edmonton symposium. The opening session addressed the need for co-operation between parties and returning officers and the need to inform election and party workers about election procedures.

At the first session returning officer Raphaël Richard began by pointing out the need to reduce the high cost of elections. Fixing the date for federal elections, as in the United States, would permit better election planning and organization and a better choice of polling places. He recalled an experience when a school board had authorized him to use a school gymnasium as a polling place but the school principal cancelled the permit at the last minute.

He also advised holding meetings at the beginning of an election period to permit party organizers and returning officers to discuss such topics as the selection of polling places, rules for the election period and appointment of enumerators.

Louis Lavoie of Elections Canada pointed out that Canadian election law is complex, cumbersome and often incomprehensible, because it attempts to resolve all possible electoral problems. Elections Canada should simplify its information, he said, and make it more accessible. Not only does Canada have a 25 per cent illiteracy rate, but people tend to ignore Elections Canada's public information in any event. Lavoie noted that Elections Canada's new information program will take this reality into account.

Several returning officers and the Chief Electoral Officer of Quebec described how they made special arrangements to guarantee smooth relations with candidates for purposes of election administration. One returning officer said he took this a step further and asked each candidate's organizers to designate someone for all communications with his office.

ENUMERATION AND REVISION

At the plenary session on enumeration, returning officer Jacques Charpentier outlined recent enumeration problems. Polling divisions are becoming bigger, enumerators are fearful of going door-to-door in some areas, and voters are increasingly likely to be away from home all day. Innovative ways must be found to cope with these new conditions. Participants estimated that the current enumeration system lists between 85 and 97 per cent of voters. However, some felt that people left off the voters lists often do not want to be listed anyway.

> "... enumerators are fearful of going door-to-door in some areas, and voters are increasingly likely to be away from home all day."

Charpentier suggested that Elections Canada publicize the need for enumerators and invite voters to apply to political parties for this work. Although the current system of nominating enumerators is efficient, he said, parties should be careful to select people who meet certain minimum physical and intellectual standards. He saw no benefit in training enumerators before a writ is issued because parties constantly change their lists of nominees. It would also be unprofitable to enumerate before a writ is issued because Canada's population is highly mobile, and too many changes to the preliminary list would be needed.

Charpentier contended that paying enumerators according to the number of voters enumerated is not fair; people work as hard in small polling divisions as in large ones but they get less pay. Also, enumerators get paid for repeat calls only if they eventually register voters. Enumerators in small polling divisions should receive a guaranteed minimum salary, and all enumerators' salaries should be tax-exempt. If these changes are made, he said, many more people would volunteer to be enumerators. He also pointed out that revising agents are underpaid and that the pay of returning officers should be based on the final list, not the preliminary one, because revision often raises as many problems as the original enumeration.

The discussion then turned to alternative systems for voter registration. Alain Gauthier, a consultant to the Commission, described Revenue Ontario's preliminary voters list used at the municipal and school board levels and British Columbia's permanent voters list. Enumeration was becoming increasingly difficult in these provinces and the validity of some lists was dubious. Under the new systems there should be fewer problems.

Gauthier was conducting a study that compared these systems, their problems and corrective measures. He discussed door-to-door canvassing, in which enumerators have trouble covering all voters in apartment buildings, and the Ontario experience with drawing up voters lists based on tax data and property purchase agreements. Locating home-owners is easier with this method, but it does not improve registration of dependants and tenants. He suggested preparing a preliminary list by the Ontario method and revising it by door-to-door canvassing.

Andrée Lortie of Elections Canada said computerizing returning officers' offices would not cause major problems because Elections Canada's systems do not require them to be expert operators. The 1988 election produced good and bad experiences, but it showed that all elections across Canada should be computerized. In the next election, enumeration will be done with index cards and an index book, the forms will be in different colours, enumerators will not have to type the voters lists, information will be entered on computers, and revision will be done from the index cards prepared for the preliminary list. Elections Canada would like to appoint – and pay for – one staff person in each returning officer's office to manage computer lists.

Jean-Paul Laperrière, another Commission consultant, reviewed the permanent voters lists used in British Columbia and Ontario's municipal voter register. According to the British Columbia elections organization, their system compares favourably with American systems, as it can be used for elections at any level, municipal to federal, thereby reducing duplication of effort and saving money.

In Ontario, the Ministry of Revenue had a mandate to develop and process municipal and school board voter registration. The public responded well to the new system, which produced more accurate information on voters.

Laperrière noted that a preliminary Commission study looked at the feasibility of using information from other government departments and agencies. One working group was investigating the possibility of using Revenue Canada data to prepare and maintain a permanent voters list. Representatives of Elections Canada, Canada Post and Statistics Canada formed a second group to evaluate geomatic data-matching, using information from their combined data banks, to produce electoral maps.

The enumeration workshops produced several conclusions. Participants did not generally question partisan nomination of enumerators, but they agreed that returning officers should make the appointments and maintain lists of people who should not be appointed again. Most participants agreed that to increase the pool of willing enumerators, enumerators' pay should not be taxable. Many enumerators are unemployed or on welfare. If they have to declare their income from enumeration, they will not want to work during elections because their pay will be deducted from their benefits.

Several participants approved of the Quebec practice of appointing supervisory enumerators to supervise enumeration in 20 to 25 polling divisions and check preliminary lists for accuracy before sending them to returning officers. Participants preferred to continue using two enumerators in each poll, to reassure voters of the integrity of the process and to keep up the enumerators' confidence.

"... returning officers should make the appointments and maintain lists of people who should not be appointed again."

Returning officers and party representatives found they had conflicting objectives in the appointment of enumerators. Returning officers generally accepted the current appointment system despite its problems, but they protested that incompetent enumerators are sometimes appointed and parties refuse to co-operate by nominating more suitable individuals. Party representatives admitted that they do not want to lose their best campaign volunteers during enumeration. To resolve this problem, participants proposed expanding the sources of potential enumerators by inviting applicants from smaller parties or outside sources, such as schools and colleges. They also suggested that returning officers and parties could co-operate more closely, even before the election is called; that the public should be informed about the importance of enumeration; and that the two leading parties in each riding should appoint representatives to assist the returning officer.

ADVANCE AND PROXY VOTING

In the sessions on advance and proxy voting, participants differed on whether to maintain the proxy vote but agreed on introducing a mail ballot. Several returning officers suggested eliminating voting in their offices because it causes administrative problems, unless the voting process can be modified to lighten their load. Many participants favoured abolishing the proxy vote because it

"... the mail ballot ... guarantees secrecy by requiring voters to mark their own ballots and seal them in envelopes."

is complex and used infrequently, but some said it is useful for voters in outlying regions. Some participants pointed out that students and military personnel have the opportunity to vote twice with current arrangements; mail ballots would pose the same risk.

The Chief Electoral Officer of Manitoba, Richard Balasko, contended that for voters who cannot get to a polling station, the mail ballot is the best way to exercise the franchise; it guarantees secrecy by requiring voters to mark their own ballots and seal them in envelopes. He suggested keeping the proxy vote for people who do not have easy access to mail service, such as trappers and others working in remote areas. Allowing automatic registration of people who vote by mail would improve this system.

Participants approved of mobile polls for hospitals and other institutions. At present, Elections Canada authorizes hospital polls only in some instances. Participants felt it would be impractical to keep these polling stations open all day if everyone has already voted.

VOTERS WITH DISABILITIES AND SPECIAL NEEDS

In the session considering voters with disabilities and special needs, participants discussed literacy and access to the vote. Rachel Bélisle of the Canadian Institute for Adult Education described illiteracy in Quebec, emphasizing that reading and writing problems often affect voters with other disabilities, such as deafness.

Concentrating on illiteracy problems and possible solutions to them, Bélisle discussed the accessibility of the ballot and other election-related forms, as well as access to political ideas and issues, which, she said, are rarely presented in simple language. She pointed out that using colours, numbers and simple, clear language would be a first step to removing obstacles to persons with reading difficulties.

Bélisle encouraged participants to remember the needs of about 25 per cent of the population by sticking as closely as possible to everyday language, using very simple sentence structures to express messages, and supplementing written messages with other audiovisual means whenever possible.

Sylvie Godbout, a member of the board of directors of the Office des personnes handicapées du Québec, noted that the obstacles facing voters with disabilities may not be readily apparent to people without disabilities. Yet everyone has the right to vote, regardless of their level of ability. People with disabilities have every right to a voice in who will represent them in Parliament.

> "People with disabilities have every right to a voice in who will represent them in Parliament."

Level access to polling stations is a priority, Godbout said, but returning officers are not the only ones with a responsibility in this regard. Candidates should also ensure that their offices, meeting halls and other facilities are accessible. How can candidates aspire to represent persons with disabilities if they can't even bother to ensure that their offices are accessible? Godbout therefore suggested that level access become a condition for the reimbursement of candidates' expenses.

Current efforts to hire persons with disabilities as election officials are useful, Godbout suggested, but participation will be discouraged and the purpose defeated if election offices are not accessible. In addition, sign language interpretation for hearing-impaired voters should be available at polling stations and on television. After so many years of neglect, said Godbout, no effort should be spared to give persons with disabilities everything they need to know in order to vote.

In discussion, participants agreed that access ramps are now perceived as normal, not remarkable. Barrier-free buildings exist, and no effort should be spared to find and use them as polling places. The Act should make this a requirement.

Andrée Lortie remarked that Elections Canada's study of ways to eliminate obstacles has resulted in a new voting booth, which has no written instructions, only illustrations. Participants considered using candidates' photos on ballots, but abandoned the idea because voters know party leaders better than candidates. They did agree that adding party colours and symbols to ballots would address these problems.

ELECTION DAY

In the workshops on election-day problems, discussion focused on the choice of election day. Unlike their colleagues who met in Edmonton, this gathering strongly favoured Sunday voting and discounted objections on religious or other grounds.

During her presentation, returning officer Céline Bernier described problems in finding adequate election-day facilities. She believes that Sunday elections would make returning officers' work easier because problems, such as recruiting qualified staff, would be reduced. She suggested allowing returning officers to recruit replacement staff for employees who are absent on election day. She also advocated election-day voter registration but suggested that election-day registrants should register and vote at the office of the returning officer to prevent double voting.

Several returning officers opposed election-day registration, in rural and urban constituencies alike, suggesting longer revision periods as an alternative. Few rural voters exercise their right to be registered on election day, they said. Other participants said that extensive voting-day registration would lead to abuse, and that rural and urban ridings should be treated similarly in this respect.

Jean Jolin, Assistant to the Chief Electoral Officer of Quebec, noted that in Quebec deputy returning officers are appointed by the governing party while poll clerks are appointed by the opposition. These officials are trained together and can fill in for one another. Each polling station also has an information and control officer who helps manage the polling station on election day. This officer acts as the eyes of the returning officer in the polling station and stays in close contact with the returning office. When the vote has been counted, the deputy returning officer communicates the results to the information and control officer, who in turn communicates them to the returning officer's office, where they are posted and made available to the media. The results are usually available 45 minutes after the close of the polls.

At the last election, Quebec used mobile polls for the first time in senior citizens' homes and hospitals where many people are unable to travel. The mobile polling team was similar to a regular polling station team.

In the workshops most returning officers disagreed with a proposal to postpone the opening of ballot boxes so as to delay the transmission of eastern Canada's results to western Canada. They argued it would create confusion in the polling stations, and election officials might leak information. Some, however, thought a half-hour delay might be possible. Morning voting hours could be shorter, but extending evening voting hours would be difficult because poll staff would be tired and impatient. Several participants concluded that the time zone problem is unsolvable and that the status quo should remain. Others noted that Sunday voting would allow more flexibility in voting times.

6

SYMPOSIUM ON POLITICAL PARTIES

Halifax, Nova Scotia
February 7–8, 1991

T HE SYMPOSIUM WAS divided into six sessions:

- The Internal Dynamics of Parties: Candidate and Leadership Selection
- The Internal Dynamics of Parties: Party Organization
- Parties, Representation and Alternative Forms of Participation
- Responsiveness, Volatility and the Electoral System
- Parties as National Institutions
- Parties as Primary Political Organizations

The Commission devoted part of its research effort to examining the performance of political parties as the main vehicles of political participation and representation in Canada. This research seminar focused on political parties as the most direct means Canadians can use to represent their interests and become involved in politics. The objective was to provide opportunities for the Commission, senior representatives of political parties and the media, and academic researchers to discuss the Commission's preliminary research findings and possible reforms. Overall, the Commission sought input from participants on ways to affirm the importance of national political parties to political participation, representation and integration. Advice was also sought on possible reforms to electoral law to improve political parties' performance in these areas and on the limitations of such reform.

CANDIDATE AND LEADERSHIP SELECTION

The first session, moderated by Kenneth Carty of the University of British Columbia, reviewed the pros and cons of reforming the candidate selection process at the constituency and national levels, particularly regarding spending limits. Should the law regulate these processes or should they be regulated mainly by the parties?

Each of the three largest parties has its own approach to leadership selection. The New Democratic Party biennial convention is technically a leadership convention, although the incumbent leader is rarely challenged.

The Liberals and Progressive Conservatives, however, have separate policy and leadership conventions. It was suggested that any attempt to regulate leadership selection must recognize the distinct processes of all the parties.

A brief overview of the recent New Democratic Party and Liberal leadership conventions was provided by Keith Archer of the University of Calgary. It was noted that both parties have used the tax credit system to assist leadership candidates in fund raising. This means the leadership selection process is subsidized from public funds.

Reference was made to the three parties' recent efforts to reform the leadership selection process. For example, at their last national policy convention, the Liberals adopted a resolution to move toward allowing all party members to elect the leader. Some expressed concern that electing the leader directly would not necessarily strengthen the party. Direct elections would give constituency interest groups more opportunities to influence the outcome, and this approach may not always result in greater participation by party members.

Lynda Erickson of Simon Fraser University identified several controversial aspects of the candidate selection process, including membership requirements, the timing of selection meetings by the party executive, and the increasing cost of a few nomination contests. Spending limits imposed by public regulation, some suggested, could open up the selection process to candidates of all socio-economic backgrounds.

Panelists generally agreed that some level of public regulation of this process is justified when public funding is involved. However, on specific issues like membership requirements, they agreed that the parties would strongly resist such efforts.

_____

> "... the combination of public funding, spending limits and disclosure gives Canada's electoral system a high measure of public confidence and legitimacy."

_____

Michael Robinson of the Liberal Party suggested that the combination of public funding, spending limits and disclosure gives Canada's electoral system a high measure of public confidence and legitimacy. Extending this combination to leadership and candidate selection could make the process more democratic.

PARTY ORGANIZATION

At the second session, moderated by Steven Wolinetz of Memorial University, participants discussed how the parties' organization and policy-making capacities could be improved. Panelists were also asked whether linkages between the parties' federal and provincial wings should be tightened or loosened.

Participants were told that the organization of Canadian political parties reflects their preoccupation with electoral competition. Their proficiency in organizing elections tends to be stronger than their ability to develop policy. William Chandler of McMaster University suggested that Canadian parties need more resources to do policy research.

Internal party processes should be concerned with more than just policy development, argued Jack Graham of the Liberal Party. These processes also give members the opportunity to express views to party leaders, develop policy support among members and educate members about policy issues. Others felt that the grassroots model of policy development is unrealistic – the grassroots membership gives direction to policy makers, rather than developing detailed policy.

Several panelists supported the establishment of party foundations such as those found in Germany and the Netherlands. Party foundations could let parties develop long-term policy alternatives and could allow parties to tap regularly into networks of policy experts and research institutes. One participant said that the foundations must remain relatively autonomous if they are to work as envisaged. Others argued that the short-term and highly partisan policy needs of political parties mean that they would want to control party foundation activities.

Steven Wolinetz noted that party foundations in several western European nations were sensitive to the partisan political climate in which they functioned. One participant suggested that foundations could make parties more credible and visible between elections. In Europe, foundations are not simply think tanks. They also educate and get party members more involved between elections.

In Germany, parties have a privileged position enshrined in the constitution, and consequently receive public support. One panelist stated that as private organizations, parties should not be given public funds. Another panelist responded that party foundations are a controlled way of encouraging policy development and suggested that directly giving funds to parties to perform certain functions would be more effective.

There was a general discussion about why Canadian political parties have not created institutions like party foundations. One panelist replied that party preoccupation with elections precludes this; another suggested that parties simply have not thought of the idea, while another argued that limited resources force parties to concentrate on elections.

Panelists reviewed the strength and direction of organizational linkages between the federal and provincial wings of the political parties. Rand Dyck of Laurentian University argued that these linkages should not be changed. It was suggested that dividing these wings would force volunteers, whose numbers are declining, to choose between them. In addition, the fracturing caused by separate organizations in the Quebec Liberal party was highlighted as a potential pitfall of such weak linkages.

PARTIES AND REPRESENTATION

Jane Jenson of Carleton University moderated the third session in which panelists discussed whether the major parties are in danger of being replaced by interest groups or single-issue groups. They also addressed changes in public opinion on political parties and reviewed ways to channel new forms of participation into the mainstream parties, as successfully achieved in some European countries.

The moderator noted that political parties are crucial because they represent the electorate. However, this role is complicated by higher levels of public cynicism and distrust and increasing recourse to single-issue activities that bypass the parties and inhibit the compromise necessary for party representation. Consequently, parties are less able to link people and government and to generate a national political language. The suggestion was made that some believe this is inevitable because social change creates a more individualistic, consumer society or because the *Canadian Charter of Rights and Freedoms* encourages using the courts rather than elections to resolve conflicts. It was also argued that political parties handicap themselves by failing to give voters clear, consistent policy alternatives.

> "... parties are less able to link people and government and to generate a national political language."

Although parties still have an important representational role, Canadians' identification with political parties has diminished, agreed Neil Nevitte of the University of Calgary. Critical public attitudes reflect the value changes of advanced industrial societies. These societies enjoy unprecedented prosperity and security, as well as geographic and occupational mobility, and through technological and informational changes they have more political knowledge. In addition, the gap between the general public and the elite has been narrowed by increasing public access to political information and dissemination of skills for autonomous decisions. A new political agenda has emerged on the quality of life (for example, the environment), and equality for Aboriginal people, women and other marginalized groups. This agenda competes with the old one, concerned with redistributive politics, and has led to a new style of political participation that demands direct action on issues.

Val Sears, formerly of *The Toronto Star*, suggested that we should not be concerned with integrating interest groups with parties, but rather with balancing interest group and party activities. Politics should be seen as groups operating in a marketplace of ideas or a collection of interests that many can share.

Another panelist, Tom Axworthy of the CRB Foundation, cautioned that increasing public cynicism should be put into perspective. Political decisions are collective choices of people who disagree. Everybody – including the Cabinet, Parliament and the public – loses most of the time because the position that is adopted will always be a compromise. Hence, in a diverse society, it is not surprising that many are cynical. One participant asserted that despite the system, most people lose, so the important question is how to give everyone a fair opportunity to influence. Another suggested that of the four traditional functions of political parties, only one has been transformed. Parties still act as organizers of electoral choice, promoters of value systems and aggregators of interests. However, because of the rise of single-issue groups, parties play a lesser role in interest articulation. To support the role of parties as promoters of values, some argue, there is a case for having an ideological basis for parties.

Panelists agreed that although levels of political participation in Canada have remained relatively stable, individuals are increasingly channelling their political activism toward special-interest groups. The effect of communication technology on the behaviour of political parties and interest groups was also discussed. Someone suggested that the government's increasing use of public opinion surveys encourages special-interest groups to try to mobilize public support in a visible and confrontational style. This approach increases the visibility of certain issues and increases the probability of sympathetic public support.

Panelists discussed how the processes used recently by political parties to select leaders and candidates had contributed to declining public confidence in parties as primary political organizations. Someone suggested that the political parties had demonstrated limited internal reform, and that only public regulation would force parties to adjust their practices to meet changing public expectations. It was noted that political parties view themselves as private organizations made up of volunteers; as such, they would not welcome state regulation of internal processes and activities.

There was general agreement that parties must present themselves to the public as effective, credible political forums, a function performed increasingly by special-interest groups. It was noted that although the government funds and gives tax credits for educational, charitable and other interest groups, it provides little funding for political advocacy and education.

> "How responsive is the Canadian electoral system to changes in voter sentiment?"

RESPONSIVENESS AND VOLATILITY

The next session, moderated by Richard Johnston of the University of British Columbia, dealt with some of the properties of the electoral system and how they relate to party performance. How responsive is the Canadian electoral system to changes in voter sentiment? Are high turnover and reduced incumbency necessarily good things? Does the system force parties to focus too much on short-term goals?

Research on electoral volatility and legislative turnover in Canada was summarized by Michael Krashinsky of the University of Toronto as "parties matter, regions matter and incumbency matters." These three factors explain most of the constituency-by-constituency swing in votes. The incumbency effect has not changed over the past 40 years, but Canadian elections are becoming increasingly regional. Regional effects on election outcomes are great and are much more important than incumbency. It was estimated that incumbency has a 4 to 5 per cent effect on electoral outcomes. The trend toward media and leader-oriented national campaigns decreases the effect of incumbency, while the increasing resources available to Members of Parliament that assist them in their communication and constituency service roles may increase the impact of incumbency. Commission research shows that size, whether the character of the constituency is rural or urban and the region do not influence the effect of incumbency. Overall, the incumbency effect is not strong in Canada.

Incumbency in the United States is a serious problem, noted panelist Brian Gaines of Stanford University, largely because of the way legislators garner personal votes through constituency service and pork-barrelling. Research shows that this phenomenon also occurs in the United Kingdom, but not in Canada. Incumbency in Canada is reduced by a consistently high turnover for parties and candidates; there are many marginal seats, and the number has not decreased. Electoral swings do not change significantly, suggesting that it is not the candidate that matters. Survey data suggest, however, that constituency service does have a limited effect. The conclusion was that low incumbency is a measure of the responsiveness of the Canadian system, and that this is a positive characteristic of Canadian politics.

David Gotthilf of Viewpoints Research suggested that there is a dichotomy between electoral and political responsiveness. Electoral responsiveness involves election results; political responsiveness involves policy and law. The American system, characterized by low turnover and opinion-driven policy development, is politically responsive but not electorally responsive. In Canada, the electoral system is very responsive while the political system is not. There are three reasons for this electoral responsiveness:

- The combination of a single-member plurality electoral system and a three-party system means that a small vote swing can cause a seat to change hands.
- Party identification among voters, particularly those under the age of 45, is declining.
- Politics is becoming increasingly professional, through the integration of marketing techniques and political strategy.

Canadian electoral responsiveness makes the political system less responsive. Politicians know how volatile public opinion is and soon learn that the campaign matters more than what they did in the preceding four years. The task is to balance electoral and political responsiveness. Following the presentations, panelists debated whether having experienced career politicians is more desirable than high legislative turnover in ensuring that politicians are constantly responsive to their constituents. Although no consensus was reached, panelists did agree that there is no apparent trade-off between having experienced legislators and ensuring the political process is accessible to new candidates. They also agreed that limiting a politician's term, an idea that is somewhat popular in the United States, is inappropriate in Canada because of high legislative turnover.

> "... there is no apparent trade-off between having experienced legislators and ensuring the political process is accessible to new candidates."

PARTIES AS NATIONAL INSTITUTIONS

The session on parties as national institutions, moderated by Brian Crowley of Dalhousie University, examined the ability of the national parties to play an integrative role and incorporate diverse views. Panelists offered conflicting interpretations of the parties' ability to serve as primary national institutions. David Elkins of the University of British Columbia observed that Canada is difficult to govern because of the presence of linguistic and regional cleavages. The expectation that parties can solve this problem may be unrealistic. He suggested that parties are good at selecting leaders, nominating candidates, competing in elections and presenting policy alternatives. But parties will be overburdened if they are expected to also serve nation-building functions.

Maureen Covell of Simon Fraser University countered that Canadian political parties do bring together diverse interests; this feature distinguishes the Canadian system from other party systems where interest aggregation occurs in the legislature or in the corporate system. In Europe, this occurs through mediation between political parties representing specific interests. The Canadian system expects parties to be open to interest groups while developing policy ideas. Denis Pageau of the Progressive Conservative Party noted that parties wanting to govern must be national in scope and accept responsibility for mediating and accommodating competing regional interests.

Several panelists noted that even when parties enjoy strong regional representation, tension between promoting national interests and advancing local interests is inevitable. A participant argued that political parties have been fairly successful at balancing these interests through leadership selection, policy conventions, and policy research and development. One panelist contended that the national integration role of parties is weak because various interest groups avoid joining political parties.

The integrative and nation-building abilities of political parties could be strengthened if Members of Parliament were allowed to represent their constituents more effectively in the House of Commons, argued one person. Another argued that parties could have a greater electoral presence in more regions if Canada adopted a system of proportional representation rather than single-member plurality. In response, several panelists noted that experience shows that the regional presence of national parties does not depend on proportional representation.

A number of panelists noted that the possibility of members representing regional parties joining the House of Commons after the next federal election could further undermine the national parties' ability to represent various regional interests. Michael Robinson pointed out that projects like the goods and services tax and the Meech Lake Accord have made parties reticent about embracing national projects. This reluctance has made the policies of regionally based parties and special-interest groups more popular.

"... because the current system is tied to election spending, the three major parties have an advantage."

The session closed with a general discussion of whether the current system of public funding gives parties enough resources to represent diverse interests, and whether this system favours existing parties at the expense of newer or smaller parties with alternative policy ideas. There was no consensus on whether current levels of public funding are adequate or excessive. Most panelists did agree, however, that because the current system is tied to election spending, the three major parties have an advantage. The exclusion of other parties from the public funding system could restrict voters' electoral choices.

PARTIES AS PRIMARY POLITICAL ORGANIZATIONS

In the final session, panelists were asked by Herman Bakvis of Dalhousie University to address leadership and candidate selection; party funding at the national and constituency level; and how to strengthen national parties.

Several panelists disagreed on the need for greater public regulation of candidate and leadership selection processes. Kenneth Carty argued these processes are of public interest and should therefore be regulated. Dalton Camp suggested these processes are internal party affairs. Neil Young, a New Democratic Party Member of Parliament, suggested that if public funds are used, there should be full disclosure and surpluses could be returned. A Liberal Member of Parliament, Peter Milliken, argued that full financial disclosure on contributions would be a step toward ensuring public confidence in the integrity of these processes.

Participants were asked to consider parties' private and public dimensions and whether they can be separated to determine which activities should be regulated. Several participants said the selection processes were important enough to justify some public regulation. Another participant objected to any public regulation that interfered with the basic voluntaristic ethos of political parties.

There was general agreement that the current requirements for election reimbursements for candidates are too restrictive. One person suggested that the 15 per cent of the constituency vote required to qualify for partial reimbursement of election expenses should be removed. Another suggestion was that parties should be reimbursed according to their national electoral performance, leaving individual candidates to be reimbursed on the basis of their local performance.

Participants then reviewed the role interest groups should play during federal election campaigns. Concern was expressed about these groups' increasing participation at the constituency level. If interest groups can make independent expenditures during federal elections, the integrity of election spending limits imposed on political parties could be undermined. Without such restrictions, Canadian elections would move closer to the system in the United States, where numerous political action committees have become key participants by raising and spending money for candidates.

The argument was advanced that spending money on advertising during elections is an issue of freedom of speech, although reasonable limits may be justified under the *Canadian Charter of Rights and Freedoms*. Most participants agreed, however, that some restrictions on independent expenditures by interest groups during federal elections are necessary and defensible.

7

SYMPOSIUM ON MEDIA AND ELECTIONS

**Toronto, Ontario
February 20–22, 1991**

THE SYMPOSIUM CONSISTED of seven sessions:

- Media and Parties: Setting the Campaign Agenda
- Leaders Debates: Significance and Potential
- Polling, Campaigns and the Media
- The Regulatory Framework
- Local Campaigns: Improving the Information Environment
- New Approaches to Campaign Communication
- Issues and Lessons

The objective of this symposium was to bring together researchers preparing reports for the Commission and practitioners from the political parties, the media, and the polling industry to discuss the preliminary findings of the research. Although the symposium covered a wide range of issues, discussion revolved around two central questions: (1) the appropriate role of regulation of political communication in electoral reform, and (2) the extent to which competition would serve the needs of candidates and voters.

Pierre Lortie, Chairman of the Commission, emphasized two points in his opening remarks:

1. The consensus of scholarly research is that the media play a central role in election campaigns.
2. Television has transformed elections.

He also noted that interveners at the Commission's public hearings had raised concerns about the role of the media and asked participants to advise the Commission as to how it could ensure the public has a fair chance of getting a clear message during campaigns.

MEDIA AND PARTIES

The first session focused on the relationship between party strategists and journalists. Topics discussed included the balance between style and substance in campaign information, the effects of the growth of political marketing on voter information and behaviour, and the influence of changes in media technologies and practices.

Michael Nolan of the University of Western Ontario described the evolution of the relationship between the media and parties in the conduct of federal election campaigns. In discussing the evolution of media technology, he noted the increasing importance of party advertising and identified three ages of political journalism: (1) the partisan age, from before Confederation to the 1950s, (2) the adversarial age, best exemplified by the pipeline debate, and (3) the age of political cynicism or irreverence. He also underscored the importance of providing free time as a supplement to paid time and news coverage.

Elly Alboim of the CBC summarized the coverage of elections as a struggle between politicians and journalists to set the agenda. He argued that the move to paid advertising by the political parties results from their belief that they can no longer communicate with their electorate through the news media. At the same time, journalists have begun to tire of old models of election campaign coverage. This is partly because of the inability of the media to accept the parties' view of election campaigns as "exercises in repetitiveness in trying to establish, educate, and convince people of central messages – a process that has nothing to do with news as the media see it." The media are losing interest in covering leaders' tours, and are increasingly suspicious that the mandates articulated during election campaigns have little to do with governing.

> "The media are ... increasingly suspicious that the mandates articulated during election campaigns have little to do with governing."

Newer media outlets, such as CBC television's Newsworld, will perpetuate this pattern, Alboim argued. Through live access to most of the political campaign on the ground, Newsworld will steadily assume the mandate for routine coverage. This will result in "less and less reporting of the substance of the parties and political platforms." In all likelihood, future election coverage will concentrate on "the major events of the campaign, the debates, the accidents, the mistakes." Increasingly, he predicted, the national media "will begin to treat elections more and more as an irrelevancy."

One participant argued that paid advertising is the only method by which parties can send an unfiltered message to voters. The role of the media, in part, should be to educate the voter about what is being done with and through paid advertising.

William Gilsdorf of Concordia University reported finding increasing cynicism in relation to election coverage in a recent survey of journalists across the country.

Research by Jean Crête of Université Laval indicates that short spots on television are a very effective means of getting messages across to people. Crête argued that spots are considered good if issues are addressed, people are not alienated, and positions on issues are made clear. His research also indicates that it is better to address issues than sell candidates. He recommended that free time could be made available and allocated through a system of credits allowing parties to choose the way they use their time.

Another participant suggested that even negative advertising by parties during the campaign – which he predicted will become more common, as in the United States – must resonate somewhere to be effective, and the media have the responsibility to analyse advertisements of this type. He argued that average Canadians are very capable of accepting or rejecting such advertising.

Another participant restated the idea that free-time broadcasting was more of a burden than a benefit to political parties and that paid time reaches the audiences parties wish to reach. It was also stated that radio can be very effective, since people can be left with impressions whether they realize it or not. Narrowcasting is the most important trend for party strategists. It was this participant's view that the voters have become increasingly sophisticated and that negative ads risk a backlash.

Elly Alboim suggested that the Commission should work to ensure a level playing field. He argued that to cover and critique party advertising campaigns, journalists require better access to information, and that the Broadcasting Arbitrator should collect and release information on the details of media purchases by parties and other aspects of campaign advertising.

According to one party official, a major task for the Commission is to find a balance among the many elements of the campaign and to ensure that money is not a dominant factor. It was suggested that all networks could be required to provide suitable time slots for free-time party broadcasts and to devote a reasonable amount of time to election coverage. As well, the Commission should "regulate the role of the media – or at least the amount of information the media provide during a campaign – how much time they devote to the coverage of what is, after all, one of the most important times in our country." This participant also recommended a shorter campaign period and an effort to make information available to voters at times when they are ready to receive it and in a format suitable to their information needs.

> "... there is an assumption ... that whatever is good for the media, is good for the politicians and political parties, and is good for the public interest. And I'm not necessarily sure about that."

Another participant suggested that the public interest should be considered in the discussion. "I think there is an assumption in this debate, and elsewhere, that whatever is good for the media, is good for the politicians and political parties, and is good for the public interest. And I'm not necessarily sure about that."

One participant spoke against regulatory control of the media on the basis that media cynicism and irreverence alone do not shape the messages in an election campaign. Both the media and politicians set the agenda for elections, he claimed. The Commission's role, he suggested, should be "to encourage the media to pursue its own separate and useful role in scrutinizing the broader context of a political campaign."

LEADERS DEBATES

In the second session Cathy Widdis Barr of Wilfrid Laurier University summarized her research on televised leaders debates in Canada, based on statistical analysis of the 1984 and 1988 National Election Study data. She noted that debates influence voter choice, participation rates, voters' perceptions of leaders' qualifications, and citizens' understanding of election issues. Those voters who gain most knowledge are those who use few other information sources.

Drawing on his comparative study of televised leaders debates, Robert Bernier of École nationale d'administration publique argued that the absence of regulations governing leaders debates has favoured the major parties and that, because debates are an important source of voter information, they should be institutionalized. He suggested that debates should be held at the end of the campaign, when voter interest is at its height, and that there should be a separate debate for the leaders of smaller parties.

Terry Hargreaves of the CBC rejected outright the idea of a regulatory framework for the debates. If we want to impose rules, he asked, where do we begin and where do we end? How can legislation be worked out that is suitable in all circumstances? He also rejected the idea of debates for smaller parties, citing the problem of identifying who would participate.

Several participants called for some form of access to the debates for minor or regional parties. One participant noted, however, that the attempt to regulate a leaders debate in Quebec had been a disaster, resulting in no debate being held during a recent election campaign.

A Liberal party strategist claimed that "the new over-regulated industry is going to be elections." However, he favoured the suggestion of having someone from outside the broadcasting sector involved in organizing the leaders debates, perhaps as convener.

Commissioner Pierre Fortier commented that the focus on the pros and cons of regulation in the morning session had restricted thinking about the larger picture. He characterized participants as saying, "Please leave us alone, we're doing fine, don't meddle, don't regulate. From Quebec came the cry – we tried to regulate; it failed, so don't try it." Fortier's response was that "I don't fear regulation, but on the other hand I'm not foolish enough to think that we should regulate for the sake of regulating." He asked that participants consider the broader picture in their deliberations.

POLLING, CAMPAIGNS AND THE MEDIA

Guy Lachapelle of Concordia University led off the third session, presenting the results of his research on the publication of opinion polls during election periods. He reviewed public concern about the issue, cited legal opinion that publication could be regulated under the Charter, summarized existing codes of ethics adopted by pollsters, journalists and broadcasters, and reported his finding that reports published during the 1988 Canadian federal election campaign often failed to live up to these standards. Among his major recommendations were (1) that the publication of polls on polling day and the two days preceding it be prohibited; (2) that all opinion polls published or broadcast during the election period be accompanied by specific technical information; (3) that exit polls be banned; and (4) that a polling commission, on the French model, be established to enforce professional standards.

Donna Dasko of Environics Research argued that placing restrictions on polling would be "an outright assault on freedom of information and freedom of speech," expressing the view that it would be better to encourage polls, which provide important information. The requirement that technical information be provided would limit the dissemination of polling data and make the publication of short excerpts impossible. She argued that competition and self-regulation has worked well and that a polling commission would have little benefit.

> "Placing restrictions on polling would be 'an outright assault on freedom of information and freedom of speech...' "

Christopher Waddell of *The Globe and Mail* argued that if media polls were to be regulated, all polls should be regulated. He noted that a requirement that methodological information be published whenever poll data were cited would preclude the use of such data in many forms of journalism. One participant, a pollster, maintained that opinion polls influence the voters, and that journalists do not receive proper training to interpret the data so that the public can be adequately informed. He called into question the ethics of certain polling firms that produce opinion polls for the media one day and work as consultants for certain political parties the next. He favoured some form of regulation.

Elly Alboim remarked that the debate was confusing methodology and analysis and that much of the information disclosed to the public would, in his view, not be understood by them. The real point of argument in the debate over polling, he claimed, is how individual polling organizations and media organizations reach their conclusions. To hide behind methodological disclosure as something that is going to resolve the real issue – competent or incompetent analysis and its effect – sidesteps the question in Alboim's view.

He then responded to Commissioner Fortier's earlier remarks on the defensive tone of the seminar. "There is defensiveness? Yes, there is because, in my view, the Commission is failing to articulate what its analytical framework is here. To bring all of us into a room, particularly broadcasters and politicians, knowing that you have leverage and power and the ability to make regulations or propose regulations, and not to understand your analytical framework leaves us in a defensive and uncomfortable position. I find it very hard to respond. I believe in regulation of debates, but I'm not sure how much I want to talk about them until I know what your point of departure is." Fortier responded that a review of the electoral process occurs only every 20 to 25 years and that it is important to examine every relevant issue without a preconceived agenda.

Other participants noted that polling has had a significant effect on Canadian politics and that this suggests the need for some form of regulation. One participant admitted he was reconsidering his position on the issue. "When I heard Professor Lachapelle's recommendations, I was still thinking we could go ahead with self-regulation. And now that I've heard from three members of the polling community, I guess I was wrong." The resistance of the pollsters to regulation, he said, had convinced him that legislation was required, despite his general reluctance to regulate.

> "It is shocking to me how most of the discussion we have had to date accepted regulation as a starting point."

Another participant noted that there are no professional standards; anyone can start a polling organization and presumably, with access to the media, publish polling reports. "It is difficult for me to subscribe totally to the position that there should be no regulation whatsoever if there are no professional standards within that industry." One participant responded by indicating there is self-regulation and that self-selection goes on within many of the media outlets; the participant cautioned against proceeding too quickly to regulation. "It is shocking to me how most of the discussion we have had to date accepted regulation as a starting point."

THE REGULATORY FRAMEWORK

The fourth session focused on the framework of laws and regulations governing election broadcasting and advertising. Discussion topics included the fairness and effectiveness of current regulations covering free and paid political time, broadcast news and public affairs coverage, and alternative regimes and possible reforms.

David Spencer of the University of Western Ontario noted that the guiding principle of the 1936 *Broadcasting Act* – that political broadcasting should be more information-driven and less sales-driven – remains today. Radio has been overtaken by television as the principal actor in political broadcasting, with the possible exception of local coverage in smaller communities. He suggested that a special network for political broadcasting, both during and between elections, might meet some of the communication needs of voters and parties. He also argued that free time should be provided for political and election broadcasting by all broadcasters as a condition of licensing.

Pierre Trudel of Université de Montréal began his discussion by referring to the distinction in Canadian law between broadcast and print media. Print media have traditionally had more unfettered freedom of expression because of the ease of starting a newspaper. Broadcast media, using scarce public airwaves, have typically faced more regulation. Trudel suggested that the editorial freedom of the media to decide the content of their messages may exclude some participants from receiving equitable coverage. The efforts of the Canadian Radio-television and Telecommunications Commission (CRTC) to promote equity in election coverage may be most effective through encouraging self-regulation and the establishment and monitoring of directives rather than by detailed, inflexible regulation.

Catherine Thompson-Pyper provided an overview of the implications for election broadcasting of the new *Broadcasting Act*. Of particular note are the elimination of the requirement to identify the sponsor and political party associated with a political program or announcement, and the extension of the paid-time requirements of the elections act to include pay and specialty services.

Christopher Dornan of Carleton University stated that the accountability of the print media in elections is low because they are not governed by formal mechanisms. Existing methods of redressing unfair or biased coverage through a letter to the editor or a complaint to the ombudsman or a press council are ineffective. The issue of the accountability of the print media stems from the contradiction of the principle of freedom of the press and the principle that no social authority should go unchecked. The print media, especially subject to concentrated ownership by large corporations, have become a social authority. Dornan argued that the only feasible check is increased press criticism.

John Coleman of the Canadian Advertising Foundation claimed he was "struck by the tone of some, if not all, of the presentations, and indeed the whole inquiry into the idea of reforming the electoral process. It was as if someone had said, 'Let's put the rules in place in case we need them.' " Coleman argued that party advertising during election campaigns should be subject to the same regulatory procedures and industry self-regulation that govern other advertising. He saw no way to ban advertising by advocacy groups during campaigns.

"It was as if someone had said, 'Let's put the rules in place in case we need them.' "

Another participant argued that such advertising must be constrained because the political parties face controls on advertising while interest groups do not. He noted that failure to restrain special-interest and advocacy groups would undermine the whole system. Co-ordination between a party and interest groups would allow a party to evade spending and advertising limits. It was alleged that such co-ordination took place in 1988 with respect to the free trade debate. Pierre Trudel argued that, just because advocacy advertisements can influence opinion and the vote, this is not a good reason to prohibit them. He noted that from a constitutional point of view, any limit on advertising by other than the political parties would have to be well thought out and form part of an integrated system of election regulation.

William Howard of the CRTC stated that other speakers had confused the right of expression with the right to be informed. Broadcast media are more regulated because not everyone can have access to the airwaves. He said that smaller parties have argued that the CRTC is an ineffective control because it cannot force changes before the fact, but only examines cases after the fact.

The panelists were asked whether restrictions on the access of pressure groups to the media could apply to provincial governments during federal elections and vice versa. Pierre Trudel said that it may be possible for the federal government to decide whether provincial governments can become interveners in federal elections.

One of the participants said that the Christian Heritage Party faces the difficulty of getting on the air because of the high cost of producing a television advertisement for use during its four minutes of allocated free time. In addition, he felt the party's news events receive little coverage.

One journalist acknowledged that the press may be considered a player in elections, but asserted that it was unlike any other because of its attempt to provide balanced coverage and to be accountable to its readers. This role should not attract regulation, he argued, adding that special election press councils would be dangerous.

The difficulty in distinguishing between small groups speaking out and powerful groups buying ads during elections was also raised by one participant.

LOCAL CAMPAIGNS

The fifth session examined local campaign communications, particularly their impact in rural and remote communities. Among the issues discussed were (1) the impact of spending limits, (2) problems of media market fit with constituency boundaries, (3) problems of access in remote areas, (4) the appropriate balance of local, regional and national campaign information, (5) alternative mechanisms for effective communications at the local level, and (6) media treatment of minor parties.

David Bell of York University argued that the Commission could have some impact on the level of democratic involvement in Canada by promoting more vibrant and meaningful local politics. In urban constituencies the media give scant attention to local issues during elections. Most coverage focuses on polling results, on national issues and on leadership politics. Large increases in constituency size (with 10 times more voters than 100 years ago) and the emergence of highly sophisticated national media have contributed to the declining importance of local campaigns in urban areas. In rural constituencies, the media, especially newspapers, report local issues in more detail, even though the quality of the coverage is often poor. Most national issues have important local implications, but the links are rarely made. Bell suggested workshops for local media, summer research internships to prepare background material on local issues, and more media access for local candidates.

Marcel Côté of SECOR Inc. listed three objectives of local election campaigns: (1) to get the candidate known in the constituency; (2) to get the candidate well positioned to win; and (3) to develop a style and method consistent with the local media environment. The achievement of these objectives depends on whether the candidate is an incumbent or a challenger, on campaign spending limits, and on the quality of the constituency organization. Pamphlets, billboards, canvassing and other direct forms of communication are available to local organizations.

"The management of a local campaign is shaped, in part, by the quality of the local media."

Côté argued that the management of a local campaign is shaped, in part, by the quality of the local media. While there is considerable variability in the competence of local media, he believes they try generally to be fair and balanced. He did not want the candidate selection process regulated. Local nomination races are not driven by money, he argued, but by organizational skills and capacities. Moreover, through internal reform, parties are addressing some of the contentious areas in the current selection process.

There was a lengthy discussion of the influence of local candidates and campaigns on voting decisions. The consensus was that the candidate's 'personal vote' accounts on average for about 7 or 8 per cent of the total vote.

Canadians in general, it was argued, want their local politicians to have a greater representational role in the policy process. Other participants agreed that local issues and local campaign strategies are more important in rural constituencies. The primary difference between rural and urban constituencies is the way information and ideas are communicated to voters.

One participant cautioned against simplistic interpretations on how voters make choices. The interplay between local and national issues and factors is difficult to document. It was said that local candidates do not know much about local issues. They take their policy cues from the national party. It is difficult to identify the dominant local issues in most constituency campaigns, and the media are not offering adequate and competent coverage of local issues and candidates.

Valerie Alia of the University of Western Ontario summarized her research on the role of the media in the local campaigns in the Yukon, the Northwest Territories and northern areas of the provinces. She argued that interdependency among remote northern communities makes politics personal, casual and small-scale, yet the nature of the circumpolar North also makes its politics global. In short, local and national dimensions of northern politics cannot be separated. Alia made several recommendations to remove barriers to electoral participation by Aboriginal people in the North, emphasizing the importance of recognizing the special needs of Aboriginal, northern and remote communities. The recommendations covered three crucial areas: (1) the need to amend regulations to permit new technologies to be used more widely to help overcome distance; (2) recognizing the special educational needs of voters, journalists and candidates in these areas; and (3) recognizing the special needs of these voters with respect to language and literacy. It was her view that the Aboriginal people in the territories and the northern regions of provinces should be fully involved in any changes to their communication and electoral environments.

Lorna Roth of Concordia University presented her research on the CBC Northern Service and the federal electoral process. She reviewed the problematic features of the CBC Northern radio and television services: (1) lack of access by all political candidates to free airtime; (2) limitations of CBC electoral coverage; (3) inadequate coverage of election issues in Aboriginal languages; (4) inconsistent radio coverage of northern issues; and (5) dissatisfaction with the CBC's policy of not allowing the Inuit Broadcasting Corporation to sell advertising time while using CBC's satellite channel.

Roth listed several recommendations designed to improve local access for all parties and candidates to northern media during election campaigns. In general, she said, the CBC Northern Service should be given a legislated special status and a mandate different from that of CBC's national service. She wanted the activities and coverage of the electoral process in the North by the CBC Northern Service tailored to meet the complex but divergent linguistic, cultural and geographic needs of the various Aboriginal peoples.

She underscored the fact that Aboriginal people in the North want more control over the design and production of paid political advertisements and more autonomy from the national parties in the management of local constituency contests.

It was noted that the broadcast time allocation issue in the North provides a useful reference point for assessing how broadcast time in general should be allocated. What is the appropriate trend? Should political advertising strategies be national in scope and controlled by the national parties, or should there be more opportunity for locally focused advertising? Finally, should these trends and strategies be regulated through the *Canada Elections Act* or the *Broadcasting Act*?

> "Aboriginal people in the North want more control over the design and production of paid political advertisements..."

Robert Hackett of Simon Fraser University reviewed the role of the local media in election campaigns, with special attention to the coverage of smaller parties. He said community weeklies were relatively fair in their coverage of local issues and candidates and were an important source of information for their readers. However, the quality of coverage was limited by a shortage of resources. The smaller parties receive about 5 per cent of the total coverage of elections and parties provided by the large media institutions. Community newspapers provide more extensive coverage. The Green Party, the Christian Heritage Party and the Confederation of Regions Party have had some success in getting media coverage of their policy platforms. He said representatives of the media argue that they provide serious and adequate coverage of emerging parties. Although local coverage of smaller parties may be more detailed, the quality is weak. Further, smaller parties are unable to make effective use of free airtime because they lack the financial and technical resources to produce credible presentations.

Hackett found that television – even though it is regulated with a mandate to provide balanced access for different points of view on matters of public concern – actually provides less coverage of smaller parties than does the daily press. As well, every representative of a smaller party expressed dissatisfaction with the current allocation of free broadcast time. They made the point that "free time is not as free as it appears, because there are production costs associated with producing ads for free time."

One media representative commented that his paper had offered equal space to all candidates in a 1988 federal general election supplement. A member of the Christian Heritage Party said his experience suggests the media are biased in their coverage of emerging parties. It was said that the smaller parties want fair treatment, but free airtime is made available to smaller parties only in non-prime periods, when the viewing audience is small.

A representative of the Reform Party said smaller parties are not treated fairly by the media and claimed that the parties do not want special treatment, just objective, balanced coverage. "I think the Commission should be looking at equal treatment for smaller parties. And that is saying that every party has an equal right to purchase broadcast time. No party has a special claim to power, or a special right to have their message heard by the Canadian public."

"No party has a special claim to power, or a special right to have their message heard by the Canadian public."

A media representative argued that it takes time for new and growing parties to establish adequate public profiles. The key to greater media coverage is the election of members to Parliament. "If it wants to be recognized and covered as though it is a national party rather than a regional party, then it needs to elect some members in more than one region."

NEW APPROACHES TO CAMPAIGN COMMUNICATION

The sixth session focused on the increasing rate of change in communication technologies and practices. Among the issues discussed were trends in media use, competing views on the responsibility of the state to ensure that voters are adequately informed, new communication systems that might improve voter information and participation, and the potential of information services delivered through cable television systems.

Robert MacDermid of York University indicated that according to his research, a significant number of Canadians pay little attention to media coverage of politics and that those paying more attention tend to be older and male. Educational level is also an important factor determining newspaper readership. He felt that "our concern really should be with how to broaden communication and how to [reach] the vast majority of people who pay no attention to politics and the messages of the media whatsoever." MacDermid suggested that more diverse channels of campaign communication may be needed to encourage participation.

David Hogarth of Concordia University suggested that Newsworld will not provide any real alternative to the kind of election coverage Canadians receive on regular broadcast channels. He recommended that Newsworld provide a service that is distinct from that of the CBC, particularly in its regional election coverage, and that it broaden access to include smaller parties and interests.

Peter Desbarats of the University of Western Ontario noted that cable television still has flexibility to expand, unlike mainstream media. He wondered why the United States, with the world's most developed system of political communication, is facing a decline in voter participation. Their electoral campaigns are making some use of cable television since it offers the impact of television, at less cost, and the targeting advantage of direct mail. Desbarats advocated regulations governing the use of cable television to ensure access to the widest possible range of political candidates and opinions. Otherwise, "to open up our cable system to paid political advertising would simply hurry along the process of making it prone to the same problems that mainstream television has when it comes to election campaigns." He advocated free time on community channels and an accountability mechanism for cable.

Lyndsay Green reported that most significant efforts to increase the level of partisan information available to voters have been carried out mainly by intermediaries, rather than by the state. She suggested that programs for improving voter information should be publicly funded and give priority to meeting the needs of those with the least access to information, because participation in the democratic process should not be based on ability to pay.

Catherine Murray from Decima Research contended that it is wrong to claim that Canadians pay little attention to the news when there is growing attention to broadly defined news programs, including entertainment. Referring to the previous presentation, she wondered whether public funding of information transmission would merely reinforce informational disparities and reach only the politically converted and informed. While seeing the potential of the community channels, Murray advocated more public notice of program time and program availability. In addition, recommendations should be made to the cable associations to speed up their process of developing new standards of quality and fairness with respect to representing community groups; all too often, Murray argued, the community channel is becoming a forum for local organized interests. One participant commented that the interactive possibilities of cable television could lead to instant polls, which might be even more troublesome than exit polls.

Robert MacDermid responded to a question on voter participation, noting that participation is related to efficacy. "People will participate so long as they feel they can have an effect on politics." While people may well continue to participate, he said, many choose to participate outside political parties because they do not believe that political parties are able to represent their interests. He provided the example of environmental groups, many of which have chosen to work the political system from outside political parties.

"People will participate so long as they feel they can have an effect on politics."

ISSUES AND LESSONS

The final session featured summaries of the symposium proceedings. John Harvard, Member of Parliament for Winnipeg St. James, began by asking the Commission to keep the interests of voters foremost in their minds during the process of arriving at recommendations. "Do not be stampeded by the political parties, do not be stampeded by the politicians, do not be stampeded by the media," he said. Pointing to the political alienation and low turnout in the United States, Harvard emphasized the importance of getting voters involved in the electoral process. He suggested that the Parliamentary Channel and CBC Newsworld present exciting opportunities to provide information about elections. As a politician, he said, he wanted to be able to express himself and to present his message – whether on his own behalf or on behalf of his political party – with the least possible expense. "The other thing I want as a politician is fairness." He would also like to see more local coverage. Finally, Harvard recommended barring interest group advertising during election campaigns and ensuring that negative advertising does not make campaigns "orgies of character assassination."

Rather than drawing conclusions from the symposium's many sessions, Lynn McDonald, a former Member of Parliament, chose instead to remind participants of the main themes of each. The responses to many issues, such as the proposal for a mandatory leaders debate, "were very predictable by sector.... Nobody broke ranks with the sector they came from." Among other points, McDonald noted that most participants favoured some form of self-regulation among pollsters and journalists, acknowledging that polls do affect voting behaviour. She stated that self-regulation for polling appears to be non-existent at present. "Nobody who is actually in the business suggested any way that they might do their job better or control their colleagues, or encourage or require them to do a better job." She noted that smaller parties want more and better coverage of their activities, while journalists felt the smaller parties get what they deserve. In addition, McDonald added her support to those favouring regulation of the nomination process and strengthening of the spending limits and called for greater gender parity at events such as this symposium.

Jodi White agreed with other participants that the "heavy air of regulation" was hanging over the symposium. In her view, there are areas where regulation is needed. "But I think we must also be sure it is not regulation for regulation's sake. There are areas that should be left alone." She said that Canada's low incumbency rate and high voter turnout gave her good reason to be optimistic about the electoral process in this country. She argued that although parties are public institutions, they are in competition with one another and must be given some latitude for privacy. Further, she expressed concern that parties not be saddled with spending limits that do not take into account the cost of new technologies or with equity provisions that do not acknowledge the central role of the major parties in maintaining the Canadian political system.

White also mentioned that transparency will be "a key issue in ensuring the trust of the Canadian people in the system that is set up." Along with transparency, however, the phrase 'a level playing field' appeared. "I think that should not be confused with the lowest common denominator.... We must not create a system that would penalize the major parties.... We must aim to have a House of Commons that is workable." She stated that the election law ought to be made as simple and clear as possible, and that it ought to come down on one side or the other on the issue of advertising by interest groups.

A discussion followed on the idea of allowing parties to buy unlimited amounts of broadcast advertising; participants offered opinions on both sides of the issue. One participant cautioned that Canada must mediate between democracy, which demands equality, and the free market, which demands that money and power be left to find their own equilibrium. Another asserted that the Commission's task was one of fine-tuning an essentially sound system. He said the Commission should look for balance between regulation and deregulation in addressing the three most important issues in the area of media and elections: interest group advertising, leaders debates, and polling practices. He went on to say that the Commission's role is more to educate the public about certain dangers in the process than to regulate it.

Commissioner Gabor observed that all participants – journalists, pollsters and party officials – tended to protest any regulation of their profession but recommend regulation of the others. He wondered how the participants could be persuaded to "lower the veil of self-interest" and appealed for understanding among the participants.

8

SYMPOSIUM ON
POLITICAL ETHICS

Hull, Quebec
April 11–12, 1991

T HE SYMPOSIUM WAS organized around six sessions:

- What Is Meant by Fairness and Equity?
- Money and Influence in the Political System
- Codes of Ethics for Political Parties
- Campaign Advertising: The Ethics of Political Marketing
- Problem Areas in Campaign Communication
- Ethics and Elections: Observations and Recommendations

The Commission organized this symposium to give the Commission, its staff, academic researchers, representatives from Canada's political parties, labour and business organizations an opportunity to examine the research findings on political and media ethics. The Commission's research on ethics was designed to assess standards of political behaviour and to identify the directions, values and principles that characterize the highest standards of ethical conduct. The goal was to develop an understanding of ethical concerns and political practices; fairness and equity, the overarching principles of the Canadian electoral system; and the benefits of self-administered codes of ethics. The six sessions began with panel presentations led by moderators, followed by discussion from the floor.

FAIRNESS AND EQUITY

In the first session, on the implications of evolution in the meaning of fairness and equity for the regulation of elections, Kathy Brock of the University of Manitoba argued that the *Canadian Charter of Rights and Freedoms* has affected Canadians' ethical perceptions significantly and contributed to a new discourse on rights. It introduced fairness, equity, openness and representativeness as public policy criteria. Under the Charter, equality rights reinforce democratic rights. Although parties are technically exempt from the Charter as private associations, their privileged place in Canadian politics makes them subject to scrutiny.

Public bodies and political parties are mechanisms to supplement and correct the inequities that result from market relations, suggested Jane Jenson of Carleton University. Equal access to the electoral system for voters and candidates is a major equity issue today, but the concept of equity has changed over time. Between 1919 and 1939, the concept of equity was based on regional identity; since 1945, equity for individuals and concern about the influence of financial resources on access to the political system have become more important. The specific concerns of women and minorities have not been considered in this development, however. Jenson downplayed the effect of the Charter, arguing that social change has led to a conception of equity based on social groups such as women, Aboriginal people and persons with disabilities. Concern for equal representation now takes into account many discriminatory barriers other than poverty. Political parties are expected to accept this new interpretation of equity and modify their activities to reflect it.

> "Concern for equal representation now takes into account many discriminatory barriers other than poverty."

Alan Cairns of the University of British Columbia agreed that the Charter can be overemphasized but warned against discounting its impact. He suggested that recent court challenges to disparities in constituency size indicate that the Charter is leading to a mathematical concept of equality that places the emphasis on individuals, rather than territorial communities. The Charter has also given constitutional identity to interest groups attached to certain Charter clauses that feel entitled to participate in changing the Charter. The declining significance of territorial representation conflicts with executive federalism, which gives regional concerns priority over individual equity. For example, the ethnic origin and sex of Supreme Court justices is now as significant as their geographical origin. The idea that "you have to be one to know one to represent one" is growing in importance and focuses more attention on the composition of representative bodies.

In the discussion that followed, participants debated whether the adoption of proportional representation would lead to a broader representative mix in the House of Commons. Some argued that proportional representation, or some variant of it, would bring fairer and more equitable representation than the first-past-the-post system. Others suggested that the Senate could provide more effective representation for marginalized groups and regions. The German model, which consists of proportional and first-past-the-post representation combined in a single chamber, was proposed as an alternative.

Arguments were put forward that such changes do not necessarily ensure equity; increased representation of women in European legislatures was not produced by proportional representation but by political parties that put women on their electoral lists. Proportional representation would also weaken the attachment of Members of Parliament to their ridings, which is particularly strong for those representing other than large metropolitan areas. Further, many people would resent giving parties control over candidate selection through party lists.

Although consensus was not reached on the strengths and weaknesses of the proportional representation and single-member plurality systems, there was agreement that some measures are needed to ensure better representation of marginalized groups, which in turn would make policy makers more sensitive to the experiences of these groups. The process should not be regulated, but specific affirmative action was felt to be worthy of consideration. Some participants argued that fairness and equity are best guaranteed by competition, not regulation. Competition compels parties to be fair and equitable, so regulation based on "the values of the day" is not necessary. New groups claiming to be more representative of a group or area can contest elections.

"... fairness and equity are best guaranteed by competition, not regulation."

Others contended, however, that competition does not always produce fairness because it takes considerable resources to be an effective participant. For example, nomination and election of candidates from a variety of socio-economic backgrounds are hampered in part by the highly decentralized nature of political parties. Central party organizations have limited influence over the choices constituency associations make.

MONEY AND INFLUENCE

In the second session, on money and influence in the political system, participants focused on whether direct financial involvement by corporations and unions in political parties and elections undermines belief in full and meaningful public participation in candidate selection and representative government.

Speaking on undue influence, Ian Greene of York University stated that since 1981, more than 130 Canadian newspaper stories have tackled this subject. The largest group of print stories focused on the relationship between donations and favours; the second largest group concerned breaches of rules. Greene argued that the public is increasingly concerned about these issues because concern for social equality is growing: the idea of special privilege is repugnant to Canadians. He suggested that a $3000 limit on contributions from any source would be a good compromise.

Participants were asked by Robert Parker of the Royal Bank of Canada to consider what values are served by corporate or union involvement in the political process. He suggested that business tries to affect the course of public policy because public policy affects it, not because business is partisan. While not suggesting business interests are identical to the national interest, he argued that their proposals are as legitimate and valuable as those of the political parties or other special-interest groups.

On the question of corporate and union contributions he noted that political funding, in itself, ought to be a positive factor in the democratic process. The current system of corporate and union political fundraising by contrast seems to support the system without advancing it. He advocated banning corporate contributions on the basis that if our political system needs anything at the moment, it is the hearts and minds of Canadians.

Gordon Wilson of the Ontario Federation of Labour argued that there is a place for corporations and unions in the political process, provided there are proper limitations. He emphasized that, for the most part, labour gets involved within the party system rather than outside it. Full financial disclosure, he argued, would allow the public to determine the motives and objectives of contributors.

Participants generally agreed that timely disclosure is critical to ensuring public confidence in the electoral process. Requiring parties to submit quarterly reports of political contributions would give the public useful information. The Commission was advised to think seriously before recommending limits on the source of contributions, however, because the law cannot anticipate changes in normative assumptions about ethical behaviour.

On the question of how money affects politics and who contributes money to campaigns and parties, participants concluded that, depending on policy objectives, financing can be regulated by limiting either contributions or expenditures. Limiting contributions aims at controlling undue influence, whereas limits on expenditures aim at ensuring fairness. Survey data suggest that 80 per cent of Canadians favour limiting expenditures; they consider fairness the most important value. About 50 per cent of Canadians favour banning union contributions, but they are somewhat more accepting of the legitimacy of corporate contributions. Participants were reminded that when all corporations are considered alike, inadequate policy prescriptions result, because most contributions come from smaller enterprises. The validity of many arguments for allowing only individual contributions was questioned; for example, if contributions are limited enough to eliminate the risk of undue influence, why would a corporate contribution buy influence and not an individual contribution of the same amount?

CODES OF ETHICS

The next session addressed the benefits of codes of ethics for political parties and what concerns such codes should address. The efficacy of self-enforcement of codes by parties and media scrutiny of codes were also discussed. Moderator Brian Crowley of Dalhousie University opened the session by asking David Mac Donald the following question: why should the idea of party codes of ethics be discussed?

Mac Donald replied that parties are quasi-public – rather than totally private – institutions, because they receive public funds and because they are uniquely suited to integrate competing interests, thus performing a vital public function. Increasingly, Canadians ascribe public characteristics to parties. He argued that the current cynicism about parties and other political institutions is exacerbated when the public perceives a discrepancy between what parties do and what they should do. A code of ethics, he said, would not only help parties change unethical behaviour, but would also signal a commitment to change that would be important in rebuilding public confidence.

Indicating he had been sceptical about the utility of codes of ethics for political parties at first, Michael Atkinson of McMaster University said he had begun to rethink his position. His initial concerns about the content of a code have been replaced by apprehension about getting parties to accept the idea of a code. No code of ethics can succeed, he said, unless the party leadership and membership consider the code to be their own. He emphasized that parties need not share a uniform code; indeed, he suggested parties formulate their own, perhaps competing to develop the best code.

There is no precedent for a comprehensive national code for political parties, pointed out William Chandler, also of McMaster, and the unfamiliar nature of the code would make it difficult to enforce. If a code of ethics is to be successful, he said, parties must accept it voluntarily. He suggested an all-party consultative process to decide its content and meaning. A code of ethics could also produce disputes over enforcement; an ombudsman might therefore be necessary. David Mac Donald pointed out the fundamental conflict between a reflective, value-oriented code of ethics and the dynamic, results-oriented practice of politics. He suggested that politicians would be unlikely to set a high priority on obeying a code of ethics if it meant losing political advantage during election campaigns.

Ian Greene of York University offered three reasons why private organizations have codes of ethics: to increase public credibility, to resolve recurring ethical problems and to avoid government regulation. He noted that they share these goals with political parties. He asserted that parties would benefit from having separate codes because they foster grassroots concern with ethical issues; on the other hand, a party with a strict code of ethics could be outmanoeuvred by a less scrupulous party.

> "No code of ethics can succeed unless the party leadership and membership consider the code to be their own."

To address declining public confidence in political institutions, alternative suggestions to a code of ethics included maintaining the status quo and regulating party activity through some kind of comprehensive law. Some party representatives were sceptical of the code of ethics solution, suggesting that it would be merely cosmetic and would not change their behaviour. They argued that a code could become a source of internal party conflict if party members transgressed. In particular, most party representatives questioned the effectiveness and credibility of a single code covering all parties. They suggested that such an approach would deny the parties' distinct internal political cultures, each party being dedicated to a unique set of ideas and values.

Participants were reminded that Commission research shows that Canadians display a high level of cynicism toward political parties. The Commission needed to develop a flexible instrument that allows parties to solve their ethical problems in ways that recognize their ideological distinctiveness. It was noted that leaders of other complex, diverse organizations have used codes of ethics to instil a sense of appropriate behaviour in their members. Parties could also achieve this by adopting their own codes of ethics.

THE ETHICS OF POLITICAL MARKETING

The fourth session, on campaign advertising, centred on the ethical limits of political advertising content and the fairness of current regulations that allocate advertising time for parties during election campaigns and limit the advertising period. Moderator Christopher Dornan of Carleton University began the session by presenting a videotape of a CBC *Journal* documentary on the rise of negative advertising in U.S. election campaigns and the prospect that such advertising will gain popularity in Canada. The documentary showed that after many years of relative quiet, advertising attacking the policy, record or character of a candidate and paid for by another – or by an advocacy group – is now used heavily in American political campaigns. Similar advertising appeared in the last Ontario provincial election. The documentary argued that once political consultants have introduced this aggressive type of advertising into a campaign, it is so effective that all candidates feel forced to respond in kind or risk defeat.

Dornan then asked Walter Soderlund of the University of Windsor whether this sort of advertising is likely to spread in Canada. Soderlund believes it will, but its importance will be comparatively limited. He said the approach works in the U.S. system because most elections are two-way races based on issues or candidates' personalities; Canada's multi-party system and the importance of party in determining voting behaviour diminish the effect of such advertising. He conceded, though, that negative information is more easily processed, making negative advertising a high-impact campaign tactic.

The ethical issues raised by negative advertising were addressed by Stephen Kline of Simon Fraser University. These issues range from impairment of the consumer's capacity for rational choice to creation of unfair advantages for candidates supported by outside interest groups.

Dornan asked participants whether negative advertising presents a problem. One panelist suggested that parties tend not to adopt new negative advertising techniques, but are often forced to because of negative advertising by interest groups. Several participants commented that many advertisements are designed to elicit an emotional response. Some argued that the visceral effect achieved by negative ads raises questions of manipulation; others argued that when an ad elicits such a response, it means that it points to a real concern.

Although party representatives showed limited concern about negative advertising per se, they did express dismay over misleading advertising. Definitions of 'unethical' advertising clearly varied between parties, but participants generally agreed that truth is essential in advertising. Many participants recognized attacks on policy positions and leadership capability as legitimate and central to effective campaigning.

It was noted that most American campaign trends migrate to Canada very quickly. Negative advertising has worked well for national parties and individual candidates in the United States, and it could work well in Canada. Americans' high level of cynicism about politics has encouraged negative ads, and similar conditions now prevail in Canada.

Some participants argued for strengthening existing regulatory bodies and increasing public education about political advertising. Others argued that transparency is the ingredient missing from modern advertising campaigns; people ought to be reminded more forcefully about who pays for the ads. Still others cautioned against limiting the parameters of debate too severely. Some said that ethical advertising cannot be legislated but will have to be guaranteed by the parties themselves.

CAMPAIGN COMMUNICATION

In the session on problems in campaign communication participants questioned the relationship between the objectives and conduct of news gathering and dynamic campaigning on one hand, and ethical expectations of the political process on the other.

William Gilsdorf of Concordia University suggested that there are three main concerns regarding campaign communication. First, new technology can be abused, especially to breach poll confidentiality. Second, marginal voters tend to receive more of their campaign information from television, a medium that is not information-driven. Third, campaign coverage is oriented to novelty, events and mistakes, rather than to substantive information and innovation.

Media treatment of ethno-cultural communities and people with disabilities during the 1988 federal election was the focus of comments by Eileen Saunders of Carleton University. Typically, the media did not give these groups a positive image as political actors. The information offered on ethnic minorities centred on recruitment and nomination of ethnic candidates and the parties' pursuit of the ethnic vote. Coverage tended to imply that the parties were "under attack by a third force." The main concerns of both groups did not figure prominently in media coverage, and they had little opportunity to use the media to advance their concerns.

"The media confer legitimacy on individuals, parties and groups by imposing their own 'ruthless definition' of news coverage."

CBC National News Editor Elly Alboim stated that he could not speak for all journalists or for the CBC, but would describe how the media cover election campaigns and how the parties want to be covered. He contended that political parties do not share the democratic need for an informed choice because they want unfettered communication of their agendas. The media resist this pressure and respond to the pressure of external competition, which does not change during elections.

Journalists have to edit and homogenize their reports in a way that can be destructive to political journalism. Because both media and parties favour packaged information, they collude to produce campaigns that the media can understand and afford to cover. The media confer legitimacy on individuals, parties and groups by imposing their own "ruthless definition" of news coverage. During elections, this definition often has little to do with others' definition of elections because the media are not committed to the election as a process and do not accept that elections create different constraints on reporting.

Campaign coverage offers the public what it wants and expects, including its cynicism about the process. This is because media values are not driven by public education, but by the audience's wants and needs. Alboim suggested that the main ethical problem is that the media should be more willing to reveal that their purpose in election coverage is not what people think it is.

"Voters want unmeditated information, so they value leaders debates on television."

The panel were asked whether unethical political marketing is a slippery slope or merely a different strategy. If it is the latter, extensive regulation may not be required. Once interest group advertising is dealt with, limits on party expenditures should eliminate many marketing abuses. One panelist said we still do not know how direct mail will affect media advertising and the fragmentation of television markets. Another participant stated that, like television, direct mail can elicit strong political responses.

Participants were reminded that the objective of a critical examination of media operations in the electoral process was not to see what benefits might accrue to the media, but to see what changes can be made to benefit voters. Voters want unmediated information, so they value leaders debates on television. Media activities should reflect Canadians' values and expectations in the information they seek and the ways they collect it.

ETHICS AND ELECTIONS

The last session identified key issues raised earlier and examined possible reforms. Hugh Segal of the Progressive Conservative Party expressed concern about regulatory and ethical "overreach", arguing that fairness and equity cannot be legislated. A better approach, he suggested, would be to introduce more transparent and timely disclosure for nominations, groups, leadership campaigns and financial loans to parties. The *Criminal Code* already deals with influence peddling, but more effort could be spent on securing convictions. Segal suggested that negative advertising is a normal marketing technique that thrives on short advertising periods. He also argued that spending limits at the constituency level favour incumbents at the cost of new participants and that making parties beholden to the state through elaborate public funding schemes is a mistake.

David Gotthilf of Viewpoints Research said Canada is now engaged in a very healthy discussion of fundamental issues. He suggested that parties need a mechanism that encourages them to discuss issues. On the subject of campaign advertising, he argued that the media produce some good coverage. He also suggested that parties should get serious about self-regulation or they will pay a heavy price in declining public confidence and support. He suggested that the parties should get together to establish a "Geneva Convention" for campaigns.

The goal of electoral reform is a healthy democracy, stated Liberal Party president Donald Johnston, and to achieve this we need strong, well-financed political parties and a level playing field. He argued that too few people take advantage of the generous tax credit, that the public does not see corporate contributions as payment for special favours, and he stated that access to power is the centre of that issue. Codes of ethics would be honoured only in the breach, he suggested, adding that dishonest advertising, not negative advertising, is the problem in campaign publicity.

It was suggested that party activists do not know how negatively the public reacts to political parties' ethics. In response to Johnston's comments about the tax credit, a participant suggested that people are unwilling to contribute to parties they consider corrupt. If parties adopted codes of ethics, the public might view them more positively and feel more comfortable about contributing.

The discussion then turned to the usefulness of codes of ethics. Several participants suggested that although there are difficulties in enforcing them, codes can help clarify right and wrong and encourage parties to find the higher ground. One participant suggested that the discussion of ethics focused too narrowly on party competition and that the discussion should be expanded. Donald Johnston responded that too many people criticize parties unfairly and that people should get involved in the parties if they believe they can improve the system.

9

SYMPOSIUM ON ELECTION AND PARTY FINANCE

Ottawa, Ontario
April 18–19, 1991

T HE SYMPOSIUM WAS divided into five sessions:

- Developments in Election and Party Financing
- Interest Groups' Election Activities
- Options for Reform: Enhancing Openness and Participation
- Options for Reform: Regulating Political Parties' Spending and Finance
- Symposium Review

The symposium on election and party finance was the last of a series bringing together the Commission and its staff with journalists, academics, politicians and party representatives. It was an opportunity for the Commission to share preliminary research findings and to discuss options for reform in political finance.

ELECTION AND PARTY FINANCING

The first session dealt with developments in election and party financing. William Stanbury of the University of British Columbia outlined important changes in political fund raising and spending since the adoption of the 1974 *Election Expenses Act*. Before 1974, 90 per cent of the revenues of the Progressive Conservative and Liberal parties came from the corporate sector. The New Democratic Party was dependent on union contributions and small donations from individuals. Since 1974, all parties have come to rely much more on donations from individuals.

Large increases in party revenues and spending have also resulted. Between 1985 and 1989, the Progressive Conservatives had revenues of $92.9 million, the Liberals $54.5 million and the New Democratic Party $63.9 million. In each year since 1977, spending by the Progressive Conservative Party has exceeded that of the other two parties combined.

The most significant development in fund raising since 1974 has been the use of direct mail. The Progressive Conservatives began to use direct mail not long after the 1974 reforms and have since relied on it to raise a significant portion of party revenues. The Liberals have not found direct mail as lucrative, while the New Democratic Party has been reasonably successful in its use of direct mail since 1983.

Stanbury cautioned that the effectiveness of fund raising by direct mail may be compromised if 'donor fatigue' develops and contributors begin to resist the many petitions for money they receive from parties. At present, only a small portion of Canadians (3 per cent in a peak year) make political donations. If the apex of individual contributions has been reached, it may be necessary to adjust the tax credit scale to reflect its lag behind inflation.

———

"The most significant development in fund raising since 1974 has been the use of direct mail."

———

These changes in patterns of individual giving have been accompanied by changes in the pattern of business contributions to parties. The parties are less dependent on the top 500 corporations than previously. The parties – especially the Progressive Conservatives – have received more money from a large number of small to medium size companies. Both the Liberals and the Progressive Conservatives make extensive use of fund-raising dinners and donor clubs. The New Democratic Party does not use either of these instruments, but it receives many donations that exceed $1000.

Since 1974, election spending by all three major parties has moved closer to statutory limits. Election spending by the New Democratic Party grew most rapidly in this period. Broadcast advertising is the single greatest expense for the three largest parties. Other major expenditures include polling and research, election training programs, fund-raising costs, and policy development. Stanbury argued that the definition of election expenses should cover election-related spending that is now exempt.

———

"Since constituency associations are not registered entities and have no legal standing, there is no public financial accountability as to how they raise and spend money."

———

Constituency associations, he said, are the "black hole of party finance" in Canada. After the 1988 federal general election, constituency associations had a surplus of $9.6 million, most of which came from the reimbursement candidates received. Since constituency associations are not registered entities and have no legal standing, there is no public financial accountability as to how they raise and spend money.

Herbert Alexander of the University of Southern California noted that political scandals frequently lead to election finance reform. In 1974, both the United States and Canada enacted major party finance legislation. U.S. legislation, enacted in the aftermath of Watergate, reflected the candidate-centred culture of electoral competition, while the Canadian reform package recognized parties as integral participants in the electoral process.

Alexander assessed the consequences of the 1974 party finance laws in the United States. First, limits on the size of contributions mean politicians can no longer secure funds from a small number of sources: they have had to expand their search for contributions. After 1974, the pattern of contributions shifted "from big givers to big solicitors." Second, contribution limits have accelerated the rise and proliferation of Political Action Committees. Third, politicians began using fund-raising techniques such as special breakfasts to reach a large number of individual donors.

In the United States, Alexander said, government can constitutionally impose spending limits only if they are tied to public funding. No spending limits exist for congressional and senatorial races. The cumulative effect of these different regimes is a fragmented electoral regulatory framework. Although there is public pressure to contain the role of money and Political Action Committees in American politics, the Senate and the House of Representatives have been unable to agree on legislation.

In assessing expenditure limits for presidential elections Alexander noted that presidential candidates have several ways to spend money outside the limits. In addition to public funding, candidates can benefit from 'soft' money, independent expenditures, parallel campaigns by unions, and expenditures by the national parties. The number of individuals participating in the tax check-off has declined (and is now at 20 per cent of American taxpayers), and its value has not been adjusted for inflation. Consequently, the public money available may not be enough to cover the costs of the 1992 presidential campaign. Alexander concludes that disclosure has been the most effective policy instrument. The financial information compiled by the Federal Election Commission is well organized and widely used.

David Johnson of McMaster University reviewed the different approaches to election and party finance law in the provinces. New Brunswick, Ontario, the Northwest Territories and Quebec have registration, require disclosure, provide tax credits and other subsidies, and have expenditure and contribution limits. Proposed legislation in Newfoundland would place it in this category; at present, it has disclosure requirements only. Manitoba, Nova Scotia, Prince Edward Island and Saskatchewan oblige parties to register and disclose, provide access to tax credits and/or other public funding, and have expenditure limits. Alberta requires registration and disclosure, gives parties and candidates access to tax credits, and has contribution limits. British Columbia and the Yukon also have tax credits.

Johnson reviewed the factors contributing to the rise of the different systems of party finance law. First, there is partisan politics: the incumbent government will design party finance laws to advance its electoral interest. Second, parties seek to gain administrative or organizational advantages. Third, party finance laws are frequently adopted in response to political scandal. In this regard, public and media opinion about the state of political ethics may prompt governments to introduce reform packages. Fourth, there is a demonstration effect: legislation adopted by the federal government or by another province may spark a province to enact similar legislation.

Participants debated the effectiveness of expenditure limits as the primary instrument for limiting the role of money in elections. It was suggested that the value of expenditure limits depends on how election expenses are defined and on how numerous and intricate the regulations are. Federally, the presence of an "other expenses" category allows candidates to spend outside the spending limits for certain kinds of expenses.

Two general approaches to expenditure limits were discussed. The first approach calls for a comprehensive definition of election expenses. Such an approach, it was submitted, would be more straightforward and would enhance public confidence in the electoral process. To be credible, expenditure limits would have to reflect the real cost of electoral competition. Severe penalties would have to be in place to deter violations, although it was suggested the adjudication process should be civil, not criminal. The potential pitfalls of a comprehensive definition of election expenses were highlighted. No precise criteria exist to determine what activity or expenditure could be credibly classified as an election expense. However, those who defended this approach noted that it would ensure that all significant electoral activities were regulated.

> "To be credible, expenditure limits would have to reflect the real cost of electoral competition."

The alternative approach to expenditure limits would limit spending on those activities primarily responsible for pushing up election expenses. Media advertising would be the prime candidate for such limits; secondary activities such as travel and administrative costs would not be subject to limits. One participant suggested such limits would not be workable. Participants agreed that either approach to expenditure limits would have to be accompanied by comprehensive disclosure requirements.

The discussion shifted to appropriate levels and formulas for the public funding of parties. Some participants criticized the existing system of reimbursements in Canada, which rewards parties and candidates for spending money during elections, favours existing players and creates barriers to new ones. Some suggested that parties and candidates should receive public funding based on the share of votes received, using either national or regional results.

The potential value of a tax check-off system for Canada was discussed. Although the use of the tax check-off is declining in the United States, the percentage of American taxpayers using the system far exceeds the percentage of Canadian taxpayers claiming political tax credits. The role of money in American politics has altered popular perceptions of the values that dominate political life. Politicians are seen as selling out to the highest bidder, and fewer individuals are joining parties or volunteering as fundraisers.

"... negative perceptions are reinforced by relentless media scrutiny of the way campaigns are funded."

One intervener said negative perceptions are reinforced by relentless media scrutiny of the way campaigns are funded. Adroit reform of election and party finance laws could be a first step in recasting the popular image of politics and politicians. Overall, participants emphasized the importance of ensuring that party finance regulations and public funding provisions are fair but realistic.

INTEREST GROUPS AND ELECTIONS

The second session dealt with the election activities of interest groups. Janet Hiebert of the Commission said that the spending by interest groups in the 1988 election was estimated to have exceeded $4.7 million – 40 cents for every advertising dollar spent during the election by the three major parties combined. Seventy-six per cent of this spending was to promote free trade, while 14 per cent of the total was to oppose it.

Hiebert pointed out that the *Canadian Charter of Rights and Freedoms* must be considered in any effort to regulate the role of interest groups in federal elections. The 1983 prohibitions on independent advertising were struck down as contrary to the Charter in the 1984 National Citizens' Coalition case. These prohibitions allowed interest groups to advertise on issues but not to target candidates or parties. The Supreme Court of Canada would have to be satisfied that any new regulation impairs freedom of expression as little as possible. Some submissions to the Commission suggested that interest groups should be subject to the same kinds of spending limits and other regulations as candidates and parties. In Hiebert's view, however, this would not address the fundamentally different nature of parties and interest groups and the capacity of interest groups to multiply into new organizations, each with the ability to spend up to any limit set.

A commonly suggested solution is to return to the intent of the 1983 legislation. But experience in Canada and other jurisdictions has demonstrated how difficult it is to establish a meaningful distinction between issue and partisan advertising. Hiebert suggested that the best alternative would be to allow a modest amount of spending by interest groups.

Brian Tanguay of Wilfrid Laurier University presented research on the activities of 89 interest groups, in 12 ridings in four provinces. Generally, these groups were not involved in political activity. At the last election, only 5 per cent of them endorsed or targeted candidates, and about 20 per cent undertook an activity such as publishing a newsletter on election issues. Labour and anti-abortion groups were the most active. Groups that received government funding, particularly those with a charitable status, tended to remain non-partisan. Groups with limited resources contacted their Members of Parliament more frequently and used unconventional media and political strategies. Paradoxically, the most dissatisfied groups, and those with the most limited resources, tended to be most in favour of unrestricted spending by interest groups.

According to Richard Johnston of the University of British Columbia, interest group advertising had a significant bearing on the 1988 federal election result. The timing of advertisements was particularly important. Most advertisements in favour of free trade began the week after the leaders debate, which had been followed by a drop in the voting intentions in favour of the Progressive Conservatives in the opinion polls. The recovery of the government's popularity was remarkably sudden and occurred as interest group advertising began to increase. Johnston estimated these advertisements were worth four or five percentage points – and perhaps as much as seven points – in the vote difference between the Progressive Conservatives and the Liberals.

Participants discussed whether the scale of intervention by interest groups seen in 1988 was unique or the beginning of a trend. According to one intervener, interest groups became involved in the 1990 Ontario provincial election because they had seen how effective such activity was during the federal election. Another participant pointed out that Canada still does not have the same magnitude of interest group involvement as the United States.

"... interest groups perform the healthy role of urging politicians and the public to deal with certain issues."

One participant suggested that interest group advertising during the 1988 election pertaining to issues would have been legal because of the good faith defence in the 1974 legislation. But that defence would not have allowed the advertisements opposing a party, which came mostly from those opposing free trade. Another participant indicated that in the United States the only organizations barred from making independent expenditures are political parties, because they are assumed incapable of doing so without co-operating with the candidates.

Some pointed to Quebec's ban on interest group advertising as a model; however, it was suggested there is some doubt whether the ban would survive a Charter challenge. Several interveners said that interest groups perform the healthy role of urging politicians and the public to deal with certain issues. Another participant said that there is ample opportunity for these groups to intervene outside election periods but that money can skew the fairness of electoral contests. Participants generally agreed that unfettered interest group advertising during elections would put political parties at an unfair disadvantage. However, there was also general concern that free speech not be unduly diminished. Participants differed on the relative importance of each, however.

> "... unfettered interest group advertising during elections would put political parties at an unfair disadvantage."

ENHANCING OPENNESS AND PARTICIPATION

In session three, options for reform to enhance openness and participation were considered. Michael Pinto-Duschinsky of Brunel College, England, explained that the German party foundations are charged with party building, research and public education. They hold political education courses; sponsor about 3500 scholarships at any given time; annually carry out $250 million in foreign political aid operations in more than 100 countries; and conduct long-term research. The foundations cost about $400 million per year to operate and receive 97 per cent of their funds from the German government.

The foundations have been effective in promoting democracy and German national interests in their international operations. Domestically they have been useful in building national unity in what was post-war West Germany. Reviews are mixed on the utility of the foundations' political education function. Pinto-Duschinsky criticized the foundations for not being member-based, transparent or accountable. He added that heavy public funding for both foundations and political parties has made German parties almost indistinguishable from the state.

In contrast, Jane Jenson of Carleton University suggested there are lessons to be learned from Western Europe. She said the European parties in the 1970s experienced some of the problems that Canadian parties face today in sustaining their representational capacity. In Europe, however, these problems diminished during the 1980s.

Looking at Canada, Jenson noted that the 1983 changes to the provisions for reimbursing parties a portion of their election expenditures mean public funding for parties depends on ability to spend; this provision sends a message that new parties are not welcome. The present public funding regime concentrates most funding on the election period and creates a public perception of parties as election-oriented. That the preponderance of public funding goes to candidates instead of parties, Jenson said, is inconsistent with the crucial importance of parties in the Canadian political system.

All these characteristics contrast starkly with the characteristics of European funding regimes, which emphasize parties over candidates. Parties there are seen as playing an important role outside election periods. Public funding for parties depends upon the level of popular support they can achieve, not on the amount spent. Jenson recommended that Canada reward votes instead of spending.

Carole Campolo of the New York City Campaign Finance Board described that city's experience with campaign finance legislation. The *Campaign Finance Act*, passed in 1988 in an atmosphere of frustrated public demands for reform, aimed to remove money as a barrier to running for public office and to encourage small contributions from a large number of sources. The public funding program is voluntary, covers both primary and general elections, and links public funding to compliance with certain rules. The program's central features are matching grants of up to $1000, full disclosure, and contribution and spending limits. Public funding payments and disclosure reports are made public frequently during the campaign itself, allowing timely media coverage of both. Computerization of the system allows for quick processing of donations and matching grants, as well as easy access by reporters.

Lisa Young evaluated several options for reforming disclosure provisions. Inclusion of the contributor's address and the date of the contribution is mandatory in many U.S. jurisdictions, she said, and ought to be considered for Canada. The disclosure of a contributor's employer's name, necessary in the United States because of legislation governing contribution limits, would not be as important in Canada. However, Young favoured shortening the reporting period and the time lag between contribution and disclosure. These improvements are desirable because reporters, academics and the public rarely have access to the information disclosed under the present system. Fuller and more accessible disclosure – perhaps aided by computerized records – could spark greater public interest.

During the ensuing discussion, participants supported fuller and more frequent disclosure. Some emphasized the virtues of pre-election disclosure; others expressed concern that the nature of current campaign practices would make disclosure during the campaign difficult. Unlike the situation in New York before the 1988 reforms, contributions greater than $2000 are rare in Canada, and options for reform ought to be kept in perspective. A participant suggested that disclosure by constituency associations and more prompt disclosure rules would be two practical forward steps.

David Taras of the University of Calgary focused on free-time advertising. He characterized such ads as weak, tedious and ghettoized out of prime time. Recent innovations such as cable and satellite television and the videocassette recorder have freed viewers from the schedules imposed on them by broadcast advertisers. Given such a wide range of options, few people will choose to watch free-time political advertisements. Taras concludes that free-time ads are not an effective means of communication.

At the same time, he lamented the lack of communication between voters and their Members of Parliament. The focus of campaign coverage in the media is on national issues, ignoring local issues; candidates are virtually locked out of commercial television airtime. Meanwhile, door-to-door canvassing has become less effective with changes in Canadians' lifestyles and schedules. This severing of ties between Members of Parliament and constituents increases public cynicism. A new form of free-time advertising for candidates could successfully address these problems, Taras argued. Candidates should receive vouchers for a certain value of airtime, to spend as they wish. In return, candidates should have to produce ads locally, discuss local issues and appear in the advertisement.

In the brief discussion that followed, a participant suggested that the Parliamentary Channel and local cable channels are under-used resources for candidates. He went on to suggest that the content and demeanour of advertisements ought not to be regulated, leaving judgement on such matters to viewers.

PARTY SPENDING AND FINANCE

The next session dealt with regulating parties' spending and finances. David Butler of Nuffield College, Oxford University, discussed the effectiveness of spending limits, restrictions on television advertising and the issue of independent expenditures in Britain. Regarding candidates' spending limits, the consensus is that most people abide by the laws. Because of high postage costs and charges for local telephone calls, direct mail and telephone canvassing are not a significant part of British election campaigns.

Candidates and parties are not allowed to buy radio or television advertising time in Britain. Although this is a limit on freedom of expression, Butler said that free time is allocated fairly. The Americanization of British campaigns has increased expenses significantly, however. In the last four days of the 1987 general election in Britain, the Conservative Party bought 11 full pages of advertising in daily newspapers at a cost of £9 million. Butler noted that opinion polls are very important tools for political parties and candidates and that they are quite expensive. Interest group advertising is not a big problem in Britain, however, because the law prohibits any outside advertising aimed at promoting the election of a candidate.

Réjean Pelletier of Université Laval discussed the evolution of election finance laws in Quebec, the effects of the system of *financement populaire* and the potential for Quebec's system to be exported to other jurisdictions. He said the 1963 election finance law in Quebec came about in the wake of a number of scandals and unethical activities. The Quebec Liberal party included election finance reform in its platform in the early 1960s, and in 1963 a new *Election Act* was adopted that restricted election expenses of parties and candidates and provided for the reimbursement of candidates. The Parti québécois introduced new legislation in 1977 that included disclosure requirements for parties, constituency associations and independent candidates, as well as a political contribution tax credit system. As a result of these reforms, only qualified voters are allowed to contribute to parties and candidates. Following passage of the law, political parties began to encourage members to become more active in fund raising and to broaden their membership to assure themselves of adequate financing.

Pelletier contended that the legislation could be exported, but that political will is necessary. He suggested that the source of political contributions be as clear as possible, but that the $100 threshold for disclosure at the federal level is too low. Unions and businesses should be allowed to contribute to political parties and candidates, and the limit should be lower than $10 000. The tax credit system should encourage modest contributions rather than large contributions.

William Stanbury noted that the Quebec tax credit is much less generous than the federal system. He described potential problems in the Quebec system. First, at public rallies when the hat is passed for contributions it is difficult to determine how much a single anonymous donor has given. Second, the ban on contributions from anyone but electors may be circumvented by businesses that reimburse individuals contributing to parties.

Stanbury noted that the regulatory regime can alter the ability of parties and candidates to raise money. Consumer Price Index adjustments do not adequately reflect rapidly increasing campaign costs. He suggested a more comprehensive definition of election expenses, an increase in election expense limits, and a more precise definition of candidates' personal expenses. He suggested reducing the level of candidate reimbursement for election expenses to 33.3 per cent from 50 per cent and increasing the party reimbursement from 22.5 per cent to 33.3 per cent.

Donald Blake of the University of British Columbia discussed his research on party competition in Canada over the last 20 years. In Canada approximately 20 per cent of Members of Parliament are replaced from one election to the next, compared with 10 per cent in the United Kingdom and just 5 per cent in the United States. Members of the Canadian House of Commons are very vulnerable, because about 30 per cent of the ridings are won by a margin of only 10 per cent of the vote. Blake added that there is no clear relationship between spending limits and competitiveness in Canadian elections.

> "... there is no clear relationship between spending limits and competitiveness in Canadian elections."

Leading off the symposium review, David Angus, chairman of the P.C. Canada Fund, said, "I think the mandate of this Commission is to try to give Canadians confidence in our system of democracy. I have been very impressed with the fact that exhaustive studies by those who are not intimately involved in politics on a day-to-day basis have concluded that our system is a very good system." Turning to specifics, he suggested the Commission must convince the public that political fund raising is a necessary element of a democratic system. He expressed satisfaction with the three parts of the existing political finance laws: modest public funding, campaign spending limits, and disclosure of spending and revenue sources. For registration of constituency associations, Angus noted that the current law allows the chief agent of the national party to designate regional or local agents to issue tax receipts. He therefore questioned whether there was a need to register local associations or allow them to issue tax receipts.

Noting the need for fiscal restraint, Angus spoke against increasing the public funding available to parties and candidates, although he agreed that the value of the tax credit has been eroded by inflation. Because direct mail is an effective means of soliciting small contributions from individuals, he was against any regulation of direct mail. He also opposed any restriction on contributions from businesses, suggesting that businesses should be encouraged to make contributions to political parties as an act of corporate citizenship. He added that there is no need to limit the size of contributions as long as there is full disclosure.

Angus suggested that only those expenditures that directly promote the party in electoral competition should be included in the definition of election expenses. He also advocated reconsideration of the 15 per cent threshold for candidate reimbursement and removal of the criminal penalties for violations of spending limits or disclosure.

Michael Robinson of the Liberal Party noted, "I personally have been able to attend all of the seminars except one. I have found them tremendously informative. I think we all come away ... with a great deal of confidence and respect for this system that we have developed here in Canada. I also think we benefited enormously from the research that has been done for the Commission." He perceived two major threats to the integrity of the Canadian electoral system: the definition of election expenses and interest group advertising during elections. He noted that technological change has jeopardized the integrity of the expenditure limits. Specifically, if polling and direct mail are not included in the definition, he predicted the increased use of polling, followed up by targeted direct mail in every riding. He also supported restriction on interest group activities sufficient to not impair competition between parties.

Parties and candidates already receive sufficient public funds, and rather than increasing the funds available, Robinson suggested, some of these funds from the local level should be reallocated to the national level.

He also suggested basing funding on votes received, rather than on the amount of money spent. Maintaining that business donations are essential sources of funding, he advocated no ban on business or union contributions. He recommended that the use of the tax credit for leadership and nomination campaigns be allowed explicitly in the law. It should be voluntary, however, and accompanied by full disclosure.

Finally, Robinson endorsed the idea of party foundations, arguing that political parties perform their election and brokerage functions well but are weak on articulating their values and underlying ideology. To enable parties to do this, party foundations should be created and publicly funded for their first 10 years.

Cliff Scotton of the New Democratic Party said, "We have been treated to a range of solid information. The papers ... have detailed the hopes and aspirations of the draftees of the original *Election Expenses Act* and subsequent amendments. The practical experience of party officials and electoral officials has brought about the inputs for consideration of change. There is a great deal of common concern." He noted that the 1974 legislation was drafted by members of the party elites and tends to alienate volunteers, from whom the parties now ask money instead of time. The definition of election expenses should be expanded to include polling, and spending limits should be increased commensurately. Scotton also argued for better disclosure, penalties for electoral law infractions, speedy publication of disclosed information, and restrictions on interest group advertising during elections – whether on time or on dollars spent.

PART 3

THE PATH TO ELECTORAL EQUALITY

~

Reprinted from
the report of
**The Committee for
Aboriginal Electoral Reform**

ACKNOWLEDGEMENTS

ON BEHALF OF the Committee for Aboriginal Electoral Reform, I would like to extend special thanks to the many individuals and organizations involved in the work leading up to this report.

I commend the efforts of the Royal Commission on Electoral Reform and Party Financing which recognized the problems encountered by Aboriginal people in the electoral system and understood the need for improved representation of Aboriginal peoples in Parliament. Its Chairman, Mr. Pierre Lortie, deserves praise for elevating Aboriginal electoral reform to the top of the Commission's working agenda.

I commend the contributions of the Committee members who shared their invaluable insights and experience as MPs of Aboriginal ancestry in shaping and refining the proposal for Aboriginal Electoral Districts. I regret that our colleagues from the NDP could not participate in our work due to prior commitments; however, I am confident that this report will reflect the cooperative, non-partisan spirit in which Committee members tackled the challenge of making the electoral system responsive to the interests of Aboriginal people.

A special word of appreciation should be extended to staff members for their ability to organize and bring to fruition an extensive consultative process in such a tight timeframe. Marc LeClair played a pivotal role from the beginning, conducting the preliminary research, conducting the coast to coast consultations under the auspices of my office in January and then repeating this tireless performance during the latest round of consultations under the auspices of the Committee. His efforts were greatly appreciated.

Rob Milen of the staff of the Royal Commission joined Marc in this extraordinary effort and also played an invaluable liaison role between the Committee and the Royal Commission. John Weinstein made a significant contribution to the report and its many drafts as editor. A special word of thanks should go to Margaret Bartle and Lorraine Rochon for their strong support services.

Finally, I wish to thank the many Aboriginal organizations from coast to coast that provided us with a forum for the Aboriginal Electoral Reform concept through their assemblies and private meetings. Without their interest and insights, this report would not have been possible.

Senator Len Marchand
Chairman, Committee for
Aboriginal Electoral Reform

Committee for Aboriginal Electoral Reform

Chairman Senator Len Marchand

Room 307, Victoria Bldg.
Ottawa, Ontario
K1A 0A4
(613) 996-7282
FAX: (613) 996-9943

Mr. Pierre Lortie
Chairman
Royal Commission on Electoral Reform
   and Party Financing
Suite 1120, 171 Slater St.
P.O. Box 1718, Stn. B
Ottawa, Ontario
K1P 6R1

Dear Mr. Lortie:

We have the honour to submit the following report on behalf of the Committee for Aboriginal Electoral Reform. As a group of Aboriginal MPs, both sitting and retired, the Committee is committed to reforming the federal electoral system to redress the structural inequalities which have blocked the effective participation and representation of Aboriginal people in the process of Canadian electoral democracy. Within the confines of the existing constitutional structure, we believe our goals can best be achieved through the creation of Aboriginal Electoral Districts.

Since its inception in May 1991, the Committee has canvassed the views of Aboriginal people on its proposal for Aboriginal Electoral Districts. Consultations were conducted across the country with national, regional and local Aboriginal leaders by way of on-site visits and correspondence. The views of Aboriginal individuals were solicited by way of an advertisement containing the Committee's proposal which appeared in Aboriginal newspapers across the country. The Committee also heard from Parliamentarians and the media on its proposal.

This report documents the response of Aboriginal people to the proposal for Aboriginal Electoral Districts. It sets out recommendations to make the electoral system responsive to the Aboriginal community of interest and to overcome impediments to Aboriginal participation in the federal electoral system.

Willie Littlechild   Ethel Blondin   Jack Anawak   Gene Rheaume

Our consultations confirmed that self-government is the priority issue of Aboriginal people. The Committee supports the constitutional recognition of self-government and has developed the AED concept so as not to detract from this fundamental objective. However, our Committee consultations have revealed a deep-seated conviction among many Aboriginal leaders that the electoral system since Confederation has weakened and marginalized the Aboriginal position in the Canadian political process and hence needs reform to accommodate Aboriginal interests.

It is our firm belief that Aboriginal electoral reform should be a priority recommendation of the Royal Commission in its report to Parliament. The Committee is prepared to continue its work with the Royal Commission and the Aboriginal community to ensure that the final report to Parliament contains concrete measures to put Aboriginal Electoral Districts into effect.

Yours sincerely,

Jack Anawak
MP, Nunatsiaq

Ethel Blondin
MP, Western Arctic

Willie Littlechild
MP, Wetaskiwin

Len Marchand
Former MP
Kamloops–Cariboo

Gene Rheaume
Former MP,
Northwest Territories

CONTENTS

1

THE COMMITTEE AND ITS PURPOSE

THIS DOCUMENT EMBODIES the findings and recommendations of the Committee for Aboriginal Electoral Reform. The Committee is a group of current and former Aboriginal Members of Parliament who have joined together to increase the participation and representation of Aboriginal people in the process of Canadian electoral democracy.

We propose to do this by means of Aboriginal Electoral Districts (AEDs). Accordingly, Aboriginal voters would elect Members of Parliament who would represent them and be accountable directly and exclusively to them through the electoral process. The proposal would provide a mechanism whereby upwards of 4% of the members of the House of Commons could be Aboriginal people, a number that corresponds to our proportion of the Canadian population.

The Government of Canada has signalled its intention to reform the electoral system, appointing the Royal Commission on Electoral Reform and Party Financing to recommend change. The Royal Commission's report is to be submitted to the government in the fall of 1991. It is our hope that the recommendations of the Committee will form an integral part of the Royal Commission's report and that Parliament will act to redress a fundamental inequality within the Canadian electoral system – the systematic under-representation of Aboriginal people in the House of Commons.

In pursuing Aboriginal electoral reform, it is not our purpose to detract in any way from the attainment of Aboriginal self-government. We recognize the concern of some Aboriginal leaders that the proposal for AEDs could divert the attention of governments and the public away from self-government or could, if implemented, exhaust public support for self-government.

We emphasize that AEDs are not a substitute for Aboriginal self-government but a complementary form of political representation. Our proposal is not designed specifically to address the special place of Aboriginal nations within Canada but is designed to take advantage of the opportunity created by the work of the Royal Commission to redress the inequality of Aboriginal people within the electoral system. In this sense, we were buoyed by the opinion of many Aboriginal leaders that although the attainment of self-government must remain their primary pursuit, structural inequalities in the electoral system as it affects Aboriginal people is a long-standing and fundamental problem that must be acted upon.

2

THE WORK OF THE COMMITTEE

T HE IDEA OF increasing Aboriginal participation in Parliament is not new. The Maori in New Zealand have had four guaranteed electoral districts since 1867. The late George Manuel, one of the driving forces behind the National Indian Brotherhood (now the Assembly of First Nations), proposed guaranteed Aboriginal representation in Parliament more than 30 years ago. Guaranteed representation in Parliament also formed a central part of the Native Council of Canada's constitutional report in the early 1980s and was one of the agenda items in the 1983 political and constitutional accord reached with First Ministers.

The recent establishment of the Committee for Aboriginal Electoral Reform and its proposal for Aboriginal Electoral Districts evolved out of earlier efforts by Senator Len Marchand of British Columbia. Senator Marchand appeared before the Royal Commission on Electoral Reform on March 13, 1990, outlining the case for electoral equality of Aboriginal people and AEDs. His office also conducted research into impediments to Aboriginal participation in the federal electoral system.

As a result of Senator Marchand's submission and those of Aboriginal organizations, the Royal Commission asked Senator Marchand to lead a series of consultations with Aboriginal leaders on the AED concept. These consultations, conducted during January 1991 by the office of Senator Marchand with national and regional Aboriginal leaders, found considerable support for establishing AEDs as a way of achieving more effective Aboriginal representation in the House of Commons.

A recurring theme heard from Aboriginal leaders in these discussions was the need for further, more in-depth consultations as a vehicle for validating community support and for developing a model that could serve as a basis for draft legislation in the Royal Commission's report. The leaders also viewed the Royal Commission's response to an ongoing process as an indication of its seriousness in pursuing the issue.

The Royal Commission responded to the report on the Marchand round of consultations by asking for the continued assistance of the Senator in guiding further consultations with the Aboriginal community. These consultations would be directed to determining whether there was sufficient support for an AED proposal that could be included in the Royal Commission's recommendations.

The Royal Commission and Senator Marchand agreed that a most effective instrument for guiding further work on AEDs would be a non-partisan committee of Aboriginal people who have served or are currently serving as members in the House of Commons. The Committee for Aboriginal Electoral Reform was established in May of 1991 to advise on and evaluate the consultative process.

In response to the Aboriginal leadership's desire for a more concrete AED proposal, the Committee developed a consultative paper on AEDs, proposing a design for AEDs and a process for implementing the concept. This consultation document, "Aboriginal Electoral Districts: The Path to Electoral Equality", was featured as a four-page advertisement in Aboriginal newspapers across Canada. It invited written responses from readers and also provided a toll-free telephone number for verbal responses.

The Committee wrote directly to Aboriginal communities and regional leaders and arranged on-site meetings with provincial, regional and national organizations; these meetings were held in May, June and July. (See Appendix 1 for the list of organizations consulted.) As the discussions progressed, the Committee was able to produce and distribute among Aboriginal leaders a question and answer summary addressing some of the key Aboriginal concerns and priorities emerging from the talks. (See Appendix 2.)

The consultative document was also sent to Members of Parliament, Senators and the news media, prompting considerable response. In addition to extensive media coverage of the Committee's participation in Aboriginal organizations' assemblies, a number of newspaper editorials focused on the AED concept, prompting Committee responses that were also published.

3

IMPEDIMENTS TO ABORIGINAL PARTICIPATION IN THE FEDERAL ELECTORAL SYSTEM

T HE FAILURE OF the existing electoral system to provide for equal and effective Aboriginal representation in Parliament is clear. Since Confederation, only 12 self-identifying Aboriginal people have occupied seats in Parliament, out of approximately 11 000 available seats. Three Métis, including Louis Riel, were elected in Manitoba in the 1870s when Métis electors were the majority. Of the nine Aboriginal people elected this century, only three have been elected in districts where Aboriginal people do not constitute a majority. The remaining six Aboriginal people have come from the Northwest Territories, where Aboriginal people form a majority in the constituency.

In exploring the root causes of Aboriginal underrepresentation in Parliament, the Committee reviewed the findings of earlier research conducted by the office of Senator Marchand. This research identified four major factors contributing to negative Aboriginal perceptions of Parliament and to Aboriginal underrepresentation:

- the historical use of the federal franchise as a means of assimilation;
- the failure of the federal electoral system to recognize the Aboriginal community of interest;
- impediments to Aboriginal participation in political parties; and
- the failure of federal electoral administration to meet the needs of Aboriginal electors and to practise employment equity.

HISTORICAL FACTORS

The skepticism and suspicion with which Aboriginal people view the electoral franchise can be traced to the historical use of the federal franchise as a means of assimilating Aboriginal people. In order to exercise the federal franchise, Indians were expected to surrender their distinct identity and status and to assimilate into settler society. Appendix 3 sets out the terms of surrender required of Indians in order to vote in federal elections until 1960, including the loss of their right to be registered under the *Indian Act*, their treaty rights, and their statutory right to property tax exemption. The Inuit did not receive the right to vote until 1950. However, no ballot boxes were placed in Inuit hamlets until 1962.

The arguments advanced in parliamentary debates to deny the franchise to Indians from Confederation until 1960 provide valuable insight into the treatment of Aboriginal people in the electoral system. Parliamentarians took aim at four elements of Aboriginal distinctiveness:

- Aboriginal socio-economic conditions were cited as a reason for denying the franchise to Aboriginal people. This included arguments that Aboriginal people were not "civilized" or "literate", that they were "wards" of the government and susceptible to voter manipulation by the government in power and thus not worthy of the right to vote.
- The distinct legal status of Indian people under the *Indian Act* and the treaties were also cited as reasons for withholding fundamental citizenship rights. In particular, treaty payments and annuities, exemption from taxation, and the prohibition on Indians entering into contracts or buying and selling were all used to deny Aboriginal people the right to vote.
- The distinct land tenure system on reserves was a concern in the early part of the century, particularly when the franchise was viewed as an incident of proprietary ownership (reserve lands were designated as federal lands).
- Finally, the distinct political consciousness of Aboriginals was used by non-Aboriginal politicians to deny Aboriginals the right to vote on the self-serving grounds that Indian sovereignty was inconsistent with any Aboriginal participation in Parliament.

The problems with the electoral system cannot be viewed in isolation from the historical difficulties that Aboriginal peoples have had with Canadian political institutions. The failure of the Canadian government to work out constitutional accommodations recognizing inherent collective Aboriginal and treaty rights, coupled with Canada's history of assimilationist policies, have had an adverse impact on Aboriginal perceptions of Parliament and the value of participating within it. This has created a dilemma for many Aboriginal Canadians. Not wanting to legitimize the constitutional structure in place in Canada, many Aboriginal leaders have argued against assuming voting rights.

FAILURE OF THE ELECTORAL SYSTEM TO RECOGNIZE THE 'ABORIGINAL COMMUNITY OF INTEREST'

The primary reason for Aboriginal underrepresentation in Parliament stems from the failure of current electoral laws to recognize the Aboriginal community of interest. While current electoral law allows for group interests to be taken into account in the drawing of electoral boundaries and has worked to the benefit of official language minority groups and geographically concentrated ethnic communities, the existing law is not capable of accommodating the broad geographic distribution of Aboriginal peoples.[1]

While Aboriginal peoples constitute upward of 4% of the overall Canadian population, their population distribution across the country has left them numerical minorities in all but the two territorial ridings. As a result, it makes it difficult for Aboriginal people to influence the outcome of an election. According to the Federal Electoral Districts – 1987 Representation Order, there are only two ridings south of the 60th parallel where Aboriginal peoples constitute more than 20% of the federal electoral district: Churchill, Manitoba (42%) and Prince Albert–Churchill River, Saskatchewan (25%). Of the remaining federal electoral districts, only seven have more than 10% of the population identified solely as Aboriginal: Kenora–Rainy River, Ontario (14%); Abitibi, Quebec (16%); Labrador, Newfoundland (10%); the Battlefords–Meadow Lake, Saskatchewan (17%); Athabaska, Alberta (12%); and Skeena, B.C. (16%). An additional seven electoral districts have an Aboriginal population of more than 5% but less than 10%.

In fact, federal electoral boundaries have served to dilute the strength of the Aboriginal vote in the hinterland. This results from the north-south axis on which the boundaries of northern electoral districts have been drawn, allowing the non-Aboriginal population in the more populous towns in the southern parts of a constituency to outvote the Aboriginal population forming the majority in the rest or most of the constituency.

The result of this structural problem was confirmed by the 1988 federal election. Leaving aside the two territorial ridings, there is only one Member of Parliament of Aboriginal descent south of the 60th parallel. When one considers that more than 900 000 Aboriginal people live south of 60, it is no surprise that Aboriginal people question the legitimacy of the electoral system and the capacity of Parliament to deal effectively with Aboriginal issues. Clearly, the application of electoral boundaries legislation has served to partition the Aboriginal community of interest into different electoral districts, thereby diluting the Aboriginal vote and rendering it ineffective.

IMPEDIMENTS WITHIN THE PARTY SYSTEM

The electoral system is dominated in large part by the three main political parties which have not been notably receptive to Aboriginal people. Low Aboriginal participation rates within the parties are especially important when considering the large role played by the parties in getting voters to the polls. A major impediment to increased Aboriginal participation in the parties has been the perception that Aboriginal people do not vote, a perception that has discouraged political activity in the Aboriginal community and the nomination of Aboriginal candidates. As long as the Aboriginal vote remains diluted and partitioned, political parties have little incentive to field Aboriginal candidates to win the Aboriginal vote.

Of the three main political parties, the Liberal Party of Canada has gone furthest in increasing Aboriginal participation, amending the party constitution to guarantee proportional representation of Aboriginal peoples within the Party. At the 1990 Liberal leadership convention, this resulted in approximately 4% of delegate positions (182 delegates) being reserved for Aboriginal Liberals. These structural adjustments were made because the existing riding association structure failed to produce Aboriginal delegates in proportion to their number.

The Progressive Conservative Party recognizes the National Aboriginal Progressive Conservative Caucus as one of its national associations, but the party's Constitution guarantees only two delegate positions for Aboriginal peoples at conventions. The party does, however, attempt to encourage Aboriginal participation at the riding level.

The New Democratic Party encourages Aboriginal people to participate at the riding level, but makes no structural accommodation for Aboriginal peoples within the party constitution.

THE FAILURE OF FEDERAL ELECTORAL ADMINISTRATION

The administration of the federal electoral system has not been responsive to the special needs and problems of Aboriginal electors. The enumeration of Aboriginal electors has been impeded by transience, homelessness, reliance on Indian band lists, and the tendency of single parents on social assistance to hide the presence of co-habitants for fear of losing their social assistance benefits. Participation in elections is impeded by distance from polling stations and the lack of public transportation on reserves, by insufficient awareness because of poor communications, particularly in isolated communities lacking electricity, and by the fear of political retribution on the part of poor communities dependent on federal fiscal transfers. In addition, the disenfranchisement of inmates in federal penal institutions under the *Canada Elections Act* has had a particular impact on Aboriginal peoples who are disproportionately represented in federal penitentiaries.

The Chief Electoral Officer is responsible for the administration of federal elections and reports directly to Parliament. The administration of an election involves approximately 450 000 people and costs approximately $100 000 000, yet few Aboriginal persons participate in the process. This is particularly the case with senior positions such as the returning officer who is responsible for administering the electoral machinery within his or her electoral district and for subdividing the district into polling divisions. Research was unable to identify any returning officer, past or present, of Aboriginal descent.

Research did uncover some representation of Aboriginal people among subordinate election officers. These include the deputy returning officers responsible for polling stations within an electoral district, election clerks, and enumerators. It can be argued that the absence of Aboriginal representation among returning officers results from a paucity of skills to undertake the functions of that position, but the fact is that 253 of the 295 returning officers appointed for the 34th General Election had no previous experience managing elections.

NOTE

1. The *Electoral Boundaries Readjustment Act* provides for the creation of 11 electoral boundaries commissions, which are responsible for readjusting federal electoral boundaries in each province and the Northwest Territories. To ensure that each constituency in a province has a roughly equal number of voters, the Commission determines the electoral quotient for that province by dividing the total population by the number of constituencies allocated to the province under the formula set out in the *Constitution Act*.

   The commissions are allowed to deviate from this electoral quotient by 25% in order to respect the *"community of interest or community of identity in the historical pattern of an electoral district"* and to maintain a "manageable size for districts in sparsely populated, rural and northern regions of the province." They may exceed the 25% variance rule under "extraordinary circumstances" which have now been invoked five times by boundaries commissions.

4

THE CASE FOR ABORIGINAL ELECTORAL DISTRICTS

WHY AEDs?

WHEN A COMMUNITY of interest or identity is spread out geographically, as Aboriginal people are in most of Canada, it is unlikely that their interests will be represented directly or that candidates of their identity will be elected. This is because their numbers in each constituency are too small to form a majority – or even a significant minority – of the population in any given area.

This is the situation facing Aboriginal people in Canada today. The proposal for AEDs aims to overcome the effects of the geographic dispersal of Aboriginal people. There has been a general feeling among Aboriginal people that the electoral system is so stacked against them that AEDs are the only way they can gain representation in Parliament in proportion to their numbers.

Direct representation of Aboriginal people would help to overcome long-standing concerns that the electoral process has not accommodated the Aboriginal community of interest and identity. Aboriginal electors would elect Members of Parliament who would represent them and be directly accountable to them at regular intervals. MPs from AEDs would understand their Aboriginal constituents, their rights, interests, and perspectives on the full range of national public policy issues.

MPs from AEDs could pursue the concerns and interests of Aboriginal people with concentrated attention and vigour. Moreover, they could do so without fear of alienating non-Aboriginal constituents, a problem that sometimes arises for Aboriginal people elected under the current system.

MPs from AEDs would help to educate non-Aboriginal MPs and the Canadian public on issues of direct concern to Aboriginal people. No longer would Aboriginal leaders have to spend time and energy educating non-Aboriginal MPs on Aboriginal issues – only to have to start again when those MPs are replaced in the House of Commons.

REDRESSING STRUCTURAL INEQUALITY

The proposal to create Aboriginal Electoral Districts is designed to redress the structural inequality within the present electoral system. Aboriginal people are not looking for special rights in the electoral system. They are merely seeking equality within the electoral system.

If Aboriginal people were represented in Parliament in proportion to their numbers, they would be entitled to approximately 12 members or 4% of the current 295 members; yet there are only three current Aboriginal MPs, two of them elected in the Aboriginal majority constituencies in the Northwest Territories. In short, the proposal for AEDs is designed to place Aboriginal electors on an equal footing with non-Aboriginal Canadians.

Some would argue that there is no discrimination because the electoral law treats everybody equally. But the Supreme Court of Canada, in its landmark equality ruling, recognized that "identical treatment may frequently produce serious inequality" and that "a bad law will not be saved merely because it operates equally upon those to whom it has application". The Court indicated that "in approaching equality issues, the main consideration must be the impact of the law on the individual or the group concerned." In examining areas of discrimination, the Court suggested:

> I would say then that discrimination may be described as a distinction, whether intentional or not but based on grounds relating to personal characteristics of the individual or group, which has the effect of imposing burdens, obligations, or disadvantages on such individual or group not imposed upon others, or which withholds or limits access to opportunities, benefits and advantages available to other members of society.[1]

Although Aboriginal people are not singled out explicitly in the current electoral law, the impact of electoral legislation creates burdens and disadvantages for Aboriginal people. The electoral law withholds and limits Aboriginal access to the opportunity to participate in Parliament and deprives them of benefits and advantages available to other members of Canadian society. The principles underlying the Supreme Court's decision apply to the situation of Aboriginal people in the electoral system. This is why the Canadian Human Rights Commission, while not offering a definitive legal opinion on the compatibility of AEDs and the Charter of Rights and Freedoms, was of the opinion that the current electoral system has not resulted in the effective or equal representation of Aboriginal people.

One of the fundamental tenets of liberal democracy is to ensure that numerical minorities are represented in legislative assemblies in proportion to their number. This principle was recognized and set out by John Stuart Mill in an article entitled "Of True and False Democracy: Representation of All, and Representation of the Majority Only". Mill argued that

> In a representative body actually deliberating, the minority must of course be overruled; and in an equal democracy (since the opinions of the constituents, when they insist on them, determine those of the representative body) the majority of the people, through their representatives, will outvote and prevail over the minority and their representatives. *But does it follow that the minority should have no representation at all? Because the majority*

ought to prevail over the minority, must the majority have all the votes, the minority none? Is it necessary that the minority should not even be heard? Nothing but habit and old association can reconcile any reasonable being to the needless injustice.

In a really equal democracy every or any section would be represented, not disproportionately, but proportionately. A majority of electors would always have a majority of the representatives, but a minority of the electors would always have a minority of the representatives. *Man for man, they would be as fully represented as the majority. Unless they are, there is not equal government, but a government of inequality and privilege:* one part of the people rule over the rest; there is a part whose fair and equal share of influence in the representation is withheld from them, contrary to all just government, but, above all, contrary to the principle of democracy which professes equality as its very root and foundation. (emphasis added)[2]

Mill's argument is as forceful today as it was more than a century ago. Should Aboriginal people have virtually no representation at all? Because the majority ought to prevail over the minority, must the non-Aboriginal majority have all the votes, the Aboriginal minority none? Aboriginal people must, person for person, be as fully represented as the majority. This is not the case today. As a result, we do not have equal government, and we do not have equal government because the electoral system does not promote equality – only habit, old associations and privileges.

Some opposition to the AED proposal is based on a fear that it would open the floodgates for ethnic minorities to seek similar measures. However, as the Canadian Ethnocultural Council has stated, ethnocultural minorities are addressing the issue of political representation through integration and increased inclusion in political parties. The Council does not foresee ethnocultural communities pursuing provisions similar to the ones in the AED proposal – a proposal which it supports for Aboriginal people.

WHY NOW?

There are a number of reasons why now is the time to move on the creation of AEDs.

- First, AEDs can be established by Parliament alone, without the consent of the provinces.
- Second, the Royal Commission on Electoral Reform will submit its report to the federal government this fall and will be recommending reform of the electoral system; our proposal could become part of that report.
- Third, we should act before the process of redefining the boundaries of electoral districts gets under way.

NOTES

1. *Andrews* v. *Law Society of British Columbia*, S.C.C. 1989 34BCLR (2nd. Edition) pp. 273–319.

2. John Stuart Mill, *Considerations on Representative Government*, Bobbs-Merrill, Indianapolis 1958. pp. 103–104.

5

The Proposal for Aboriginal Electoral Districts

I NON-DEROGATION FROM ABORIGINAL SELF-GOVERNMENT
IN THE CONSULTATION document, the Committee suggested that Aboriginal Electoral Districts be established to redress the imbalance and inequality experienced by Aboriginal people in the federal electoral system and not as an alternative to Aboriginal and treaty rights, including the inherent right of Aboriginal people to self-government. The Committee suggested that effective parliamentary representation and self-government were complementary forms of representation. The approach of the Committee was to suggest that specific measures be taken to ensure that the legislative enactment of AEDs in no way derogates from the Aboriginal and treaty rights of Aboriginal people.

REFORM WITHIN THE EXISTING CONSTITUTIONAL STRUCTURE

In undertaking its work, the Committee chose to pursue the creation of AEDs without having to resort to amending the Constitution. The Committee proposes that Aboriginal Electoral Districts be established by the Parliament of Canada acting on its own constitutional authority. This act of Parliament would not require the formal agreement of the provinces, but it would require that three conditions be met. First, AEDs must be contained within provincial boundaries. Second, no additional House of Commons seats could be created. Third, the number and size of Aboriginal electoral districts would have to be determined by the electoral quotient (there must be a minimum number of Aboriginal people residing in the district).

DETERMINING THE NUMBER OF AEDs

The committee believes that the best way to achieve equality within the electoral system is to guarantee a process where Aboriginal people would be represented in Parliament in proportion to the Aboriginal population. Recalling Mill's words, "In a really equal democracy every or any section would be represented, not disproportionately but proportionately." The Committee's proposal is designed to achieve proportionality.

With the exception of the Atlantic provinces, the number of AEDs to be created in a province would depend on two factors: the number of Aboriginal people that choose to participate in AEDs and the size of the province's electoral quotient. The process would be as follows:

1. The number of electoral districts are allotted to the provinces according to the formula set out in the Constitution;
2. The electoral quotient of the province is determined by dividing the total population of the province by the number of electoral districts allotted to the province under the Constitution;
3. After a province's electoral quotient is determined, this quotient is used to calculate the number of AEDs in the province.
4. The number of AEDs would be equal to the number of self-identifying Aboriginal people divided by the electoral quotient. For example if there were 150 000 Aboriginal people in a given province and that province's electoral quotient was 75 000, then two AEDs could be created $(150\,000 \div 75\,000 = 2)$.

It should be noted that, as AEDs would cover large geographic areas, it is expected that the population in AEDs would generally be lower than the province's electoral quotient.[1] This is because electoral boundaries commissions can exceed or fall short of the electoral quotient by 25% in any district in order to accommodate a community of interest or to maintain a manageable size for districts in sparsely populated rural and northern regions. Boundaries commissions may even deviate further in extraordinary circumstances (usually related to geography). For instance, in the above example, if the population size of AEDs were allowed to deviate from the provincial electoral quotient, then more AEDs could be created. If the AED quotient was lowered from 75 000 to 50 000, then three AEDs could be created $(150\,000 \div 50\,000 = 3)$.

The Committee's proposal would guarantee the right of Aboriginal people to have one or more Aboriginal Electoral Districts in each province when the number of self-identifying Aboriginal people reached the required threshold. To avoid the New Zealand situation, where the number of Maori seats has been frozen since 1867, the number of AEDs would vary in step with the growth of the Aboriginal population.

DETERMINING AED BOUNDARIES

To avoid difficulties in managing the electoral process, the Committee suggested that the procedure for establishing Aboriginal Electoral Districts should fit as closely as possible with the general framework in which elections are conducted in Canada. This approach assures Aboriginal people, as well as others in Canada, that the integrity of the electoral process will be preserved.

The Committee's proposal suggested that if a province were to have more than one Aboriginal Electoral District, then the boundaries of the districts would have to be determined by the electoral boundaries commission for that province. In such cases, the Committee suggested that the boundaries commission would be required to consult with the Aboriginal people concerned and give significant consideration to the criteria of comparable population and community of interest and identity.

The Committee suggested that boundaries criteria could include geographic boundaries or take into consideration the cultural and political differences between Aboriginal peoples. The Committee noted the example of a province with two Aboriginal districts and two distinct Aboriginal peoples. Rather than creating two districts covering separate geographical regions (for example a northern and a southern district), the Committee suggested that two province-wide districts could be established, one for each Aboriginal people, if this were the expressed wish of these peoples.

The law creating Aboriginal Electoral Districts would state this criterion – the existence of distinct Aboriginal people – as an example of the general criterion of community of identity.

THE REGISTRATION PROCESS

The conduct of elections requires an electoral list on which voters' names appear. This practice is the norm in every democracy. Establishing the voters list for Aboriginal Electoral Districts would be part of the general voter registration process carried out by Elections Canada. Aboriginal people would not be required to initiate or manage the voter registration process on their own. But Elections Canada would be expected to involve Aboriginal people and their associations in the process.

The Committee noted that the establishment of AEDs would not in itself overcome the difficulties associated with enumerating Aboriginal voters who are poor, homeless or transient, or who are engaged in the traditional pursuits of hunting and trapping in remote areas. However, the Committee suggested that the participation of Aboriginal organizations would permit greater and more meaningful Aboriginal involvement in the electoral process. Aboriginal people could advertise in Aboriginal media, conduct voter registration drives, and involve Aboriginal people conversant in Aboriginal languages to assist in the process.

Under the Committee's proposal, those who wish to vote in an Aboriginal Electoral District would be required to self-identify as Aboriginal persons. If challenged, they would have to be able to provide proof of Aboriginal ancestry or community acceptance. The Committee's reliance upon this criterion stemmed from the growing national and international recognition of this approach to Aboriginal identification. An appeals body, composed of Aboriginal people and governed by the principles of natural justice, would also be necessary. Its decisions could be appealed to the Federal Court of Canada.

Individuals would have the right not to identify themselves as Aboriginal persons for electoral purposes. They would then vote in the general electoral district in which they live. Aboriginal people could not vote in both the Aboriginal Electoral District and the general electoral district during the same election.

ABORIGINAL CANDIDATES AND POLITICAL PARTIES

Under the Committee's proposal, voters in Aboriginal Electoral Districts would have the right to nominate as candidates and elect anyone they wished, provided they met the usual conditions for candidacy. Candidates in Aboriginal Electoral Districts could be official candidates for recognized political parties or independent candidates. The choice would be one for Aboriginal candidates and Aboriginal voters to make. However, it was suggested that Aboriginal candidates would have the same rights and privileges as non-Aboriginal MPs with regard to public funding and the reimbursement of election expenses.

ATLANTIC CANADA AND THE TERRITORIES

The Committee's suggested approach would not change the situation of the electoral districts already established for the Northwest Territories and Yukon. These seats are provided for in the Constitution and would remain as they are.

The Committee's proposal would not result in Aboriginal Electoral Districts in any of the four Atlantic provinces at this time. This is because the Aboriginal population in each province falls short of the threshold required to establish an Aboriginal Electoral District under existing constitutional arrangements. For Aboriginal people in these four provinces, the Committee suggested that a special constitutional provision, such as exists for the Northwest Territories and Yukon, would be required.

Given the Aboriginal population in Atlantic Canada, the consultative paper suggested that one approach would be to create one Aboriginal Electoral District for the entire region. However, the Committee noted that establishing this approach would require a constitutional amendment and hence the consent of some of the provinces.

PROCESS FOR IMPLEMENTATION

Appendix 4 sets out a proposed process for implementing AEDs. Essentially, it is suggested that the legislation to create AEDs could be in place prior to the next election. However, AEDs would not come into effect until after the next election. The delayed implementation is caused by the need to wait for Statistics Canada to publish census results (expected in 1992) and by the fact that it takes boundaries commissions two years to complete the process of boundaries readjustment.

The Committee also suggested Canada's electoral system is likely to see fundamental change as a result of the report of the Royal Commission on Electoral Reform and Party Financing, expected in the fall of 1991. The Committee anticipates that the Royal Commission will change the process for determining electoral district boundaries to make it more responsive to patterns of population growth and migration in Canada. The process set out in Appendix 4 is built on this anticipated change in the overall process for determining electoral district boundaries.

NOTE

1. In the consultative paper, the Committee left open the question of the size of the maximum allowable deviation from provincial electoral quotients. The consultative paper suggested that the maximum allowable deviation is likely to change as a result of the Royal Commission's report.

6

THE CONSULTATIVE PROCESS
Findings and Recommendations

T HIS SECTION PRESENTS the findings of extensive consultations with Aboriginal leaders across the country on the key elements of the AED proposal. The findings are followed by the Committee's recommendations.

AED IMPACT ON SELF-GOVERNMENT

During the first phase of consultations in January 1991, Senator Marchand found that most leaders took the position that Aboriginal parliamentary representation can complement self-government and would be helpful in supporting Aboriginal self-governing institutions. This general view continued during consultations conducted by the Committee.

In its consultation paper, the Committee drew an analogy with the European Community where strong sovereign governments have believed it proper and effective to give their people the ability to elect representatives to the European Parliament. Elected representatives from each member country are thus in a position to advance their common interests and to deal effectively with issues that cut across their individual boundaries. This suggestion hit a responsive chord with Aboriginal leaders, even with those leaders who appeared to be concerned about the potential negative impact of AEDs on the recognition of self-government. Several respondents suggested that future Aboriginal Members of Parliament would act as ambassadors for their nations and would facilitate their needs in Ottawa.

During the Royal Commission's public hearings in the summer of 1990, Ovide Mercredi, then Manitoba Regional Vice-Chief of the Assembly of First Nations, told the Commission that it was possible to have collective rights while participating in the political life of the state. Phil Fontaine of the Assembly of Manitoba Chiefs also told the Commission that First Nations sought a distinct order of government, while at the same time being able to participate and have greater influence in the electoral process. The former National Chief of the Assembly of First Nations, Georges Erasmus, said in a recent interview with the *Globe & Mail* that he doesn't believe that electoral reform conflicts with Aboriginal sovereignty and self-government.

Some representatives from the Métis National Council and the Native Council of Canada clearly see AEDs complementing their right to self-government. The Métis have long endorsed guaranteed parliamentary representation as a historical position dating back to Riel's provisional governments which sought political autonomy for the Métis as well as representation in Parliament.

Although the vast majority of leaders do not believe that AEDs are inconsistent with self-government, some leaders were concerned that the creation of AEDs might exhaust public support for Aboriginal issues or be falsely portrayed to the Canadian public as a 'solution' to the political marginalization of First Nations. Others suggested that although there was significant merit in the Committee's proposal, the timing of the proposal is not appropriate and that it should wait until further constitutional recognition of Aboriginal and treaty rights.

The Committee does not share this view. The Committee believes that Canadians understand the need to settle long-standing Aboriginal issues, including the need to make fundamental changes in the way Canada's political institutions are structured. The fact that two-thirds of Canadians support setting aside seats for Aboriginal people is strong evidence for this view. (Angus Reid poll, October 1990)

The Committee believes that if Canadians are going to learn to live together, the Canadian federation must recognize Aboriginal self-government and must also provide an opportunity for Aboriginal people to share in the governing of Canada. Moreover, denying Aboriginal people effective voting rights at this time makes about as much sense as denying Aboriginal people effective social and economic benefits and programs until constitutional accommodations are made.

Moreover, Aboriginal people stand to benefit if there were more Aboriginal MPs. They would be in a position to press the case for Aboriginal self-government. Aboriginal MPs would be in a position to promote the Aboriginal position on issues that go beyond the boundaries of Aboriginal lands but have a particular impact on Aboriginal people. Aboriginal MPs can help in the appointment of qualified Aboriginal people to the approximately 3000 Order in Council appointments made through parliamentary institutions. Aboriginal people have much to offer in the transportation, communications and resource sectors, in the field of art and cultural policy, as well as in many other areas.

Recommendation 1

There is a genuine concern among some Aboriginal people that the achievement of AEDs could be used by non-Aboriginal politicians as an excuse not to deal with the Aboriginal priority of self-government. This concern must be addressed by making it clear in federal legislation that the creation of AEDs does not abrogate or derogate from Aboriginal and treaty rights and other rights or freedoms of Aboriginal peoples, including the inherent right of Aboriginal self-government.

The principle that existing rights are not to be abrogated or derogated from is a recurring one in the Canadian Charter of Rights and Freedoms and was acknowledged during the First Ministers Conferences on Aboriginal Constitutional Matters. It is also an approach which the Right Honourable John Diefenbaker pursued in extending the franchise to all Aboriginal people. He stated:

> I say this to those of the Indian race, that in bringing forward this legislation the Minister of Citizenship and Immigration (Mrs. Fairclough) will reassure, as she has assured to date, that existing rights and treaties, traditional or otherwise, possessed by the Indians shall not in any way be abrogated or diminished in consequence of having the right to vote. That is one of the things that throughout the years has caused suspicion in the minds of many Indians who have conceived the granting of the franchise as a step in the direction of denying them their ancient rights.[1]

DETERMINING THE NUMBER OF AEDs

Throughout all phases of the consultative process, a recurring theme was the desire of Aboriginal groups to have AEDs established in a manner that recognizes the diversity of Aboriginal peoples and that respects their traditional territories. Suggestions ranged from tying the number of AEDs to the number of treaties to establishing one AED for each of the 53 distinct linguistic and cultural groups. It would be impossible to accommodate fully the diversity of Aboriginal identities and political interests in the electoral system within the existing limited number of parliamentary seats. After careful consideration, the Committee believes that a generous allowable deviation from the electoral quotient is the most effective way of recognizing the diversity of the Aboriginal peoples.

Under the Committee's proposal, the number of AEDs would depend upon both the size of the Aboriginal population and the size of the allowable deviation from the electoral quotient. The higher the allowable deviation, the greater the possibility of accommodating Aboriginal political boundaries and interests.

The Committee supports a generous allowable deviation from the electoral quotient in determining the number of AEDs and is buoyed by the recent decision of the Supreme Court of Canada. The Committee was concerned that the Supreme Court might reduce the allowable deviation, but just the opposite occurred. In the recent decision *Carter* v. *Saskatchewan* (Attorney General), the Supreme Court reaffirmed the legality of a broad deviation principle and acknowledged, among other things, the ability to recognize minority interests in applying it.[2]

In that case, the Court was faced with a constitutional challenge to Saskatchewan electoral legislation, which pre-allocated seats to urban and rural areas. It is to be noted that the Court did not rule unconstitutional the 50% deviation for the two northern ridings in the province. In determining whether the legislation violated section 3 of the Charter, which guarantees every citizen the right to vote, the Court examined the fundamental principles of parliamentary democracy. In the examination, the majority of the Court decided as follows:

- the purpose of the right to vote enshrined in section 3 of the Charter is not equality of voting power per se, but the right to "effective representation";
- while a citizen's vote should not be unduly diluted, it is a practical fact that effective representation often cannot be achieved without taking into account countervailing factors like geography, population growth, community history, community interests and minority representation;
- the purpose of section 3 is not to effect perfect voter equality insofar as that can be done, but the broader goal of guaranteeing effective representation;
- the values and principles animating a free and democratic society are arguably best served by a definition of the section 3 right that places effective representation at the heart of the right to vote.

The Committee believes that a generous deviation for AEDs is necessary to achieve effective representation for Aboriginal people. Reducing the deviation and/or abolishing the extraordinary circumstances exception would result in inequities within the AED system. For example, a reduction in the deviation would result in larger ridings and make it difficult to recognize the distinct political differences between Aboriginal peoples and the cultural differences between various Indian nations.

Métis and Indian leaders on the Prairies spoke to the need for each people to have its own representatives. They suggested that only through separate representation would they be able adequately to pursue their distinct agendas in Parliament. Without a generous deviation, these political differences would not be accommodated.

Finally, a reduction in the deviation could very well result in AEDs with inordinately high populations, thus denying effective representation in Parliament. It would also make it difficult to accommodate rising growth rates in the Aboriginal population. Accordingly, only with more generous deviation rules can effect be given to the factors that, in aggregate, go to the heart of effective representation:

- geographical differences;
- political differences between Aboriginal groups (e.g., Indians and Métis) and within Aboriginal peoples (e.g., different Indian Nations);
- Aboriginal population growth; and
- ensuring that Aboriginal people on a national level are represented in Parliament in proportion to their numbers.

Recommendation 2

Given the population distribution of Aboriginal people, the size of the AEDs and the recent Supreme Court decision, the Committee recommends that the existing allowable deviation rule be retained or increased.

DETERMINING AED BOUNDARIES

A recurring theme among respondents was that the Aboriginal community of interest must be respected when drawing federal electoral boundaries. A number of leaders cited the practice of electoral boundaries commissions in respecting the community of interest of official language and other minorities, but not Aboriginal peoples, in drawing electoral boundaries.

During the Royal Commission hearings, Treaty 7 and the Grand Council of the Crees suggested that electoral boundaries should coincide with treaty and land claims boundaries. The Grand Council of the Crees in Quebec and the Métis Society of Saskatchewan recommended the establishment of northern electoral districts with Aboriginal majorities even though the population would fall below the electoral quotient by more than the allowable deviation.

In the context of AEDs, concerns were raised during the consultations conducted by Senator Marchand about the criteria for determining AED boundaries in provinces that would be entitled to more than one AED. On the Prairies, Métis provincial leaders sought separate AEDs for Métis and Indians, a view shared by Indian leaders.

Concerns about the criteria for determining boundaries also surfaced during the Committee consultations. Several treaty groups wanted their treaty boundaries respected if seats were to be established in their traditional territories. One Chief from New Brunswick suggested that it was a "non-Indian thought process" to suggest that all of the Aboriginal people in Atlantic Canada could participate in one Aboriginal Electoral District.

During the consultation process, it became clear that many Aboriginal people had given up on making presentations to electoral boundaries commissions. Several northern leaders expressed frustration that their proposals to redraw boundaries to create Aboriginal majority districts in the northern parts of their provinces had fallen on deaf ears. For the most part, however, Aboriginal leaders knew very little about the composition and mandate of boundaries commissions.

Recommendation 3

The Committee recommends that the following criteria be set as guidelines for the establishment of AED boundaries:

- recognition of treaty boundaries;
- recognition of regional council boundaries;
- recognition of the composition of the Aboriginal population, i.e., Indian, Métis, Inuit; and
- recognition of the local Aboriginal history and relationship to the land.

It is further recommended that the rules now in place for setting federal constituency boundaries in the Northwest Territories also be applicable to AEDs. These rules require that special consideration be given to the following factors:

- ease of transportation and communication within constituencies;
- geographical size and shape of the constituencies relative to one another; and
- community or diversity of interests of the inhabitants of the various regions.

Composition of Boundary Commissions

The application and interpretation of the boundaries criteria are also important. Under the existing *Electoral Boundaries Readjustment Act*, each boundaries commission consists of three members, with the chairman appointed by the provincial Chief Justice and the other two appointed by the Speaker of the House of Commons. The Committee believes that Aboriginal people can assist in the determination of boundary criteria and makes the following recommendations concerning the composition and process for boundaries commissions.

Recommendation 4

The Committee recommends that the Speaker of the House of Commons appoint two additional Aboriginal people to sit on boundaries commissions for the purpose of determining the Aboriginal boundaries in provinces that have more than one AED.

Procedures to be Followed in Setting AED Boundaries

The *Electoral Boundaries Readjustment Act* sets out a procedure providing for public input and the Committee believes that it is essential for Aboriginal people to be involved in this process.

Recommendation 5

The Committee recommends the following changes to the electoral boundaries determination process:
- **a requirement that AED boundaries commissions hold a reasonable number of public hearings and that submissions in writing may be given within a prescribed period of time;**
- **a requirement that a preliminary report be prepared by the boundaries commission that cannot be sent for approval by Parliament unless and until the Aboriginal community has had an opportunity to respond and input from the Aboriginal community has been considered;**
- **a requirement that public hearings be held over a sufficiently long period of time to allow accessibility by a population burdened by distance and communication problems;**
- **generous requirements for the giving of notice of public hearings and of the opportunity to submit written briefs and make oral presentations; and**
- **consideration should be given to providing funding for witnesses where appropriate.**

The Committee believes that this approach would ensure real public involvement in the boundary-setting process, with the desired result that the final resolution would more closely approximate the views of those to be represented by members elected from AEDs.

THE REGISTRATION PROCESS

The Committee's consultations with Aboriginal leaders did not produce disagreement over the premise in the AED proposal that Aboriginal self-identification must be a requirement for registration on the Aboriginal electoral list and that those whose identity is challenged would have to provide proof of Aboriginal ancestry or community acceptance. The Committee did discover a stronger emphasis on the self-identification qualification from organizations whose members had suffered in the past from arbitrary definitions of who is an Aboriginal person.

Women's associations felt strongly that the onus for disqualifying an elector on the basis of identity or ancestry should be on those making the challenge rather than on those being challenged. These associations suggested that the handling of challenges and the appeals process included in the AED proposal must be controlled by Aboriginal communities. These groups also wished to leave open the question of whether non-Aboriginal women who gained Indian status through marriage to Indians would be entitled to participate in Aboriginal Electoral Districts.

Recommendation 6

The Committee recommends that Aboriginal self-identification be the critical factor in qualifying as an Aboriginal elector in addition to the standard electoral qualifications of all Canadian voters.

The burden of proof in challenges to those seeking to register on an Aboriginal voters list should rest with those making the challenge.

Furthermore, the Committee recommends that an appeals body or tribunal should be controlled by Aboriginal people and should consist of Aboriginal men and women together with eminent elders.

There appeared to be a general acceptance of the AED proposal's provision for Aboriginal individuals to have the right to vote in AEDs or in general electoral districts but not both. However, a concern was raised that effective Aboriginal participation in the electoral system required two votes for Aboriginal electors: one in AEDs and one in the general electoral district in which they reside. The Committee cannot accept this latter view as it infringes on the "one-person, one-vote" principle underlying our electoral democracy. Our AED proposal is designed to correct an existing inequality, not create a new one. It also ensures freedom of choice for those Aboriginal electors who may not wish to participate in AEDs.

ABORIGINAL CANDIDATES AND POLITICAL PARTIES

The Party System

An important issue for all respondents was whether Aboriginal candidates would become part of the conventional party system or run as independents in the House of Commons. In the Marchand round of consultations, several leaders strongly favoured party alignment so as to have the opportunity to participate in the governing caucus and Cabinet decisions if the party to which they belonged formed the government. Some leaders suggested that Aboriginal people should form their own political party, while others were concerned that the existence of an Aboriginal party could generate a backlash against Aboriginal people.

Some leaders expressed the opinion that Aboriginal candidates would lose credibility with their electors by associating with a mainstream party. Others were more blunt, suggesting that because of the poor treatment of Aboriginal people, none of the parties was worthy of Aboriginal support. Some leaders even suggested that the Committee recommend a legislative ban on political party activity within the AED system.

The Committee does not agree with this suggestion. One of the fundamental rights of people is to choose their political representatives freely. To water down this principle or to restrict this right in any way would not be in the best interests of Aboriginal people.

Other Aboriginal leaders said they could live with or without party alignment. It was generally agreed that the Aboriginal electorate would decide whether party affiliation was an asset or a liability. However, most leaders agreed that party affiliation would not be the main selection criterion and suggested that individuals would be elected on the strength of their character and their commitment to the community. No clear consensus has emerged on this issue.

Relationship between Aboriginal MPs and Non-Aboriginal MPs

Several leaders were concerned that non-Aboriginal MPs could disregard Aboriginal issues if Aboriginal people had their own MPs and that Aboriginal people would be ignored by non-Aboriginal MPs. Others were concerned that Aboriginal MPs might become second-class MPs. Still others suggested that the existence of Aboriginal MPs would limit Aboriginal people from lobbying other MPs and ministers of the Crown.

There was a more widely held view that rather than alienating non-Aboriginal MPs, having a larger number of Aboriginal people in Parliament would sensitize and educate non-Aboriginal MPs and the public through their promotion of an Aboriginal agenda and their common sense approach on other issues. Many respondents believe that even though there have been non-Aboriginal MPs who have been helpful in the past, they were no substitute for an increased number of Aboriginal MPs.

Several leaders in western Canada noted that Aboriginal MLAs from northern ridings were very helpful in communicating their needs and advancing their concerns in provincial legislatures. Other respondents noted that Aboriginal MPs in Parliament did make a difference in terms of the rights of Aboriginal people. Several leaders believed that the establishment of AEDs would greatly facilitate the process of communicating the concerns of Aboriginal associations representing Aboriginal people living in urban and off-reserve rural areas.

The Committee does not have a concrete recommendation to address this concern; the Committee anticipates, however, that all MPs will work together to ensure that the needs of all constituents are met. No prescription can force MPs to work with one another, but all representatives must understand that the reason for creating Aboriginal Electoral Districts is the failure of the present system to produce effective representation for all Aboriginal people. Cooperation is required to ensure that the entire democratic process is responsive to the needs of all Canadians, whether Aboriginal or non-Aboriginal.

Moreover, MPs from Aboriginal Electoral Districts would have the same rights and privileges as other Members of Parliament and would participate in the full range of issues before Parliament. This common denominator ought to ensure, as it has in the past, that MPs will continue to work together on the wide range of public policy issues facing Parliament, including Aboriginal issues.

Relationship between Aboriginal MPs and Aboriginal Organizations

There was some concern that Aboriginal MPs could usurp the role of Aboriginal organizations. This view was not shared by a majority of respondents. Nor does the Committee share this view. The Committee believes that the non-derogation provision set out in Recommendation 1 addresses these concerns.

The Committee believes that even after our inherent right of Aboriginal self-government is recognized in the Constitution, the socio-economic conditions of Aboriginal communities will require the federal government to provide continuing financial support (similar to support for have-not provinces). While some Aboriginal communities would be self-supporting, their number would be limited. Thus it can be expected that Aboriginal governing institutions will have a continuing and long-term relationship with the Government of Canada. It makes sense to ensure that there are as many Aboriginal representatives as possible in the House of Commons, to ensure that resource appropriations are secured for Aboriginal governments as well as to ensure that Aboriginal people have a voice in the affairs of the country.

FINANCING OF ABORIGINAL ELECTORAL DISTRICTS

The subject of election financing in AEDs raises the concerns of how to facilitate meaningful campaigns over vast areas by people largely of limited means. Leaders' concerns revolved around the smaller pool of resources within the Aboriginal community and the absence of meaningful tax incentives to fuel the electoral process. (Tax credits are of little value when there is no income to declare.) During the consultations, the smaller pool of resources was a particular concern to those who believed that AEDs would generate a significant number of candidates, all of whom would have to draw upon this limited pool. It also raised the concern that one candidate with a financial backer could unduly influence the electoral process. This was of particular concern to Aboriginal women.

Several leaders suggested that increased levels of public financing would offset the impact of candidates supported by a financial backer and the better-endowed political parties. Others, particularly in the hinterland areas, wanted to guard against third-party interests (primarily the resource industries) influencing the outcome of elections. Still others wanted to ensure that the system would not impede elders and young Aboriginal people from running for election to the House of Commons.

The current legislation limits a candidate's election expenses based on the population of the electoral district, with exceptions made in sparsely populated areas to take into account the geographic size of the constituency. Given the size of the proposed AEDs and the diverse locations of voter populations, existing expense ceilings may have to be increased. This view has also been expressed to the Royal Commission by various parties in connection with rural and northern constituencies.

Recommendation 7

To encourage Aboriginal people with diverse views and economic backgrounds to become candidates without the fear of financial ruin, the Committee recommends that consideration be given to increasing the expense limitations and financing available for all larger electoral districts, including Aboriginal Electoral Districts.

In addition, the Committee recommends that the winner and all losing candidates gaining a specified percentage of the vote be reimbursed. The percentage of the vote required for reimbursement would have to be on a sliding scale, taking into consideration the number of candidates, the number of ballots cast, and the total vote garnered by a particular candidate.

This latter provision is required to discourage frivolous candidates and to ensure that when a number of candidates run for elected office in an AED, they are not punished financially if the vote is significantly split among all candidates.

ATLANTIC CANADA

The Committee's proposal suggested that a special constitutional provision be made for a single Aboriginal Electoral District for the Aboriginal people of Atlantic Canada. This proposal met with a mixed response.

There was no consensus on the number of seats to be created in Atlantic Canada but all leaders felt that more than one seat was necessary. Atlantic leaders felt that population figures should not be the sole determining factor in determining the number of seats. As one leader stated, "We're tired of being told that we can't have a street light because our population is too small."

Representatives from the Métis and non-status Indians argued that at least four seats should be created – one for each of the four peoples: the Micmacs, Maliseet, Innu and Métis. Several leaders pointed out that creating more than one AED in Atlantic Canada would conform with the historical practice of providing Atlantic Canadians with effective voting strength (the Senate floor rule). Aboriginal leaders were firmly of the view that the number of future seats should not be fixed, but should be capable of growth as the Aboriginal population in Atlantic Canada grows.

The majority of leaders felt that, because the creation of AEDs in Atlantic Canada requires a constitutional amendment, the matter should be left open for further negotiation between the Government of Canada, Aboriginal leaders and the provinces.

Recommendation 8

The Committee recommends that the number of seats to be created in Atlantic Canada be the subject of further discussion between Atlantic Aboriginal leaders and the federal and provincial governments. The Committee firmly believes that a strong case can be made for more than one AED in Atlantic Canada.

CONSULTATION AND PROCESS FOR IMPLEMENTATION

The consultations did not generate detailed suggestions on the more technical aspects of the proposal. At this stage, Aboriginal people are still focusing on the fundamentals and merits of the AED concept. It is not anticipated that comprehensive suggestions on the more technical aspects will be forthcoming until the legislative stage.

The Committee's proposed process for implementing AEDs is premised on a shift in the method of determining the size of electoral districts, from one based on total population to one based on registered electors only. The Committee sees some advantages in this shift because it reduces the size of the electoral quotients and makes the system more responsive to Aboriginal population growth. This latter point is particularly important given the comparatively higher Aboriginal birth rate and the relatively young age of the Aboriginal population. Moving to an electors-based system, coupled with a voter registration process sponsored by the Aboriginal community, would also help overcome the problems Aboriginal people have had with the enumeration and census process.

Several Aboriginal leaders suggested that should the Royal Commission or Parliament decide not to change the boundaries readjustment process to an electors-based system, a system for creating AEDs within the current boundaries readjustment process should be developed.

Recommendation 9

The Committee recommends that the boundaries readjustment process be conducted more often to be more responsive to population growth and migration.

In the event that Parliament does not move to establish a boundaries readjustment process based on registered electors, the Committee recommends that legislation establish AEDs within the existing boundaries readjustment process.

Throughout the consultation process Aboriginal leaders spoke of the need for increased participation in the legislative and administrative design and implementation of the AED concept. Several leaders suggested that there should be a further opportunity for Aboriginal input at the legislative stage. Some leaders believed it necessary to have another round of consultations before the proposal is recommended to Parliament. The Committee takes the view that further consultation is necessary and that this should be undertaken in the context of the legislative process.

Recommendation 10

The Committee recommends that the parliamentary committee charged with considering new electoral legislation actively solicit Aboriginal involvement in the review of legislation creating AEDs.

ELECTORAL ADMINISTRATION

The creation of AEDs and Aboriginal voters lists would not in themselves overcome the barriers that many Aboriginal people encounter in the administration of federal elections. The Committee therefore paid special attention to concerns about electoral administration expressed during the consultations. The Committee's interviews with respondents revealed major barriers to Aboriginal participation in enumeration, revision of voters lists and voting and confirmed earlier research findings. Among the barriers cited are

- homelessness, transience, and the tendency of single parents on social assistance not to report a companion resident for fear of losing benefits;
- distance from polling stations and lack of public transportation;
- absence of Aboriginal officials in electoral administration;
- language and literacy; and
- lack of public education and awareness.

The Committee has addressed these concerns with several proposed changes to the electoral law designed to overcome impediments to Aboriginal participation in the enumeration and voting process.

Recommendation 11

1. Homelessness
The Committee endorses submissions to the Royal Commission advocating that the concept of residency contained in the *Canada Elections Act* be broadened to incorporate homeless persons including the suggestions that

- **homeless persons be entitled to identify a local shelter or hostel as their residence; and**
- **voters who have not been enumerated be allowed to register on election day.**

The Committee recommends that homeless Aboriginal people also be entitled to identify a local Aboriginal community office, such as a band office, Métis local or friendship centre, as their place of residence.

2. Transience

The Committee recommends that an Aboriginal person be able to be enumerated in the AED where he or she is living at the time of enumeration. However, once enumerated, the Aboriginal elector would be able to vote in another district, provided he or she was in the riding for a specified period of time. Given the size of AEDs, voter lists for an entire AED should be provided to all polling stations in the AED in order to facilitate voting by the traveller.

3. The Failure to Enumerate Co-Habitants of Persons on Social Assistance

The Committee recommends that addresses on enumeration lists be kept confidential for purposes of the election only and not be allowed to be used for the purpose of denying social assistance or other benefits.

Though such a provision would be useful, it may fail to account for the distrust and fear of people in such a situation, most of whom will in all likelihood not know of the prohibition and not believe it even if they were told.

The Committee recommends that any Aboriginal person could give as his or her address any Aboriginal community office.

Recommendation 12

4. Distance

The Committee recommends the following measures to overcome the problem of distance from polling stations in AEDs:

- allow for proxy voting in any case where a voter lives beyond a pre-determined distance from the nearest polling station;
- provide self-explanatory proxy materials to all voters beyond such distance, such materials to be in both official languages as well as the local Aboriginal language where requested by the Aboriginal community;
- hold voting over a longer period;
- make advance polling available over a longer period of time than is now allowable;

- expand the availability of advance polling to all voters who live beyond the pre-determined distance from the nearest polling station, or who intend on election days to be beyond such distance from the nearest polling station;
- allow for mobile polling stations during the election period, with the itinerary posted well in advance in conspicuous public facilities, published in community newspapers, and broadcast over local radio (itinerary should be required by the Act to provide for stops at communities beyond a specified distance from the nearest polling station and having a minimum aggregate population);
- polling stations should be located by a returning officer only after consulting local groups and officials, thus avoiding potential trouble spots and identifying accessible locations; and
- to ensure an adequate number of convenient polling stations, a legislative provision should require that polling stations be located so that a certain percentage of the voting population does not live beyond a set distance from the nearest polling station (for purposes of population location, the most recent census figures should provide the necessary information).

Recommendation 13

5. Aboriginal Employment in Electoral Administration
The Committee recommends that new legislation incorporate strong employment and appointment equity provisions, together with the training necessary to ensure that Aboriginal people have the opportunity to participate in all facets of the administration of the electoral system.

Recommendation 14

6. Language and Literacy
The Committee recommends that:

- all AED election materials (notices, brochures, ballots, etc.) be provided in both official languages and in the local Aboriginal language where requested by the Aboriginal community; and
- symbols be printed on ballots, a practice used in other countries, such that political parties and/or candidates are represented by symbols.

Recommendation 15

7. Public Education and Voter Registration

If the fundamental goal of Aboriginal voter participation is to be achieved, the changes we recommend must be implemented, together with a legislatively mandated community-based voter registration and education campaign by Elections Canada during each election. History has shown a vast array of reasons for the lack of Aboriginal awareness of the electoral system; only through such efforts can this problem begin to be addressed. Public education is needed to dispel the tremendous amount of suspicion and frustration resulting from generations of exclusion in the political process.

The Committee recommends that a joint public education and awareness program be implemented by Elections Canada and Aboriginal organizations.

Recommendation 16

8. Report of Chief Electoral Officer

Any suggested changes must be monitored to assess their effectiveness. The Committee therefore recommends that the Chief Electoral Officer be required to report after each election as to the effectiveness of the electoral system in getting the Aboriginal vote out and suggesting any recommendations to improve the situation.

NOTES

1. The Right Honourable John Diefenbaker, *Hansard*, January 18, 1960.

2. *A.G. for Sask.* v. *Roger Carter*, Q.C. SCC Court Site 22345, June 6, 1991.

CONCLUSION

THE COMMITTEE BELIEVES that increased Aboriginal participation in Parliament can make a major difference in the lives of all Canadians. Parliament is a place to exchange information and ideas, to learn from one another, and to reinforce Canadian unity. Parliament and all Canadians have been short-changed by the electoral system's failure to provide for effective Aboriginal representation. Increasing the number of Aboriginal people in Parliament is not the full answer to all Aboriginal issues, but it can be an effective means to promote many Aboriginal aspirations.

The absence of Aboriginal voices in the House of Commons undermines the Canadian commitment to pluralism and forces Aboriginal concerns and opinions onto the lawns of the Parliament buildings where more often than not they are heard but not heeded. Aboriginal views will continue to be expressed by Aboriginal leaders and their organizations and through Aboriginal governments. But Aboriginal people are also citizens of Canada and have as much right as any other citizen to participate freely in the parliamentary process on an equal footing with other Canadians.

If Canadians are serious about building bridges with the Aboriginal community, the electoral process must be designed to ensure that Aboriginal people not only have the opportunity to participate, but also the right to participate effectively. The Committee believes that Canadians will agree that the adoption of its recommendations will provide for effective Aboriginal voting rights. They are long overdue.

SUMMARY OF RECOMMENDATIONS

Recommendation 1

There is a genuine concern among some Aboriginal people that the achievement of AEDs could be used by non-Aboriginal politicians as an excuse not to deal with the Aboriginal priority of self-government. This concern must be addressed by making it clear in federal legislation that the creation of AEDs does not abrogate or derogate from Aboriginal and treaty rights and other rights or freedoms of Aboriginal peoples, including the inherent right of Aboriginal self-government.

Recommendation 2

Given the population distribution of Aboriginal people, the size of the AEDs and the recent Supreme Court decision, the Committee recommends that the existing allowable deviation rule be retained or increased.

Recommendation 3

The Committee recommends that the following criteria be set as guidelines for the establishment of AED boundaries:

- recognition of treaty boundaries;
- recognition of regional council boundaries;
- recognition of the composition of the Aboriginal population, i.e., Indian, Métis, Inuit; and
- recognition of the local Aboriginal history and relationship to the land.

It is further recommended that the rules now in place for setting federal constituency boundaries in the Northwest Territories also be applicable to AEDs. These rules require that special consideration be given to the following factors:

- ease of transportation and communication within constituencies;
- geographical size and shape of the constituencies relative to one another; and
- community or diversity of interests of the inhabitants of the various regions.

Recommendation 4

The Committee recommends that the Speaker of the House of Commons appoint two additional Aboriginal people to sit on boundaries commissions for the purpose of determining the Aboriginal boundaries in provinces that have more than one AED.

Recommendation 5

The Committee recommends the following changes to the electoral boundaries determination process:

- a requirement that AED boundaries commissions hold a reasonable number of public hearings and that submissions in writing may be given within a prescribed period of time;
- a requirement that a preliminary report be prepared by the boundaries commission that cannot be sent for approval by Parliament unless and until the Aboriginal community has had an opportunity to respond and input from the Aboriginal community has been considered;
- a requirement that public hearings be held over a sufficiently long period of time to allow accessibility by a population burdened by distance and communication problems;
- generous requirements for the giving of notice of public hearings and of the opportunity to submit written briefs and make oral presentations; and
- consideration should be given to providing funding for witnesses where appropriate.

Recommendation 6

The Committee recommends that Aboriginal self-identification be the critical factor in qualifying as an Aboriginal elector in addition to the standard electoral qualifications of all Canadian voters.

The burden of proof in challenges to those seeking to register on an Aboriginal voters list should rest with those making the challenge.

Furthermore, the Committee recommends that an appeals body or tribunal should be controlled by Aboriginal people and should consist of Aboriginal men and women together with eminent elders.

Recommendation 7

To encourage Aboriginal people with diverse views and economic backgrounds to become candidates without the fear of financial ruin, it is recommended that consideration be given to increasing the expense limitations and financing available for all larger electoral districts, including Aboriginal Electoral Districts.

In addition, the Committee recommends that the winner and all losing candidates gaining a specified percentage of the vote be reimbursed. The percentage of the vote required for reimbursement would have to be on a sliding scale, taking into consideration the number of candidates, the number of ballots cast and the total vote garnered by a particular candidate.

Recommendation 8

The Committee recommends that the number of seats to be created in Atlantic Canada be the subject of further discussion between Atlantic Aboriginal leaders and the federal and provincial governments. The Committee firmly believes that a strong case can be made for more than one AED in Atlantic Canada.

Recommendation 9

The Committee recommends that the boundaries readjustment process be conducted more often to be more responsive to population growth and migration.

In the event that Parliament does not move to establish a boundaries readjustment process based on registered electors, the Committee recommends that legislation establish AEDs within the existing boundaries readjustment process.

Recommendation 10

The Committee recommends that the parliamentary committee charged with considering new electoral legislation actively solicit Aboriginal involvement in the review of legislation creating AEDs.

Recommendation 11

1. Homelessness
The Committee endorses submissions to the Royal Commission advocating that the concept of residency contained in the *Canada Elections Act* be broadened to incorporate homeless persons including the suggestions that:

- homeless persons be entitled to identify a local shelter or hostel as their residence; and
- voters who have not been enumerated be allowed to register on election day.

The Committee recommends that homeless Aboriginal people also be entitled to identify a local Aboriginal community office, such as a band office, Métis local or friendship centre, as their place of residence.

2. Transience
The Committee recommends that an Aboriginal person be able to be enumerated in the AED where he or she is living at the time of enumeration. However, once enumerated, the Aboriginal elector would be able to vote in another district, provided he or she was in the riding for a specified period of time. Given the size of AEDs, voter lists for an entire AED should be provided to all polling stations in the AED in order to facilitate voting by the traveller.

3. The Failure to Enumerate Co-Habitants of Persons on Social Assistance
The Committee recommends that addresses on enumeration lists be kept
confidential for purposes of the election only and not be allowed to be used
for the purpose of denying social assistance or other benefits.

The Committee recommends that any Aboriginal person could be entitled to give as his or her address any Aboriginal community office.

Recommendation 12

4. Distance
The Committee recommends the following measures to overcome the problem of distance from polling stations in AEDs:

- allow for proxy voting in any case where a voter lives beyond a pre-
  determined distance from the nearest polling station;
- provide self-explanatory proxy materials to all voters beyond such distance, such materials to be in both official languages as well as the local
  Aboriginal language where requested by the Aboriginal community;
- hold voting over a longer period;
- make advance polling available over a longer period of time than is
  now allowed;
- expand the availability of advance polling to all voters who live beyond
  the pre-determined distance from the nearest polling station, or who
  intend on election days to be beyond such distance from the nearest
  polling station;
- allow for mobile polling stations during the election period, with their
  itinerary posted well in advance in conspicuous public facilities,
  published in community newspapers and broadcast over local radio
  (itinerary should be required to provide for stops at communities beyond
  a specified distance from the nearest polling station and having a minimum aggregate population);
- polling stations should be located by a returning officer only after consulting local groups and officials, thus avoiding potential trouble spots
  and identifying accessible locations; and
- to ensure an adequate number of convenient polling stations, a legislative provision should require that polling stations should be located
  so that a certain percentage of the voting population does not live beyond
  a set distance from the nearest polling station (for purposes of population location, the most recent census figures should provide the necessary information).

Recommendation 13

5. Aboriginal Employment in Electoral Administration

The Committee recommends that new legislation incorporate strong employment and appointment equity provisions, together with the training necessary to ensure that Aboriginal people have the opportunity to participate in all facets of the administration of the electoral system.

Recommendation 14

6. Language and Literacy

The Committee recommends that:

- all AED election materials (notices, brochures, ballots, etc.) be provided in both official languages and in the local Aboriginal language where requested by the Aboriginal community; and
- symbols be printed on ballots, a practice used in other countries, such that political parties and/or candidates are represented by symbols.

Recommendation 15

7. Public Education and Voter Registration

The Committee recommends that a joint public education and awareness program be implemented by Elections Canada and Aboriginal organizations.

Recommendation 16

8. Report of Chief Electoral Officer

Any suggested changes must be monitored to assess their effectiveness. The Committee therefore recommends that the Chief Electoral Officer be required to report after each election as to the effectiveness of the electoral system in getting the Aboriginal vote out and suggesting any recommendations to improve the situation.

The Report of
the Committee for
Aboriginal Electoral Reform

APPENDICES

APPENDIX 1
Consultation List

FIRST ROUND CONSULTATION LIST

John Amagoalik
Inuit Tapirisat of Canada

J'net August
Aboriginal Youth Council of
    Canada

Roger Augustine
Union of NB Indians

Gary Bohnet
Métis Association of the NWT

Réal Boudrias
Native Alliance of Quebec

Paul Chartrand
Dept. of Native Studies,
    University of Manitoba

Bentley Cheechoo
Nishnawbe-Aski Nation

Matthew Cooncome
Grand Council of the Crees

Regina Crowchild
Indian Association of Alberta

Roland Crowe
Federation of Saskatchewan
    Indian Nations

Larry Desmueles
Métis Association of Alberta

Russell Diabo
Algonquins of Barrière Lake

Dwight Dorey
Native Council of Nova Scotia

Yvon Dumont
Manitoba Métis Federation Inc.

Ruby Durno
Labrador Métis Association

Adam Eneas
First Nations Congress

Georges Erasmus
National Chief, Assembly of First
    Nations

Phil Fontaine
Assembly of Manitoba Chiefs

Phil Fraser
Native Council of Canada (NB)

Ray Funk
Member of Parliament

Ron George
United Native Nations

Keith Goulet
Member of Saskatchewan
    Legislative Assembly

Joe Hare
Union of Ontario Indians

Many Jules
Kamloops Indian Band

Andrew Kirkness
Indian Council of First Nations
   of Manitoba

Chris Lafontaine
Gabriel Dumont Institute

Harry Laforme
Indian Commission of Ontario

Joe Miskokomon
Union of Ontario Indians

Chief Bill Monture
Six Nations

Dave Nawegahbow
Indigenous Bar Association

Ron Rivard
Métis National Council

Viola Robinson
Native Council of Canada

Doris Ronnenberg
Native Council of Canada (Alta)

Konrad Sioui
AFN Regional Vice Chief

Saul Terry
Union of BC Indian Chiefs

Ken Thomas
SIAP

Graham Tuplin
Native Council of PEI

Gerard Webb
Federation of Newfoundland
   Indians

Bill Wilson
First Nations Congress

Don Worme
Indigenous Bar Association

Chief Peter Yellowquill
Dakota Ojibway Tribal Council

Harvey Young
Native Council of Saskatchewan

SECOND ROUND CONSULTATION LIST*

Alliance Tribal Council
Athabasca Tribal Council
Atlantic All Chiefs Assembly
Atlantic Regional Vice-Chiefs
Pearl Calahassen, MLA
Cariboo Tribal Council
Carrier Sekani Tribal Council
Council of Haida Nation
Dakota Ojibway Tribal Council
Edmonton *Journal* Editorial
   Board

Federation of Saskatchewan
   Indian Nations
   Battlefords Treaty #6 Tribal
      Council
   Beardy–Okemasis Band #96
      & 97
   Confederation of Tribal
      Nations
   Meadow Lake Tribal Council
   Prince Albert District Tribal
      Council

---

* Organizations where the Committee made presentations and/or held *in camera*
   meetings. Meetings included discussions at annual general meetings, board
   meetings or discussions with the executive(s) of the organization.

Saskatoon District Tribal
  Council
Touchwood/File Hills/
  Qu'Appelle District
Gitksan Wet'suet'en Tribal
  Council
Grand Council Treaty #3
High Level Tribal Council
Indigenous Bar Association
Interlake Reserve Tribal Council
Inuit Tapirisat of Canada
Island Lake Tribal Council
Kaske Dena Tribal Council
Keewatin Tribal Council
Ktunaxa/Kinbasket Tribal
  Council
Kwakiutl District Council
Lesser Slave Lake Indian
  Regional Council
Manitoba Keewatinowi
  Okimakanaks
Manitoba Métis Federation
Métis Association of Alberta
Métis Association NWT
Métis Society of Saskatchewan
Mid Island Tribal Council
Musgamagw Tribal Council
National Association of Native
  Friendship Centres
National PC Aboriginal Caucus
Native Council of Canada
  Labrador Métis Association
  Native Alliance of Quebec
  Native Council of Alberta
  Native Council of Manitoba
  Native Council of NS
  Native Council of PEI

Native Council of Saskatchewan
NB Aboriginal Peoples Council
United Native Nations
Native Women's Association
  of Canada
Nicola Valley Tribal Council
Nisga'a Tribal Council
North Coast Tribal Council
Nuu-Chah-Nulth Tribal Council
Okanagan Tribal Council
Ontario Métis and Aboriginal
  Association
Quebec Chiefs Assembly
Regina *Leader Post* Editorial Board
Saskatoon *Star Phoenix* Editorial
  Board
Shuswap National Tribal Council
Mary Sillett, Inuit Women's
  Association
Mary Simon, Inuit Circumpolar
  Conference
South Island Tribal Council
Sto:Lo Tribal Council
Swampy Cree Tribal Council
Toronto *Globe & Mail* Editorial
  Board
Tribal Chiefs' Association
Tsilhquot'in Tribal Council
Tsimshian Tribal Council
Union of BC Indian Chiefs
Union of NB Indians
Union of Ontario Indians
Senator Charlie Watt, Makivik
  Corporation
Whe-La-La-U Tribal Council
Women of the Métis Nation
Yellowhead Tribal Council

WRITTEN AND ORAL RESPONSES AND COMMENTS

Philip Adams, Government
of Yukon

Curtis Ahenakew, Shell Lake,
Saskatchewan

The Honourable Warren
Allmand, MP

Gorden Antoine

Senator Jack Austin

The Honourable Lloyd Axworthy,
PC, MP

Alcie Bear, Senator MMF

Gertrude Bear, La Ronge,
Saskatchewan

The Honourable Perrin
Beatty, PC, MP

Brian Beaudry

Tony Belcourt

Cynthia Bertolin

Don Blenkarn, MP

Senator Sidney Buckwold

The Honourable Charles
Caccia, MP

The Honourable Kim
Campbell, PC, MP

L. Andrew Cardozo, Canadian
Ethnocultural Council

Glenna Cayen, Saskatoon,
Saskatchewan

Clem Chartier

The Honourable Jean
Chrétien, PC, MP

The Right Honourable
Joe Clark, PC, MP

Darren Cook, La Ronge,
Saskatchewan

Sheila Copps, MP

Marian Daniels, Saskatchewan

Christine Deom

The Honourable Consiglio
Di Nino

Phillip Dorion

George Eckalook, Resolute
Bay, NWT

Edmonton *Journal* Editorial
Board

Georges Erasmus

Michelle Falardeau-Ramsay,
Canadian Human Rights
Commission

Douglas Fisher, *Ottawa Sun*

Senator Royce Frith

Ray Funk, MP

Richard J.N. Gamble, Chief,
Beardy–Okemasis Band

Chief Wendy Grant

Deanna Greyeyes, Regina,
Saskatchewan

Jack Grieves

Walter Guppy, Kenora, BC

John Harvard, MP

Jim Hawkes, MP

Felix Holtmann, MP

Marilyn Jones

Chief Harvy Jules

Chief Many Jules

Lucie Kalula, A/Mairess,
Municipality of Tuaktaq

Stan Keyes, MP

James Larocque, LaRonge,
Saskatchewan

Chief Robert Louie, Westbank
Indian Council

Chief Patrick Madahbee,
Little Current, Ontario

Chief Joyce Manuel, Neskonlith
Indian Band

Keith Mathiew

Chief Nathen Mathiew

Audrey McLaughlin, Leader,
NDP

Cynthia McNab

Kathleen McNab

Myriam McNab
Fina McNeil
Gordon R. Miller, Ottawa,
    Ontario
Dennis Mills, MP
Senator Hartland Molson
Ken Monteith, MP
Don Moses
Chief Joe Norton
Roger Obonsawin
Dr. Rey D. Pagtakhan, MP
The Honourable Steve
    Paproski, PC, MP
Daniel Paul, Confederacy of
    Mainland Micmacs
Gorden Peters, Chiefs of Ontario
Sophie Pierre, Ktunaxa/
    Kinbasket Tribal Council
Ross Reid, MP
Claire Riddle
Ron Rivard, Métis National
    Council
Viola Robinson, President, NCC
Don Ross

Billie Russell, Okanagan Tribal
    Council
Chief Steve Sacobie, Kingsclear
    Indian Band
Marjorie Sandercock,
    Yellowknife, NWT
Robert Sheppard, *Globe & Mail*
The Honourable Tom Siddon,
    PC, MP
Robert E. Simon, Savona, BC
Jim Sinclair, Assembly of
    Aboriginal Peoples of
    Saskatchewan
Chief Saul Terry, Union of
    BC Indian Chiefs
Ken Thomas
Toronto *Sun* Editorial Board
Mary Ellen Turpel
Vancouver *Sun* Editorial Board
David Walker, MP
George Watts
Ruth Williams
Donald Worme, Indigenous Bar
    Association

APPENDIX 2
Questions and Answers

Are Aboriginal Electoral Districts a substitute for self-government?

No. A voice in the House of Commons is not inconsistent with the goal of self-government. One form of representation does not preclude the other. Rather, they are complementary forms of representation. For example, in Europe the citizens of sovereign states elect their own representatives to the European Parliament. Representatives from each sovereign state speak to matters of common interest and deal with issues that cut across state boundaries.

Are Aboriginal Electoral Districts a form of apartheid?

Even to suggest that Aboriginal Electoral Districts are a form of apartheid is misleading and inflammatory. First, the proposal works within the existing framework of electoral laws. In its essence, the proposal is intended to include Aboriginal people more effectively in the political system, not to exclude them. Second, the proposal does not guarantee separate seats; it puts in place and guarantees that a process will be available whereby Aboriginal people can be represented more effectively in the House of Commons. Finally, the proposal is premised on full freedom of choice for Aboriginal people about where and how they participate in the electoral process.

Wouldn't implementation of this proposal result in a flood of requests from other groups for similar consideration?

First, let's be clear. Aboriginal people have a defined status under the Constitution of Canada. But when it comes to achieving fair representation of Aboriginal people in the political institutions of our country, we have a particular difficulty: we have the numbers, but our numbers are geographically dispersed across the country.

This proposal attempts to redress that situation by adding flexibility to the current system to allow for the creation of Aboriginal Electoral Districts based on our numbers. The underlying principles of the current legislation already recognize the need to reflect communities of interest and identity in establishing electoral districts and to promote the efficacy of the vote. Our proposal aims to allow Aboriginal people to benefit from these principles in a way that we have not done before because of our geographic dispersal.

Will Aboriginal *seats* be guaranteed in legislation or in the Constitution?

No. The proposal seeks to establish a process in federal legislation whereby Aboriginal Electoral Districts could be created if this is the wish of Aboriginal people. Aboriginal people will decide whether they want Aboriginal Electoral Districts.

Couldn't we just redraw the boundaries of federal electoral districts to create districts with an Aboriginal majority?

This does not appear to be possible because Aboriginal people are dispersed across vast geographic areas. Currently there are only four electoral districts with an Aboriginal population greater than 25% of the total.

How many Aboriginal Electoral Districts could be created?

The number of electoral districts that could be created depends upon the number of Aboriginal people in a given province and the size of the province's electoral quotient. There will be at least one in each province except in Atlantic Canada. In those provinces with large Aboriginal populations, British Columbia, Ontario and the Prairies, it may be possible to create two Aboriginal Electoral Districts. The final determination will depend upon obtaining more accurate and reliable statistical information.

Can Aboriginal Electoral Districts be created before the next election?

Probably not. New electoral boundaries cannot be drawn until release of the required 1991 census information in late 1992. The redrawing of electoral boundaries, under existing legislation, then takes approximately two years to complete. We do believe, however, that the proposal can be implemented for the general election immediately following the next one.

Are the Aboriginal people in Atlantic Canada excluded from this proposal?

The size of the Aboriginal population in these provinces would not permit the creation of an Aboriginal Electoral District in each province. We therefore recommend a constitutional amendment to create one Aboriginal Electoral District covering all of Atlantic Canada.

Will the number of seats in the House of Commons increase as a result of creating Aboriginal Electoral Districts?

No. Under present constitutional arrangements seats are allocated to the provinces. Aboriginal Electoral Districts would come out of these allocations.

Will Aboriginal Electoral Districts cross provincial boundaries?

No. The Constitution requires that electoral districts be contained within provincial boundaries. We do propose, however, that there be a single electoral district covering all the Atlantic provinces. This will require a constitutional amendment.

If Aboriginal Electoral Districts are established, will an Aboriginal person have two votes?

No. Aboriginal voters will have the right to choose whether they wish to vote in an Aboriginal Electoral District or in the general electoral district in which they live. This kind of choice is already available in the law to students who move away from home to attend college or university and to members of the Armed Forces and the foreign service posted abroad. Therefore a precedent already exists.

Will Aboriginal people have a say in establishing the boundaries of each Aboriginal Electoral District?

Yes. Where more than one Aboriginal Electoral District is to be created in a province, the independent electoral boundaries commission will consult with Aboriginal people in determining the boundary. This could mean that separate electoral districts could be created within a province for Indian and Métis people, for example, provided both have the number of electors that meet the province's electoral quotient.

Will Aboriginal people have to participate in political parties?

They may choose whether to do so. Aboriginal people in an Aboriginal Electoral District would have the right to nominate and elect anyone they choose. Candidates could be independents or could be official candidates from a recognized political party.

Will Aboriginal Electoral Districts create incentives for aboriginal people to participate in the electoral system?

It stands to reason that the participation of Aboriginal people will be enhanced if they know that the system may result in Aboriginal MPs being sent to the House of Commons. There are a number of examples of increased Aboriginal participation in the electoral system where there are Aboriginal candidates running for elected office. The level of Aboriginal participation in federal elections in the Northwest Territories is testimony to that effect.

Will a system of Aboriginal Electoral Districts have the effect of politically isolating Aboriginal people?

Given the number of Aboriginal representatives elected to date, it is obvious that Aboriginal people are isolated now. The creation of Aboriginal Electoral Districts will be a step towards eliminating the political isolation of Aboriginal people and encouraging greater participation in the governance of Canada.

Will the system isolate MPs elected from Aboriginal Electoral Districts? Will other MPs ignore Aboriginal constituents? Will they tell them to see their Aboriginal MP?

It is anticipated that all MPs will work together to ensure that the needs of all constituents are met. While no prescription can force MPs to work with one another, all representatives must understand that the rationale for creating Aboriginal Electoral Districts is the failure of the present electoral system to produce effective representation for Aboriginal people. Co-operation is required to ensure that the entire democratic process is responsive to the needs of all Canadians, whether Aboriginal or non-Aboriginal.

Will Aboriginal MPs deal only with Aboriginal issues?

No. MPs from Aboriginal Electoral Districts would have the same rights and privileges as other Members of Parliament and would participate in the full range of issues before Parliament. Aboriginal people are citizens of Canada, and their MPs will deal with all issues that are of interest to Canadians.

Will the limited number of Aboriginal Electoral Districts accommodate the interests of less numerous aboriginal groups within an Aboriginal Electoral District?

This is an important consideration which will be discussed by the leadership across the country. Aboriginal people have a history of making decisions by consensus and it is likely that this will continue.

How will this proposal benefit the small number of Inuit in northern Quebec and northern Manitoba?

Inuit people would have the right to vote in an Aboriginal Electoral District along with all other Aboriginal people who wished to participate. It would be necessary for the MP elected to represent and work on behalf of all Aboriginal constituents. An MP elected in an Aboriginal Electoral District should be sensitive to the aims and aspirations of all Aboriginal people within the Aboriginal Electoral District.

Won't Aboriginal Electoral Districts be too large to manage?

Aboriginal Electoral Districts may indeed cover large areas. There are already special provisions in federal electoral legislation for the expenses of MPs in constituencies with large geographic areas. It is our understanding that the Royal Commission on Electoral Reform and Party Financing is reviewing those provisions.

If the electoral system is to treat everyone equally, why should Aboriginal people receive special treatment?

There is no special treatment. Aboriginal Electoral Districts deal with structural discrimination in the electoral system. All electoral rules would apply to Aboriginal Electoral Districts. The proposal is designed to ensure that

Aboriginal people will be represented in the House of Commons in proportion to our share of the Canadian population. Such is not the case today. Only 12 self-identified Aboriginal MPs have ever sat in the House of Commons out of the 10 966 available seats in all general and by-elections since Confederation.

How would the proposal be implemented?
An important advantage of this proposal is that it could be implemented by Parliament through amendments to existing electoral legislation.

Is the consultation paper a "take it or leave it" document?
No. The purpose of the consultative document is to seek Aboriginal views on a comprehensive proposal for Aboriginal representation in Parliament. The Committee invites suggestions on ways to improve the proposal. The Committee is seeking consensus in the Aboriginal community and invites the active participation of all interested Aboriginal people and other Canadians.

Will Aboriginal people be consulted on this proposal?
Yes. In January Senator Len Marchand led a round of consultations with the leadership of national and regional Aboriginal organizations. These organizations requested further and more in-depth consultations. These are now being launched.

Who will be undertaking these consultations?
The consultations will be undertaken by a group of current and former Aboriginal Members of the House of Commons. These individuals have formed the Committee for Aboriginal Electoral Reform.

What will be the nature of these consultations?
There will be a direct mailing of the proposal to Aboriginal First Nations and representatives of Aboriginal service delivery organizations. The Committee will be placing an advertisement in Aboriginal newspapers to inform individuals and organizations. The views of the executive of Aboriginal political organizations at the national and regional levels will be sought through on-site visits.

What will the Committee do at the end of the consultation process?
A final report with recommendations will be prepared. The report will incorporate the views of Aboriginal individuals and organizations expressed during the consultation process. The report will be presented to the Royal Commission on Electoral Reform and Party Financing for its consideration.

Is this an initiative by the government or one of the political parties?

Neither. This initiative is being led by current and former Members of the House of Commons who are seeking to change the electoral system to ensure that Aboriginal people have the opportunity to be represented in the House of Commons in proportion to their numbers.

What is the position of the Royal Commission on Electoral Reform and Party Financing in this proposal?

The Committee for Aboriginal Electoral Reform has met with the Royal Commission. The Royal Commission is providing technical support to the committee and awaits with interest our report on the level of consensus in the Aboriginal community on our proposal.

APPENDIX 3
Chronology of Aboriginal Electoral Voting Rights

1867   Parliamentarians elected in accordance with electoral laws of the provinces. All provinces exclude Indians from voting.

1875   British Columbia expressly disqualifies "Indians and Chinamen" from voting.

1876   Ontario expressly prohibits on reserve Indians from voting.

1881   NWT disqualifies enfranchised Indians.

1884   Ontario prohibits off reserve Indians from voting where individuals receive treaty payments, annuities or money from the band.

1885   *Electoral Franchise Act* provides Indians in Eastern Canada with right to vote provided that they meet a low property test.

1886   Manitoba disqualifies Indians and persons of Indian blood from receiving any annuities from voting.

1889   New Brunswick enacts legislation disqualifying Indians from voting.

1898   *Electoral Franchise Act* is repealed and the electoral laws of the provinces are reinstated. All provinces exclude Indians from voting.

1908   Saskatchewan disqualifies Indians from exercising the franchise.

1909   Alberta disqualifies all persons of Indian blood who belonged or reported to belong to any Indian Band.

1915   Quebec disqualifies Indians and mixed bloods domiciled on lands reserved for Indians.

1917   *War-Time Elections Act/Military Voters Act* extend franchise to Indians in active military service.

1919   Yukon disqualifies Indians from voting.

1920   *Dominion Elections Act* – On reserve Indians disqualified unless the Indian served in the Navy, Military, or the Air Force in the First World War.

1922   PEI disqualifies Indians on reserve from voting.

1934   Esquimaux (Inuit) disqualified from federal franchise (no exemption for Armed Forces service).

1944	An Act to Amend the *Dominion Elections Act* provides voting rights to Indians who participated in World War II and their spouses.
1949	British Columbia extends provincial franchise to Indians.
1950	An Act to Amend the *Dominion Elections Act* provides voting rights to Indians who waive their tax exempt status with respect to personal property.
	Inuit receive unqualified right to vote in federal elections.
1952	Manitoba extends provincial franchise to all Indians.
1954	Ontario extends provincial franchise to all Indians.
1960	Saskatchewan extends provincial franchise to all Indians.
	Federal Universal Indian Suffrage granted to Indians.
1963	PEI and New Brunswick extend provincial franchise to all Indians.
1965	Alberta extends provincial franchise to all Indians.
1969	Quebec extends provincial franchise to all Indians.
1982	Liberal Party of Canada establishes 12 member Standing Committee for Native and Original Peoples.
1983	Progressive Conservative Party recognizes a National Progressive Conservative Aboriginal Association.
1989	The National Executive of the Liberal Party of Canada endorses the establishment of an Aboriginal Peoples' Commission within the Liberal Party.

APPENDIX 4
Scenario for Implementation

The following scenario provides an overview of how Aboriginal Electoral Districts could be implemented within this context of electoral reform:

1. The decennial census has been conducted in 1991.

2. After the census results are published in 1992, each province will be allocated its seats in the House of Commons.

3. Later that year, the potential number of Aboriginal Electoral Districts would be announced when census figures on Aboriginal people become available.

4. Calling of the next general election will trigger the compilation of a list of all citizens of voting age by Elections Canada through the usual enumeration method.

5. To overcome historical difficulties in enumerating Aboriginal people, Elections Canada would work jointly with Aboriginal organizations in the next election to ensure that Aboriginal electors are registered.

6. Following the election, a new electoral quotient for each province would be determined as a basis for allocating seats to the province.

7. An electoral boundaries commission for each province will be established for the purpose of drawing a new electoral map.

8. The first order of business for the commissions would be to determine how many Aboriginal Electoral Districts would be formed in each province.

9. The commissions will rely on the number of Aboriginal electors registered on the Aboriginal electoral list for the previous election and on the results of a special registration drive co-ordinated by Elections Canada in conjunction with Aboriginal organizations.

10. Once the list of registered Aboriginal electors is completed and submitted to the electoral boundaries commissions, they would establish the number of Aboriginal Electoral Districts by dividing the number of registered Aboriginal electors by the provincial electoral quotient. (For example, if the electoral quotient for the province was 40 000 people and there were 81 000 registered Aboriginal electors, then the electoral boundaries commission would be required to create two Aboriginal Electoral Districts.)

11. If more than one Aboriginal Electoral District can be created in a province, the boundaries of each district would be determined through consultations between the electoral boundaries commission and the Aboriginal people concerned.

12. After each general election, Elections Canada would determine whether electoral boundaries should be redrawn as a result of population changes.

13. In making this determination, Elections Canada would consider whether there was an increase in the number of registered Aboriginal electors sufficient to create new Aboriginal Electoral Districts.

14. If Elections Canada determined that boundaries of electoral districts in a province had to be redrawn after an election, a new electoral quotient would be calculated for the province.

15. The Electoral Boundaries Commission for the provinces affected would proceed to draw boundaries for general and Aboriginal Electoral Districts, hold public hearings and report to the Speaker of the House of Commons as under the present system.

PART 4

APPENDICES

~

APPENDIX A
Orders-in-Council

C O M M I S S I O N

appointing   nommant

Pierre Lortie,   Pierre Lortie,
Elwood Lorrie Cowley,   Elwood Lorrie Cowley,
Pierre Wilfrid Fortier,   Pierre Wilfrid Fortier,
Donald H. Oliver,   Donald H. Oliver,
and   et
Lucie Pépin   Lucie Pépin

Commissioners under Part I of the   Commissaires en vertu de la
Inquiries Act, to inquire on the   partie I de la Loi sur les
appropriate principles and process   enquêtes, chargés de faire
that should govern the election of   enquête sur les principes et
members of the House of Commons and   procédures qui devraient régir
the financing of political parties   l'élection des députés et le
and of candidates' campaigns.   financement des partis
                                         politiques et des campagnes des
                                         candidats.

DATED ...... 8th December, 1989   DATÉE le ...... 8 décembre 1989

RECORDED ... 8th December, 1989   ENREGISTRÉE le 8 décembre 1989

Film 627 Document 205

David D. Kirchmayer

DEPUTY REGISTRAR   SOUS-REGISTRAIRE
GENERAL OF CANADA   GÉNÉRAL DU CANADA

Canada

ELIZABETH THE SECOND, by the Grace of God of the United Kingdom, Canada and Her other Realms and Territories QUEEN, Head of the Commonwealth, Defender of the Faith.	ELIZABETH DEUX, par la Grâce de Dieu, REINE du Royaume-Uni, du Canada et de ses autres royaumes et territoires, Chef du Commonwealth, Défenseur de la Foi.

DEPUTY ATTORNEY
GENERAL

SOUS-PROCUREUR
GÉNÉRAL

TO ALL TO WHOM these Presents shall come or whom the same may in anyway concern,

À TOUS CEUX à qui les présentes parviennent ou qu'icelles peuvent de quelque manière concerner,

GREETING:

SALUT :

WHEREAS, by Order in Council P.C. 1989-2290 of November 15, 1989, the Committee of the Privy Council has advised that a Commission do issue under Part I of the Inquiries Act, chapter I-11 of the Revised Statutes of Canada, 1985, appointing Pierre Lortie of St-Lambert, Quebec, Elwood Lorrie Cowley of Saskatoon, Saskatchewan, Pierre Wilfrid Fortier of Ottawa, Ontario, Donald H. Oliver of Halifax, Nova Scotia, and Lucie Pépin of Montreal, Quebec, to be Our Commissioners to inquire into and to report on the appropriate principles and process that should govern the election of members of the House of Commons and the financing of political parties and of candidates' campaigns;

Attendu que, aux termes du décret C.P. 1989-2290 du 15 novembre 1989, le Comité du Conseil privé a recommandé que soit émise, en vertu de la partie I de la Loi sur les enquêtes, chapitre I-11 des Lois révisées du Canada (1985), une commission nommant Pierre Lortie, de Saint-Lambert (Québec), Elwood Lorrie Cowley, de Saskatoon (Saskatchewan), Pierre Wilfrid Fortier, d'Ottawa (Ontario), Donald H. Oliver, d'Halifax (Nouvelle-Écosse) et Lucie Pépin, de Montréal (Québec), à titre de Nos commissaires chargés d'enquêter et de présenter un rapport sur les principes et procédures qui devraient régir l'élection des députés et le financement des partis politiques et des campagnes des candidats,

NOW KNOW YOU that We, by and with the advice of Our Privy Council for Canada, do by these Presents nominate, constitute and appoint Pierre Lortie, Elwood Lorrie Cowley, Pierre Wilfrid Fortier, Donald H. Oliver and Lucie Pépin to be Our Commissioners to conduct such an inquiry;

Sachez que, sur et avec l'avis de Notre Conseil privé pour le Canada, Nous désignons, constituons et nommons, par les présentes, Pierre Lortie, Elwood Lorrie Cowley, Pierre Wilfrid Fortier, Donald H. Oliver et Lucie Pépin, Nos commissaires pour mener cette enquête;

TO HAVE, HOLD, exercise and enjoy the said office, place and trust unto you Pierre Lortie, Elwood Lorrie Cowley, Pierre Wilfrid Fortier, Donald H. Oliver and Lucie Pépin, together with the rights, powers, privileges and emoluments unto the said office, place and trust of right and by law appertaining during Our Pleasure;

AND WE DO HEREBY advise that Our Commissioners inquire into and report on the appropriate principles and process that should govern the election of members of the House of Commons and the financing of political parties and of candidates' campaigns, the inquiry include an examination of

(a) the practices, procedures and legislation in Canada,

(b) the means by which political parties should be funded, the provision of funds to political parties from any source, the limits on such funding and the uses to which such funds ought, or ought not, to be put,

(c) the qualifications of electors and the compiling of voters' lists, including the advisibility of the establishment of a permanent voters' list;

À titre de commissaires de cette enquête, vous, Pierre Lortie, Elwood Lorrie Cowley, Pierre Wilfrid Fortier, Donald H. Oliver et Lucie Pépin, jouirez, à titre amovible, de tous les droits, pouvoirs, privilèges et avantages conférés de droit et de par la loi à ces fonctions.

Nous recommandons que Nos commissaires enquêtent et présentent un rapport sur les principes et procédures qui devraient régir l'élection des députés et le financement des partis politiques et des campagnes des candidats, et que l'enquête porte notamment sur les questions suivantes :

a) les pratiques, les procédures et la législation canadiennes;

b) les moyens par lesquels les partis politiques devraient être financés, leurs sources de financement, les limites à ce genre de financement et les fins auxquelles ces fonds devraient ou ne devraient pas être destinés;

c) la qualité d'électeur et l'établissement des listes électorales, notamment l'opportunité de créer une liste électorale permanente.

AND WE DO HEREBY authorize Our Commissioners

(a) subject to paragraph (d), to adopt such procedures and methods as they may consider expedient for the proper conduct of the inquiry and to sit at such times and such places as they may decide,

(b) to engage the services of such experts and other persons as are referred to in subsection 11(1) of the Inquiries Act as well as the former elected representatives referred to in paragraph (d), at such rates of remuneration and reimbursement as may be approved by the Treasury Board,

(c) to rent office space and facilities for the purposes of the inquiry in accordance with Treasury Board policies;

AND WE DO HEREBY direct Our Commissioners

(d) in order to assist them to develop workable proposals based on practical electoral experience, to establish an advisory panel of such former elected representatives, including those who have served at the federal and provincial levels of government in Canada, as are in their opinion necessary for the purposes of the inquiry,

Nous autorisons Nos commissaires :

a) sous réserve de l'alinéa d), à adopter les méthodes et les procédures qu'ils considèrent les plus indiquées pour la conduite de l'enquête et à siéger aux endroits et aux moments qu'ils jugent convenir;

b) à retenir les services d'experts et d'autres personnes comme le prévoit le paragraphe 11(1) de la Loi sur les enquêtes, ainsi que d'anciens représentants élus mentionnés à l'alinéa d), aux taux de rémunération et de remboursement qu'approuvera le Conseil du Trésor;

c) à louer les bureaux et les installations nécessaires à l'enquête, conformément aux politiques du Conseil du Trésor;

Nous ordonnons à Nos commissaires :

d) de constituer, pour les aider à élaborer des propositions fondées sur une expérience électorale pratique, un conseil consultatif composé d'anciens représentants élus dont des personnes qui ont servi aux paliers fédéral et provincial de gouvernement du Canada, en nombre suffisant pour les fins de l'enquête;

(e) to submit their report in both official languages to the Governor in Council, and

(f) to file their papers and records with the Clerk of the Privy Council as soon as reasonably may be after the conclusion of the inquiry;

AND WE DO FURTHER designate Pierre Lortie as Chairman of the Commission.

IN TESTIMONY WHEREOF, We have caused these Our Letters to be made Patent and the Great Seal of Canada to be hereunto affixed.

WITNESS:

Our Right Trusty and Well-beloved Jeanne Sauvé, a Member of Our Privy Council for Canada, Chancellor and Principal Companion of Our Order of Canada, Chancellor and Commander of Our Order of Military Merit upon whom We have conferred Our Canadian Forces' Decoration, Governor General and Commander-in-Chief of Canada.

e) de présenter un rapport dans les deux langues officielles au gouverneur en conseil;

f) de remettre leurs dossiers et documents au greffier du Conseil privé le plus tôt possible après la fin de l'enquête.

Nous nommons Pierre Lortie président de la Commission.

EN FOI DE QUOI, Nous avons fait émettre Nos présentes lettres patentes et à icelles fait apposer le grand sceau du Canada.

TÉMOIN:

Notre très fidèle et bien-aimée Jeanne Sauvé, Membre de Notre Conseil privé pour le Canada, Chancelier et Compagnon principal de Notre Ordre du Canada, Chancelier et Commandeur de Notre Ordre du Mérite militaire à qui Nous avons décerné Notre Décoration des Forces canadiennes, Gouverneur général et Commandant en chef du Canada.

AT OUR GOVERNMENT HOUSE, in Our City of Ottawa, this eighth day of December in the year of Our Lord one thousand nine hundred and eighty-nine and in the thirty-eighth year of Our Reign.

À NOTRE HÔTEL DU GOUVERNE-MENT, en Notre ville d'Ottawa, ce huitième jour de décembre en l'an de grâce mil neuf cent quatre-vingt-neuf, le trente-huitième de Notre règne.

BY COMMAND,   PAR ORDRE,

DEPUTY REGISTRAR   SOUS-REGISTRAIRE
GENERAL OF CANADA   GÉNÉRAL DU CANADA

COMMISSION

appointing   nommant

Robert Thomas Gabor   Robert Thomas Gabor
and   et
William Knight   William Knight

Commissioners under Part I of the   Commissaires en vertu de la
Inquiries Act, to inquire on the   partie I de la Loi sur les
appropriate principles and process   enquêtes, chargés de faire
that should govern the election of   enquête sur les principes et
members of the House of Commons and   procédures qui devraient régir
the financing of political parties   l'élection des députés et le
and of candidates' campaigns.   financement des partis
                                         politiques et des campagnes des
                                         candidats.

DATED ...... 2nd November, 1990   DATÉE le ...... 2 novembre 1990

RECORDED ... 2nd November, 1990   ENREGISTRÉE le   2 novembre 1990

Film 644 Document 6

DEPUTY REGISTRAR   SOUS-REGISTRAIRE
GENERAL OF CANADA   GÉNÉRAL DU CANADA

Canada

ELIZABETH THE SECOND, by the Grace of God of the United Kingdom, Canada and Her other Realms and Territories QUEEN, Head of the Commonwealth, Defender of the Faith.	ELIZABETH DEUX, par la Grâce de Dieu, REINE du Royaume-Uni, du Canada et de ses autres royaumes et territoires, Chef du Commonwealth, Défenseur de la Foi.

DEPUTY ATTORNEY GENERAL	SOUS-PROCUREUR GÉNÉRAL

TO ALL TO WHOM these Presents shall come or whom the same may in anyway concern,

GREETING:

WHEREAS, by Order in Council P.C. 1990-2167 of October 3, 1990, the Committee of the Privy Council has advised that a Commission do issue under Part I of the Inquiries Act, chapter I-11 of the Revised Statutes of Canada, 1985, appointing Robert Thomas Gabor of Winnipeg, Manitoba, and William Knight of Ottawa, Ontario, to be Our Commissioners to inquire into the matters described in Our Commission issued pursuant to Order in Council P.C. 1989-2290 of November 15, 1989, vice Our Commissioners Elwood Lorrie Cowley of Saskatoon, Saskatchewan, and Donald H. Oliver of Halifax, Nova Scotia, who have resigned;

NOW KNOW YOU that We, by and with the advice of Our Privy Council for Canada, do by these Presents nominate, constitute and appoint Robert Thomas Gabor and William Knight to be Our Commissioners to inquire into the matters described in Our Commission issued pursuant to Order in Council P.C. 1989-2290 of November 15, 1989;

À TOUS CEUX à qui les présentes parviennent ou qu'icelles peuvent de quelque manière concerner,

SALUT :

Attendu que le Comité du Conseil privé recommande, en vertu du décret C.P. 1990-2167 du 3 octobre 1990, que soit prise, en vertu de la partie I de la Loi sur les enquêtes, chapitre I-11 des Lois révisées du Canada (1985) une commission visant la nomination de Robert Thomas Gabor, de la ville de Winnipeg (Manitoba), et de William Knight, de la ville d'Ottawa (Ontario), à titre de commissaires chargés de faire enquête sur les questions décrites dans Notre commission prise en vertu du décret C.P. 1989-2290 du 15 novembre 1989, en remplacement d'Elwood Lorrie Cowley, de la ville de Saskatoon (Saskatchewan), et de Donald H. Oliver, de la ville de Halifax (Nouvelle-Écosse), commissaires démissionnaires,

Sachez que, sur et avec l'avis de Notre Conseil privé pour le Canada, Nous désignons, constituons et nommons Robert Thomas Gabor et William Knight commissaires chargés de faire enquête sur les questions décrites dans Notre commission prise en vertu du décret C.P. 1989-2290 du 15 novembre 1989;

TO HAVE, HOLD, exercise and enjoy the said office, place and trust unto you Robert Thomas Gabor and William Knight, together with the rights, powers, privileges and emoluments unto the said office, place and trust of right and by law appertaining during Our Pleasure.

IN TESTIMONY WHEREOF, We have caused these Our Letters to be made Patent and the Great Seal of Canada to be hereunto affixed.

WITNESS:

Our Right Trusty and Well-beloved Ramon John Hnatyshyn, a Member of Our Privy Council for Canada, Chancellor and Principal Companion of Our Order of Canada, Chancellor and Commander of Our Order of Military Merit, One of Our Counsel learned in the law, Governor General and Commander-in-Chief of Canada.

AT OUR GOVERNMENT HOUSE, in Our City of Ottawa, this second day of November in the year of Our Lord one thousand nine hundred and ninety and in the thirty-ninth year of Our Reign.

À titre de commissaires de cette enquête, vous, Robert Thomas Gabor et William Knight, jouirez, à titre amovible, de tous les droits, pouvoirs, privilèges et avantages conférés de droit et de par la loi à ces fonctions.

EN FOI DE QUOI, Nous avons fait émettre Nos présentes lettres patentes et à icelles fait apposer le grand sceau du Canada.

TÉMOIN:

Notre très fidèle et bien-aimé Ramon John Hnatyshyn, Membre de Notre Conseil privé pour le Canada, Chancelier et Compagnon principal de Notre Ordre du Canada, Chancelier et Commandeur de Notre Ordre du Mérite militaire, l'un de Nos conseillers juridiques, Gouverneur général et Commandant en chef du Canada.

À NOTRE HÔTEL DU GOUVERNE-MENT, en Notre ville d'Ottawa, ce deuxième jour de novembre en l'an de grâce mil neuf cent quatre-vingt-dix, le trente-neuvième de Notre règne.

BY COMMAND,   BY COMMAND,

DEPUTY REGISTRAR   DEPUTY REGISTRAR
GENERAL OF CANADA   GENERAL OF CANADA

APPENDIX B
Schedule of Written Submissions

Adams, Mr. and Mrs. Ian
Adamson, Agar
Adkin, Dennis W.
Adsett-Macintyre, Rebecca
Ainsworth, William C.
Alberta Federal and
    Intergovernmental Affairs
Alberta Federation of Labour
Alberta Liberal Party
Alberta Medical Association
Allen, Phyllis
Altenhof, E.J.
Anderson, D.M.
Anderson, Judith
Andrews, Kenneth
Angell, Harold M.
Armishaw, Irene M.
Armstrong, Patricia
Assad, Mark
Assembly of First Nations
Association canadienne de la
    radio et de la télévision de
    langue française Inc.
Association de la presse
    francophone
Association des centres d'accueil
    du Québec
Association des éditeurs de la
    presse hebdomadaire régionale
    francophone
Association des médecins
    psychiatres du Québec
Association des professeurs pour
    des programmes universitaires
    internationaux
Association des propriétaires
    de tavernes et brasseries
    du Québec Inc.

Association néo-démocrate
    de la circonscription de
    Hull–Aylmer
Association of Canadian
    Advertisers Incorporated
Association of Canadian
    Distillers
Association progressiste-
    conservatrice de la
    circonscription de Roberval
Atkins, The Honourable Senator
    Norman K.
Avram, Lee
Axworthy, Chris
Axworthy, The Honourable Lloyd
Backholm, Irene
Baffin Regional Council
Baffin Region Inuit Association
Bagot, H.
Baird, Bessie E.
Baldwin, William Archie
Balshaw, Marguerite, and
    Frances Esler
Barabas, Joe
Barabas, Susan
Barnes, Adele
Barrett, Douglas
Barrett, Howard
Barron, R.E.
Battlefords–Meadow Lake
    Progressive Conservative
    Riding Association
Beamish, Daniel
Belsher, Ross
Benzvy-Miller, Shereen
Bernier, Céline
Bevilacqua, Maurizio
Birchard, Guy

Bissonnette, Elaine
Blair, Margaret
Blair, Richard M.L.
Blenkarn, Don
Bloomfield, Garnet M.
Bohlen, J.C.
Boisvert, Jacques
Boland, Patrick W.
Boroudjerdi, Mohammad
Bourgault, Lise
Bouwmeester, Ralph
Bowd, Alex J.
Bowes, Russell D.F. and Roberta
Boyer, Patrick
Boyle Street Community Services
    Co-operative
Brams, Steven J.
Brant Liberal Association
Brasser, Margaret and John
Brazzell, Gary T.
Breaugh, Mike
Brick, Frank A.
Bridges, A.J.
British Columbia and Yukon
    Hotels Association
British Columbia Association for
    Community Living
British Columbia Association of
    Broadcasters
British Columbia Civil Liberties
    Association
British Columbia Coalition of
    the Disabled
British Columbia Corrections
    Branch, Adult Institutional
    Services
British Columbia Council of
    Federal New Democratic Party
    Ridings
British Columbia Federation
    of Labour
Broadhurst, Carol
Brooks, O.J.
Brown, Dianna

Brown, Jerry
Brown, Michael
Buck, Evelyn M.
Bujold, The Honourable Rémi,
    and Louis Duclos
Bulkowski, Peter
Bundgard, Paul M.
Burnaby–Kingsway New
    Democrat Riding Association
Burnett, James E.
Burnie, Mary and Helen
Burrows, William
Business and Professional
    Women's Club of Thompson
Business Council for Fair Trade
Butcher, John
Byers Casgrain
Byl, Pete
Caccia, The Honourable Charles
Cairns, Rosemary
Caldwell, Rev. R. Quincy
Calgary Chamber of Commerce
Calgary Southeast Progressive
    Conservative Riding
    Association
Callaway, Paul C.
Cameron, Don
Campbell, D.M.
Canadian Advisory Council on
    the Status of Women
Canadian Alliance for Trade and
    Job Opportunities
Canadian Association for
    Community Living
Canadian Association of
    Broadcasters
Canadian Association of
    Elizabeth Fry Societies
Canadian Association of
    Friedreich's Ataxia
Canadian Association of Liquor
    Jurisdictions
Canadian Association of the Deaf
Canadian Bar Association

Canadian Broadcasting
Corporation, Northern Service,
Eastern Arctic
Canadian Broadcasting
Corporation, Parliamentary
and National Community
Relations
Canadian Cable Television
Association
Canadian Chamber of Commerce
Canadian Daily Newspaper
Publishers Association
Canadian Disability Rights
Council
Canadian Ethnocultural Council
Canadian Federation of Labour
Canadian Federation of Students
Canadian Forces Base Alouette,
Bagotville
Canadian Home and School and
Parent-Teacher Federation
Canadian Human Rights
Commission
Canadian Human Rights
Foundation
Canadian Institute of Chartered
Accountants
Canadian International Civil
Service Association
Canadian Judicial Council
Canadian Labour Congress
Canadian Lord's Day Association
Canadian Lord's Day Association,
Brantford Auxiliary
Canadian Lord's Day Association,
Norwich Auxiliary
Canadian Mental Health
Association
Canadian Mental Health
Association, Alberta Division
Canadian Mental Health
Association, Moncton
Region Inc.
Canadian Mental Health
Association, Quebec Division

Canadian National Institute for
the Blind
Canadian Paraplegic Association,
Manitoba Division
Canadian Paraplegic Association,
Newfoundland Division
Canadian Paraplegic Association,
Nova Scotia Division
Canadian Paraplegic Association,
Prince Edward Island Division
Canadian Restaurant and
Foodservices Association
Capilano–Howe Sound
Progressive Conservative
Riding Association
Capp, Geoffrey B.
Carleton–Gloucester New
Democrat Riding Association
Carll, David J.
Carlson, Adele D.
Carrière, Suzanne
Carruthers, Edward R.R.
Catterall, Marlene
C.D. Howe Institute
Centre Alpha de Jonquière
Centre psychiatrique de
Roberval, L'Envol
Chaba, Eugene P.
Chadwick, Harry
Chalmers, Douglas
Chamber of Commerce of
Metropolitan Montreal
Charest, Paul
Charpentier, Jacques
Chief Election Officer for Ontario
Chief Electoral Officer and City
Clerk, City of Sudbury
Chief Electoral Officer of the
City of Ottawa
Chief Electoral Officer of
British Columbia
Chief Electoral Officer of Canada
Chief Electoral Officer
of Manitoba

Chief Electoral Officer
of Newfoundland
Chief Electoral Officer of
Nova Scotia
Chief Electoral Officer of Quebec
Chief Electoral Officer of
Saskatchewan
Chief Electoral Officer of Yukon
Child, Mable C.W.
Chown, Robert S.D.
Christian Heritage Party of
Canada
Christian, William
Churchill New Democrat Riding
Association
Churchill Progressive
Conservative Riding
Association
Citizens Concerned About
Free Trade
City of Saskatoon
Clark, Alan L.
Clark, Keiron
Clarke, Andrew
Clarke, John
Clarke, Laurie
Coalition of Provincial
Organizations of the
Handicapped
Coimbra, Carlos A.
Coll, Philip
Collin, Ken
Collins, A. Bruce
Coman, Mickey
Commissioner of Official
Languages
Commissioner of the Royal
Canadian Mounted Police
Commission scolaire des
Draveurs
Committee for '94
Communist Party of Canada
Concerned Citizens for Civic
Affairs in North York Inc.

Confederation of Canadian
Unions
Confederation of Regions,
Manitoba Party
Confederation of Regions,
Western Party
Congdon, Earl
Cook, Harry
Cook, Marie
Cook, Ronald
Cornish, S.J.
Correctional Service Canada
Corrigan, R. Dennis
Côté, Joseph
Côté, Suzanne
Cottam, K. Jean
Council of Canadians
Council of Elizabeth Fry Societies
of Ontario
Council of the Students' Union,
Memorial University of
Newfoundland
Council of the Town of Vaughan
Council on Aging,
Windsor–Essex County Inc.
Courtney, John C.
Cowie, Ian B.
Craig, Susan R.
Craven, Barbara A.
Crawford, David
Crawford, David S.
Crawford-Macaulay, Erma G.
Creelman, June
Crouchman, Joseph A.
Crow, David
Crow, Stanley
Crozier, S.J.
CTV Television Network Ltd.
Cumberland–Colchester Liberal
Riding Association
Cunningham, Glenn
CUSO
Dahlo, Al
Dakota–Ojibway Tribal Council

Daley, George
Dalton, Jeremy and Leah
Dashwood, Elizabeth
Davis, Mr. and Mrs. Ken
Dawson, J.W.
Day, M.
de Blieck, Nellie
Decarie, Graeme
Deighan, Pauline
Derick, Herbert R.
Desbarats, Peter
Deschenes, Sylvie M.
Desrosiers, Jean-Maurice
de Walle, Frank
Dick, Francine
Dingwall, David C.
Donaghey, Samuel
Donald, G. Cameron
Douglas Hospital Centre,
    Beneficiaries' Committee
D.R.
Droogendyk, Jan
Drul, Terry
Drysdale, Carolyn
Dubuc-Vaillancourt, Monique
Duchesne, Martine, United
    Nations Secretariat
Du Couturier-Nichol, Garrfield
Dugaro, Ed
Dumart, Jean-Thomas
Dunn, Sally A.
Dunn, Will B.
Duport, Philippe
Duyzer, Mr. and Mrs. Gary
Dziubinski, Andrew
Earl, Doug
Easton, R. Bruck
Eckgren, Betty
Edmonton East New Democrat
    Riding Association
Elizabeth Fry Society of Calgary
Elizabeth Fry Society of
    Edmonton
Elizabeth Fry Society of
    Greater Vancouver

Elizabeth Fry Society of
    New Brunswick Inc.
Elizabeth Fry Society of Ottawa
Elizabeth Fry Society of
    Saskatchewan Inc.
Elizabeth Fry Society of Toronto
Elmer, Diane
Emberley, Kenneth C.
End Legislated Poverty
Engelmann, Frederick C.
Environics Research Group Ltd.
Etobicoke Centre Progressive
    Conservative Riding
    Association
Evans, Hertta
Falardeau, Denise
Fangrad, Dave
Farwell, Lance
Fath, Ruth
Federated Anti-Poverty Groups
    of British Columbia
Fédération des femmes
    du Québec
Federation of Canadian
    Municipalities
Fédération professionnelle des
    journalistes du Québec
Fee, Doug
Ferguson, John D.R.
Ferguson, The Honourable Ralph
Fewster, W. Jean
Field Operations Division,
    United Nations
Finnis, David
Flagel, Frank
Fleming, Stephen
Flis, Jesse
Flynn, Maureen A.
Fogarty, David B.
Foley, Sandra, Paul Hyland and
    Jessie MacDonald
Foreign Service Community
    Association
Foster, Maurice
Fowler, Donald M.

Fraser, Doug
Fraser, James C.
Friesen, Benno
Fritz, R.E.
Frontenac Law Association
Furber, Roy F.
Gabor, Robert
Gaffiero, Carmel
Gallup Canada Inc.
Garant, Patrice
Gardom, Garde B.
Garneau, Raymond
Gavin, Don
Gearing, William R.
Gelade, Brian
Gellman, M.A.
General Hospital (Grey Nuns)
  of Edmonton
Gérin, François
Gillespie, Gil
Gilmore, W.J.
Glazer, Diane
Godwin, Coral Thelony
Goede, Ina
Gomolchuk, Sheldon
Goodison, Jack W.E.
Graham, Gerry
Graham, Jean
Grand Council of the Crees
  (of Quebec)
Gray, The Honourable Herb
Greater Moncton Association for
  Community Living Inc.
Greater Moncton Chamber of
  Commerce
Greater Moncton Literacy Council
Greater Vancouver Libertarian
  Party Association
Greene, Barbara
Green Party, British
  Columbia/Yukon Region
Green Party of British Columbia
Green Party of Canada
Green Party, Toronto
Grolle, E. Hendrik

Grondin, Conde R.
Groody, Eric P.
Grossman, Larry
Guarnieri, Albina
Guthrie, Joan
Hadley, Eleanor L.
Haehnel, Ruth
Hahn, Thomas
Hale, Frank
Halifax Progressive Conservative
  Riding Association
Hall, Muriel
Hamel, Jean-Marc
Hamilton, David M.
Handicapped Action Committee
Harb, Mac
Harvard, John
Harvey, Ross
Harvey, William E.
Hawkes, Job J.
Heather, Larry
Heisey, Alan
Henderson, Douglas
Henry, W.H.
Herman, Jerry E.
Hertel, Paul
Hipperson, Greg
Hockin, The Honourable Tom
Hodder, Mary J.
Hoffman, Kenneth L.
Holmes, Grant S.
Holtby, John
Hôpital Louis-H.-Lafontaine,
  Comité de bénéficiaires
Hopkins, Len
Horvath, Louis
Hosier, Leslie
Hotel Association of Canada Inc.
Hotham, Gordon W.
Hughes, Gary
Hughes, Opal L.
Hume, Mark
Hunter, Ian
Hunter, Patricia
Hurley, Pat

Hutchison, Margaret
Hutmacher, Wayne A.
Hyslip, Doug
Hyson, Stewart
Indian and Northern Affairs
  Canada
Institute for Political
  Involvement
Institute of Canadian Studies
Iqaluit and Baffin Regional
  Chambers of Commerce
Ireland, Clive
Ireland, John R.
Irwin, Eric B.
Iscoe, Steve
Island New Democrats
Ivanyshyn, John
Jacklin, C.M.
Jansen, Julie
Jean, Margot
Jefferson, Clara
Jelinek, The Honourable Otto
Jenkins, Garry R.
Jerome, Florence and Maxwell J.
John Howard Society of Alberta
John Howard Society of Kingston
  and District
John Howard Society of
  Manitoba
John Howard Society of
  New Brunswick Inc.,
  Moncton Branch
John Howard Society of
  Saskatchewan
Johnson, Harold W.
Johnson, Jeanette
Johnson, Richard
Johnson, Sara E.
Johnston, Archie
Johnston, Howard
Johnstone, William
Jonkman, Fred and Arlene
Joseph, Brian
Juniper Centre Inc.

Kaeppner, W.M.
Kamloops Liberal Riding
  Association
Kamloops New Democrat Riding
  Association
Kamloops Progressive
  Conservative Riding
  Association
Kaneb, T.A.
Kaplan, The Honourable Robert
Kativik Regional Development
  Council
Kent, Tom
Kester, Maive
Kholopov, Alexander V.
Kingsclear Indian Band
Kirk, D.
Klaassen, Cora
Klewchuk, Iris
Knaus, Jakob
Knight, Al D.
Knight, Donald I.
Kotyk, Ted
Koutroulides, Anastase
Koutstaal, Jeremy
Kuivenhoven, Peter
Labelle, Marc
Lachapelle, Guy, and
  Édouard Cloutier
Ladysmith Green Party
Lafferty, H.J.
Lait, Andrew
Landry, Linda
Langlois, Charles A.
Langlois, Denis, Marc-André
  Lévesque and Roger Jobin
Lapointe, Cyril Malcolm
Laporte, Rod
Lasichuk, Andrey
Laurentian University Students'
  General Association
Lavoie, Jacques
Lawrence, A.G. Lief
Lawrence, Gwen

Lea, Chris
Learning Disabilities Association
of the Yukon
LeBlanc, Francis
LeDuc, Lawrence
Lee, J.W.
Leeson, Howard
Legge, Derek
Lemieux, Marc
Lemieux, Vincent
Letcher, Gordon C.
Lethbridge Federal New
Democrats
Levenson, Christopher
Lévesque, Laurier
Lewans, Paul J.
Lewis, Deryck
L'Heureux-Giguère, Jo-Anne
Liberal Party of Canada
Liberal Party of Canada, Alberta
Liberal Party of Newfoundland
and Labrador
Liberal Riding Associations of
London West, London East and
London Middlesex
Libertarian Party of Canada
Locally-Engaged Staff
Association, Embassy of
Canada, Washington, D.C.
Loewen, John
London Cross Cultural Learning
Centre
London Greens
London West New Democrat
Riding Association
London West Progressive
Conservative Riding
Association
Lucier, The Honourable
Senator Paul
Lund, William J.
Lundgren, Bruce
Lunn, Janice
Lyle, May and William
MacDonald, Mary I.

MacDougall, John A.
MacIsaac, Alex
MacLean, Mary Margaret
MacLeod, David E.
MacNaughton, R.P.
MacPhail, Cecil E.
MacPherson, Paul
Madden, Wayne
Mailly, Claudy
Maindonald, Wayne T.
Malone, Arnold
Manitoba Anti-Poverty
Organization Inc.
Manitoba Association for
Community Living
Manitoba Federation of Labour
Manitoba Keewatinowi
Okimakanak Inc.
Manitoba Libertarian Association
Manley, John
Manois, George
Marchand, Marie
Marchand, The Honourable
Senator Len
Marica, Carol
Mario, Dean W.
Marois, André
Marsh, Fred G.
Martell, Jay
Martin, Robert
Maston, E.R.
Matrai, Geza
Mawhinney, J. Gordon
Maynard, Joanne
McConnell, Howard
McConney, Allan E.
McCrossan, W. Paul
McDonald, Lynn
McDougald, James D.
McDowell, R.R.
McEwan, Jane
McGowan, Laurie
McGrath, Judy
McKean, Frances G.
McManus, E.

McNair, Shirley
McRae, Ken
McRobie, Alan
McTeer, Maureen A.
Meindl, Poldi
Melin, Corby Dale
Melin, Deon
Métis Society of Saskatchewan
Metro Tenants Legal Services
Mid-Canada Communications
    Corp.
Mifflin, Fred
Miller, Jay
Mills, Scott D.
Ministry of Municipal Affairs,
    Municipal Government
    Structure Branch, Ontario
Mississauga West Progressive
    Conservative Riding
    Association
Moddejonge, Bert
Mongeau, Patrice
Monière, Denis
Montreal Collaborating Centre
    for Research and Training in
    Mental Health, World Health
    Organization
Moreau, A.J.
Morin, André
Morrison, Allan D.
Morrison, Denise, Bob and Jeff
Mouck, Zella
Moxley, W.J.
Munro, Michael R.
Murchie, Alex Donald
Murdoch, Sharon
Murphy, Ted, and Rénald Guay
Murray, David
Mynders, Christine
Nanaimo Regional General
    Hospital, Volunteer Services
National Anti-Poverty
    Organization
National Citizens' Coalition

National Pensioners' and Senior
    Citizens' Federation
Native Council of Canada
Native Council of Nova Scotia
Nayman, Bernard G.
New-Age Political Association
    of Canada
New Brunswick Aboriginal
    Peoples' Council
New Brunswick Association for
    Community Living
New Brunswick Liberal Party
New Brunswick Progressive
    Conservative Youth Federation
New Brunswick Redistribution
    Committee
New Democratic Party
    of Canada
New Democratic Party of
    Canada, New Brunswick
    Section
New Democratic Party of
    Canada, Ontario Section
Newfoundland and Labrador
    Computer Services Ltd.
Newfoundland Association for
    Community Living
New Populist Party of British
    Columbia
New, R. Rickhart
New Westminster–Burnaby New
    Democrat Riding Association
Nicholson, Rob
Nickerson, Mike
Nixon, Major Douglas
Nixon, Winifred
Northwest Territories Council for
    Disabled Persons
Nova Scotia Advisory Council on
    the Status of Women
Nova Scotia Civil Liberties
    Association
Nova Scotia Federation of Labour
Nova Scotia Hospital

Nova Scotia Liberal Association
Nova Scotia New Democrats
Nova Scotia Progressive
   Conservative Association
O'Dowd, Michael
Office des personnes
   handicapées du Québec
Okanagan–Shuswap New
   Democrat Riding Association
Oldham, Robert W.
Omnifacts Research Ltd.
Ontario Advisory Council for
   Disabled Persons
Ontario Advisory Council on
   Senior Citizens
Ontario Association for
   Community Living
Ontario Association of Interval
   and Transition Houses
Ontario Commission on Election
   Finances
Ontario Federation of Labour
Ontario Federation of Students
Ontario Hotel and Motel
   Association
Ontario Literacy Council
Ontario Ministry of Health,
   Psychiatric Branch
Ontario New Democrats
O'Reilly, Kevin, and Anne
   McKracken
Osborne, Les and June
Osterman, John
Osterwoldt, Siegfried
Packwood, Prudence
Pagtakhan, Rey
Palda, Filip, and Kristian S. Palda
Pamenter, Jean
Paquette, Peter D.
Paradis, Émilien
Paris, Edward B.
Parish, G.C.
Parkdale–High Park Liberal
   Riding Association
Parrott, Glen

Parti nationaliste
Parti nationaliste du Québec
Parti Rhinocéros
Pasis, Harvey
Patriquin, Larry
Payne, Finlay J.
Payne, Robert
Peck, Robert D.
Peever, Richard
Penicud, Alfred and Mrs. D.A.
Pentecostal Assemblies of
   Canada
Perkins, Stanley A.
Petrik, Denny Z.
Phelan, Charles J.
Phillips, The Honourable
   Senator O.H.
Piccinin, Nillo A.
Picken, D.M.
Pigott, Margaret
Pilon, Dennis
Pilon, Kenneth V.
Plourde, Léon
Policy Concepts
Pollard, Anthony P.
Populist Party of Canada
Porter, John H.
Pottinger, B.M.
Poulton, Patrick W.
Premier's Council on the
   Status of Disabled Persons,
   New Brunswick
Priebe, Klaus H.E.
Prince Edward Island Council of
   the Disabled
Prince Edward Island Federation
   of Labour
Prince Edward Island Literacy
   Council
Prince Edward Island New
   Democratic Party
Prince Edward Island
   Progressive Conservatives
Prince Edward Island Restaurant
   and Foodservices Association

Prince George–Peace River
Progressive Conservative
Riding Association
Prisoners' Rights Committee
Progressive Conservative Party
of Canada
Progressive Conservatives of
New Brunswick
Provincial Advisory Council on
the Status of Women for
Newfoundland and Labrador
Psychiatric Patient Advocate
Office
Public Curator of Quebec
Public Service Alliance of Canada
Pynn, John
Quebec Cerebral Palsy
Association Inc., Saguenay–
Lac St-Jean Division
Quebec Human Rights
Commission
Quebec New Democrats
Quebec Paraplegic Association
Quennell, Frank
Quesnel, Louise
Quittner, Joseph
Rabstein, Lothar
Raby, Alain
Radio Québec
Ray, A.K.
Reagh, Elizabeth S.
REAL Women of Canada
Redway, The Honourable Alan
Reformed Christian Business and
Professional Organization
Reform Party of Canada
Regina–Wascana Progressive
Conservative Riding
Association
Regroupement des associations
de personnes handicapées de
l'Outaouais
Regroupement des groupes
populaires en alphabétisation
du Québec

Reimer, John
Reruie, Frank
Réseau d'aide aux personnes
seules et itinérantes de
Montréal Inc.
Ressl, Bill
Restaurant and Foodservices
Association of British
Columbia
Revenue Canada, Taxation
Rhiness, Brian J.
Ridley, Jim
Riis, Nelson
Rissling, Nels
Roberts, James L.
Robinson, Grant C.
Rodriguez, John
Roe, Dave
Ross, David F.
Ross, Michael
Roth, Robert M.
Roth, Rudolf E.
Roy, Jean-Pierre
Royal Canadian Legion
Royal Ottawa Hospital
Rozendaal, Joanne
Ruff, Norman J.
Ryan, Diane
Ryksen, Sara
Rymer, K.W.
Rymer, Mr. and Mrs. Howard C.
Saanich–Gulf Islands Liberal
Riding Association
Saint John Hearing Society
Salmon, Ross
Salvation Army, Bermuda
Sancton, Andrew
Saskatchewan Action Committee
on the Status of Women
Saskatchewan Association of
Rural Municipalities
Saskatchewan Coalition for
Social Justice
Saskatchewan New Democrats

The Grand Theatre (London)
The Pas Health Complex Inc.
Thiele, John J.
Thompson Chamber of
  Commerce
Thompson, J. Walter
Thomson, Rachel
Thorkelson, Scott
Todd, William G.
Tourism Ontario Inc.
Treiger, Seymour
Trudgen, Johana
Turtle Island Confederation
Twigg, Gordon
Tyssen, Richard, and
  Minnie de Jong
Tzovaras, Michos
Ubriaco, Rita
Unincorporated Village District
  of Cranberry Portage
Union of British Columbia
  Municipalities
University of Western Ontario
  Students' Council
Van Brugge, Linda
Vancouver Board of Trade
Vancouver Centre Progressive
  Conservative Riding
  Association
Vancouver Island Progressive
  Conservative Riding
  Associations
Vandenberg, Tim
Van Den Bosch, George E.
Van Manen, Jennifer
Van Neste, Mary K.
van Roggen, The Honourable
  Senator George C.
Varaleau, Darlene
Varzeliotis, A.N. Thomas
Verduijn, Arie
Vermeulen, Elizabeth
Vertes, John
Veterans' Affairs Canada
Vetterli, John and Elsie

Victoria Civil Liberties
  Association
Victoria Labour Council
VOCM Radio
Vrugteveen, Irene
Waddell, Ian
Wagemans, Victor
Waldron, Debbie
Walker, David
Walker, F.H.
Walker, Michael
Wall, Robert B.
Warnke, Allan
Watt, The Honourable
  Senator Charlie
Watt, W.R.
Wattam, N. Richard
Weber, Jean
Weber, Mae
Weir, W.J.
Wellington–Grey–Dufferin–
  Simcoe Progressive
  Conservative Riding
  Association
Western Arctic Liberal Riding
  Association
Western Arctic New Democratic
  Party
Western Arctic Progressive
  Conservative Riding
  Association
Western Independence Party
Wheatley, Michael
Whelan, Ed
Wigle, Robert M.
Wilkins, John
Williams, Marc
Willowdale New Democrat
  Riding Association
Wilson, Constance
Wilson, G.S. Lowen
Wilson, Sandra
Wilson, Terry G.
Windsor Homeless Coalition
Winninger, David

Wittick, Joseph R.
Wolf, R.E.
Women's Association for
  Education and Social Action,
  Saguenay–Lac St-Jean–
  Chibougamau–Chapais Region
Wong, Debra
Woodard, Douglas
Woods, Margaret
World Sikh Organization
Woytowich, Cory
Yellowknife Chamber of
  Commerce

Yorkton–Melville Progressive
  Conservative Riding
  Association
Yu, Andrew James
Yukon Association for
  Community Living
Yukon Liberal Riding
  Association
Yukon Literacy Council
Yukon New Democrats
Yukon Progressive Conservative
  Riding Association
Zalinko, I.R.
Zelenietz, Marty
Ziegler, S.

ISSUE PAPERS

Harold M. Angell — Provincial Party Financing in Quebec, 1963 to date

Keith Archer — An Exploration of the Principles Governing Election

Jerome H. Black — National Voter Turnout in Canada: Problems and Challenges

Donald E. Blake — Electoral Reform and Party Financing in Canada: Issues and Alternatives

Janine Brodie — The Regulation of the Spending Practices of Political Parties, and Third-party Participation in Electoral Campaigns

Alan C. Cairns — Representation and the Electoral System: Some Possible Questions for Research

R. Kenneth Carty — Does Canada Need a Permanent Voters List?

William Christian — Issues for Electoral Reform

Stephen Clarkson — Contribution Towards an Agenda for Research

John C. Courtney — Questions Concerning Electoral Reform

Jean Crête	Notes pour un agenda
Gurston Dacks	The Aboriginal Peoples and the Electoral Process of Canada
Peter Desbarats	News Media and Elections
Frederick C. Engelmann	Fairness, Equality and Dispatch: Taking the Crown out of Elections and Other Topics
Frederick J. Fletcher	The Mass Media and Elections in Canada: An Overview
Pierre Fortin	Quelques réflexions sur les enjeux éthiques
Patrice Garant	L'âge du vote depuis la Charte
William O. Gilsdorf	Reflections on Media, Political Parties and Election Campaigns in Canada
Raymond Hudon	Démocratie, élections et exercice du droit de vote
William P. Irvine	Financing Elections in Canada: Applying Some Basic Principles
Liss Jeffrey and Gertrude J. Robinson	Mass Media and the Electoral Process
Jane Jenson	Maximizing Equity and Innovation in Canada's Elections
Richard Johnston	Some Research Prospects with Existing Data Sets
J.A. Laponce	Distinguishing Two Types of Campaigns: The Parliament-like and the Advertising Campaigns
Lawrence LeDuc	A New Proposal for Reviving the Spirit of Canadian Democracy
William Leiss	Media and Elections
Vincent Lemieux	Réflexions sur la réforme électorale

Vaughan Lyon	Suggested Issues for the Commission's Consideration
Don MacNiven	Issues in Electoral Morality
Louis Massicotte	Le financement populaire des partis au Québec: analyse des rapports financiers, 1977–1988
Alex C. Michalos	Ethical Considerations Regarding Public Opinion Polling during Election Campaigns
F.L. Morton and Rainer Knopff	The Charter and Constituency Size
Jan Narveson	Some Thoughts on Elections and Democracy
Michael Nolan	The Media and Elections
Filip Palda and Kristian S. Palda	Campaign Spending and Campaign Finance Issues: An Economic View
Jon H. Pammett	Third-party Advertising
Jon H. Pammett	Voting Turnout in Canada
Réjean Pelletier	La réforme électorale au Canada: droit de vote et financement des partis
Andrew J. Petter	Electoral Reform, Party Financing and the Canadian Charter of Rights and Freedoms
Kent Roach	Constitutional Standards for Electoral Districting
Liora Salter	The Boundaries and Limitations of Electoral Reform
Bryan Schwartz	Patronage as an Election Financing Issue
Carolle Simard	Les groupes ethniques au Canada et le système politique
David E. Smith	Canada's Electoral System

Jennifer Smith — Brief Observations on Enumeration, Registration, Interest-group Spending, Redistribution, and the Right to Vote

Walter C. Soderlund and Walter I. Romanow — A Research Agenda for the Study of Mass Media and Elections in Canada

W.T. Stanbury (with Sandra Carter and Gary Clark) — The Financing of Political Parties and Election Campaigns in Canada: A Bibliography

Michael B. Stein — Minor Political Parties and Reform of Federal Election Finance Legislation in Canada

Ian Stewart — Public Confidence and Canadian Elections

A. Brian Tanguay — The Transformation of Political Parties in Canada: Implications for Electoral Reform

H.G. Thorburn — Thoughts on Elections, Candidates and Party Leadership Selection

J. Wearing — Party Finance Legislation: A Reassessment

Alan Whitehorn — Problems and Suggestions on Electoral Reform

Appendix C
Schedule of Participants in Public Hearings, 1990

**OTTAWA, ONTARIO
MARCH 12, 1990**

Jean-Marc Hamel, Former Chief Electoral Officer of Canada

Progressive Conservative Party of Canada
The Honourable Gerry St. Germain, President
Jean-Carol Pelletier, National Director
Rosemary Dolman, Director of Operations
Elaine Collins, Director of the Women's Bureau

New Democratic Party of Canada
Rod Murphy, Member of Parliament for Churchill
Richard Proctor, Federal Secretary

Kristian S. Palda, Department of Business, Queen's University
Filip Palda, Department of Economics, University of Ottawa

Liberal Party of Canada
The Honourable Herb Gray, Acting Leader
Marc Desmarais, Executive Assistant to the President
Charles King, Co-ordinator for Constituencies

François Gérin, Member of Parliament for
   Megantic–Compton–Stanstead

Commissioner of Official Languages
D'Iberville Fortier, Commissioner
Michel Robichaud, Assistant Director, Complaints and Audits
Anna Blauveldt, Division Chief
Marcel Charlebois, Complaints and Audits Officer

Canadian Cable Television Association
Michael Hind-Smith, President and Chief Executive Officer
Jay Thomson, Director of Government Relations
Gérald Lavallée, Vice-President of Regulatory Affairs

Scott Thorkelson, Member of Parliament for Edmonton–Strathcona

Royal Ottawa Hospital
Chris Henderson, Associate Executive Director

Bob Roth, School of Journalism, Carleton University

Commission scolaire des Draveurs
Gaston Poiré, Chairperson
Jean-Guy Binet, Executive Director
Gilbert Prévost, Director of Adult Education
Raymond Bélanger, Literacy Instructor
Diane Pouliot, Literacy Instructor

Mark Assad, Member of Parliament for Gatineau–La Lièvre

Scott D. Mills, Student, Carleton University

OTTAWA, ONTARIO
MARCH 13, 1990

Royal Canadian Mounted Police
Norman Inkster, Commissioner

The Honourable Senator Norman K. Atkins

Council of Canadians
Maude Barlow, Chairperson
John Trent

Canadian Association of Elizabeth Fry Societies
Bonnie Diamond, Executive Director
Shereen Benzvy-Miller
Sharon Waddell

Association of Canadian Distillers
Tim Woods, Vice-President of Communications and Public Relations
Donna Chislett, Research Assistant

Canadian University Service Overseas
Chris Bryant, Executive Director

John Reimer, Member of Parliament for Kitchener

Canadian Alliance for Trade and Job Opportunities
Thomas d'Aquino, Member of the Executive Committee
Lorne H. Walls, Manager, Public Affairs, Alcan Aluminum Ltd.

Canadian Labour Congress
Nancy Riche, Executive Vice-President
Pat Kerwin, Director of Political Action

Grand Council of the Crees (of Quebec)
Grand Chief Matthew Coon-Come
Bill Namagoose, Executive Director

Aboriginal Peoples' Commission of the Liberal Party of Canada
The Honourable Senator Len Marchand
Marc LeClair

Len Hopkins, Member of Parliament for Renfrew–Nipissing–Pembroke

Claudy Mailly, Former Member of Parliament for Gatineau–La Lièvre

Suzanne Carrière, Returning Officer for Hull–Aylmer

Prudence M.A. Packwood, Returning Officer for Ottawa West

John Bromley, Returning Officer for Renfrew–Nipissing–Pembroke

Guy Bergeron, Chief Electoral Officer of the City of Ottawa

FREDERICTON, NEW BRUNSWICK
MARCH 19, 1990

Conde R. Grondin, Department of Political Science, University
of New Brunswick

Confederation of Regions Party of New Brunswick
Brent Taylor, Research Director
Greg Hargrove, Former candidate, North York

New Democratic Party of New Brunswick
Allan Sharp, Executive Member

Progressive Conservative Party of New Brunswick
David MacDonald, President of Fredericton Association
Bill Lebans, Chief Agent

J. W. Bud Bird, Member of Parliament for Fredericton–York–Sunbury

Erma G. Crawford-Macaulay, Returning Officer for Fundy–Royal

C. Keith Alward, Deputy Returning Officer for Fundy–Royal

Premier's Council on the Status of Disabled Persons
Randy Dickinson, Executive Director

New Brunswick Progressive Conservative Youth Federation
Craig P. Astle

Job J. Hawkes, Former member of the Department of Humanities and Languages, University of New Brunswick

Gary Hughes, Department of Psychology, University of New Brunswick

Théo Noël, Returning Officer for Gloucester

Stewart Hyson, Former member of the Department of Political Science, University of New Brunswick

E. R. Maston, Returning Officer for Fredericton–York–Sunbury

Alfred Crossman, Returning Officer for Saint John

Liberal Association of New Brunswick
Léopold Mallet, President
Elaine Wright, Vice-President

MONCTON, NEW BRUNSWICK
MARCH 20, 1990

Greater Moncton Association for Community Living Inc.
Kayle Eno, Executive Director
Deanna Gaston, Community Liaison Officer

William Mott Stewart, Student, University of New Brunswick

New Brunswick Redistribution Committee
Jean A. Cadieux

George A. Daley

Saint John Hearing Society
Ellen Flemming, Executive Director
Percy Anthony
Arthur Boyle
Thérèse Robitaille, Interpreter

Société des Acadiens et Acadiennes du Nouveau-Brunswick
Martin Aubin, President, Petitcodiac
Alonzo Le Blanc

Canadian Mental Health Association, New Brunswick Division
Marthe Léger, Executive Director
Tom Blanchard

Our Place
Nancy Smith, Director

R.L. Smith

David Ross

Greater Moncton Literacy Council
Marian Zaichkowski, Chair

John Howard Society of Moncton
Wendy Amos, Executive Director

Elizabeth Fry Society of New Brunswick
Jean Steeves, President

Dorchester Penitentiary
Claude Dumaine, Warden

Greater Moncton Chamber of Commerce
Chuck F. Steeves, Head of the Government Relations Committee

CHARLOTTETOWN, PRINCE EDWARD ISLAND
MARCH 21, 1990

Island New Democrats
Judy Whitaker, Former candidate

Harry Cook, Returning Officer for Hillsborough

Lorne Cudmore, New Democratic Party Official Agent (Cardigan)

Prince Edward Island Literacy Council
Laura Mair, Co-ordinator of the Provincial Literacy Volunteers' Project

Liberal Party of Prince Edward Island
Gordon L. Campbell, President

Prince Edward Island Restaurant and Foodservices Association
Don Cudmore, President

Canadian Paraplegic Association, Prince Edward Island Division
Brian Bertelsen, Executive Director

Redistribution Committee of Prince Edward Island
Elizabeth S. Reagh

Prince Edward Island Council of the Disabled
Anne Lie-Nielson, Executive Director

Canadian National Institute for the Blind
Bernard MacDonald, District Administrator

Cecil E. MacPhail, Returning Officer for Malpeque

Prince Edward Island Advisory Council on the Status of Women
Angie Cormier, Acting Administrator

**Progressive Conservative Federal Constituency Associations of
   Prince Edward Island**
Mike Burge

Prince Edward Island Federation of Labour
Sandy MacKay, President

Pauline Deighan, Returning Officer for Egmont

VICTORIA, BRITISH COLUMBIA
MARCH 26, 1990

Robert Patterson, Deputy Chief Electoral Officer of British Columbia

Norman Ruff, Department of Political Science, University of Victoria

Victoria Civil Liberties Association
Tom Gore, President

British Columbia Ministry of the Solicitor General
Jim Cairns, Program Analyst, Adult Institutional Services

Handicapped Action Committee
Joanne Neubaur, President

Victoria Labour Council
Steve Orcherton, Secretary-Treasurer

Progressive Conservative Federal Constituency Associations of Vancouver Island
Donald F. Wheeler, Regional Director, Federal Organization Committee, Vancouver Island

Marguerite Balshaw, Election official

Saanich–Gulf Islands Liberal Constituency Association
Paul McKivett, Former President

David Crawford, Former candidate for the Libertarian Party of Canada

Barbara A. Craven, Returning Officer for Saanich–Gulf Islands

Socialist Party of Canada
John George Jenkins, General Secretary

Jane McEwan

VANCOUVER, BRITISH COLUMBIA
MARCH 27, 1990

City of Vancouver
Gordon Campbell, Mayor

British Columbia Association of Broadcasters
Chris Weafer, Counsel

Ian Waddell, Member of Parliament for Port Moody–Coquitlam

William T. Stanbury, Faculty of Commerce and Business Administration, University of British Columbia

British Columbia Federation of Labour
Ken V. Georgetti, President
John Weir

British Columbia Coalition of the Disabled
Margo Massie, President and Chairperson of the Board
Mary Williams, Board Executive

End Legislated Poverty
Jean Swanson, Co-ordinator

Federated Anti-Poverty Groups of British Columbia
Gus Long

British Columbia Council of Federal New Democratic Party Constituencies
Dominique Roelants, President
Johanna den Hertog, Former President of the National Party
Glen Sanford, Campaign Organizer

Surrey–White Rock Liberal Constituency Association
Kenneth J. E. Jones, President
Bruce Torrie

Surrey–White Rock Progressive Conservative Constituency Association
Doug G. Stewart, President
Scott Thompson, Executive Member

Green Party of Canada
Kathryn Cholette, Party Leader
Steve Kisby, Executive Secretary
Richard James Bidwell, Chief Agent

British Columbia Civil Liberties Association
Robert D. Holmes, Secretary of the Board of Directors
Erin Shaw, Policy Analyst

Libertarian Party of Canada
Wayne Marsden, Former candidate
Bill Tomlinson, Former candidate

Christian Heritage Party of Canada
Allan Garneau, Executive Director
Rita Waenink, National Campaign Director

Ian Hunter, Student

William Ressl, Gladstone Secondary School

Jeremy Dalton, Election official

Ed Dugaro

MONTREAL, QUEBEC
APRIL 9, 1990

Confédération des syndicats nationaux
Gérald Larose, President
Peter Bakvis, Executive Assistant
Michel Rioux, Information Services

Harold M. Angell, Department of Political Science, Concordia University

Public Curator of Quebec
Nicole Fontaine, Curator
Marie Boivin, Lawyer

Liberal Party of Canada, Quebec Branch
The Honourable Francis Fox, President
Gilles Dufour, Executive Director
The Honourable Serge Joyal, President, Policy Commission

Jean-Pierre Roy, Former Official Agent for the Liberal Party of Quebec

SORECOM Inc.
Soucy Gagné, Consultant

M. Graeme Decarie, Department of History, Concordia University

Canadian Association of Friedreich's Ataxia
Pierre Asselin, Public Relations

Association des centres d'accueil du Québec
Michel Clair, Executive Director
Christiane Lepage, Legal Adviser
Jean-Louis Vaillancourt, President, Regional Council
Jacques Houde, Executive Director of a centre

Senior Citizens' Forum of Montreal
J. Léo Hudon, President
Michel Magnan

Jacques Lavoie, Former Member of Parliament for
    Hochelaga–Maisonneuve

Quebec Paraplegic Association
René Dallaire, President
Daniel Lapointe, Executive Director

MONTREAL, QUEBEC
APRIL 10, 1990

Correctional Service Canada, Quebec Region
Jacques Dyotte, Assistant Deputy Commissioner, Operations

Prisoners' Rights Committee
Jean-Claude Bernheim, Co-ordinator

Réseau d'aide aux personnes seules et itinérantes de Montréal Inc.
Jocelyne Vaillant, Co-ordinator

Canadian Mental Health Association, Quebec Division
Michel Trottier, Executive Director
Lucien Landry, Member, Montreal Administrative Council

Douglas Hospital Centre
Joyce Boillat, Executive Director
Peter Steibelt, Social Director
Martha Bishop, Secretary

Lise Bourgault, Member of Parliament for Argenteuil–Papineau

Raymond Garneau, Former Member of Parliament for Laval-des-Rapides

Sylvain Auclair, Green Party, Rosemont

Canadian Human Rights Foundation
Suzanne Birks, President

Chamber of Commerce of Metropolitan Montreal
Jacques Ménard, President
Luc Lacharité, Executive Vice-President

Michael Spencer

Émilien Paradis, Election official

Jean-Maurice Desrosiers

Céline Bernier, Returning Officer for Saint-Laurent

Henriette Guérin, Returning Officer for Outremont

Jocelyne Lavoie, Returning Officer for Laval

MONTREAL, QUEBEC
APRIL 11, 1990

Association des propriétaires de tavernes et brasseries du Québec Inc.
Roland Turcotte, President

Regroupement des groupes populaires en alphabétisation du Québec
Christiane Fabiani, Information Officer

Monique Dubuc-Vaillancourt, Returning Officer for Ahuntsic

St-Henri–Westmount Liberal Constituency Association
Jan Davis, Vice-President

Jo-Anne L'Heureux-Giguère, Election official

Carolle Simard, Department of Political Science, Université du Québec
à Montréal

Lower Canada College Student Council
Michael Richmond
Michael Sheppard
David Soriand

SASKATOON, SASKATCHEWAN
APRIL 17, 1990

John C. Courtney, Department of Political Science, University
of Saskatchewan

Citizens Concerned About Free Trade
Marjaleena Repo, National Organizer

Liberal Federal Constituency Associations of Saskatoon
Vic Karwacki, President

Rod Laporte, Member of Parliament for Moose Jaw–Lake Centre

Métis Society of Saskatchewan
Gérald Morin, President
Clem Chartier, Consultant
Max Morin, Representative, Cross-Bow Valley
Ron Campone, Representative, Saskatoon

Frank Quennell, Campaign Organizer, Saskatoon

**Progressive Conservative Federal Constituency Associations
of Saskatoon**
Lori Isinger
Pat W. Pitka

Chris Axworthy, Member of Parliament for Saskatoon–Clark's Crossing

Howard McConnell, College of Law, University of Saskatchewan

Voice of the Handicapped, Saskatoon Division
Fred Curths, Vice-President

Dennis W. Adkin

**Saskatoon–Clark's Crossing Progressive Conservative
Constituency Association**
Madge McKillop

Bill Werezak, Returning Officer for Saskatoon–Dundurn

Joyce Brown, Returning Officer for Saskatoon–Clark's Crossing

Margaret Woods, Returning Officer for Saskatoon–Humboldt

REGINA, SASKATCHEWAN
APRIL 18, 1990

University of Regina
Dan de Vlieger, Dean, Faculty of Arts
Howard Leeson, President, Political Science Professors' Association
Lorne Brown, Department of Political Science
Ray Sentas, Department of Political Science
Gerry Sperling, Department of Journalism and Political Science

Saskatchewan Association of Rural Municipalities
Bernard Kirwan, President
David Nederhoff, Director
Lorne Wilkinson, Former Executive Director

Saskatchewan New Democrats
Carol Y. Bryant, Co-ordinator, Election Planning Support

John Howard Society of Saskatchewan
Dave A. Tickell, Executive Director

Keith Lampard, Chief Electoral Officer of Saskatchewan

Saskatchewan Pro-Life Association
Thomas Schuck, President

Canadian Association of Liquor Jurisdictions
Ted Urness, Chairperson and Chief Executive Officer

Station CKCK-TV
Frank Flegel, News Editor

Regina–Wascana Progressive Conservative Constituency Association
Fred Yeo

Saskatchewan Coalition for Social Justice
Blair Wotherspoon

Ed Whelan

Alex J. Bowd, Returning Officer for Regina–Wascana

Jerry E. Herman and **Carla Herman**, Former candidates

Paul J. Lewans, Former candidate

WINNIPEG, MANITOBA
APRIL 19, 1990

Canadian Paraplegic Association, Manitoba Division
George Dyck, President
John Lane, Executive Director

Stoney Mountain Institution
Ted Kotyk, Inmate

The Honourable Lloyd Axworthy, Member of Parliament for Winnipeg
  South Centre
Irwin Corobow, President, Winnipeg South Centre Liberal Association
Phil Knight, Winnipeg South Centre Liberal Association

Dakota–Ojibway Tribal Council
Chief Ernie Daniels, Tribal Executive Officer
Carl Roberts, Personnel Chief

Angus Reid Group
Angus Reid, President and Chief Executive Officer

Assembly of First Nations
Ovide Mercredi, Vice-Chief

Robert Gabor, Lawyer

Gary T. Brazzell, P.C. Canada fundraiser

Coalition of Provincial Organizations of the Handicapped
Laurie Beachell, Executive Director
Doreen Demas, Executive Member
Frank Enns, National Council Member

Kenneth Emberley

Manitoba Libertarian Association
Clancy Smith

Canadian Disability Rights Council
Jim Derkson, Executive Member
Yvonne Peters, National Co-ordinator

Carole Scrivener, Returning Officer for Winnipeg South Centre
Bev Ann Scott, Election assistant

S. Jo Lopuck, Returning Officer for Winnipeg Transcona

Lucille Bouvier, Returning Officer for St. Boniface

John Howard Society of Manitoba
Graham Reddoch, Executive Director
Tracey K. Lewis, Director of Research and Education
Wendy Nassar

THOMPSON, MANITOBA
APRIL 20, 1990

City of Thompson
Don MacLean, Mayor

Leona Mayer, Constituency Assistant to Rod Murphy, MP

Churchill Progressive Conservative Constituency Association
Richard Whidden, President

Alexander Donald Murchie, Liberal Party Official Agent (Churchill)

Thompson Business and Professional Women's Club
Jan Zebrinski, President

Lyle Robert Walsh, Returning Officer for Churchill

Manitoba Keewatinowi Okimakanak Inc.
David Merasty, Director for the Health Liaison Program

Robert Wall, Progressive Conservative Party fundraiser

Juniper Centre Inc.
Lynda Mulligan, Supervisor
Jean Smith, Manager
Sarah Ross, Client

Thompson Progressive Conservative Constituency Association
Ken Collin

Thompson Chamber of Commerce
Margaret Pronyk, President
Bunny Cane, Director

QUEBEC CITY, QUEBEC
APRIL 30, 1990

Pierre-F. Côté, Chief Electoral Officer of Quebec
Eddy Giguère, Assistant Chief Electoral Officer
Jean Jolin, Director of Polling Operations

Vincent Lemieux, Department of Political Science, Université Laval

Fédération professionnelle des journalistes du Québec
Claude Robillard, Secretary General
Alain Saulnier, Vice-President

Louis Duclos and **The Honourable Rémi Bujold**

Office des personnes handicapées du Québec
Paul Mercure, President
Sylvie Godbout, Administrative Council
Gaetan Bibeau, Research Director

Jacques-Marie Gaulin, New Democratic Party Official Agent (Chambly)

Patrice Garant, Department of Law, Université Laval

Association canadienne de la radio et de la télévision de langue française Inc.
Gilles Grégoire, President
Bernard Montigny, Secretary General
Michel Héroux, President of TVA
Charles Bélanger, Vice-President of CFCF

Jacques Charpentier, Returning Officer for Louis-Hébert

Louise Quesnel, Department of Political Science, Université Laval

Paul Charest, Returning Officer for Trois-Rivières

André Marois, Returning Officer for Megantic–Compton–Stanstead

CHICOUTIMI, QUEBEC
MAY 1, 1990

Centre psychiatrique de Roberval
Christianne Côté, Director of Professional Services
Huguette Dufour, Day Manager
Henri Laplante, President, Clients' Committee

Bertrand Tremblay, Vice-President, Saguenay Press Club

Centre Alpha de Jonquière
Andréa Bouchard, Training and Development

Regroupement des radiodiffuseurs
Marc-André Lévesque, Radio Roberval Inc. (CHRL)
Roger Jobin, CJPM Television
Denis Langlois, CKRS and CFRS Television

Fern Coulombe, Former Mayor of Jonquière

Women's Association for Education and Social Action
Monique Larouche-Morin, President

Jacques Boisvert, Returning Officer for Jonquière

Canadian Forces Base Alouette, Bagotville
Captain Louise Leblanc

Suzanne Côté, Returning Officer for Roberval

Saguenay–Lac St-Jean Cerebral Palsy Association
Serge Leblanc, Executive Director

Denise Falardeau, National Vice-President, Progressive Conservative
Party of Canada

TORONTO, ONTARIO
MAY 7, 1990

Don Blenkarn, Member of Parliament for Mississauga South

Bernard Nayman, Chartered Accountant

Lynn McDonald, Former Member of Parliament for
Broadview–Greenwood

Harry Chadwick, Member of Parliament for Brampton–Malton

William Christian, Department of Political Science, University of Guelph

Metro Tenants Legal Services
Marnie Hayes, Community Legal Worker

Toronto Christian Resource Centre
Michael Shapcott, Community Development Worker

Church of the Holy Trinity and Basic Poverty Action Group
Kevin Barrett, Community Development Worker

Canadian International Civil Service Association
Ronald Fegan
Ken Lasiuk

Warren R. Bailie, Chief Election Officer of Ontario
Alan Stewart, Legal Adviser

Commission on Election Finances (Ontario)
Gordon Kushner, Executive Director

Province of Ontario
Michael O'Dowd, Ministry of Revenue
George Manios, Ministry of Municipal Affairs

Lawrence LeDuc, Department of Political Science, University of Toronto

Ruth Haehnel, Returning Officer for Scarborough–Rouge River

REAL Women of Canada
Gwen Landolt, National Vice-President
Joan Pimento, Campaign Worker
Patrick M. Redmond, Consultant

Ontario Association for Community Living
Harry Zwerver, Executive Director
Anna-Rae Fishman, Assistant to the Executive Director

TORONTO, ONTARIO
MAY 8, 1990

Larry Grossman, Former Leader of the Ontario Progressive
  Conservative Party

Environics Research Group Ltd.
Michael Adams, President

National Citizens' Coalition
David Somerville, President

Canadian Association of Broadcasters
Tony Scapillati, Corporate Counsel

CTV Television Network Ltd.
Rose Oushalkas, Director of Government Relations and Business Affairs
Tim Kotcheff, Director of News and Public Affairs

Patrick Boyer, Member of Parliament for Etobicoke–Lakeshore

Canadian Daily Newspaper Publishers Association
Paul Wilson, Chairperson
John E. Foy, President

Communist Party of Canada
George Hewison, Party Leader

Canadian Association for Community Living
Ron Smith, President
Diane Richler, Vice-President

Ontario Ministry of Health
J. Howard Danson, Acting Director, Psychiatric Hospitals Branch
Mary Beth Valentine, Provincial Co-ordinator, Psychiatric Patient
  Advocate Office

Ontario Advisory Council on Senior Citizens
Mary Tate, Executive Director

Policy Concepts
Peter Regenstreif, President

Committee for '94
Libby Burnham

Libertarian Party of Canada
R. Dennis Corrigan, Leader
Richard Prendiville, Legal Adviser

Marie Marchand, Former candidate for the Progressive Conservative
  Party of Canada

SUDBURY, ONTARIO
MAY 9, 1990

Sudbury Business and Professional Women's Club
Rachel Proulx, President

Mid-Canada Communications Corp.
Michael G. Keller, Station Manager for Pembroke and Ottawa

Ward Skinner, Progressive Conservative Official Agent (Sudbury)

Sudbury Progressive Conservative Constituency Association
James V. Bubba, President

Sudbury Literacy Council, Cambrian College Literacy Program
Heather Segsworth, Literacy Instructor
Dee Goforth, Co-ordinator
Margaret Janveau, Client

City of Sudbury
W.F. Dean, Solicitor

Sudbury Provincial New Democrats
Sharon Murdoch, President
Elmer McVey

Women's Centre
Anna L. Proulx

John A. MacDougall, Member of Parliament for Timiskaming

John Rodriguez, Member of Parliament for Nickel Belt

John R. Didone, Former official agent for the Progressive Conservative
  Party of Canada

John DeDiana, Former candidate for the Progressive Conservative Party
  of Canada

Laurentian University Students' General Association
Lee Jeanotte, Vice-President
Dawn Anderson

LONDON, ONTARIO
MAY 10, 1990

Garnet Bloomfield, Former Member of Parliament for
  London–Middlesex

Liberal Federal Constituency Associations of London
Patrick Boland, President
Susan Barnes, Former President, London West
Douglas D. Ferguson, Campaign Manager
Michael Eizenga

London West New Democrats
Atul Kapur

Anastase and **Pamela Koutroulides**

Bruce Lundgren, Department of English, University of Western Ontario

The Grand Theatre (London)
Helen Moore-Parkhouse, Director of Marketing

London Cross Cultural Learning Centre
Kathleen Kevaney, Centre Co-ordinator

Robert J. Mahar, Locally-Engaged Staff Association, Canadian Embassy
in Washington, D.C.

London Greens
Ken Bovey, Co-ordinator
Peter Robbinson, Co-ordinator

Ontario Advisory Council for Disabled Persons
Shirley Van Hoof

London West Progressive Conservative Constituency Association
Mort Glanville, President

Peter Desbarats, Dean, Graduate School of Journalism, University of
Western Ontario

University of Western Ontario Students' Council
Robert J. L. Wright, External Affairs Researcher
Dean Beltsis
Steven Deighton

David Winninger

Robert Martin, Department of Law, University of Western Ontario

Andrew Sancton, Department of Political Science, University of
Western Ontario

WHITEHORSE, YUKON
MAY 14, 1990

The Honourable Senator Paul Lucier

Patrick Michael, Chief Electoral Officer of the Yukon

Jean Graham, Returning Officer for the Yukon

Yukon New Democratic Party Constituency Association
Graham McDonald, President

Yukon Progressive Conservative Constituency Association
Tim Preston, President
Michael J. Lauer

Yukon Liberal Constituency Association
H. Shayne Fairman, President

Yukon Association for Community Living
Janice L. Wood, Co-ordinator
Robert Walker, National Representative

Learning Disabilities Association of the Yukon
Susan Walker, Executive Director
Elinore Frederickson, Past President

Yukon Literacy Council
Mary Louise Fournier, Co-ordinator

KAMLOOPS, BRITISH COLUMBIA
MAY 15, 1990

Nelson Riis, Member of Parliament for Kamloops

Don Gavin, New Democratic Party Official Agent (Kamloops)

Shuswap Nation Tribal Council
Chief Ron Ignace, Chairman
Robert Manuel, Tribal Director

Green Party of Canada
Trudy Frisk, Regional Spokesperson, British Columbia/Yukon Region
Connie Harris, Election Co-ordinator

Progressive Conservative Party of Canada, British Columbia Branch
Richard Blair, President, Federal Organizing Committee

Laurie Clarke, Returning Officer for Kamloops

KAH-Ed Institute Inc.
Al D. Knight, President

Gordon C. Letcher

Kamloops New Democratic Party Constituency Association
Ron Hamilton, Vice-President

Kamloops Progressive Conservative Constituency Association
Vince Croswell, President

Kamloops Liberal Constituency Association
Gordon Hoffman, Vice-President
Agnes Halliday, Former President

Don Cameron

Howard Johnston, Former Member of Parliament for
Okanagan–Kootenay

Reform Party of Canada in Kamloops
Ted Maskell

GLEICHEN, ALBERTA
MAY 16, 1990

Siksika Nation Tribal Council
Chief Strater Crowfoot
Andrew Bear Robe, Administrator
Fred Breaker, Council Member
Ann McMaster, Council Member
Ronald Many Heads, Council Member
Clifford Many Guns, Council Member
Chief Gwendora Bear, Council Member
Angelina A. Youngman, Council Member
Leonard Good Eagle, Council Member
Lena Running Rabbit, Secretary
Chief Karla Water, Secretary
Lucy Wright, Secretary
Maria Black, Youth Chief
Blaine Favel, Student
Adrian Stimson, Co-ordinator
Russell Wright, Elder
Wayne Courchêne, Native Newspapers

VANCOUVER, BRITISH COLUMBIA
MAY 17, 1990

Union of British Columbia Municipalities
Bill Krug, Local Government Adviser
Frank Storey, Research Officer

Don Ursaki, Former candidate for the Liberal Party of Canada

Restaurant and Foodservices Association of British Columbia
Don Bellamy, Executive Director
D. Adrian Cownden, President, Oak Bay Marina Restaurant

Hotel Association of Canada Inc.
Jack Sirrs, Executive Vice-President

Downtown East Side Residents' Association
Jim Green, Organizer

Capilano–Howe Sound Progressive Conservative Constituency Association
John Lakes, Vice-President, Progressive Conservative Party of British Columbia

Dennis Pilon

New Westminster–Burnaby New Democratic Party Constituency Association
Pat Portsmouth, Vice-President

Greater Vancouver Libertarian Party Association
Paul Geddes, Vice-President, Libertarian Party of Canada
Chris Blatchley, Past President

New Populist Party of British Columbia
Gerald Kirby, Party Leader

Andrey Lasichuk

British Columbia Association for Community Living
Patty Gibson, Communications Co-ordinator
Jean Bennett, Self Advocacy Adviser

Al Dahlo, Returning Officer for North Vancouver

Don Knight, Former independent candidate in 1984

VANCOUVER, BRITISH COLUMBIA
MAY 18, 1990

Dianna M. Brown, Returning Officer for Port Moody–Coquitlam

Burnaby–Kingsway New Democratic Party Constituency Association
Jean B. McMurdo, President

Margot Jean

Eleanor L. Hadley, Election officer

CALGARY, ALBERTA
MAY 22, 1990

Reform Party of Canada
Preston Manning, Party Leader
Siân M. Stephenson, Vice-President

Eric Groody, National Citizens' Coalition

Confederation of Regions, Western Party
Elmer Knutson, Party Leader

Galvanic Analytical Systems Ltd.
Doug Fraser, President

Liberal Party of Canada, Alberta
Robert D. Hallett

Debra Wong, Campaign worker

Progressive Conservative Party of Canada, Southern Alberta Branch
Ted Carruthers

Calgary Southeast Progressive Conservative Constituency Association
Magne Housken
Carol Laird

Jennifer Taylor

Robert W. Oldham

Calgary Chamber of Commerce
Harold Millican, President
Eden Oliver, President, Economic and Governmental Affairs Committee
Colin MacDonald, Economic and Governmental Affairs Committee
Ron Nicholls, Economic and Governmental Affairs Committee

Harold W. Johnson, Accountant

Lethbridge Federal New Democrats
Don Ferguson, President

Mary Hornett-Twigg, Returning Officer for Calgary North

Liberal Party of Canada
Bert Moddejonge, National Vice-President
Terry Gibson

EDMONTON, ALBERTA
MAY 23, 1990

Patrick D. Ledgerwood, Chief Electoral Officer of Alberta

Ross Harvey, Member of Parliament for Edmonton East

Edmonton East New Democratic Party Constituency Association
Jim Crowell, President

New Democratic Party of Canada
Jim Gurnett, Federal Executive
Lyle Bleich, Provincial Secretary

Edmonton Northwest New Democrats
Ken C. Nixon, Vice-President

Reform Party of Canada
Preston Manning, Party Leader

Liberal Party of Canada, Alberta
Patricia Spencer, President

Alberta Federal and Intergovernmental Affairs
Morris Maduro, Director, Asia-Pacific International Division

Boyle Street Community Services Co-operative
Larry Brockman, Community Development Worker

Alberta Medical Association
Sandy J. Murray, Past President

Alberta Hospital, Edmonton
Lynn Jones, Director of Public Relations

Canadian Mental Health Association, Alberta Division
Tony Hudson, Associate Executive Director

John Howard Society of Alberta
Howard Sapers, Executive Director
Gerry O'Neill, Board Member
Michael Lignitsky, Research Director

Harvey Pasis, Department of Public Administration,
Athabaska University

Sara E. Johnson

Alberta Federation of Labour
Audrey M. Bath, Secretary-Treasurer
Winston Gereluk, General Services Director

Frederick C. Engelmann, Department of Political Science,
University of Alberta

Samuel Donaghey, Returning Officer for Edmonton North

Alan Clark, Returning Officer for Yellowhead

Alice A. Killam, Former Returning Officer for Peace River

John Patrick Day, Former Returning Officer for Edmonton West

Brian J. Rhiness, Campaign worker

G. Cameron Donald, Campaign worker

Mr. X, Former inmate

YELLOWKNIFE, NORTHWEST TERRITORIES
MAY 24, 1990

Legislative Assembly of the Northwest Territories
David M. Hamilton, Clerk

Yellowknife Chamber of Commerce
Dorothy Barkley, Executive Director

Margo McDiarmid

Kevin O'Reilly

Rosemary Cairns, Returning Officer for Western Arctic

Western Arctic New Democratic Party
Stephen Whipp, Secretary
Rici Lake

Northwest Territories Council for Disabled Persons
Dale Robinson, Executive Director

Western Arctic Progressive Conservative Constituency Association
John Vertes, President

Western Arctic Liberal Constituency Association
Ewan Cotterill, President
Lynda Sorenson, Former candidate

Don Scott, Former Manitoba MLA

WINNIPEG, MANITOBA
MAY 29, 1990

Assembly of Manitoba Chiefs
Grand Chief Phil Fontaine
Shirley Olson, Executive Director

Winnipeg North Centre Liberal Constituency Association
Karin Kuhl

Manitoba Association for Community Living
Dale Kendel, Executive Director

Cyril Keeper, Former Member of Parliament for Winnipeg North Centre

Terry R. Stratton, Campaign Manager

Richard Balasko, Acting Chief Electoral Officer of Manitoba
Judy Thompson, Acting Assistant Chief Electoral Officer of Manitoba

Manitoba Anti-Poverty Organization Inc.
Patricia Morrison, Lawyer
Suhad Bisharat, Office Manager

Progressive Party of Manitoba
Sid Green, Party Leader

Manitoba Federation of Labour
Susan Hart-Kulbaba, President
John Doyle, Communications Co-ordinator
Rob Hilliard

Wardrop Engineering
Grant S. Holmes, Manager of Business Development

A.J. Moreau

Ted Murphy, Businessman, and **Rénald Guay**, Lawyer

TORONTO, ONTARIO
MAY 30, 1990

Gallup Canada Inc.
Lorne Bozinoff, Vice-President
Peter MacIntosh, Research Analyst

Canadian Institute of Chartered Accountants
David Hector, President
Donald E. Sheehy, Senior Manager, Research Studies
Dana Clarence
Bernard Nayman

National Pensioners' and Senior Citizens' Federation
Edith Johnston, Secretary

Gregory H. Vezina, Official Agent, Green Party of Canada

Ontario Literacy Council
Tracy Westell, Public Educator and Grants Co-ordinator

St. Paul's Progressive Conservative Constituency Association
Harry Katz, Spokesperson

Canadian Restaurant and Foodservices Association
Walter Oster, Chairman of the Board
Douglas Needham, President

Institute for Political Involvement
Alex Jupp, President
The Honourable Alastair W. Gillespie, Vice-President

Elizabeth Dashwood, Returning Officer for Rosedale

Charles Caccia, Member of Parliament for Davenport

Ralph Bouwmeester and **Jeff Shapiro**

Reformed Christian Business and Professional Organization
Hans Vander Stoep, Executive Director
Ray Pennings, Public Policy Analyst

Rita Ubriaco

N. Richard Wattam

TORONTO, ONTARIO
MAY 31, 1990

Ontario Federation of Labour
Julie Davis, Secretary-Treasurer
Ross McClellan, Political and Legislative Director

Etobicoke Centre Progressive Conservative Constituency Association
Douglas Robson, President
John D. McElwain, Vice-President, Finance

New Democratic Party, Ontario Section
Brian Harling, Provincial Secretary
Jill Marzetti

Concerned Citizens for Civic Affairs in North York Inc.
Colin J. Williams, President
Terry Sawyer, Executive Member

Ontario Federation of Students
Edith Garneau, Chair
Tim Jackson, Treasurer and Chair-Elect
Chris Lawson, Campaign Researcher

Ryerson Students' Union
Diane Dyson, Information Officer

Wellington–Grey–Dufferin–Simcoe Progressive Conservative Constituency Association
Douglas Maund, President
Eleanor Taylor

Canadian Hellenic Federation
Constantine Karayannopoulos, President, Public Relations Committee
Peter Dotsikas

HALIFAX, NOVA SCOTIA
JUNE 4, 1990

Nova Scotia Civil Liberties Association
Walter Thompson

A. Bruce Collins, Election worker

Alexander Kholopov, Department of Physiology and Biophysics, Dalhousie University

Patrick Nowlan, Member of Parliament for Annapolis Valley–Hants

Howard E. Crosby, Member of Parliament for Halifax West

George Cooper, former Member of Parliament for Halifax

Sandra Foley, Returning Officer for Halifax

Paul F. Hyland, Returning Officer for Halifax West

Jessie MacDonald, Returning Officer for Dartmouth

Agar Adamson, Department of Political Science, Acadia University

Nova Scotia Advisory Council on the Status of Women
Debi Forsyth-Smith, President
Marie Crooker
Pauline D'Entremont

Clara E. Jefferson, Campaign Manager, Progressive Conservatives (Annapolis Valley–Hants)

Nova Scotia Liberal Association
Gerald F. Blom, President
Francine J. Cosman, Executive Director

Nova Scotia Hospital
William O. McCormick, Clinic Director

Nova Scotia New Democrats
Michael Coyle

Cumberland–Colchester Liberal Constituency Association
Dennis James, Former candidate

Halifax Progressive Conservative Constituency Association
Camille Garant, Treasurer
Mike Casey, Accountant

SYDNEY, NOVA SCOTIA
JUNE 5, 1990

David C. Dingwall, Member of Parliament for Cape Breton–
East Richmond

Canadian Paraplegic Association, Nova Scotia Division
John Rogers, Executive Director

Royal Canadian Legion
James C. Lovelace

Francis G. LeBlanc, Member of Parliament for Cape Breton
Highlands–Canso

Alex MacIsaac, New Democratic Party Official Agent (Cape Breton–
East Richmond)

Student Committee for Electoral Reform, Mount St. Vincent University
Michael Haynes

Students' Union of Nova Scotia
Jeffrey Phelps

Native Council of Nova Scotia
Viola M. Robinson, President

New Brunswick Aboriginal Peoples' Council
Gary P. Gould, President

United Mine Workers
Brad McIsaac, Vice-President

Mary Margaret MacLean, Returning Officer for Cape Breton
 Highlands–Canso

Nova Scotia Progressive Conservative Association
Blair Mitchell, Executive Vice-President
John Abbass, Past President

Kenneth Andrews, Returning Officer for Cape Breton–East Richmond

Brian Joseph, Department of Development Studies, University College
 of Cape Breton

ST. JOHN'S, NEWFOUNDLAND
JUNE 6, 1990

Garfield Warren, Member of the House of Assembly (Torngat Mountains)

**Provincial Advisory Council on the Status of Women for Newfoundland
 and Labrador**
Wendy Williams, President
Martha Muzychka, Researcher

VOCM Radio
Randy Simms, Director of Community Affairs

Omnifacts Research Ltd.
Gloria Robbins, Vice-President

Newfoundland and Labrador Association of the Deaf
Myles Murphy, President

Dermot F. Whelan, Chief Electoral Officer of Newfoundland

Fisheries, Food and Allied Workers
Richard Cashin, President

St. John's East New Democratic Party Constituency Association
Tara Ivanochko, Spokesperson of the President, Youth New Democrats

**Progressive Conservative Constituency Associations of
 Newfoundland and Labrador**
Stephen J. Delaney, President

Liberal Party of Newfoundland and Labrador
Norman Whalen, President

Canadian Paraplegic Association, Newfoundland Division
Sean E. Fitzgerald, Executive Director
Adrian Battcock, Member of the Board
Dave W. Scott, Executive Director, *The Hub*
Leona Hogan, Researcher

Council of the Students' Union, Memorial University of Newfoundland
Wade Brake

Mary J. Hodder, Returning Officer for Burin–St. George's

Newfoundland Association for Community Living
Don P. Barnes, Executive Director

Province of Newfoundland
Marvin McNutt, Director of Adult Corrections Division,
   Department of Justice

Dave Roe

OTTAWA, ONTARIO
JUNE 11, 1990

Maurice Foster, Member of Parliament for Algoma

Canadian Advisory Council on the Status of Women
Glenda Simms, President
Ginette Busque, Vice-President
Elly Silverman, Director of Research
Tina Head, Legal Analyst

Veterans Affairs Canada
Fernand Breton, Hôpital Ste-Anne

Canadian Bar Association
John J. Jennings, National President
Terence Wade, Director

Mary Van Neste

June Creelman

Hull–Aylmer New Democratic Party Constituency Association
Robert Dupuis, President
Dany Gravel

Parti nationaliste du Québec
Louis Gravel, Party Leader
Denise Laroche

Maurizio Bevilacqua, Member of Parliament for York North

National Anti-Poverty Organization
Havi Echenberg, Executive Director
Cheryl Boon, Advocacy Researcher

Fédération des femmes du Québec
Chantal Maillé, Member of the Committee of Political Action
Cécile Coderre, Treasurer

Marlene Catterall, Member of Parliament for Ottawa West

Canadian Home and School and Parent-Teacher Federation
Maybelle Durkin, Executive Director
Helen Koeppe

W.M. Kaeppner

OTTAWA, ONTARIO
JUNE 12, 1990

The Honourable Robert Kaplan, Member of Parliament for York Centre

Canadian Association of the Deaf
James D. Roots, Executive Director

William Burrows

Association de la presse francophone
Wilfred Roussel, Director General

Fergus J. O'Connor, Frontenac Law Association

Simon de Jong, Member of Parliament for Regina–Qu'Appelle

Native Council of Canada
Robert Groves, Special Adviser

Albina Guarnieri, Member of Parliament for Mississauga East

Derek Lee, Member of Parliament for Scarborough–Rouge River

Maureen A. McTeer, Candidate in 1988 for the Progressive Conservative
Party of Canada in Carleton–Gloucester, Ontario

W.B. Snarr, Consultant

Canadian Federation of Students
Jane Arnold, Chairperson
Sylvia Sioufi, Researcher
Todd Smith, Member

Taddle Creek Greens
James R.M. Harris, Provincial candidate in Ontario

OTTAWA, ONTARIO
JUNE 13, 1990

Canadian Ethnocultural Council
Andrew Cardozo, Executive Director
Alex Munter, Director

Guy Lachapelle, Department of Political Science, Concordia University

Public Service Alliance of Canada
Daryl T. Bean, National President
Steven Jelly, Assistant to the Executive Committee

John Manley, Member of Parliament for Ottawa South

Jill Vickers, Institute for Canadian Studies, Carleton University

World Sikh Organization
Attar S. Chawla, Finance Director
Alice Basarke, Executive Assistant
Atit Singh

John Harvard, Member of Parliament for Winnipeg St. James

Canadian Broadcasting Corporation
Michael McEwen, Executive Vice-President
James R. Messel, Legal Counsel

Canadian Human Rights Commission
Michelle Falardeau-Ramsay, Deputy Chief Commissioner
Harvey Goldberg, Acting Director, Research and Policy Branch
James Meddings, Policy Analyst, Research and Policy Branch

Federation of Canadian Municipalities
Patricia Hunsley, Director of Policy and Research

Carleton–Gloucester New Democratic Party Constituency Association
Michael Martin, President
Melissa Coleman

Ian Cowie, Management Consultant

**National Organization of Immigrant and Visible Minority Women
of Canada**
Madonna O. Larbi, Executive Director
Elizabeth Milan
N. Nzegwu

Comité des bénéficiaires de l'Hôpital Louis-H. Lafontaine
Lucien G. Landry, Secretary
Denise Champagne, Archives Officer
Daniel St-Onge, Law Student

K. Jean Cottam, Party Representative

Rey D. Pagtakhan, Member of Parliament for Winnipeg North

Lucien Saumur

IQALUIT, NORTHWEST TERRITORIES
JULY 23, 1990

Nunatsiaq Liberal Constituency Association
Al Woodhouse

Abe Okpik, Campaign worker

Iqaluit Chamber of Commerce
Cheri Kinnear, Past President

Iqaluit Office of the Returning Officer for Nunatsiaq
Jeanne Mike, Former Elections Clerk

Baffin Region Inuit Association
Duncan Cunningham, President's Assistant

Nunatsiaq News
Matthew Spence, Managing Editor

Inuit Broadcasting Corporation
Lynda Gunn, Regional Director for Baffin Division

Canadian Broadcasting Corporation, Northern Service
Simon Awa, Director of Operations, CBC Eastern Arctic, Iqaluit
Patrick Nagle, Regional Director

Bryan Robin Pearson, Former Mayor of Iqaluit

Baffin Women's Association
Yvonne Earle

Baffin Regional Council
Pudloo Mingeriak, Mayor of Cape Dorset
Meeka Kilabuk

KUUJJUAQ, QUEBEC
JULY 24, 1990

Tikile Kleist

Kativik Regional Development Council
Jean-Guy Bousquet

Makivik Corporation
Zebedee Nungak, Vice-President
Sam Silverstone, Lawyer

OTTAWA, ONTARIO
SEPTEMBER 19, 1990

Liberal Party of Canada
The Honourable Don Johnston, National President
Peter Milliken, Member of Parliament for Kingston and the Islands
Sheila Gervais, Acting Secretary General
Gordon Ashworth, Senior Consultant
The Honourable John Reid, Member of the Consultative Committee on
    the Revision of the *Canada Elections Act*

Social Credit Party of Canada
Harvey Lainson, Former Party Leader
Kathy Kanters, National Secretary
Graydon Meek, National Executive Director

Libertarian Party of Canada
Stan Tyminski, Party Leader
Daniel Hunt, Director

Parti nationaliste du Québec
Louis Gravel, Party Leader
Marc Authier, Treasurer

Communist Party of Canada
Glen Beddell
John MacLennan
Tom Morris

OTTAWA, ONTARIO
SEPTEMBER 20, 1990

New Democratic Party of Canada
Rod Murphy, Member of Parliament for Churchill
Richard Proctor, Federal Secretary
Anne Davis, Special Adviser
Louise O'Neill, Former candidate in 1988 in the constituency of
    Outremont (Quebec)

Green Party of Canada
Chris Lea, Party Leader
Steve Kisby, Executive Secretary
Len Busch
Frank De Jong

Janice Lunn, Returning Officer for Oshawa

Reform Party of Canada
Preston Manning, Party Leader

Confederation of Regions, Western Party
Elmer Knutson, Party Leader
Colonel (Ret'd) Gary H. Rice, Regional Director (Ontario)
James Webb, Regional Director (Atlantic)

Marxist-Leninist Party of Canada
Arnold August, Chief Agent
Serge Lafortune

OTTAWA, ONTARIO
SEPTEMBER 21, 1990

Progressive Conservative Party of Canada
The Honourable Gerry St. Germain, President
W. David Angus, President of the P.C. Canada Fund
Jennifer Lynch, President of the National Progressive Conservative
Women's Federation

Christian Heritage Party of Canada
E. J. Vanwoudenberg, Party Leader
Allan Garneau, Executive Director
Rita Waenink, National Campaign Director

Populist Party of Canada
John C. Turmel, President (Ontario)
Tom Kennedy

Elections Canada
Jean-Pierre Kingsley, Chief Electoral Officer of Canada
Ron Gould, Assistant Chief Electoral Officer of Canada
Yvon Tarte, Executive Director and General Counsel

APPENDIX D
Schedule of Participants in the Symposiums and Other Consultation Meetings

SYMPOSIUM ON THE ADMINISTRATION OF ELECTIONS AT THE CONSTITUENCY LEVEL

Edmonton, Alberta
October 21, 22 and 23, 1990

Program

First day

Evening Session:
Running a Local Election

Second day

Morning Session:
Enumeration and Revision: Doing it Right

Afternoon Session:
Advance Ballots and Proxies: Improving the Process

Evening Session:
Serving Voters with Disabilities and Special Needs

Third day

Morning Session:
Election Day Headaches and How to Solve Them

Afternoon Session:
Improving the Local Election Process: Where Do We Go From Here?

Panelists

Richard Balasko   Chief Electoral Officer of Manitoba
Larry Brockman   Boyle Street Community Services
                                   Co-operative, Edmonton, Alberta
Rosemary Dolman   Acting National Director, Progressive
                                   Conservative Party of Canada, Ottawa,
                                   Ontario

Rolly Forget — Returning Officer for Timiskaming, Ontario

Elsie Gallagher — Returning Officer for Fraser Valley West, British Columbia

Ruth Haehnel — Returning Officer for Scarborough–Rouge River, Ontario

Cheryl M. Hewitt — New Democratic Party of Canada, Edmonton, Alberta

Keith Lampard — Chief Electoral Officer of Saskatchewan

Linda Landry — Returning Officer for St. Catharines, Ontario

Major Arthur Lawrence — Returning Officer for Annapolis Valley–Hants, Nova Scotia

Patrick D. Ledgerwood — Chief Electoral Officer of Alberta

Andrée Lortie — Assistant Director of Operations, Elections Canada, Ottawa, Ontario

Joy Miller — Returning Officer for Vancouver Centre, British Columbia

Richard Rochefort — Director of Communications, Royal Commission on Electoral Reform and Party Financing

Jack Siegel — Liberal Party of Canada, Toronto, Ontario

Lesley Singer — Returning Officer for Trinity–Spadina, Ontario

Terry Stratton — Progressive Conservative Party of Canada, Winnipeg, Manitoba

Discussion Leaders

Rosemary Cairns — Returning Officer for Western Arctic, Northwest Territories

Al Dahlo — Returning Officer for North Vancouver, British Columbia

Gordon Mawhinney — Returning Officer for Moncton, New Brunswick

Judith McArthur — Returning Officer for Brampton–Malton, Ontario

Participants

Harry Atkinson — Returning Officer for Cariboo–Chilcotin, British Columbia

Tony Barry — Liberal Party of Canada, Fredericton, New Brunswick

Margaret Birrell — New Democratic Party of Canada, Vancouver, British Columbia

John W. Bromley — Returning Officer for Renfrew–Nipissing–Pembroke, Ontario

Eugene Chaba	Returning Officer for Beaver River, Alberta
Heather Chiasson	Liberal Party of Canada, Halifax, Nova Scotia
Pauline Deighan	Returning Officer for Egmont, Prince Edward Island
Jane Frost	Progressive Conservative Party of Canada, Vancouver, British Columbia·
Gordon H. Goodrow	Returning Officer for Burlington, Ontario
William J. Harris	Returning Officer for St. John's East, Newfoundland
Paul Hyland	Returning Officer for Halifax West, Nova Scotia
John B. Kane	Returning Officer for Guelph–Wellington, Ontario
Grant Kippen	Director of Organization, Liberal Party of Canada, Ottawa, Ontario
Denis Lussier	Assistant Director of Administration, Elections Canada, Ottawa, Ontario
Jessie MacDonald	Returning Officer for Dartmouth, Nova Scotia
André Marois	Returning Officer for Mégantic–Compton–Stanstead, Quebec
Ruth Matthews	Returning Officer for Waterloo, Ontario
William L. McDiarmid	Returning Officer for Hamilton Mountain, Ontario
Judy McGrath	Returning Officer for Labrador, Newfoundland
Jeanne Mike	Election Clerk for Nunatsiaq, Northwest Territories
Bill Mukanik	Returning Officer for Edmonton East, Alberta
Libby O'Driscoll	Returning Officer for Winnipeg North, Manitoba
Geoff Pardoe	Returning Officer for Swift Current–Maple Creek–Assiniboia, Saskatchewan
Ray Pennings	Christian Heritage Party of Canada, Stoney Creek, Ontario
Neil Weir	Reform Party of Canada, Sherwood Park, Alberta
Mary Jane White	New Democratic Party of Canada, Halifax, Nova Scotia
Gloria Wilde	Green Party of Canada, Burks Falls, Ontario
Andrew C. Wilton	Returning Officer for Brandon–Souris, Manitoba
David Woodbury	Provincial Secretary, New Democratic Party of Canada, Winnipeg, Manitoba
Margaret Woods	Returning Officer for Saskatoon–Humboldt, Saskatchewan
Robyn Youell	Progressive Conservative Party of Canada, St. Albert, Alberta

Royal Commission

Pierre Lortie	Chairman
Pierre Fortier	Commissioner
Robert Gabor	Commissioner
William Knight	Commissioner
Lucie Pépin	Commissioner
Guy Goulard	Executive Director
Peter Aucoin	Director of Research
Michael Cassidy	Research Co-ordinator and Symposium Moderator
Richard Rochefort	Symposium Co-ordinator

SYMPOSIUM ON THE
ACTIVE PARTICIPATION OF WOMEN IN POLITICS

Montreal, Quebec
October 31, November 1 and 2, 1990

Program

First day

Opening Session:
Speakers:
Sheila Copps, Member of Parliament for Hamilton East, Ontario
Pierre Lortie, Chairman of the Royal Commission on Electoral Reform and Party Financing
Lucie Pépin, Commissioner, Royal Commission on Electoral Reform and Party Financing

Second day

Morning Session:
Women and Electoral Politics in Canada
Speaker:
Janine Brodie, Department of Political Science, York University

Afternoon Session:
Women's Participation in Political Parties
Speaker:
Sylvia Bashevkin, Department of Political Science, University of Toronto

Evening Dinner:
The Challenge of Electoral Reform
Speaker:
Pierre Lortie

Third day

Morning Session:
Women and their Candidacy to the House of Commons
Speaker:
Lynda Erickson, Department of Political
  Science, Simon Fraser University

Afternoon Session:
Women Politicians and the Media
Speakers:
Gertrude J. Robinson, Graduate Program in
  Communications, McGill University
Armande Saint-Jean, Department of
  Communications, Université du Québec
  à Montréal

Panelists

Rosemary Brown | Executive Director, Match International,
  Ottawa, Ontario

Libby Burnham | Member of Committee for '94, Toronto, Ontario

Denise Falardeau | National Vice-President, Progressive
  Conservative Party of Canada (Quebec)

Albina Guarnieri | Member of Parliament for Mississauga, Ontario

Aldéa Landry | Deputy Premier of New Brunswick,
  Fredericton, New Brunswick

Ami Lönnroth | Journalist, *Svenska Dagbladet*, Stockholm,
  Sweden

Eleanor Smeal | President, The Fund for the Feminist Majority,
  Washington, D.C.

Joseph Thornley | Consultant, Public Affairs International,
  Toronto, Ontario

Participants

Laura Balas | Candidate in 1988 for the New Democratic
  Party of Canada in Swift Current–Maple
  Creek–Assiniboia, Saskatchewan

Nicole Bélanger	Regional Director, Société Radio-Canada, Montreal, Quebec
Shari Burnard	Ontario regional representative, National Women's Liberal Commission, Liberal Party of Canada, Toronto, Ontario
Marlene Catterall	Member of Parliament for Ottawa West, Ontario
Mary Clancy	Member of Parliament for Halifax, Nova Scotia
Erminie Cohen	Progressive Conservative Party of Canada, Saint John, New Brunswick
Hon. Mary Collins	Minister Responsible for the Status of Women and Member of Parliament for Capilano–Howe Sound, British Columbia
Francine Cosman	Executive Director, Nova Scotia Liberal Party
Johanna den Hertog	Former President of the New Democratic Party of Canada, Vancouver, British Columbia
Marion Dewar	Former Member of Parliament for Hamilton Mountain, Ontario
Dorothy Dobbie	Member of Parliament for Winnipeg South, Manitoba
Hon. Judy Erola	Former Member of Parliament and Cabinet Minister, Ottawa, Ontario
Sheila Gervais	Secretary General, Liberal Party of Canada, Ottawa, Ontario
Connie K. Harris	Election Co-ordinator, Green Party of Canada, Salmon Arm, British Columbia
Jon Leah Hopkins	Representative for the Yukon Status of Women Council, Whitehorse, Yukon
Nancy Jackman	Progressive Conservative Party of Canada, Toronto, Ontario
Jane Jenson	Department of Political Science, Carleton University
Thérèse Killens	Former Member of Parliament for St-Michel–Ahuntsic, Quebec
Julie Anne Le Gras	Representative for the Alberta Human Rights Commission, Edmonton, Alberta
Jennifer Lynch	President, National Progressive Conservative Women's Federation, Ottawa, Ontario
Shirley Maheu	Member of Parliament for St-Laurent, Quebec
Marian Maloney	Liberal Party of Canada, Etobicoke, Ontario
Rosemary A. McCarney	Former Vice-President of the Liberal Party of Canada, Toronto, Ontario
Trina McQueen	Director, News and Current Affairs, CBC, Toronto, Ontario

Maureen McTeer	Candidate in 1988 for the Progressive Conservative Party of Canada in Carleton–Gloucester, Ontario
Mary Meldrum	Director of the Women's Bureau, Progressive Conservative Party of Canada, Ottawa, Ontario
Sandra Mitchell	President of the New Democratic Party of Canada, Saskatoon, Saskatchewan
Joyce Nash	New Democratic Party of Canada, Nanaimo, British Columbia
Louise O'Neill	Candidate in 1988 for the New Democratic Party of Canada in Outremont, Quebec
Abby Pollonetsky	Director of Women's Programs, New Democratic Party of Canada, Ottawa, Ontario
Richard Proctor	Federal Secretary, New Democratic Party of Canada, Ottawa, Ontario
Diana Ryback	Past President, Liberal Party in Manitoba, Winnipeg, Manitoba
Johanne Sénécal	Vice-President, National Progressive Conservative Women's Federation, Val Morin, Quebec
Carolle Simard	Department of Political Science, Université du Québec à Montréal
Lise Thibeault	Candidate in 1984 for the Liberal Party of Canada in Gamelin, Quebec
Judy T. Whitaker	New Democratic Party of Canada, Charlottetown, Prince Edward Island
Debra L. Wong	Election volunteer, Calgary, Alberta
Valerie York	Member, National Progressive Conservative Women's Federation, Calgary, Alberta

Royal Commission

Pierre Lortie	Chairman
Pierre Fortier	Commissioner
Robert Gabor	Commissioner
William Knight	Commissioner
Lucie Pépin	Commissioner
Guy Goulard	Executive Director
Jean-Marc Hamel	Special Adviser to the Chairman
Peter Aucoin	Director of Research
Kathy Megyery	Research Co-ordinator
Richard Rochefort	Symposium Co-ordinator

CANADA–UNITED STATES CAMPAIGN
REFORM SYMPOSIUM

Joan Shorenstein Barone Center on the Press, Politics and Public Policy
John F. Kennedy School of Government
Harvard University
Cambridge, Massachusetts
November 19 and 20, 1990

Program

First day   Morning Session:
                             *The Financing of Election Campaigns in the United
                             States and Canada*

                             Afternoon Session:
                             *The Role of the Media in Election Campaigns:
                             A Discussion of Potential Reforms in the United
                             States and Canada*

Second day   Morning Session:
                             *The Role of Political Parties: A Comparative
                             Perspective*

                             Afternoon Session:
                             Symposium Review by Canadian Participants

Moderators and Panelists

The Financing of Election Campaigns

Moderator: Gary R. Orren, Professor of Public Policy and
                             Associate Director, Joan Shorenstein Barone
                             Center on the Press, Politics and Public
                             Policy, John F. Kennedy School of
                             Government, Harvard University

Jill Abramson   Staff Reporter for the *Wall Street Journal*,
                             Washington, D.C.
Phil Friedman   Associate, Ross and Hardies, Washington, D.C.
John J. Motley   Vice-President, Federal Government Relations,
                             National Federation of Business Free
                             Enterprise Political Action Committee,
                             Washington, D.C.
Marc Nuttle   Executive Director, National Republican
                             Congressional Committee, Washington, D.C.

Karl J. Sandstrom	Staff Director and Counsel, House Subcommittee on Elections, Washington, D.C.
Frank J. Sorauf	Department of Political Science, University of Minnesota
Fred Wertheimer	President, Common Cause, Washington, D.C.

The Role of the Media

Moderator:	Ellen Hume, Executive Director, Joan Shorenstein Barone Center on the Press, Politics and Public Policy, John F. Kennedy School of Government, Harvard University
Ed Fouhy	Executive Producer, Concord Communications Group and former member of Commission on Presidential Debates
James C. May	Executive Vice-President, Government Relations, National Association of Broadcasters, Washington, D.C.
Tom Patterson	Department of Political Science, Syracuse University
Ron Rosenblith	Campaign Consultant, Washington, D.C.
Paul Taylor	Staff Writer, National News, *The Washington Post*, Washington, D.C.
David Yepsen	Chief Political Writer, *Des Moines Register*, Des Moines, Iowa

The Role of Political Parties

Moderator:	Martin Linsky, John F. Kennedy School of Government, Harvard University
Jan Witold Baran	Partner, Wiley, Rein and Fielding, Washington, D.C. and General Counsel for the Republican National Committee, Washington, D.C.
Bernadette A. Budde	Vice-President of Political Education, Business Industry Political Action Committee, Washington, D.C.
Gary R. Orren	John F. Kennedy School of Government, Harvard University
Bob Shogan	Political Correspondent, *The Los Angeles Times*, Washington Bureau, Washington, D.C.
Paul Tully	Political Director, Democratic National Committee, Washington, D.C.

Concluding Panel

Thomas S. Axworthy	Executive Director, The CRB Foundation, Montreal, Quebec
Richard Proctor	Federal Secretary, New Democratic Party of Canada, Ottawa, Ontario
Suzanne Warren	Director of Operations (Ontario), Progressive Conservative Party of Canada, Toronto, Ontario

Canadian Participants

W. David Angus	Chairman, P.C. Canada Fund, Montreal, Quebec
Darryl Bricker	Special Adviser to the Prime Minister of Canada, Ottawa, Ontario
Les Campbell	Principal Secretary, New Democratic Party of Canada, Ottawa, Ontario
Penny Collenette	Liberal Party of Canada, Ottawa, Ontario
Ross Fitzpatrick	President and Chief Executive Officer, Viceroy Resource Corporation, Vancouver, British Columbia
Michel Fournier	Chief of Staff, Office of the Leader of the Opposition, Ottawa, Ontario
Sheila Gervais	Secretary General, Liberal Party of Canada, Ottawa, Ontario
Edward Goldenberg	Principal Secretary to the Leader of the Opposition, Ottawa, Ontario
Jane Jenson	Department of Political Science, Carleton University
Patrick Kerwin	National Director, Political Action, Canadian Labour Congress, Ottawa, Ontario
Allan Lutfy	Liberal Party of Canada, Ottawa, Ontario
Peter Milliken	Member of Parliament for Kingston and the Islands, Ontario
Michael G. Robinson	Chief Financial Officer, Liberal Party of Canada, Ottawa, Ontario
Bernard A. Roy	Partner, Ogilvy Renault, Montreal, Quebec
Larry Shapiro	Executive Producer, *The Editor*, Montreal, Quebec

American Participants

Edith Holway	Fellows and Program Administrator, Joan Shorenstein Barone Center on the Press, Politics and Public Policy, John F. Kennedy School of Government, Harvard University
John Howell	Deputy Director, Institute of Politics, John F. Kennedy School of Government, Harvard University
Larry Meyer	Political Reporter, *The Miami Herald*, Miami, Florida
Charles Royer	Director, Institute of Politics, John F. Kennedy School of Government, Harvard University
Hon. Mike Synar	United States Congressman, Democrat, Second District, Oklahoma
Jo-Anne Wilburn	Conference Co-ordinator, Institute of Politics, John F. Kennedy School of Government, Harvard University
Hon. Timothy E. Wirth	United States Senator, Democrat, Colorado

Royal Commission

Pierre Lortie	Chairman
Robert Gabor	Commissioner
William Knight	Commissioner
Lucie Pépin	Commissioner
Guy Goulard	Executive Director
Jean-Marc Hamel	Special Adviser to the Chairman
Peter Aucoin	Director of Research

SYMPOSIUM ON ELECTION AND PARTY FINANCING AT THE CONSTITUENCY LEVEL

Winnipeg, Manitoba
November 26–27, 1990

Program

First day	Morning Session: *Managing Candidates' Spending and Financing in Federal and Provincial Elections*

Afternoon Session:
*Presentation of Draft Proposal from Accounting
Profession Working Group on Election/Party
Finance Reporting at the Local Level*

Second day

Morning Session:
*Workshops for Official Agents and Auditors to
Discuss the Proposal of the Accounting Profession
Working Group*

Panelists

Mark T. Anderson	Canadian Institute of Chartered Accountants, Toronto, Ontario
John Buckworth	Chartered Accountant, John Buckworth and Associates, Richmond Hill, Ontario
Simon Chester	Legal Counsel, McMillan Binch, Toronto, Ontario
Pierre Dalphond	Partner, McCarthy Tétrault, Montreal, Quebec
Denis Desautels	Managing Partner, Montreal Office, Caron Bélanger Ernst and Young, Montreal, Quebec and Chairman of the Accounting Profession Working Group
Israel J. Ellis	Canadian Institute of Chartered Accountants, Downsview, Ontario
Michael Krashinsky	Division of Social Sciences, Scarborough College, University of Toronto
Frederick S. Mallett	Retired Partner, Ernst & Young, Toronto, Ontario
Bernard G. Nayman	Canadian Institute of Chartered Accountants, Downsview, Ontario
Donald E. Sheehy	Senior Manager, Research Studies, Canadian Institute of Chartered Accountants, Toronto, Ontario
David W. Smith	President, Prince Edward Island Financial Services Inc.
S. Anthony Toth	Director of Public Affairs, Certified General Accountants Association of Canada, Vancouver, British Columbia

Participants

George M. Allen	Commissioner of Canada Elections, Elections Canada, Ottawa, Ontario
Glenn A. Bedell	Communist Party of Canada, Weston, Ontario

Pierre Bourque	Progressive Conservative Party of Canada, Longueuil, Quebec
Carole Bryant	Director of Administration, New Democratic Party of Canada, Regina, Saskatchewan
R. Kenneth Carty	Department of Political Science, University of British Columbia
Ed Dale	Director of Administration, Ontario New Democrats, Toronto, Ontario
Lloyd Davis	Reform Party of Canada, Steinbach, Manitoba
Rand Dyck	Department of Political Science, Laurentian University
Jim W. Fishbourne	Reform Party of Canada, Victoria, British Columbia
Harry K. Gaffney	Progressive Conservative Party of Canada, Edmonton, Alberta
Placide Gagné	Official Agent for the Progressive Conservative Party of Canada, Baie-Comeau, Quebec
Jacques-Marie Gaulin	New Democratic Party of Canada, Saint-Basile-le-Grand, Quebec
Scott Gordon	Elections Finance Officer, Elections Manitoba
Jim Houston	Official Agent for the New Democratic Party of Canada, Halifax, Nova Scotia
Charles King	Liberal Party of Canada, Ottawa, Ontario
Reg Légère	Liberal Party of Canada, Caraquet, New Brunswick
Brian Luther	Auditor, New Democratic Party of Canada, St. Albert, Alberta
Ken Mader	Chairman, Canadian Institute of Chartered Accountants, Toronto, Ontario
Jennifer Malloy	Official Agent for the Western Arctic, Liberal Party of Canada, Yellowknife, Northwest Territories
James Matthews	President, James Matthews and Associates, Winnipeg, Manitoba
Randy Mavins	Auditor, New Democratic Party of Canada, Canadian Institute of Chartered Accountants, Winnipeg, Manitoba
Leona Mayer	Constituency Assistant to Rod Murphy, M.P., Thompson, Manitoba
Carolyn M. Maynes	Chief Financial Officer, Progressive Conservative Party of Canada, Ottawa, Ontario
D. Neil McFadgen	Progressive Conservative Party of Canada, Etobicoke, Ontario

Gordon McFarlane	Progressive Conservative Party of Canada, Winnipeg, Manitoba
Wayne McIntyre	Liberal Party of Canada, Regina, Saskatchewan
Jim B. Pealow	Society of Management Accountants of Canada, Hamilton, Ontario
Réjean Pelletier	Department of Political Science, Université Laval
Norman Peron	F.M.C.A., President, Society of Management Accountants of Canada, Hamilton, Ontario
Patrick Peters	Progressive Conservative Party of Canada, Steinbach, Manitoba
Susan Phillips	Accounting Manager, P.C. Canada Fund, Ottawa, Ontario
Ruben Richert	Official Agent for Chris Axworthy, M.P., Saskatoon, Saskatchewan
Lin Rubin	Director of Administration, B.C. New Democrats, Vancouver, British Columbia
Alan R. Siaroff	Department of Political Science, McMaster University
Frederick B. Slattery	Director of Election Financing, Elections Canada, Ottawa, Ontario
Siân Stephenson	Reform Party of Canada, Calgary, Alberta
Paul G. Thomas	Department of Political Studies, University of Manitoba
Jan Waenink	Chief Agent, Christian Heritage Party of Canada, Surrey, British Columbia
J. Glen Whaley	F.M.C.A., President, Certified General Accountants Association of Canada, Vancouver, British Columbia
Carol D. Young	Liberal Party of Canada, Halifax, Nova Scotia

Royal Commission

Pierre Lortie	Chairman
Pierre Fortier	Commissioner
Robert Gabor	Commissioner
William Knight	Commissioner
Lucie Pépin	Commissioner
Guy Goulard	Executive Director
Jean-Marc Hamel	Special Adviser to the Chairman
Peter Aucoin	Director of Research
F. Leslie Seidle	Senior Research Co-ordinator and Symposium Moderator
Herman Bakvis	Research Co-ordinator
Janet Hiebert	Research Co-ordinator
Richard Rochefort	Symposium Co-ordinator

SYMPOSIUM ON THE ADMINISTRATION
OF ELECTIONS AT THE CONSTITUENCY LEVEL

Sherbrooke, Quebec
December 9, 10 and 11, 1990

Program

First day   Evening Session:
                             *The Organization of Elections at the Constituency
                             Level*

Second day   Morning Session:
                             Enumeration and Revision: How Do We Proceed?

                             Afternoon Sessions:
                             *Advance Polls and Proxy Voting: How Can the
                             System Be Improved?*

                             *Service to Voters with Disabilities and Citizens
                             with Special Needs*

Third day   Morning Session:
                             *Problems Arising on Election Day: How Do We
                             Deal with Them?*

                             Afternoon Session:
                             *Facilitating Election Operations at the
                             Constituency Level: Where Are We Heading?*

Panelists

Richard Balasko   Chief Electoral Officer of Manitoba
Rachel Bélisle   Project Manager (Literacy), Canadian Institute
                                for Adult Education, Montreal, Quebec
Céline Bernier   Returning Officer for St-Laurent, Quebec
Pierre Bonomo   New Democratic Party of Canada, Montreal,
                                Quebec
Jacques Charpentier   Returning Officer for Louis-Hébert, Quebec
Adrien Cloutier   Returning Officer for Charlesbourg, Quebec
Sylvie Godbout   Office des personnes handicapées du Québec,
                                Sherbrooke, Quebec
Claire Gourdeau-   Returning Officer for Saint-Hyacinthe–
   Bousquet   Bagot, Quebec
Jean Jolin   Director of Polling Operations, Office of the
                                Chief Electoral Officer of Quebec

Louis Lavoie	Director of Operations, Elections Canada, Ottawa, Ontario
Andrée Lortie	Assistant Director of Operations, Elections Canada, Ottawa, Ontario
Denis Pageau	Director of Operations, Quebec, Progressive Conservative Party of Canada
Raphaël Richard	Returning Officer for Chambly, Quebec
Bernard Tanguay	Returning Officer for St-Jean, Quebec
J.L. Pamphile Tardif	Returning Officer for Frontenac, Quebec

Participants

Jeannine Blackburn-Roy	Returning Officer for Richmond–Wolfe, Quebec
Pierre Blain	Assistant Returning Officer for Hull–Aylmer, Quebec
Guy Bouchard	Returning Officer for LaSalle-Émard, Quebec
Denis Coderre	Liberal Party of Canada, Montreal, Quebec
Roland Couturier	Returning Officer for Restigouche–Chaleur, New Brunswick
Louise de Lafontaine	Co-ordinator, Office of the Chief Electoral Officer of Quebec
Marcel Douville	Returning Officer for Saint-Léonard, Quebec
Pierre Fafard	Returning Officer for Montmagny–L'Islet, Quebec
Micheline Fournier	Progressive Conservative Party of Canada, Cowansville, Quebec
Mario Gagnon	Returning Officer for Champlain, Quebec
Laurette Greenlay	Office Manager, Elections Manitoba
Lisette Levesque	Returning Officer for Argenteuil–Papineau, Quebec
Conrad Lizée	Returning Officer for Sherbrooke, Quebec
Denis Lussier	Assistant Director of Administration, Elections Canada, Ottawa, Ontario
Carson E. Payne	Progressive Conservative Party of Canada, Moose Creek, Ontario
Jean-Pierre Quéry	Election Clerk for Laval-Ouest, Quebec
Paulette Sonier Rioux	Returning Officer for Acadie–Bathurst, New Brunswick
Alain Tardif	Liberal Party of Canada, Montreal, Quebec
Michael Towsey	Liberal Party of Canada, Tingwick, Quebec

Royal Commission

Pierre Lortie	Chairman
Pierre Fortier	Commissioner
Robert Gabor	Commissioner
William Knight	Commissioner
Lucie Pépin	Commissioner
Guy Goulard	Executive Director
Michael Cassidy	Research Co-ordinator and Symposium Moderator
Richard Rochefort	Symposium Co-ordinator
Jean-Paul Laperrière	Consultant
Alain Gauthier	Consultant

SYMPOSIUM ON POLITICAL PARTIES

Halifax, Nova Scotia
February 7–8, 1991

Program

First day

Morning Sessions:
The Internal Dynamics of Parties: Candidate and Leadership Selection
Moderator:
R. Kenneth Carty, Department of Political Science, University of British Columbia

The Internal Dynamics of Parties: Party Organization
Moderator:
Steven B. Wolinetz, Department of Political Science, Memorial University of Newfoundland

Afternoon Sessions:
Parties, Representation and Alternative Forms of Participation
Moderator:
Jane Jenson, Department of Political Science, Carleton University

Responsiveness, Volatility and the Electoral System
Moderator:
Richard Johnston, Department of Political Science, University of British Columbia

Second day

Morning Session:
Parties as National Institutions
Moderator:
Brian Lee Crowley, Department of Political
Science, Dalhousie University

Afternoon Session:
Parties as Primary Political Organizations
Moderator:
Herman Bakvis, Research Co-ordinator,
Royal Commission on Electoral Reform and
Party Financing, Dalhousie University

Panelists

Keith Archer	Department of Political Studies, University of Prince Edward Island/University of Calgary
Thomas S. Axworthy	Executive Director, The CRB Foundation, Montreal, Quebec
Dalton K. Camp	Political Commentator, Queen's County, New Brunswick
William M. Chandler	Department of Political Science, McMaster University
Maureen Covell	Department of Political Science, Simon Fraser University
Rosemary Dolman	Director of Operations, Progressive Conservative Party of Canada, Ottawa, Ontario
Rand Dyck	Department of Political Science, Laurentian University
David J. Elkins	Department of Political Science, University of British Columbia/University of Ottawa
Lynda Erickson	Department of Political Science, Simon Fraser University
Brian Gaines	Department of Political Science, Hoover Institute, Stanford University
David Gotthilf	President, Viewpoints Research, Winnipeg, Manitoba
Jack Graham	Liberal Party of Canada, Halifax, Nova Scotia
Patrick Kerwin	National Director, Political Action, Canadian Labour Congress, Ottawa, Ontario
Michael Krashinsky	Division of Social Sciences, Scarborough College, University of Toronto
Réjean Landry	Department of Political Science, Université Laval

Peter Milliken	Member of Parliament for Kingston and the Islands, Ontario
Neil Nevitte	Department of Political Science, University of Calgary
Denis Pageau	Director of Operations, Quebec, Progressive Conservative Party of Canada
Richard Proctor	Federal Secretary, New Democratic Party of Canada, Ottawa, Ontario
Michael G. Robinson	Chief Financial Officer, Liberal Party of Canada, Ottawa, Ontario
Val Sears	Max Bell Visiting Professor of Journalism, University of Regina
Sharon Sutherland	School of Public Administration, Carleton University
Neil Young	Member of Parliament for Beaches–Woodbine, Ontario

Participants

Gordon Ashworth	Liberal Party of Canada, Toronto, Ontario
Chris Banman	New Democratic Party of Canada, Aberdeen, Saskatchewan
Cathy Beehan	Progressive Conservative Party of Canada, Vanier, Ontario
Roxanna Benoit	Progressive Conservative Party of Canada, Ottawa, Ontario
Margaret Birrell	New Democratic Party of Canada, Vancouver, British Columbia
Sheila Gervais	Secretary General, Liberal Party of Canada, Ottawa, Ontario
Eddy Giguère	Assistant to the Chief Electoral Officer of Quebec
Raymond Guardia	New Democratic Party of Canada, Montreal, Quebec
Sandra Houston	New Democratic Party of Canada, Halifax, Nova Scotia
Hon. Donald J. Johnston	President, Liberal Party of Canada, Ottawa, Ontario
Charles King	Liberal Party of Canada, Ottawa, Ontario
Jean-Pierre Kingsley	Chief Electoral Officer of Canada
Grant Kippen	Director of Organization, Liberal Party of Canada, Ottawa, Ontario
Hon. Robert E.M. Layton	Chairman of the National Caucus, Progressive Conservative Party of Canada, Ottawa, Ontario

Carolyn M. Maynes	Chief Financial Officer, Progressive Conservative Party of Canada, Ottawa, Ontario
J. Patrick Nowlan	Member of Parliament for Annapolis Valley–Hants, Nova Scotia
Ray Pennings	Christian Heritage Party of Canada, Stoney Creek, Ontario
W. Gerry Robinson	Liberal Party of Canada, Vancouver, British Columbia
Alan R. Siaroff	Department of Political Science, McMaster University
Neil Weir	Reform Party of Canada, Sherwood Park, Alberta
David Woodbury	Provincial Secretary, New Democratic Party of Canada, Winnipeg, Manitoba

Royal Commission

Pierre Lortie	Chairman
Pierre Fortier	Commissioner
Robert Gabor	Commissioner
William Knight	Commissioner
Lucie Pépin	Commissioner
Guy Goulard	Executive Director
Peter Aucoin	Director of Research
Herman Bakvis	Research Co-ordinator and Symposium Moderator
Frederick J. Fletcher	Research Co-ordinator
David Mac Donald	Assistant Research Co-ordinator
Richard Rochefort	Symposium Co-ordinator

SYMPOSIUM ON MEDIA AND ELECTIONS

Toronto, Ontario
February 20, 21 and 22, 1991

Program

| First day | Evening Session:
Media and Parties: Setting the Campaign Agenda |
| Second day | Morning Sessions:
Leaders Debate: Significance and Potential

Polling, Campaigns and the Media |

	Afternoon Session: *The Regulatory Framework*
Third day	Morning Session: *Local Campaigns: Improving the Information Environment*
	Afternoon Sessions: *New Approaches to Campaign Communication*
	Issues and Lessons

Moderators

Marc Raboy	Department of Information and Communication, Université Laval
David Schatzky	Executive Director, Children's Broadcast Institute, Toronto, Ontario

Panelists

Valerie Alia	Graduate School of Journalism, Middlesex College, University of Western Ontario
Cathy Widdis Barr	Department of Political Science, Wilfrid Laurier University
David Bell	Centre for International and Strategic Studies, York University
Robert Bernier	École nationale d'administration publique, Montreal, Quebec
Jean Crête	Department of Political Science, Université Laval
Peter Desbarats	Dean, Graduate School of Journalism, Middlesex College, University of Western Ontario
Christopher Dornan	School of Journalism, Carleton University
William O. Gilsdorf	Department of Communication Studies, Concordia University
Lyndsay Green	Lyndsay Green and Associates, Toronto, Ontario
Robert Hackett	Department of Communications, Simon Fraser University
David Hogarth	Department of Communication Studies, Concordia University
Guy Lachapelle	Department of Political Science, Concordia University

Robert MacDermid	Department of Political Science, York University
Michael Nolan	Graduate School of Journalism, University of Western Ontario
Catherine Thompson-Pyper	Consultant and former Senior Adviser, Ontario Ministry of Culture and Communications
Lorna Frances Roth	Department of Communication Studies, Concordia University
David Ralph Spencer	Graduate School of Journalism, University of Western Ontario
Pierre Trudel	Centre de recherche en droit public, Université de Montréal

Commentators

Elly Alboim	National News Editor, CBC-TV, Ottawa, Ontario
Marcel Côté	Senior Partner, SECOR Inc., Montreal, Quebec
Donna Dasko	Vice-President, Environics Research Group, Toronto, Ontario
Terry Hargreaves	Senior Adviser to the President, CBC, Ottawa, Ontario
John Harvard	Member of Parliament for Winnipeg St. James, Manitoba
William Howard	Legal Counsel, CRTC, Hull, Quebec
Lynn McDonald	Sociologist, Former Member of Parliament for Broadview–Greenwood, Ontario
Catherine A. Murray	Vice-President, Decima Research, Toronto, Ontario
Richard Price	Professor of Political Science and Dean of Student Affairs, University of Windsor
Michel St-Laurent	Groupe de recherche sur les industries culturelles et l'informatisation sociale, Université du Québec à Montréal
Christopher Waddell	National News Editor, *The Globe and Mail*, Ottawa, Ontario
Jodi White	Progressive Conservative Party of Canada, Toronto, Ontario

Participants

Agar Adamson	Department of Political Science, Acadia University
Arnold Amber	Executive Producer of News Specials, CBC National TV, Toronto, Ontario

Gordon Ashworth	Liberal Party of Canada, Toronto, Ontario
Warren R. Bailie	Chief Election Officer of Ontario, Toronto, Ontario
Chris Banman	New Democratic Party of Canada, Aberdeen, Saskatchewan
Cathy Beehan	Progressive Conservative Party of Canada, Vanier, Ontario
Donald Benham	Political Writer, *The Winnipeg Sun*, Winnipeg, Manitoba
Roxanna Benoit	Progressive Conservative Party of Canada, Ottawa, Ontario
Luc Bernier	Department of Political Science, Concordia University
Margaret Birrell	New Democratic Party of Canada, Vancouver, British Columbia
Catherine M. Bolan	Assistant to David Bell, Department of Political Science, York University
Robert Bragg	Editorial Writer, *Calgary Herald*, Calgary, Alberta
John Coleman	President and Chief Executive Officer, Canadian Advertising Foundation
Darrell Dexter	New Democratic Party of Canada, Dartmouth, Nova Scotia
Rosemary Dolman	Director of Operations, Progressive Conservative Party of Canada, Ottawa, Ontario
Christine Dyck	Office of Audrey McLaughlin, New Democratic Party of Canada, Ottawa, Ontario
Thérèse Fortier	Director of Communications, Office of the Chief Electoral Officer of Quebec
Paul W. Fox	Professor Emeritus, Senior Research Associate, Emmanuel College, University of Toronto
Allan Garneau	Executive Director, Christian Heritage Party of Canada, Langley, British Columbia
Sheila Gervais	Secretary General, Liberal Party of Canada, Ottawa, Ontario
David Gotthilf	President, Viewpoints Research, Winnipeg, Manitoba
Raymond Guardia	New Democratic Party of Canada, Montreal, Quebec
Steven High	New Democratic Party of Canada, Ste-Foy, Quebec
Christine Jackson	Director of Communications, Elections Canada, Ottawa, Ontario

Hon. Donald J. Johnston	President, Liberal Party of Canada, Ottawa, Ontario
Charles King	Liberal Party of Canada, Ottawa, Ontario
Grant Kippen	Director of Organization, Liberal Party of Canada, Ottawa, Ontario
Hon. Robert E.M. Layton	Chairman of the National Caucus, Progressive Conservative Party of Canada, Ottawa, Ontario
Julie Mason	New Democratic Party of Canada, Toronto, Ontario
Annie Méar	Department of Communications, Université de Montréal
John Miller	Chairman, Department of Journalism, Ryerson Polytechnical Institute, Toronto, Ontario
Jason Moscovitz	National Affairs Correspondent, CBC Radio News, Ottawa, Ontario
Jean Ouellet	Elections Ontario, Scarborough, Ontario
Denis Pageau	Director of Operations, Quebec, Progressive Conservative Party of Canada
Ray Pennings	Christian Heritage Party of Canada, Stoney Creek, Ontario
Leonard Preyra	Department of Political Science, Saint Mary's University
Richard Proctor	Federal Secretary, New Democratic Party of Canada, Ottawa, Ontario
Michael Robinson	Chief Financial Officer, Liberal Party of Canada, Ottawa, Ontario
W. Gerry Robinson	Liberal Party of Canada, Vancouver, British Columbia
Wade Rowland	Associate Producer, CTV National News, Toronto, Ontario
Anthony M. Sayers	Department of Political Science, University of British Columbia
Siân Stephenson	Reform Party of Canada, Calgary, Alberta
Geoffrey Stevens	*Sun Times of Canada*, Toronto, Ontario
Paul Taylor	Staff Writer, National News, *The Washington Post*, Washington, D.C.
André Tessier	Office of the Leader of the Official Opposition, Ottawa, Ontario
Paula Todd	Queen's Park Reporter, *The Toronto Star*, Toronto, Ontario

Tom Trbovich   National Director, Progressive Conservative
                        Party of Canada, Ottawa, Ontario
Ken Warenko   Reform Party of Canada, Calgary, Alberta
Loren A. Wells   Elections Ontario, Scarborough, Ontario
Anthony Westell   Director, School of Journalism, Carleton
                        University
Rich Willis   Progressive Conservative Party of Canada,
                        Oakville, Ontario
Hugh Winsor   National Political Editor, *The Globe and Mail*,
                        Ottawa, Ontario
David Woodbury   Provincial Secretary, New Democratic Party of
                        Canada, Winnipeg, Manitoba

Royal Commission

Pierre Lortie   Chairman
Pierre Fortier   Commissioner
Robert Gabor   Commissioner
William Knight   Commissioner
Lucie Pépin   Commissioner
Guy Goulard   Executive Director
Jean-Marc Hamel   Special Adviser to the Chairman
Peter Aucoin   Director of Research
Frederick J. Fletcher   Research Co-ordinator and Symposium
                        Moderator
Richard Rochefort   Director of Communications and Symposium
                        Co-ordinator

SYMPOSIUM ON POLITICAL ETHICS

Hull, Quebec
April 11–12, 1991

Program

First day   Morning Sessions:
                        What Is Meant by Fairness and Equity?

                        Money and Influence in the Political System

                        Afternoon Session:
                        Codes of Ethics for Political Parties

Second day

Morning Sessions:
Campaign Advertising: The Ethics of Political Marketing

Problem Areas in Campaign Communication

Afternoon Session:
Ethics and Elections: Observations and Recommendations

Moderators

Brian Crowley	Department of Political Science, Dalhousie University
Christopher Dornan	School of Journalism, Carleton University

Panelists

Elly Alboim	National News Editor, CBC-TV, Ottawa, Ontario
Michael Atkinson	Department of Political Science, McMaster University
Kathy Brock	Department of Political Studies, University of Manitoba
Alan C. Cairns	Department of Political Science, University of British Columbia
William Chandler	Department of Political Science, McMaster University
William O. Gilsdorf	Department of Communication Studies, Concordia University
Ian Greene	Department of Political Science, York University
Jane Jenson	Department of Political Science, Carleton University
Stephen Kline	Department of Communications, Simon Fraser University
Robert R. Parker	Vice-President and Chief Adviser, Government Affairs, Royal Bank of Canada
Eileen Saunders	School of Journalism, Carleton University
Walter C. Soderlund	Department of Communication Studies, University of Windsor
Gordon Wilson	President, Ontario Federation of Labour, Toronto, Ontario

Participants

Hon. Lloyd Axworthy	Member of Parliament for Winnipeg South Centre, Manitoba
Chris Banman	New Democratic Party of Canada, Aberdeen, Saskatchewan
Roxanna Benoit	Progressive Conservative Party of Canada, Ottawa, Ontario
Margaret Birrell	New Democratic Party of Canada, Vancouver, British Columbia
A. William Blaikie	Member of Parliament for Winnipeg Transcona, Manitoba
Daniel J. Blessington	Executive Assistant to Commissioner John Warren McGarry, U.S. Federal Election Commission, Washington, D.C.
Pierre-F. Côté	Chief Electoral Officer of Quebec
Darrell Dexter	New Democratic Party of Canada, Dartmouth, Nova Scotia
Rosemary Dolman	Director of Operations, Progressive Conservative Party of Canada, Ottawa, Ontario
Joe Fontana	Member of Parliament for London East, Ontario
Allan Garneau	Executive Director, Christian Heritage Party of Canada, Langley, British Columbia
Sheila Gervais	Secretary General, Liberal Party of Canada, Ottawa, Ontario
David Gotthilf	President, Viewpoints Research, Winnipeg, Manitoba
Deborah Grey	Member of Parliament for Beaver River, Alberta
John Harvard	Member of Parliament for Winnipeg St. James, Manitoba
Elwin Hermanson	Reform Party of Canada, Beechy, Saskatchewan
Hon. Donald J. Johnston	President, Liberal Party of Canada, Ottawa, Ontario
Patrick Kerwin	National Director, Political Action, Canadian Labour Congress, Ottawa, Ontario
Charles King	Liberal Party of Canada, Ottawa, Ontario
Jean-Pierre Kingsley	Chief Electoral Officer of Canada
Guy Lachapelle	Department of Political Science, Concordia University
Hon. Robert E.M. Layton	Chairman of the National Caucus, Progressive Conservative Party of Canada, Ottawa, Ontario

Maureen Mancuso	Department of Political Science, University of Windsor
Carolyn M. Maynes	Chief Financial Officer, Progressive Conservative Party of Canada, Ottawa, Ontario
Howard McCurdy	Member of Parliament for Windsor–St. Clair, Ontario
John Warren McGarry	Chairman, U.S. Federal Election Commission, Washington, D.C.
Brian McKee	New Democratic Party of Canada, Ottawa, Ontario
Michel Mercier	Secrétariat à la reforme électorale, Conseil exécutif, Quebec
Peter Milliken	Member of Parliament for Kingston and the Islands, Ontario
Richard Proctor	Federal Secretary, New Democratic Party of Canada, Ottawa, Ontario
W. Gerry Robinson	Liberal Party of Canada, Vancouver, British Columbia
Dan Rogers	Liberal Caucus Research Bureau, Ottawa, Ontario
Walter I. Romanow	Department of Communication Studies, University of Windsor
Hugh Segal	Progressive Conservative Party of Canada, Toronto, Ontario
Daiva Stasiulis	Department of Sociology, Carleton University
Siân Stephenson	Reform Party of Canada, Calgary, Alberta
John C. Surina	Staff Director, U.S. Federal Election Commission, Washington, D.C.
Yvon Tarte	Legal Counsel, Elections Canada, Ottawa, Ontario
Joseph Thornley	Consultant, Public Affairs International, Toronto, Ontario
Ed Vanwoudenberg	Leader, Christian Heritage Party of Canada, Langley, British Columbia
Neil Weir	Reform Party of Canada, Sherwood Park, Alberta
Rich B. Willis	Progressive Conservative Party of Canada, Oakville, Ontario

Royal Commission

Pierre Lortie	Chairman
Pierre Fortier	Commissioner
Robert Gabor	Commissioner
William Knight	Commissioner

Lucie Pépin	Commissioner
Guy Goulard	Executive Director
Jean-Marc Hamel	Special Adviser to the Chairman
Peter Aucoin	Director of Research
Janet Hiebert	Research Co-ordinator and Symposium Moderator
Frederick J. Fletcher	Research Co-ordinator and Symposium Moderator
David Mac Donald	Assistant Research Co-ordinator
Richard Rochefort	Symposium Co-ordinator

SYMPOSIUM ON ELECTION AND PARTY FINANCE

Ottawa, Ontario
April 18–19, 1991

Program

First day

Morning Session:
Developments in Election and Party Financing
Moderator:
Joseph Wearing, Department of Political Studies, Trent University

Afternoon Sessions:
Interest Groups' Election Activities
Moderator:
Jane Jenson, Department of Political Science, Carleton University

Options for Reform: Enhancing Openness and Participation
Moderator:
Terence Morley, Department of Political Science, University of Victoria

Second day

Morning Sessions:
Options for Reform: Regulating Political Parties' Spending and Finance
Moderator:
R. Kenneth Carty, Department of Political Science, University of British Columbia

Symposium Review

Panelists

Herbert E. Alexander	Citizens' Research Foundation, University of Southern California
W. David Angus	Chairman, P.C. Canada Fund, Montreal, Quebec
Donald E. Blake	Department of Political Science, University of British Columbia
David Butler	Nuffield College, Oxford, England
Carole Campolo	Deputy Executive Director, New York City Campaign Finance Board, New York
Janet Hiebert	Research Co-ordinator, Royal Commission on Electoral Reform and Party Financing
David Johnson	Department of Political Science, McMaster University
Richard Johnston	Department of Political Science, University of British Columbia
Réjean Pelletier	Department of Political Science, Université Laval
Michael Pinto-Duschinsky	Brunel, The University of West London, England
Michael Robinson	Chief Financial Officer, Liberal Party of Canada, Ottawa, Ontario
Clifford A. Scotton	Former Federal Secretary, New Democratic Party of Canada, Nanaimo, British Columbia
William T. Stanbury	Faculty of Business and Commerce, University of British Columbia
A. Brian Tanguay	Department of Political Science, Wilfrid Laurier University
David Taras	Canadian Studies Program, University of Calgary
Lisa Young	Research Analyst, Royal Commission on Electoral Reform and Party Financing

Participants

Gordon Ashworth	Liberal Party of Canada, Toronto, Ontario
Thomas S. Axworthy	Executive Director, The CRB Foundation, Montreal, Quebec
Chris Banman	New Democratic Party of Canada, Aberdeen, Saskatchewan
Doreen Barrie	Department of Political Science, University of Calgary
Cathy Beehan	Progressive Conservative Party of Canada, Vanier, Ontario

Roxanna Benoit	Progressive Conservative Party of Canada, Ottawa, Ontario
Patrick Boyer	Member of Parliament for Etobicoke–Lakeshore, Ontario
Pierre-F. Côté	Chief Electoral Officer of Quebec
Johanna den Hertog	Former President of the New Democratic Party of Canada, Vancouver, British Columbia
Darrell Dexter	New Democratic Party of Canada, Dartmouth, Nova Scotia
Rosemary Dolman	Director of Operations, Progressive Conservative Party of Canada, Ottawa, Ontario
John Galligan	Liberal Party of Canada, Ottawa, Ontario
Sheila Gervais	Secretary General, Liberal Party of Canada, Ottawa, Ontario
Jim Gurnett	New Democratic Party of Canada, Edmonton, Alberta
Brian Harling	New Democratic Party of Canada, Scarborough, Ontario
Hon. Donald J. Johnston	President, Liberal Party of Canada, Ottawa, Ontario
Thomas F. Josefiak	Commissioner, U.S. Federal Election Commission, Washington, D.C.
Charles King	Liberal Party of Canada, Ottawa, Ontario
Jean-Pierre Kingsley	Chief Electoral Officer of Canada
Hon. Robert E.M. Layton	Chairman of the National Caucus, Progressive Conservative Party of Canada, Ottawa, Ontario
Allan Lutfy	Liberal Party of Canada, Ottawa, Ontario
Donald C. MacDonald	Chairman, Ontario Commission on Election Finances, Toronto, Ontario
Louis Massicotte	Chief of Policy and Strategic Planning, Elections Canada, Ottawa, Ontario
Carolyn M. Maynes	Chief Financial Officer, Progressive Conservative Party of Canada, Ottawa, Ontario
Hugh Mellon	Department of Political Science, Brock University
Michel Mercier	Secrétariat à la réforme électorale, Conseil exécutif, Quebec
Peter Milliken	Member of Parliament for Kingston and the Islands, Ontario
Rodney Murphy	Member of Parliament for Churchill, Manitoba
Robert E. Mutch	Independent scholar, Washington, D.C.
Barbara Nault	Liberal Party of Canada, Lethbridge, Alberta

Ron Peacock	Executive Director, P.C. Canada Fund, Ottawa, Ontario
Ray Pennings	Christian Heritage Party of Canada, Stoney Creek, Ontario
Richard Proctor	Federal Secretary, New Democratic Party of Canada, Ottawa, Ontario
W. Gerry Robinson	Liberal Party of Canada, Vancouver, British Columbia
Frederick B. Slattery	Director of Election Financing, Elections Canada, Ottawa, Ontario
Marcel Socqué	Executive Director of the P.C. Caucus, Ottawa, Ontario
John C. Surina	Staff Director, U.S. Federal Election Commission, Washington, D.C.
Tom Trbovich	National Director, Progressive Conservative Party of Canada, Ottawa, Ontario
Jan Waenink	Christian Heritage Party of Canada, Surrey, British Columbia
Neil Weir	Reform Party of Canada, Sherwood Park, Alberta
David Woodbury	Provincial Secretary, New Democratic Party of Canada, Winnipeg, Manitoba

Royal Commission

Pierre Lortie	Chairman
Pierre Fortier	Commissioner
Robert Gabor	Commissioner
William Knight	Commissioner
Lucie Pépin	Commissioner
Guy Goulard	Executive Director
Jean-Marc Hamel	Special Adviser to the Chairman
Peter Aucoin	Director of Research
F. Leslie Seidle	Senior Research Co-ordinator and Symposium Moderator
Frederick J. Fletcher	Research Co-ordinator
Richard Rochefort	Symposium Co-ordinator

OTHER CONSULTATION MEETINGS

Members of the Commission also met or consulted with the following experts from Canada and abroad.

Canada

Michael Adams
E.W. (Ted) Anderson
Senator Gérald F. Beaudoin
Marc André Bédard
Gilbert Boddez
André Boisvenue
Pierre Boutet
Thomas R. Burger
Larry Burling
Allan Cairns
Avrum Cohen
Ken Cousineau
Charles Dalfen
The Right Honourable Brian
    Dickson
Mary Eberts
Len Farber
Ivan P. Fellegi
Sandra Foley
Edgar Gallant
Raymond Garneau
Michel Gratton
Pierre Gravelle
Richard Groot
John Groves
Jocelyne Habra
William A. Howard
Hudson Noel Janisch
Roma Kelembt
The Honourable Mr. Justice
    F.B.W. Kelly
Ed Kerr
Norbert Kilingler
Lucie Laforce
Vincent Lemieux
Jordan A. Levitin
Nick Locke
The Honourable Donald
    MacDonald

Judge Advocate General
    Robert L. Martin
David Mason
Ian McKinnon
John Meisel
John Nigh
Robert Normand
Mel Parker
Sheldon Parsons
Gilbert Payet
Layton Schurman
The Honourable Robert Stanfield
Harry S. Swain
Beth Symes
J.C. Tait
Alain Tassé
Roger Tassé
John Thompson
The Right Honourable Pierre
    Elliott Trudeau
J.S. Weintraub
Drew Westwater
Anthony W.J. Whitford
Joyce Whitman
Janet D.W. Willwerth
The Honourable Mr. Justice
    C. Ross Wimmer

Australia

John Booth
Bruce Jeffery, MP
The Honourable Elisabeth
    Kirby, MLC
John Murray, MP
Amanda Olsson
Campbell Sharman
George Souris, MP
The Honourable Max
    Willis, MLC

England

David Butler
R. Clayton
Michael Pinto-Duschinsky
G.P. Pratt
Robert Worcester

France

René Abraham
Jean-Pierre Bonin-Moulins
François Gazier
Pierre Martin
Marc Sadaoui
Michel Sapin

Germany

Klaus-Gunther Biederbick
Helmut Buschbohm
Peter Conradi
Hans Feldmann

Udo Kempf
Gerald Kretschmer
Karl Nassmacher
Irmgard von Rottenburg
Jurgen Anton Ruttgers
Peter Scheib
Mr. Speilker
Horst Wayrauf
Torsten Wolframm

United States

Lee Ann Elliott
Thomas J. Josefiak
John Warren McGarry
Ronald D. Michaelson
Lawrence M. Noble
Robert Odell
Bob Stern
John C. Surina
Scott E. Thomas

APPENDIX E
The Collected Research Studies*

VOLUME 1
Money in Politics: Financing Federal Parties and Candidates in Canada

W.T. Stanbury   Money in Politics: Financing Federal Parties
                                 and Candidates in Canada

VOLUME 2
Interest Groups and Elections in Canada
F. Leslie Seidle, Editor

Janet Hiebert   Interest Groups and Canadian Federal
                                 Elections

A. Brian Tanguay and   Political Activity of Local Interest Groups
Barry J. Kay

VOLUME 3
Provincial Party and Election Finance in Canada
F. Leslie Seidle, Editor

Louis Massicotte   Party Financing in Quebec: An Analysis of the
                                 Financial Reports of Political Parties
                                 1977–1989

David Johnson   The Ontario Party and Campaign Finance
                                 System: Initiative and Challenge

Terry Morley   Paying for the Politics of British Columbia

H. Mellon   The Evolution of Political Financing
                                 Regulation in New Brunswick

Doreen P. Barrie   Party Financing in Alberta: Low-Impact
                                 Legislation

---

* The titles of studies may not be final in all cases.

VOLUME 4
Comparative Issues in Party and Election Finance
F. Leslie Seidle, Editor

Herbert E. Alexander   The Regulation of Election Finance in the
United States and Proposals for Reform

Robert E. Mutch   The Evolution of Campaign Finance Regulation
in the United States and Canada

Jane Jenson   Innovation and Equity: The Impact of Public
Funding

Michael Pinto-   The Party Foundations and Political Finance
Duschinsky   in Germany

VOLUME 5
Issues in Party and Election Finance in Canada
F. Leslie Seidle, Editor

Lisa Young   Toward Transparency: An Evaluation of
Disclosure Arrangements in Canadian
Political Finance

Michael Krashinsky   Some Evidence on the Effects of Incumbency
and William J. Milne   in the 1988 Canadian Federal Election

R. Kenneth Carty   Official Agents in Canadian Elections:
The Case of the 1988 General Election

Keith Heintzman   Electoral Competition, Campaign Expenditure
and Incumbency Advantage

Thomas S. Axworthy   Capital-Intensive Politics: Money, Media and
Mores in the United States and Canada

Peter P. Constantinou   Public Funding of Political Parties, Candidates
and Elections in Canada

Eric Bertram   Independent Candidates in Federal General
Elections

Donald Padget   Large Contributions to Candidates in the 1988
Federal Election and the Issue of Undue Influence

Pascale Michaud and   Economic Analysis of the Funding of Political
Pierre Laferrière   Parties in Canada

VOLUME 6
Women in Canadian Politics: Towards Equity in Representation
Kathy Megyery, Editor

Sylvia Bashevkin	Women's Participation in Political Parties
Janine Brodie with the assistance of Celia Chandler	Women and the Electoral Process in Canada
Lisa Young	Legislative Turnover and the Election of Women to the Canadian House of Commons
Lynda Erickson	Women and Candidacies for the House of Commons
Gertrude J. Robinson and Armande Saint-Jean, with the assistance of Christine Rioux	Women Politicians and their Media Coverage: A Generational Analysis

VOLUME 7
Ethno-Cultural Groups and Visible Minorities in Canadian Politics: The Question of Access
Kathy Megyery, Editor

Daiva K. Stasiulis and Yasmeen Abu-Laban	The House the Parties Built: (Re)constructing Ethnic Representation in Canadian Politics
Alain Pelletier	Politics and Ethnicity: Representation of Ethnic and Visible-Minority Groups in the House of Commons
Carolle Simard	Visible Minorities and the Canadian Political System

VOLUME 8
Youth in Canadian Politics: Participation and Involvement
Kathy Megyery, Editor

Raymond Hudon, Bernard Fournier and Louis Métivier, with the assistance of Benoît-Paul Hébert	To What Extent Are Today's Young People Interested in Politics? An Inquiry among 16- to 24-Year-Olds

VOLUME 13

Canadian Political Parties: Leaders, Candidates and Organization
Herman Bakvis, Editor

VOLUME 14

Representation, Integration and Political Parties in Canada
Herman Bakvis, Editor

VOLUME 18
Media and Voters in Canadian Election Campaigns
Frederick J. Fletcher, Editor

Jean Crête	Television, Advertising and Canadian Elections
Robert MacDermid	Media Usage and Political Behaviour
Cathy Widdis Barr	The Importance and Potential of Leaders' Debates
Robert Bernier and Denis Monière	The Organization of Televised Leaders' Debates in the United States, Europe, Australia and Canada
Lyndsay Green	An Exploration of Alternative Methods for Improving Voter Information

VOLUME 19
Media, Elections and Democracy
Frederick J. Fletcher, Editor

Jacques Gerstlé	Election Communication in France
Holli A. Semetko	Broadcasting and Election Communication in Britain
Klaus Schoenbach	Mass Media and Election Campaigns in Germany
Karen Siune	Campaign Communication in Scandinavia
John Warhurst	Campaign Communication in Australian Elections
Doris A. Graber	The Mass Media and Election Campaigns in the United States of America
Frederick J. Fletcher and Robert Everett	Mass Media and Elections in Canada

VOLUME 20
Reaching the Voter: Constituency Campaigning in Canada
Frederick J. Fletcher and David V.J. Bell, Editors

David V.J. Bell and Frederick J. Fletcher	Electoral Communication at the Constituency Level: A Framework for Analysis
Anthony M. Sayers	Local Issue Space at National Elections: Kootenay West–Revelstoke and Vancouver Centre
Andrew Beh and Roger Gibbins	The Campaign–Media Interface in Local Constituencies: Two Alberta Case Studies from the 1988 Federal Election Campaign
David V. J. Bell and Catherine M. Bolan	The Mass Media and Federal Election Campaigning at the Local Level: A Case Study of Two Ontario Constituencies
Luc Bernier	Local Campaigns and the Media: The 1988 Election in Outremont and Frontenac
Leonard Preyra	Riding the Waves: Parties, the Media and the 1988 Federal Election in Nova Scotia
David V.J. Bell, Frederick J. Fletcher and Catherine M. Bolan	Electoral Communication at the Constituency Level: Summary and Conclusion

VOLUME 21
Election Broadcasting in Canada
Frederick J. Fletcher, Editor

David Ralph Spencer with the assistance of Catherine M. Bolan	Election Broadcasting in Canada: A Brief History
Pierre Trudel and France Abran	The Legal and Constitutional Framework for the Regulation of Election Campaign Broadcasting
David Hogarth and Bill Gilsdorf	The Impact of All-News Services on Elections and Election Coverage
Peter Desbarats	Cable Television and Federal Election Campaigns in Canada

APPENDIX F
Staff of the Commission

SENIOR OFFICERS

Executive Director
Guy Goulard

Director of Research
Peter Aucoin

Special Adviser to the Chairman
Jean-Marc Hamel

Research
F. Leslie Seidle
Senior Research Co-ordinator

Co-ordinators
Herman Bakvis
Michael Cassidy
Frederick J. Fletcher
Janet Hiebert
Kathy Megyery
Robert A. Milen
David Small

Assistant Co-ordinators
David Mac Donald
Cheryl D. Mitchell

Legislation
Jules Brière, Senior Adviser
Gérard Bertrand
Patrick Orr

Communications and Publishing
Richard Rochefort, Director
Hélène Papineau, Assistant
   Director
Paul Morisset, Editor
Kathryn Randle, Editor

Finance and Administration
Maurice R. Lacasse, Director

Contracts and Personnel
Thérèse Lacasse, Chief

ALPHABETICAL LISTING OF STAFF

The following individuals served the Royal Commission at some point during our enquiry.

Personnel

Arsenault, Daniel
Bertram, Eric
Bevilacqua, Anna
Bolan, Catherine M.
Bonin, Paul
Boucher, Cécile
Brose, Natalie
Burden, Patricia
Cécire, Angelo
Constantinou, Peter
Dancause, Susan
Denoncourt, Yves
DeRepentigny, Bernard
Desforges, Cécile
Dionne, Marie T.
Dumont, Luc
Garneau, Véronique
Girard, Marlène
Guy-Shea, Mary
Heintzman, Keith
Herold, Richard
Juneau, Elise
Lafrance, Denis
Langlois, France
Lauzon, Michel
LeBlanc, Paulette
Leroux, Hélène
Maheux, Lorraine
Mathieu, Jean
McArthur, Kate
McBride, Kathleen
McKay, David
McMurtie, Pierrette
McVeigh, Ruth M.
Mellon, Hugh
Miquelon, Denise
Padget, Donald
Patry, Sylvie

Pelletier, Alain
Poitras, Jacques
Prescott, Josée
Séguin, Christiane
Séguin, Jacinthe
Simard, Liette
Trani, Maria-José
Tremblay, Dominique-Christine
Tremblay, Steve
Young, Lisa

Contractors – Specialized Services

Cook, Sheila-Marie
Dagenais, Louise
Field, Caroline
Gauthier, Alain
Goldbloom, Jonathan
Johnston-McKillop, Pauline
Laperrière, Jean-Paul
Lemery, Marthe
McCoomb, Ann
Nazar, Loretta
Pétrin, Louise
Ratelle, Nicole
Reid, Mado
Rouleau-O'Toole, Claudette
Woodley, Margaret

Interns

Bélanger, Michelle
Docherty, David
Dunlop, Jane
Evans, Scott
Holmes, Paul
Labelle, Claudine
Langlois, Roch
Morissette, Chantal
Roy, Louise